Incident Response:

A Strategic Guide to Handling System and Network Security Breaches

M000236706

Incident Response: A Strategic Guide to Handling System and Network Security Breaches

Dr. E. Eugene Schultz
Russell Shumway

New Riders

www.newriders.com
201 West 103rd Street, Indianapolis, Indiana 46290
An Imprint of Pearson Education
Boston • Indianapolis • London • Munich • New York • San Francisco

Incident Response: A Strategic Guide to Handling System and Network Security Breaches

International Standard Book Number: 1-57870-256-9

Library of Congress Catalog Card Number: 20-01087072

07 06 05   7 6 5 4 3 2

Interpretation of the printing code: The rightmost double-digit number is the year of the book's printing; the rightmost single-digit number is the number of the book's printing. For example, the printing code 02-1 shows that the first printing of the book occurred in 2002.

Printed in the United States of America

Trademarks

Warning and Disclaimer

Publisher
David Dwyer

Associate Publisher
Stephanie Wall

Production Manager
Gina Kanouse

Managing Editor
Kristy Knoop

Sr. Acquisitions Editor
Jeff Riley

Product Marketing Manager
Stephanie Layton

Publicity Manager
Susan Nixon

Project Editor
Elise Walter

Copy Editor
Amy Lepore

Indexer
Cheryl Lenser

Manufacturing Coordinator
Jim Conway

Book Designer
Louisa Klucznik

Cover Designer
Brainstorm Design, Inc.

Cover Production
Aren Howell

Composition
Scan Communications Group, Inc.

The part of this book that I wrote is dedicated to the original Computer Incident Advisory Capability (CIAC) team members: Tom Longstaff, Ana Maria de Alvare, David S. Brown, and Russell Brand. These outstanding individuals worked with me, the original CIAC team manager, to overcome many obstacles, both from the outside and from within. They deserve the credit for any success that the original CIAC team enjoyed.
E. Eugene Schultz

The part of this book that I am responsible for is dedicated to my wife, Amy McBurnie, for all her encouragement throughout my career.
Russell Shumway

❖

TABLE OF CONTENTS

About the Authors

Dr. E. Eugene Schultz, founder and former manager of the U.S. Department of Energy's Computer Incident Advisory Capability (CIAC) team, is currently on the support staff of Global Integrity's REACT team—the first commercial incident response capability.

Russell Shumway is the director of intelligence and response services with Network Security Corporation, which is responsible for the management of NSEC's Incident Mitigation and Open-Source Monitoring services. Russ previously worked as the technical director of Global Integrity Corporation's REACT program, where he worked on numerous computer-security incidents for clients ranging from Fortune 100 companies to private individuals and provided consulting services to 7 of the top 10 financial services companies in the United States and 13 of the top 50 in the world. He assisted in the design and development of Global Integrity's Financial Services Incident Sharing and Advisory Center (FS/ISAC).

Dr. Terry Gudaitis is a behavioral scientist/criminologist who has 12 years of experience in research and applied practice in the discipline of behavioral assessment and profiling. She received her MA and Ph.D. from the University of Florida. Since 1987, she has provided domestic and international assessments and profiles for academia, local law enforcement, federal agencies and bureaus, and private industry.

Dr. Gudaitis has worked with the Central Intelligence Agency as a criminal psychologist at the CounterTerrorist Center. Currently, Dr. Gudaitis is responsible for the integration of behavioral/criminal profiling and computer forensics at Global Integrity Corporation, a Science Applications International Corporation (SAIC) subsidiary. Dr. Gudaitis provides consultation, human systems assessment, and profiling services to private industry. Dr. Gudaitis has recently published articles in CyberPsychology and Behavior, Imp Magazine, presented on the "Insider Threat" at SecureComm98, was a guest speaker on "Cyber Crime Profiling" for Leadership America-Greater Washington, and is an active member of the High Technology Crime Investigative Association.

About the Technical Reviewers

These reviewers contributed their considerable hands-on expertise to the entire development process for *Incident Response*. As the book was being written, these dedicated professionals reviewed all the material for technical content, organization, and flow. Their feedback was critical to ensuring that *Incident Response* fits our readers' need for the highest-quality technical information.

Patrick "Swissman" Ramseier, CCNA, CISSP, is the Chief Security Officer for the SARAA Corporation. SARAA (Secure Archive Retrieval Anytime Anywhere) is dedicated to bringing the latest in optical imaging, Internet delivery, and proprietary enabling technologies to revitalize and transform the proven business model of archive storage, management and retrieval companies nationwide in a secure manner. Patrick started out as a UNIX system administrator. Over the past 13 years, he has been involved with corporate-level security design, architecture reviews, vulnerability assessments, VPN support, physical, network and operating system security (UNIX-Solaris, Linux, BSD and Windows NT/2000), training, research and development. He has a B.A. in business and is working concurrently on his masters and doctorate in computer science.

Larry Paccone is a Principal National/Systems Security Analyst at Logicon/TASC. As both a technical lead and project manager, he has worked in the Internet and network/systems security arena for more than eight years. He has been the technical lead for several network security projects supporting a government network/systems security research and development laboratory. Prior to that, Larry worked for five years at The Analytical Sciences Corporation (TASC) as a national security analyst assessing conventional military force structures. He has an M.S. in Information Systems, an M.A. in International Relations, and a B.A. in Political Science. He also has completed eight professional certifications in network and systems security, internetworking, wide area networking, Cisco routing/switching, and Windows NT.

Acknowledgments

Many people have contributed significantly to this book. Elise Walter of New Riders, the editor, worked at all phases of our writing effort to ensure that this book was the best it could possibly be. Larry Paccone and Patrick Ramseier, the technical editors, made many insightful suggestions. Amy Lepore served as copy editor and Cheryl Lenser as indexer. And we cannot forget Jeff Riley of New Riders—manager extraordinaire. Jeff's humor and motivating comments kept us going as we wrote this book.

Jim Mellander and Russ Montello also helped by providing superb technical input when we asked them to.

Special thanks go to Dr. Terry Gudaitis who wrote Chapter 10 of this book despite her extremely busy schedule. We are confident that reading this chapter will show you why she enjoys the stellar reputation that she has.

Russ would also like to acknowledge his peers and coworkers, Tim Applby, Jennifer Braun, Dr. Terry Gudaitis, and Frank Schugar.
—Gene and Russ

Tell Us What You Think

As the reader of this book, you are the most important critic and commentator. We value your opinion and want to know what we're doing right, what we could do better, what areas you'd like to see us publish in, and any other words of wisdom you're willing to pass our way.

As the Associate Publisher for New Riders Publishing, I welcome your comments. You can fax, email, or write me directly to let me know what you did or didn't like about this book—as well as what we can do to make our books stronger.

Please note that I cannot help you with technical problems related to the topic of this book, and that due to the high volume of mail I receive, I might not be able to reply to every message.

When you write, please be sure to include this book's title and author as well as your name and phone or fax number. I will carefully review your comments and share them with the author and editors who worked on the book.

Fax:	317-581-4663
Email:	stephanie.wall@newriders.com
Mail:	Stephanie Wall
	Associate Publisher
	New Riders Publishing
	201 West 103rd Street
	Indianapolis, IN 46290 USA

Introduction

Many who read this book already know something about responding to information security–related incidents. Commonly referred to as "break-ins," "hacks," "security breaches," and other terms, these incidents have become all too commonplace. Why? One of the most important reasons is that systems, applications, and networks have become more complex and diverse and are thus increasingly difficult to defend. The Internet continues to undergo almost unprecedented growth, enabling attackers from almost anywhere in the world to probe and shortly afterward attack systems that are connected to the Internet. Compounding the problem is the tendency for senior management to be oblivious to the threat of security-related incidents, much like the proverbial "ostrich with its head in the sand."

Security-related attacks that occur often have catastrophic consequences. Chapter 2, "Risk Analysis," discusses the types of negative consequences security-related incidents can cause and the extent of each. We do not mean to claim that "the sky is falling." Instead, we present selected loss statistics when available. But we are confident that the problem is far greater than most people realize. National infrastructures are gravely at risk and have been for years. A few saboteurs could, for example, bring down or modify systems that control critical parts of these infrastructures, such as energy production and distribution systems, air-traffic control systems, and others. We have become dependent on computers but fail to take the security of computers and networks seriously. And we will continue to fail to take the security of computers and networks seriously until some event—a security-related incident of unparalleled proportion, something that shocks the public—occurs. Perhaps this will manifest itself in the form of massive and prolonged power outages or even a jumbo jet crash caused by someone tampering with a computer.

Governments are not likely to take computer security more seriously if the public does not demand better security. Corporations are also not likely to take computer security more seriously unless stockholders press them, security-related losses mount dramatically, or a proliferation of lawsuits related to poor security practices occurs.

The need to respond effectively when security-related incidents occur has also increased proportionately to the growing level of threat. The main purpose of this book is to communicate to readers what they need to know not only to set up an incident response effort, but also to improve existing incident response efforts.

The concepts and principles presented throughout this book are not simply ideas we have fabricated. The authors have spent a large portion of their careers in computer and information security, helping organizations respond to incidents. Case studies from our firsthand experiences are included throughout this book. At the same time, however, we have attempted wherever possible to present models, projected trends, and other more theoretical concepts to encourage readers to think about incident response at a more conceptual level as well. The problem we face is indeed a very multifaceted one; computer science and information technology alone can solve only part of this problem. The human side is particularly important, especially when it comes to dealing with insider attacks. This book thus presents a broad perspective, covering a variety of technical, procedural, managerial, and psychological information. This broad perspective makes this book appropriate for readers with both technical and nontechnical backgrounds.

Organization of this Book

Every chapter in this book focuses on a particular area of incident response. The chapter breakdown is as follows:

- Chapter 1, "An Introduction to Incident Response," covers issues such as what incident response is, why it is needed, and the kinds of initial considerations that must be addressed.

- Chapter 2, "Risk Analysis," covers the kinds of incidents that can occur, the types of damage that result, and the relationship between risk analysis and incident response efforts.

- Chapter 3, "A Methodology for Incident Response," presents a classic six-stage methodology for incident handing: preparation, detection, containment, eradication, recovery, and follow-up. This chapter also presents the rationale for using this methodology as well as special considerations that apply to each stage.

- Chapter 4, "How to Form and Manage an Incident Response Team," explains how to create and sustain an incident response effort.

- Chapter 5, "Organizing for Incident Response," covers how to prepare for responding to incidents. The major focus is on dealing with the various parts of an organization and enlisting support from within as well as dealing with the press. It also presents suggestions for minimizing damage to an organization's reputation if an incident occurs.

- Chapter 6, "Tracing Network Intrusions," describes intrusion-tracing techniques for networked systems and other related considerations, such as how to develop communication channels that enable those who are involved in incident response to obtain information about attacks that have occurred.

- Chapter 7, "Legal Issues," deals with basic legal considerations that surround the incident response arena as well as their applicability. These include matters such as applicable legal statutes, considerations related to individual privacy, legal risks associated with responding to incidents, how to deal with the law enforcement community, and others.

- Chapter 8, "Forensics I," covers locating evidence, determining the form of the evidence, using forensic triage, best practices, separating the collection of evidence from the analysis of it, forensic evidence handling and preservation and the rationale for each method and technique, the cost of forensic analysis versus the gain, using data forensics and evidence in court or disciplinary hearings, and other important issues.

- Chapter 9, "Forensics II," continues where Chapter 8 leaves off. Chapter 9 covers the more technical, detailed aspects of computer forensics, including covert searches, advanced searches, how to deal with encrypted data, and special considerations with laptops, older systems, UNIX hosts, and Linux hosts.

- Chapter 10, "The Human Side of Incident Response," (written by Dr. Terry Gudaitis, a criminogist who specializes in dealing with computer crime) deals with the human factor, including how to construct profiles on individuals' behavior and how to interview suspects when computer crimes have occurred.

- Chapter 11, "Responding to Insider Attacks," covers topics such as types of insiders, types of attacks, special considerations that apply to insider attacks, how to work with human relations, legal and other functions to bring insider attack cases to suitable closure, and the relationship of insider investigations to disciplinary/court hearings.

- Chapter 12, "Traps and Deceptive Measures," describes types of deceptive measures available, how to deploy them, cautions, and how to weigh costs versus benefit.

- Chapter 13, "Future Directions in Incident Response," deals with what incident response ofthe future might be like and the probable implications for the incident response community.

- Appendix A, "RFC-2196," contains the RFC that deals specifically with incident response considerations.

- Appendix B, "Incident Response and Reporting Checklist," presents a sample form for reporting security-related incidents that occur.

We are confident that this book will be of great value to you as you deal with the challenge of responding to security-related incidents.

Conventions Used in This Book

This book uses the following conventions:

- `Constant Width` represents display text, error messages, examples, email addresses, domain names, URLs, files, directories, host and domain names, and in-text references to syntax models.

- `Constant Width Italics`, in some code examples, indicates an element (for example, a parameter) that you must supply.

- In syntax examples, square brackets [] enclose optional items.

1

An Introduction to Incident Response

THE PROLIFERATION OF COMPUTING TECHNOLOGY IS one of the most pronounced trends in the second half of the twentieth century and the beginning of the twenty-first century. Not much more than novelty when first introduced, computers now are not only commonplace but also essential in much of this world. No one knows how many computers, let alone computer users, there currently are.

Computers in and of themselves have limited value. As standalone entities, they enable people to prepare reports, keep track of tax records, and so on. The power of computing lies in the capability of computers to interconnect. Interconnection allows for not only computer-to-computer but also user-to-user communications. Any mention of interconnection immediately brings to mind the Internet, which ties together regional and service-provider networks over the entire globe. Again, no one knows exactly how many Internet users there are, but at the time this book was being written, many estimates were that this number exceeds 300 million users.

During the early era of computing, little thought was given to the security of computers and data that resided on them. Very often, the only way someone could misuse them was to gain physical access—a difficult task in many settings. The need to remotely connect to computing systems grew rapidly, however. Modems were invented, and dial-in access started to become prevalent. The result was more access to authorized users but, unfortunately, increased opportunity for unauthorized persons to connect to the same systems. Dial-in connections too often tended to be slow, while advances in networking occurred at a rapid pace. Local networking evolved, followed by wide area networking. The Internet is, in many respects, the ultimate type of wide area networking.

At the same time, the Internet has proven to be a two-edged sword. On one hand, it has supported unparalleled network connectivity to the point that it is a major enabler of untold commercial enterprises, agencies, and academic institutions today. On the other hand, it has opened up opportunities for unscrupulous and misguided people who attack and disrupt systems. The Internet Preamble contains a statement saying that the Internet does not provide security. If you want security, *you* need to build it in. Period.

Many years of software development have taught us that if a particular feature or property is not built into the initial software requirements, it is generally more difficult and costly to retrofit a system to include that feature or property. This principle certainly applies to the Internet. The lack of inherent security is, in many respects, its biggest downfall. Many individuals and organizations understandably have examined the cost of achieving suitable security and backed away from it because security mechanisms are often too cumbersome, disruptive, and costly. Unfortunately, lack of adequate security has led to a multitude of security breaches that have resulted in financial loss, disruption, embarrassment, and distrust of and loss of confidence in technology.

Several things happened in the 1980s that radically increased people's awareness of the kinds of things that could happen when Internet security is not adequate. One of the most noteworthy episodes was the set of computer break-ins described in Cliff Stoll's now classic book, *The Cuckoo's Egg*. While working as a system administrator at Lawrence Berkeley Laboratory, Stoll investigated a small discrepancy between the amount of system usage calculated by the system's accounting program as compared to a custom accounting program developed at Lawrence Berkeley Laboratory. His investigation led to identification of a massive set of break-ins aimed at obtaining information from U.S. government and government-contractor computers. Stoll alleges that the attackers were supported by the KGB in the Soviet Union.

The break-ins described in Stoll's book were not limited to Lawrence Berkeley Laboratory. They also involved Lawrence Livermore National Laboratory (LLNL), U.S. nuclear weapons laboratories, MITRE Corporation, universities, and many U.S. military sites, to name a few. Few people had realized the potential for perpetrating espionage via what was then called the ARPAnet.

The U.S. Department of Energy (DOE) was particularly concerned. Meetings at various locations around the U.S. were held to discuss what had occurred and what course of action could be taken in response to it. Rick Carr, the head of unclassified security for the DOE at the time, was the first to recognize that conventional security and computer-protection programs would not be enough to stave off the kind of attacks that had ravaged Lawrence Berkeley Laboratory, LLNL, and other sites. Carr called for the formation of an incident response capability to assist sites under attack. The seminal idea of having an incident response capability was thus born. He worked in cooperation with individuals within the DOE headquarters and LLNL to obtain funding for a team that would later be known as the Computer Incident Advisory Capability (CIAC).

Meanwhile, individuals at Carnegie-Mellon's Software Engineering Institute (SEI) got wind of Carr's idea and applied for funding for what they called the Computer Emergency Response Team Coordination Center (CERT/CC), designed to serve the entire Internet community. Receiving funding from the Defense Advanced Research Projects Agency (DARPA) a little earlier than CIAC did, they announced themselves as the central coordination center for incident response efforts. Since that time, virtually hundreds of incident response teams within the commercial sector, academia, and the government arena have been formed. Incident response is now a well-entrenched capability.

What Is Incident Response?

This book covers a broad range of considerations associated with responding to security-related incidents in computing systems and networks. Before we can define "incident response," however, it is necessary to first define what "incidents" are.

Definition of Incidents

By *incidents*, we mean adverse events that threaten security in computing systems and networks. *Events* include *any* observable thing that happens in a computer and/or network. Events include connecting to another system via a network, accessing files, system shutdowns, and so on. *Adverse events* include system crashes, packet flooding within a network, unauthorized use of another user's account, unauthorized use of system privileges, defacement of one or more web pages, and execution of malicious code that destroys data. Other adverse events include floods, fires, electrical outages, and excessive heat that causes system crashes. Incidents such as natural disasters and power-related disruptions are not, however, within the scope of this guidebook. This book focuses exclusively on *security-related* incidents.

Outages

Outages and potential outages due to natural disasters, electrical failures, and so forth are the focus of an area that has traditionally been called *business continuity* and *business continuity planning*.

Types of Security-Related Incidents

What kinds of adverse events are there when security-related incidents occur? The number might surprise you. The next part of this chapter discusses types of security-related incidents.

CIA-Related Incidents

Traditionally, computer and information security efforts have focused on CIA: confidentiality (of information that needs to be protected), integrity (of information, systems, services, and so on), and availability (of information, applications, services, systems, networking, and so on). Many incidents that have occurred in the past have fit the CIA model well. Consider, for example, the many break-ins into Pentagon systems from Argentina in the late 1990s. These attacks were designed to obtain U.S. military information or, in other words, to compromise the *confidentiality* of this information. Concerns regarding integrity have been triggered by incidents in which attackers have planted remote-control programs such as Netbus, SubSeven, and BackOrifice2K into Windows systems.

In a well-publicized incident in 2000, a Microsoft employee's laptop system was compromised in this manner while the laptop was away from Microsoft premises; after the laptop was connected directly to the internal network, perpetrators then used it to gain access to resources within this network and send copies to systems outside the network. *Integrity* had been compromised. Finally, a good example of the need for *availability* is the series of distributed denial-of-service (DDoS) attacks against e-business companies in 2000 that crashed many hundreds of systems, causing huge financial losses.

Other Types of Incidents

An increasing proportion of professionals in the computer and information security arena is starting to realize that confidentiality, integrity, and availability in and of themselves provide an unduly narrow perspective. Additionally, new kinds of incidents have surfaced within the last 10 years or so; these incidents are often of a fundamentally different nature than older, more "traditional" incidents. Consider the following types of incidents in the subsections that follow.

Reconnaissance Attacks

Reconnaissance, in the context of security-related incidents, means discovering information that is useful in attacking whatever target a perpetrator has chosen. Although not a very strong form of attack, reconnaissance is usually a precursor to follow-up activity in which security-related defenses are actively breached. *Port scanning*, running a program that remotely finds ports that are open and closed on a remote system, represents one of the most common types of reconnaissance attacks, especially to cable modem and DSL users. Because cable modem and DSL connections are always "on," attackers have more time to conduct reconnaissance attacks. *Vulnerability scans* go beyond port scans by finding how services respond to connections, thereby indicating whether a particular vulnerability is (or vulnerabilities are) present.

Repudiation

Repudiation is one of the best examples of a type of incident that does not involve any of the traditional CIA. *Repudiation* means that a person or program acting on behalf of a person takes some action (which, in particular, indicates some kind of commitment) and then denies doing so later. Someone might, for example, use electronic means to order merchandise and then deny ordering the merchandise after it arrives. Repudiation presents a particular problem for the world of e-business because it can translate into major financial loss if not adequately controlled.

Harassment

Harassment means bothering, threatening, embarrassing, or intimidating someone else. Harassment occurs in everyday settings, and it is starting to occur in the cyberworld more, too. The perpetrator can, for example, use e-mail to send a series of obnoxious messages to a victim, use a chat room to do the same, use a messaging or remote screenwrite service, and so on. Extreme forms of harassment include *cyberstalking*, in which the stalker uses electronic means to follow and intimidate a victim, and cyber-predators' use of chat rooms and other avenues to make sexual advances.

Extortion

Extortion means attempting to get a victim to pay money or deliver something else of worth because of a threat the perpetrator has made. Extortion attempts are starting to become more prevalent in the cyberworld. Consider, for example, a real-life case study in which an employee used electronic means to attempt to receive money from his employer. He had the only copies of encryption keys that could decrypt files containing the company's original engineering research. The company decided to turn to law enforcement instead. In another case, two attackers broke into a corporation's network and then attempted to get this corporation to pay them a large sum of money in return for their secrecy about the break-in. The extortion attempt failed when the corporation made a public announcement about the break-in and turned the case over to law enforcement, which arrested the alleged perpetrators.

Pornography Trafficking

Computers and networks are also increasingly used to store and transport pornography. Although the definition of "pornography" might differ from one region, state, province, or country to another, it is not necessary to look very hard before finding some kind of electronic pornography-related activity that breaks the law somewhere. A particularly distressing trend is the use of computers and networks for the purpose of sending, receiving, and storing child pornography.

Dealing with suspected cases of pornography has become more difficult because of techniques offenders can use to hide pornographic images within other graphics images. This makes obtaining a copy of pornographic images by anyone but the offender extremely difficult. The most well known of these methods, steganography, is discussed in Chapter 9, "Forensics II."

Organized Crime Activity

Another category of incident that does not fit the traditional CIA mold is organized crime activity via electronic means. Organized crime can, for example, use computer technology in performing criminal acts such as drug trafficking and running prostitution rings.

Subversion

Subversion is used here to describe a type of incident in which an intended function or access appears to work as expected but does not. This might superficially seem to be simply an attack in which the integrity of a system, network, or application is violated, but it is in reality something more. Examples include putting a bogus financial server on a network to discover credit card numbers and illegal indexing of web pages. In the latter, a perpetrator modifies web links so that when anyone connects to a particular web page, the connection is actually to another, completely different, web page.

Hoaxes

Hoaxes are incidents caused by dissemination (either deliberately or unintentionally) of false information. Even though hoaxes are based on false information, they can have a huge negative impact, sometimes including damage to systems (caused by panicked users) and a significant waste of time and resources. A recent example is the hoax concerning the Virtual Card for You virus. Several organizations (particularly vendor organizations) distributed urgent bulletins warning recipients that this virus was the worst to ever surface in the wild. The virus allegedly first distributed itself to a user's mail distribution list, then froze the infected system, forcing the user to reboot the system, and then erased sector zero of the hard drive, rendering the hard drive useless. As things turned out, there was no Virtual Card for You virus, forcing many of the organizations that spread so much panic to make red-faced retractions of their previous bulletins about this virus.

Hoax Lists: Good or Bad?

Several incident response teams maintain listings of known hoaxes, such as hoaxes about new viruses that have allegedly been found. These teams claim that maintaining such listings is helpful in lessening the negative impact of hoaxes and in snuffing them out quickly. Other security professionals, however, question the value of maintaining these listings, saying that knowing whether or not a new virus or worm exists usually does little good until antivirus software vendors actually update their software to recognize the new malicious code. Furthermore, in the past, virus writers have sometimes assigned the name of a virus on a hoax list to a virus they have just created, causing massive confusion. Finally, those opposed to hoax lists say that these lists result in a greater amount of attention paid to hoaxes, something that actually encourages those who perpetrate them.

Caveat

The kinds of incidents discussed in this section are by no means mutually exclusive. Reconnaissance, for example, is likely to be followed by attempts to gain unauthorized access to data or to bring systems down. Remember, too, the case in which young perpetrators broke into a corporation's network and then attempted to extort money from the corporation. One of the troubling aspects of cybercrime trends, in fact, is the increased complexity of incidents over the years.

What Incident Response Involves

Incident response means actions taken to deal with an incident that occurs. These actions normally represent some form of intervention to negate or minimize the impact of the incident. Actions can be initiated by either humans or computer systems. In fact, one of the new trends discussed in Chapter 13, "Future Directions," is the use of automated incident response mechanisms.

Although Chapter 3, "A Methodology for Incident Response," covers the logic and flow of incident response in detail, suffice it to say at this point that incident response involves a potentially very large range of activities. Although many of these activities are direct reactions to the adverse event that occurs, many are not. Many of the facets of incident response involve preparing to handle incidents, enabling those involved in incident response efforts to work more efficiently. Many other facets involve managing the large amount of data likely to be accumulated as incidents occur.

It is also tempting to view incident response as something that is done only by technical personnel. Although it is true that technical personnel are likely to be some of the main players involved when incidents occur, incident response very frequently requires much more than application of technical knowledge. It also involves management, legal knowledge, human relations training, technical writing skills, and even knowledge of psychology (especially when it comes to dealing with insider attacks), as Chapter 11 of this book, "The Human Side of Incident Response," will detail. In short, successful incident response efforts are usually multidisciplinary efforts that involve a range of participants with a variety of skills. Effective incident response goes far beyond simply making a technical diagnosis and applying technical skills to fix the problem.

The Relationship between Incident Response and Incident Response Teams

Anyone who keeps up with vulnerability advisories is almost certainly familiar with acronyms such as CERT, AUSCERT, GIAC, DFN CERT, NASIRC, and others. These acronyms represent the names of incident response teams. For example, NASIRC stands for the NASA Automated Systems Incident Response Capability. It might thus be tempting to assume that "incident response" is equivalent to "incident response team." This kind of assumption, however, is not necessarily true. Although many incident response teams now exist, much of the actual work in responding to incidents is performed by individuals who are *not* part of any team, per se. As Chapter 4, "Forming and Managing an Incident Response Team," points out, whether or not it is possible to form an actual team depends on many factors such as funding. But effective incident response does *not* necessitate having a *team*, as you will see shortly.

Relationship to the Goals of Information and Computer Security

Virtually every discussion of information and computer security defines three goals: confidentiality, integrity, and availability (CIA). As previously mentioned, confidentiality means protecting the contents of files, network transmissions, the contents of a computer's memory, and so on from unauthorized disclosure. Integrity means keeping systems and data from unauthorized alteration. Availability means ensuring that access to systems, network services and components, and data is continuous and without interruption. But as Donn Parker pointed out in his book *Fighting Computer Crime*, computer and information security efforts that focus exclusively on the CIA objectives are doomed to fail.

CIA in and of itself excludes other important goals and considerations. Consider, for example, an electronic business transaction in which someone orders a large number of goods and then denies ordering them shortly afterward. Preventing repudiation or "nonrepudiation" of transactions is thus another critical goal of information and computer security. Additionally, establishing accountability of users—ensuring that user actions on systems and networks are properly recorded so that irresponsible, hostile, and other acts come to light—is yet another important goal.

Incident response is directly linked to the goals of computer and information security. If the controls (for example, access control permissions, firewalls, encryption) that are deployed ever should be defeated or bypassed (as will almost certainly happen in one or more circumstances), incident response can be used to restore confidentiality, integrity, or availability. In fact, as you will see shortly, effective incident response is in tune with an organization's security objectives so that the infrastructure established for incident response and the particular procedures put in place reflect the relative importance of each of the security goals for that organization.

Incident Response and the Computer/Information Security Life Cycle

In a competent computer and information security practice, incident response is an essential component of the information security life cycle. The three major parts of this cycle are countermeasures, detection, and response (see Figure 1.1).

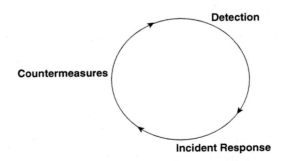

Figure 1.1   The computer/information security life cycle.

Countermeasures

Countermeasures are defenses that counter threats such as break-ins, denial-of-service attacks, repudiation, and others. Countermeasures are usually chosen and deployed as a result of conducting a risk analysis, although other approaches (such as adoption of measures deemed to be in accordance with due care standards or even "best practices") are being used increasingly as an alternative to traditional risk-based approaches. No countermeasure is foolproof, however; even if it were, resources for adopting all the countermeasures necessary to counter all identified sources of risk would undoubtedly be insufficient.

Detection

Detection of security incidents essential means providing an indication that security has been breached. Because the topic of detection is covered in detail in Chapter 3, it suffices at this point to say that effective detection provides feedback concerning the adequacy of the countermeasures that have been deployed. If a particular type of incident (for example, break-ins to Windows-based systems) occurs repeatedly and is noticed by an intrusion-detection capability, there is increased impetus to deploy countermeasures (or sometimes to increase or change the countermeasures already in place) to protect against this type of incident.

Incident Response

The next and final part of the computer/information security life cycle is *incident response*; after an incident has been noticed, incident response is the next logical step. Note that assessing the type, severity, location, and/or frequency of attacks during incident response activity can prompt the deployment of new or different types of intrusion-detection methods.

The Rationale for Incident Response

Incident response, initially an area that did little more than evoke curiosity two decades ago, keeps growing in importance. Why? This next section presents the major reasons.

Difficulty in Securing Systems and Networks

Most fundamentally, information systems, applications, and networks have become substantially more sophisticated, making them even harder to secure. Networks, in particular, are difficult to secure because of the complexity and diversity of services and protocols in today's network environments. Additionally, networks go virtually everywhere, making potential points of unauthorized access nearly ubiquitous. Distributed computing environments, which typically entail intricate relationships between servers and clients, also present nearly insurmountable challenges to security. Compounding these problems is the fact that most organizations face shortfalls in funding for cybersecurity.

As desirable as it is to place extremely high levels of countermeasures (for example, access controls) on computing resources, doing so is generally unrealistic because of cost and other practical constraints. Being able to detect and recover from incidents quickly can, in many respects, therefore be considered a protection strategy that supplements system and network protection measures.

A note of caution is appropriate at this point. Although an effective incident response effort can, to some degree, compensate for using fewer countermeasures than needed, it can never totally replace these countermeasures. Consider the consequences of failing to install any countermeasures whatsoever in favor of simply responding to any incident that occurs. The organization that takes this kind of approach makes the implicit assumption that every incident can be promptly detected—a completely unrealistic assumption given statistics from the intrusion-detection arena. Additionally, there is no guarantee that an incident that occurs can and will be immediately terminated with minimal consequences. In the worst case, the organization will devote so much time and attention to incident response (because deploying no countermeasures would virtually open the proverbial incident floodgates) that it would have been better to devote this time to a combination of countermeasures and incident response.

Nevertheless, all this translates to substantially elevated potential for security-related incidents that require the capability to deal with these incidents. Difficulties in securing computers and networks thus make incident response a necessary component in any strategy to provide security.

Abundance of Security-Related Vulnerabilities

Today's operating systems and applications typically have an abundance of flaws (see related sidebar), many of which, if exploited, result in breaches of security mechanisms. Security-related vulnerabilities of this nature are being found in great numbers and with alarming regularity. Incident response can help reduce the impact of these vulnerabilities by cutting down the potential for loss and disruption should one or more of these vulnerabilities be exploited.

Dealing with Security-Related Vulnerabilities

Hardly a week goes by before new announcements about security-related vulnerabilities in operating systems and application software appear. It is not unusual for a newsgroup such as BugTraq (www.bugtraq.com) to post several hundred vulnerability notices every year.

Keeping up with security-related vulnerabilities is extremely important in avoiding security-related incidents. For example, a number of security experts have agreed that 10 particular vulnerabilities that are not fixed in many organizations are the cause of a disproportionate number of security-related incidents (see www.sans.org/topten).

Fixing vulnerabilities is, unfortunately, not always an easy matter. Installing vendor-supplied patches is, for example, usually not a straightforward matter. Patches can cause systems and/or applications to become unstable or, at worst, totally nonfunctional. Worse yet, too often the first (or even second) patch that vendors develop does not work properly, requiring deinstallation of the original patch and installation of the most recent one.

Chapter 3 will discuss the relationship between incident response stages and the need to patch security-related vulnerabilities. Aside from all other considerations, however, it is important to realize just how closely related the problem of frequent emergence of new security-related vulnerabilities and proliferation of security-related incidents is. The "white hat" community too often learns of new vulnerabilities only after observing a new pattern of security breaches.

Much of the fault for the abundance of security-related bugs in software lies with vendors, who are in a rush to get their products to market quickly and devote too little time to quality assurance. Many security-related flaws are simply programming errors, such as a failure to check whether input that a user sends is within a defined range of values. Out-of-range input that is nevertheless accepted by a program can cause a variety of problems, depending on many factors. One possible outcome, for example, is a transition to an abnormal processing state with increasing memory consumption to the point that there is no more available memory. The result can be an application or system crash.

Much of the fault for the abundance of security-related vulnerabilities in software actually falls on all of us. We continue to buy bug-infested software and accept software flaws as a normal part of life. Until we demand better-quality software (and, frankly, refuse to buy it until it meets our quality standards), we won't get it. Unless vendors perceive economic pressure for change, they won't change.

Availability of Programs that Attack Systems and Networks

Just as an abundance of security-related vulnerabilities has emerged and continues to emerge, a large number of programs that exploit these vulnerabilities have become publicly available. Port and vulnerability scanning tools comprise just one of many categories of these tools. Some tools are designed to provide unauthorized local and/or remote access to files and directories. Others yield remote shell (interactive) access, and still others escalate privileges when some kind of shell access is established.

Tools that launch denial-of-service attacks are also in abundance. Perhaps worst of all, an increasing proportion of tools that launch attacks require little knowledge of computers or how this software works. These "kiddie scripts" in particular have increased the level of threat to computing systems and networks; now virtually anyone can launch successful attacks. The widespread availability of programs that can be used to attack other systems once again elevates the importance of incident response. Simply put, systems and networks can be attacked more efficiently and easily; effective intervention can reduce the impact of these attacks.

Actual and Potential Financial Loss

Organizations that experience security-related incidents suffer financial loss, the amount of which has escalated considerably over the years. Eighty-five percent of the respondents to the 2001 computer crime survey by the FBI and Computer Security Institute (CSI) revealed having experienced security-related breaches during the previous year. Sixty-four percent of the respondents admitted that these breaches resulted in financial loss. The cumulative loss attributed to these incidents was nearly $378 million—an eye-opening statistic given the relatively few people who responded. This amount was over $100 million more than the loss reported in the same survey the previous year.

In addition, security-related threats have become more diverse. New kinds of security-related incidents are constantly emerging, each of which has its own potential to cause financial loss. All this again points to the need for, among other things, prompt detection of security-related incidents and remedial actions that substantially diminish financial loss.

Potential for Adverse Media Exposure

Negative media exposure resulting from security-related incidents is a major concern of most organizations. Security-related news items are increasingly making headlines and are receiving major television and radio coverage. News about security-related incidents is especially savory to the media. Effective incident response strategies can reduce the potential for adverse media exposure by helping minimize the duration and magnitude of incidents.

The Need for Efficiency

When incidents occur, pandemonium too often prevails. Incidents, including security-related incidents, are generally unexpected events in computing environments that are frequently less than sufficiently stable in the first place. Regardless of the type of incident that has occurred, responding efficiently and systematically causes less negative impact and discord than if there is no orchestrated effort. Personnel need to follow all necessary steps to handle an incident correctly without performing incorrect and potentially catastrophic actions (such as needlessly reformatting hard drives to eradicate malicious code) or omitting critical steps.

Efficiency also implies using resources appropriately. When both technical and managerial personnel respond to an incident, allocating a sizeable amount of resources often becomes necessary. These resources could be assigned to a different mission more often if a typical incident's impact is blunted and the duration is short.

Limitations in Today's Intrusion-Detection Capabilities

As mentioned previously, today's intrusion-detection tools are far less than perfect. One particular problem is the tendency to miss (overlook) bona fide incidents. Another is the propensity to generate false alarms. An incident response capability can, to some degree, attenuate both problems; determining exactly what has happened and the magnitude of the problem is an important part of the incident response process. Chapter 6, "Tracing Network Attacks," discusses a few relevant considerations concerning intrusion detection, including the advantages and disadvantages of network-based and host-based intrusion detection. Intrusion detection is not, however, a central focus of this book.

Legal Considerations

Yet another impetus for incident response capability is addressing legal issues. Several considerations that apply are discussed next.

Exercise of Due Care

At the most basic level, having an incident response capability is increasingly being viewed within industry as a matter of "due care." *Due care*, in the most fundamental sense, means exercising reasonable precautions that indicate an organization is being responsible. If a corporation were to experience a major security-related incident that escalated because no incident response capability was in place, those who were adversely affected (such as stockholders, business partners, and others who suffered a significant financial loss) would have strong grounds for suing on the basis of lack of exercise of due care.

Conforming to Provisions of the Law

Additionally, responding to incidents presents many potential legal landmines. Issues such as network monitoring, keystroke capture, invasion of privacy, whether or not to construct profiles on certain users, issues related to international law, and so forth frequently present themselves. When done properly, incident response helps ensure that legal statutes are not violated and that actions performed during the course of responding to incidents are defensible in a court of law. The growing area of *forensics*, using methods of data gathering and handling that will serve as acceptable evidence in a court of law, is a particularly important part of the legal side of incident response. Chapter 7, "Legal Issues," as well as Chapter 8, "Forensics I," and Chapter 9, "Forensics II," cover legal considerations of incident response in detail.

Interfacing with the Law Enforcement Community

Finally, incident response activity is often tied in, explicitly or implicitly, with law enforcement. A question that usually looms in the minds of those who respond to incidents is whether or not a law enforcement agency will be brought in at some point in time. Again, having an incident response capability can result in a better interface with the law enforcement community.

The Fortress Mentality

In past centuries, armies built fortresses as a major part of their military strategy. Fortresses had different architectures, defense features, and so forth, and for a while they worked. Then came the advent of more powerful weaponry. Troops that stayed inside fortresses eventually became sitting ducks. Fortresses are now not much more than items of curiosity in the twenty-first century.

The term "fortress mentality," first coined by Eugene Schultz, David Brown, and Tom Longstaff in their 1990 University of California technical report on incident response, also applies to a prevalent mentality concerning how security should be achieved. Traditional approaches (based on annual loss expectancy, calculation of residual risk, controls checklists, and so on) are in many respects akin to building a fortress because they emphasize barriers at the expense of the operational side of security. It is impractical and almost certainly impossible, however, to protect systems sufficiently to make them immune against all attacks. If appropriate detection and response strategies are implemented, rapid intervention that can diminish the impact of any incident will occur. *Effective computer and information security strategies achieve balance between barriers and operational security.*

Overview of Incident Response

The next portion of this chapter provides an overview of the process of responding to incidents.

Initial Considerations

A successful incident response effort is closely linked to policy. This next subsection explains why and how.

Policy

Computer and information security begins and ends with policy. An information security policy is a high-level description of essential elements of computer and information security, including the basic requirements and infrastructure necessary for establishing security. A policy generally describes do's and don'ts for users (and possibly system administrators) and specifies punishments for failure to observe the provisions of the policy. An effective policy also describes an organization's *security stance*—whether the organization generally wants open and free access at the cost of little security, tight security controls at the cost of greater inconvenience to users and possibly loss of functionality and performance, or something in between these two extremes.

Performance Appraisal

Ideally, an information security policy will also include provisions related to each employee's adherence to the information security policy in the personnel performance-appraisal process. In most cases, this is a better approach than simply spelling out punishments for failing to comply. The prospect of punishment generally evokes strong negative emotions in humans.

A policy is a necessary part of a successful computer and information security effort. Failing to specify requirements in advance spells doom. Although the context of the coverage of policy here has been computer and information security in general, everything said so far applies equally well to the area of incident response (which is one of the many areas within the umbrella of computer and information security). Unless an organization's information security policy specifies requirements for incident response, these requirements will almost certainly not be met. Some important types of incident response requirements typically included in an information security policy are as follows:

- The sanctioning of the incident response capability, (that is, stating that it is a *required* function of the organization in question)
- The mission or objectives as well as the scope of this capability
- The authority (if any) given to this capability
- The limits of incident response (what kinds of actions are and are not permissible during the process of responding to an incident)
- The relationship to the law enforcement community (whether law enforcement should be brought in to deal with an incident and, if so, when)

Simply writing a policy, of course, does little or no good and is, in fact, an almost sure recipe for the policy being ignored. Obtaining buy-in from those who are affected by it is necessary to stave off resistance. Especially critical is approval by senior-level management; without senior-level management's support, a policy is almost certainly doomed to fail. Making the buy-in from senior-level management widely visible (for example, by having the CEO or someone who reports to the CEO sign it) to those affected by the policy is, in fact, one of the best strategies in making a policy work.

Policy Review

Having a policy is important, but policies get out of date over time. It is thus important to review an organization's information security policy, especially (in the current context) any provisions related to incident response, and make changes as needed. New types of incidents will emerge, necessitating changes in incident response–related policy provisions. Parts of an incident response effort might also prove unsuccessful, necessitating an analysis of whether certain requirements were appropriate in the first place.

Who should participate in a policy review? Normally, the manager of the incident response effort, the head of computer and information security (who might or might not also be the incident response manager), senior IT management, the head of audit, and others should participate. Note that effective policy is high level and thus does not include technical content.[1] Having technical personnel participate in a policy review is thus usually *in*appropriate.

A policy review should normally occur every six months to a year, although it is a good idea to conduct a special review whenever it is appropriate (for example, when a conflict between provisions in the policy and other requirements is discovered).

Planning and Organization

Chapter 5, "Organizing for Incident Response," covers planning and organizing for incident response in detail. This next section introduces topics covered more fully later.

Developing an Incident Response Architecture

Developing an incident response architecture is especially critical. An incident response architecture defines the components of an incident response capability and how these components are interrelated. Normally, an architecture can be represented by a pyramid with the highest (most conceptual) elements at the top, followed by more specific elements at the next level, followed by even more specific elements at the next level. Possible components include policy, procedures, technology, intrusion detection, communications, and others. Figure 1.2 illustrates one possible rendition of an incident response architecture.

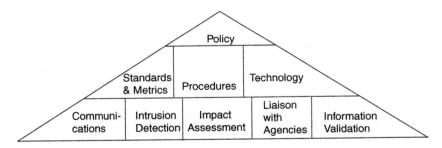

Figure 1.2   A possible incident response architecture.

1. This statement does not imply that technical requirements should go unwritten. Technical requirements should simply be embedded in another type of document (a technical standards or guidelines document) rather than in a policy.

Estimating Resources Needed

One of the downsides of incident response is that it is not cheap from a financial perspective. Many incident response efforts fail, or at least border on the brink of ruin, due to lack of resources. It is thus essential for management to attempt to accurately gauge the level of resources needed for an incident response effort and then begin to explore ways to obtain this level. Resources must cover expenditures on items such as personnel, technology, travel, training, facilities, and other categories.

Establishing the Proper Technology Base

A suitable technology base is absolutely integral to a successful incident response effort. For example, intrusion detection is an extremely important component of such an effort. To determine whether a security-related incident has actually transpired, intrusion detection software might be necessary. This kind of software is generally not cheap; without proper planning, a budget shortfall that precludes the purchase of such software is likely. Other kinds of software that might be essential are integrity-checking software that detects any change in files and directories, antivirus software (which is now virtually a necessity rather than a luxury), forensics software, database software (to archive relevant data), and other types.

Software, however, is only part of the technology base that needs to be established. Hardware such as server platforms and workstations is a necessity. Communications devices such as cellular phones and pagers are no longer just an option. Palm Pilots, dictaphones, fax machines, and other types of devices might also be necessary.

Developing Procedures

Planning and organizing for incident response also requires creating highly comprehendible, detailed procedures for responding to incidents. Such procedures offer several significant benefits, including the following:

- **Shortening the learning curve.** Incident response typically requires a steep learning curve. The availability of procedures can substantially shorten this learning curve for those who are new to the incident response arena.

- **Uniformity of response efforts.** If followed, procedures ensure that the same kinds of steps are followed by those who engage in incident response, regardless of the particular individual involved, type of incident, and so forth.

- **Quality assurance.** If well written, procedures help ensure a certain degree of adherence to established standards. This promotes quality of incident response efforts.

- **Legal considerations.** If a lawsuit or even criminal charges should grow out of an incident, evidence of the existence and deployment of standard procedures for incident response can counter certain legal allegations that might be presented.

Developing Cooperative Relationships

Security-related incidents are seldom isolated to one or two systems or networks in a single organization anymore. Increasingly, these incidents are widespread, typically even crossing international boundaries. Additionally, one never knows the next entity with which one must deal. Incident response teams, Internet service providers (ISPs), vendors, and law enforcement agencies are just a few of these possible entities. After all, "no man is an island." The incident response effort that does not heed this truism will likely not accomplish much. Building cooperative relationships with other entities is an important consideration in planning for and organizing an incident response effort.

Dealing with Organizational Considerations

Every incident response capability is part of some overall organization or, in some cases, group of organizations. To be truly effective, this capability must fit in reasonably within the organization(s). Virtually every medium- to large-size organization has, for example, an operations organization. On the downside, it is possible for an incident response effort to collide with operations, causing major fallout. On the upside, operations might deploy certain hardware and software that might be useful. A good example is hardware and software used in intrusion detection. If operations already has created an intrusion-detection capability, tapping into this capability would normally make more sense than setting up an independent one.

It is also important—to the maximum extent possible—for intrusion response capabilities to work within the cultural context of the organization to which they belong. An organizational culture that, for instance, highly values privacy is not likely to be receptive to efforts to construct profiles on individual employees.

Finally, it is critical for an incident response effort's procedures, data archival methods, and other facets of operation to coincide to those of the organization of which this capability is a part. If a conflict surfaces, modifying the team's procedures and practices to coincide with the organization's is normally the best course of action. In exceptional cases, special requirements (such as the need for forensics) might call for exemption from the organization's procedures and practices. In this case, discussing the team's particular requirements with senior management is the proper course of action.

Establishing Metrics

Metrics are measurement conventions represented in terms of numbers. Metrics in the field of computer and information security have gotten off to a rather slow start; it is, after all, often difficult to think of metrics for critical variables such as "adequacy of existing controls given levels of threat." Metrics are now starting to gain more acceptance, in part because they provide one of the most important ways to communicate with senior management.

Metrics are particularly important in the area of incident response because management is likely to ask for status reports or other queries in terms of metrics, such as "number of incidents handled." It is important to consider and evaluate possible metrics when planning and organizing for incident response. Fortunately, the incident response arena is very conducive to the use of metrics. Metrics, such as the number of incidents handled, number of business-threatening incidents handled, average time for incident detection, average time from incident onset to termination, and others are fairly intuitive.

Summary

This chapter sets the stage for the rest of this book. "Incident response" means responding to "incidents," events that happen in computing systems and networks that threaten security. "Security" has traditionally translated to the need for confidentiality, integrity and availability (CIA), so in the most fundamental sense, incidents involve some kind of compromise of CIA.

Security-related incidents have become substantially more diverse in nature, however; incidents such as reconnaissance attempts, repudiation of transactions, organized crime activity, subversion, extortion attempts, and hoaxes are becoming more common. Incident response has become increasingly important because of the growing difficulty of securing systems and networks, the proliferation of security-related vulnerabilities, the need to minimize loss and disruption when incidents occur, legal considerations, and other important reasons. Although traditional methods such as risk analysis can be used to find some kinds of risk, and although security countermeasures can be deployed to protect against these risks, traditional strategies are in and of themselves insufficient to counter the many current threats and risks.

Incident response is now a necessary component of a successful computer and network security life cycle that includes countermeasures, detection, and response. A successful incident response effort requires considerable organization and planning, starting with the appropriate provisions in an organization's information security policy and then building from there. Developing a suitable incident response architecture, planning resource needs, planning use of technology, creating incident response procedures, forming cooperative relationships with other teams and organizations, and creating appropriate metrics are also essential elements in planning and organizing for incident response.

2

Risk Analysis

COMPUTER AND INFORMATION SECURITY ALWAYS, IN some manner, deals with risk and how to manage it. In many information security professionals' minds, the beginning point in the practice of information security is risk analysis. This chapter deals with risk analysis and its relationship to incident response. Major topics include risk analysis, types of risk, obtaining data about risk, and using the results of risk analysis.

About Risk Analysis

Although *risk analysis* means many things to many people, in the most fundamental sense, it means determining the expected loss associated with each source or cause of loss in computing systems and networks. In an organization, for example, tampering with financial applications might be perceived as the greatest risk, followed by damage to or disruption of the networking infrastructure, followed by external intrusions into servers that house financial applications, followed by something else.

Risk analysis can be either quantitative or qualitative. A *quantitative risk analysis*, as the term implies, involves numbers (normally monetary figures) to represent the amount of risk believed to be present. A quantitative risk analysis in the United States, for example, would yield expected dollar losses for each source of risk. In an *annual loss expectancy (ALE)*, the expected loss associated with each individual source of risk during a year is calculated. The formula for determining the expected loss for each source of risk is the probability of occurrence multiplied by the cost of the negative outcome or loss:

$$Risk = Probability \times Loss$$

The sum of all expected losses for the year is the ALE. Table 2.1 illustrates a hypothetical ALE calculation.

Table 2.1 **Hypothetical Calculation of the ALE**

Source	Probability	Loss	Risk
Destruction of customer database	.005	$24,000,000	$120,000
Unauthorized loss of copyright data to competitors	.003	$35,000,000	$105,000
Sabotage of major network components	.001	$18,000,000	$18,000
Disruption of billing systems	.002	$8,000,000	$16,000
Worm or virus attack	.05	$90,000	$4,500
TOTAL			**$263,500**

Alternatively, other professionals prefer to simply determine whether each threat is high, medium, or low in impact—a *qualitative* approach in that the output is not quantitative. This is, in many respects, the most intuitive approach. Table 2.2 shows the results of a hypothetical qualitative risk analysis based on the same sources of threat as in Table 2.1.

Table 2.2 **Hypothetical Qualitative Risk Analysis**

Source	Risk
Destruction of customer database	High
Unauthorized loss of copyright data to competitors	High
Sabotage of major network components	Medium
Disruption of billing systems	Medium
Worm or virus attack	Low

There is little agreement within the field of computer and information security concerning exactly how to conduct a risk analysis. Controversy concerning whether quantitative risk analysis is better than qualitative risk analysis abounds. Proponents of qualitative risk analysis argue (among other things) that risk analysis implies a precision that does not really exist. Critics of the qualitative approach argue that this approach lacks precision. Still others say that risk analysis really boils down to little more than guesswork based on gut feelings at best. Those who downplay the value of risk analysis altogether are likely to embrace the previously discussed due care approach instead.

Despite spirited opposition and disagreement, risk analysis remains a fixture in the field of information security. A major reason that so many information security professionals value risk analysis so highly is not only because it provides a basis for determining the relative degree to which resources need to be protected, but also because the *process* of performing a risk analysis helps those engaged in it to better understand what they are trying to protect and why.

Assessing Risk

As should now be evident, no proven, well-accepted method of assessing risk currently exists. Several criteria are frequently applied, however, when professionals consider the degree of risk present. These criteria include the following:

1. **Monetary cost.** How expensive would it be to fix whatever has occurred as the result of an incident?

2. **Operations impact.** To what degree would critical services be lost and operational schedules disrupted?

3. **Public relations fallout.** What kind of negative publicity would occur, especially outside of one's organization?

4. **Impact on humans.** Would the incident elevate danger to humans in terms of safety, morale, loss of confidence in management and/or computing systems, and so on?

The treatment of risk analysis in this chapter represents anything but another attempt to regurgitate the principles of traditional risk analysis or to take one of the many (sometimes ludicrous) positions professionals have adopted concerning the "correct" way to perform a risk analysis. The reason that risk analysis is the theme of this entire chapter is that it is one of the most important parts of responding to incidents, as you will see shortly.

Types of Security-Related Risks

This section provides details concerning specific types of security-related risks that occur today, their impact, and how to obtain data concerning their probability of occurrence.

Risk Categories

As expected, the specific categories of security-related risks that occur today are very diverse. Here are the most common ones.

Break-ins

Break-ins are unauthorized access to one or more systems in which the attacker masquerades as a legitimate user, usually (but not always) by entering the correct username and password. When authenticated as a user, the attacker can do virtually anything that the legitimate user can do, including read email messages in the user's email queue, send messages, access the home directory and any subdirectories and files therein, and so on. In most break-ins, however, the intruder's goal is not simply to reach another user's account. The goal instead is often to gain *shell* access, meaning access to a command shell such as /bin/sh or /bin/tsh in UNIX or cmd.exe in Windows systems. With access to a shell, intruders can run programs or scripts that can expand the intruder's access to the system and/or network, usually by escalating the privilege level, as you will see shortly.

Too often, unfortunately, senior-level managers trivialize break-ins, thinking they are caused by pimply-faced teenagers who cannot really cause any damage. Sometimes this preconception is true, but a large body of evidence strongly indicates that break-ins are performed by a wide range of perpetrators, often even by members of an organized crime ring or a country's intelligence agency. Break-ins can result in theft of valuable data and/or software. Break-ins to systems of several vendors, for example, have resulted in theft of source code for operating systems and other products. Additionally, a break-in can result in compromise of integrity. Consider, for example, the break-in to a U.S. government laboratory once in which the intruders changed the value of pi in a critical scientific application to 3.8!

Even if data or programs are not stolen or altered, break-ins can result in sizeable loss. A break-in into a single system in a National Aeronautics and Space Administration (NASA) site once disrupted space flight operations for several weeks. The victim machine, operated by the Missions Operation Directorate (MOD), was critical in controlling functions for manned space flights. This machine had to be carefully inspected, restored, and tested before NASA officials approved it for use in operations again. The financial cost was high; the delay substantially ran up the cost of the launch.

Unauthorized Execution of Programs or Commands

It is not necessary to actually break into a system to accomplish an intruder's goals. A perpetrator can also exploit a vulnerability in a victim system that enables the perpetrator to run one or more rogue commands on that system. A clever perpetrator can then do almost anything on the compromised system. One of the most common ways to run rogue commands is to create a buffer overflow condition. A *buffer overflow condition* results from more input being received than there is available memory, often causing the excess input to overwrite commands in memory that are waiting to be executed. Not only can existing commands be overwritten, if done correctly, the attacker's commands will be positioned in the buffer so that they are actually executed.

One of the most common methods of running unauthorized commands on victim systems is exploiting the Berkeley Internet Name Domain server (BIND). BIND is the most commonly deployed implementation of the domain name system (DNS). DNS is an essential Internet service in that it enables systems to locate other systems simply by using hostnames (for example, system.domain.co), converting each hostname to an IP address such as 131.243.2.3 (or vice versa). Functions within certain versions of BIND, including nxt, qinv, in.named, and others, have a number of exploitable bugs

that can result in outcomes such as a buffer overflow, resulting in the capability to execute commands with root (superuser) privileges. For example, some versions of BIND
do not correctly validate NXT records. An attacker can consequently send a huge
amount of input in these records to cause a buffer overflow and then run a rogue program at the same privilege level that the name server has.

Attackers who initiate BIND attacks seldom stop after exploiting one or more vulnerabilities. They also frequently purge system logs to cover their tracks and then (if
they have not already gained root access) download and run tools to obtain a root
shell. Next they run network-scanning tools to locate other systems with the same
BIND vulnerabilities, and then they attack these systems in the same manner. The toll
in terms of number of machines compromised within a short period of time is often
very high.

BIND attacks pose a very serious risk factor because of the prevalence of BIND on
the Internet. In fact, a consensus effort to determine the exploited vulnerabilities identified BIND-based attacks as the most frequent (see the next sidebar). Both Linux and
UNIX systems are vulnerable to BIND attacks.

Unauthenticated remote users might also be able to run rogue code on systems that
run unpatched versions of LPRng. LPRng is a frequently used software package in
FreeBSD UNIX and certain versions of Linux, and it replaces the Berkeley Standard
Distribution (BSD) lpd printing service. This software has a *format string vulnerability*, a
problem caused by missing format strings in function calls. Format strings help ensure
that received input is processed properly. This vulnerability enables user-supplied arguments to be passed to a susceptible function call.

Privilege Escalation

Privilege escalation means gaining privileges without being authorized to do so. If
attackers are not able to gain privileges immediately when they access a system, they
next usually attempt to escalate privileges by running programs that exploit vulnerabilities. When the intruder becomes a superuser, that person has complete control of the
victim system (in most operating systems). Worse yet, if trusted access mechanisms
between hosts are in place, the intruder might now be able to easily gain superuser
access to other systems that trust the original victim system.

A good example is recent attacks involving the Remote Procedure Call (RPC) in
certain flavors of UNIX and Linux systems. Attackers have been exploiting RPC
weaknesses in functions such as rpc.ttdbserverd (ToolTalk), rpc.cmsd (Calendar
Manager), and rpc.statd. Successful exploitation (by running carefully constructed programs) results in unauthorized root access.

An intruder toolkit called "Ramen" is also frequently used in victim hosts. This publicly available toolkit exploits vulnerabilities in FTPD, rpc.statd, and LPRng. Ramen not
only gives unauthorized root access, it also contains a mechanism for self-propagation.

The SANS Top 10 Vulnerabilities

Vendors keep coming out with new patches, yet security breaches continue to occur at accelerating rates. Why? A group of experts determined that the overwhelming majority of known incidents occur through exploitation of a limited number of vulnerabilities. These include (in order of frequency of successful exploits) the following:

1. Vulnerabilities in BIND, particularly in nxt, qinv, and in.named, that can lead to root access in any system that runs BIND.

2. Vulnerabilities in CGI programs and application extensions in web servers that can allow unauthorized access to files and directories, execution of rogue commands, and a variety of other outcomes.

3. Remote Procedure Call (RPC) security bugs, particularly in rpc.ttdbserverd (ToolTalk), rpc.cmsd (Calendar Manager), and rpc.statd, that can enable attackers to remotely reach network services and then run commands as root in UNIX and Linux systems.

4. A Remote Data Service (RDS) security flaw in the Microsoft Internet Information Server (IIS) that can allow attackers to remotely run rogue commands with Administrator privileges on Windows NT and Windows 2000 hosts.

5. Buffer overflow problems, pipe attacks (which allow unauthorized users to execute rogue commands), and multipurpose Internet mail extension (MIME) exploits that result in root compromise in UNIX and Linux systems.

6. Buffer overflows in the sadmind and mountd programs in Solaris that can be exploited to allow attackers to gain root access.

7. File sharing through network file system (NFS) mounts and Windows shares that allows anyone to gain access to file systems and that allows too much access (in other words, write access) once access is achieved.

8. Easy-to-guess or nonexistent passwords, especially for superuser accounts.

9. Buffer overflow conditions in Internet Mail Application Protocol (IMAP) and Post Office Protocol (POP) configuration that result in unauthorized root access in Unix and Linux systems.

10. Default SNMP community strings that allow perpetrators to remotely access (and then reconfigure or take down) devices or gain access to SNMP traffic that contains sensitive network configuration and other data.

One of the single most important things an information security effort can accomplish is to ensure that at least these 10 vulnerabilities are patched whenever possible.

Exploitation of Common Gateway Interface (CGI) Programs

The majority of today's web servers have common gateway interface (CGI) programs that allow users to interact with web pages. The fact that these programs are typically so easy to find and execute at the same privilege level as the web server on which they run makes CGI programs a favorite target of attackers. Some CGI programs even allow users to start up programs by entering the name of the program or routine to invoke. Flaws in the design and/or implementation of these programs can allow attackers to breach security in a number of ways, including executing rogue commands or programs (including back door programs), defacing web pages, accessing files and directories (sometimes including system files and directories) not intended for web user access, and escalating the level of privilege.

Additionally, web servers frequently have sample CGI programs installed by default. These sample programs are usually included for demonstration purposes. Too many webmasters fail to remove these programs; weaknesses in these programs can also be exploited.

The cost incurred by organizations that experience web attacks, regardless of whether a CGI or another exploit has been used, is generally much higher than people think. Because web servers are now the foundation of e-business, CGI and other exploits can, for example, result in one or more web servers becoming nonfunctional for extended periods of time, causing a substantial loss of business.

Denial-of-Service Attacks

Denial-of-service (DoS) attacks are reported to incident response teams more than any other type of attack. Misconceptions about denial-of-service attacks abound, however. One widely held misconception is that denial-of-service attacks invariably crash applications or hosts. Although the majority of reported DoS attacks do indeed cause applications or hosts to crash, a DoS attack can also cause a system or function to slow down or not run properly. A poorly written CGI program, for example, can crash a web server through a buffer overflow or other condition, but it can also cause CPU overutilization, making the victim host unresponsive.

Several types of DoS attacks are now almost legendary because they have occurred so many times:

- **SYN flooding.** In a SYN flooding attack, a hostile host sends a flood of SYN packets to a victim host. SYN packets are sent by a host that wants to start a TCP connection with another host (which we will also call the "receiving host"). The receiving host monitors the status of the connection attempt as well as the connection itself, if a connection is established. Monitoring the status requires resources. When a connection is closed, the resources used in monitoring the connection no longer are needed. As more connections occur, more resources are allocated to monitor the state of the connections. Under normal conditions in which a normal number of connections are in place, the receiving host has more than enough resources to monitor all the connections to it.

  But what if a flood of SYN packets is sent, and the receiving host gets no subsequent packets that are part of the normal process of completing the connection? Simply put, the receiving host runs out of resources, making the victim host unresponsive in the case of moderate resource exhaustion or causing it to crash in the case of more severe resource exhaustion. Because SYN flooding attacks are easy to initiate, they occur frequently. Fortunately, most vendors of operating systems have addressed the problem by having the operating system drop partially open connections.

- **Teardrop attack.** A teardrop attack is another type of DoS attack. The IP protocol is a robust protocol designed to deal with a wide range of devices, systems, and types of networking. If a system is going to send packets that are, say, 1 kilobyte (1,024 bytes) in size, network devices such as routers might not be able to handle packets that are this large. They might instead be able to handle packets that are only half this size. In this case, IP automatically divides the original packet into tinier parts that are able to make their way through network devices that cannot handle larger packets, a process called *fragmentation*.

   When the fragmented packets arrive at the receiving host, this host reassembles them into the packet that the sending host originally created. Fragmenting packets is useful because it provides a practical and reasonably efficient way to transport data across a network while still preserving the accuracy of the data. An attacker can abuse the fragmentation process, however, by causing the receiving host to receive values in packets it is not programmed to process. In a teardrop attack, one packet fragment is placed within another so that when the receiving host receives this set of packet fragments, the resulting values (in terms of offsets) are out of range. The receiving machine goes out of control and crashes.

   There are many variations of the classic teardrop attack as well as many other types of packet fragmentation attacks. An attacker can, for example, write a program that divides packets into fragments in a manner that causes subsequent packets to overwrite portions of the initial fragment.

- **Smurf attack.** Still another kind of denial-of-service attack is a smurf attack. In this kind of attack, a target host is victimized when an attacker falsifies ("spoofs") the origination or source address to be the target host's address. The attacker (or, more properly, a program that runs on behalf of the attacker) releases a flood of ping packets or ICMP echo requests destined for all the hosts on the local network. This is accomplished by having the broadcast address as the destination. A network broadcast address of a network has a particular IP address that is used for sending packets to every host within the local network.

   When the ping or ICMP echo request packets reach the broadcast address, these packets also are sent to the other hosts. They respond by replying to the source address, the address of the targeted host. The flood of replies can have several effects, the most likely of which is causing the target host to crash or, with a little luck, perhaps slowing it down to a crawl instead due to having to process such a barrage of packets. Most operating system vendors have developed patches that correct this problem, although network filtering that limits broadcast traffic is another viable solution.

Ping

Ping, the "packet Internet groper," is a protocol designed to determine whether or not a host is alive on the network (that is, whether it is running and responsive). Ping transmits a group of characters, usually a reasonably small group (typically fewer than 100 bytes), and then waits for the host that has been pinged to respond. One of the primary uses of ping is determining whether a particular host has crashed.

- **Ping-of-death attack.** Still another classic type of DoS attack is the ping-of-death attack. This attack creates a buffer overflow condition, something that results from having too little memory available for incoming data to be processed. The exact way in which a buffer overflow condition is handled depends on a number of factors, but one possible outcome is exhaustion of memory that causes an application or system to crash.

  The trick to a successful ping-of-death attack is to send ping packets that exceed the maximum size, namely 64KB in TCP/IP. The receiving host might not be programmed to reject the oversized packets and might consequently go into a buffer overflow condition. This problem has mainly (but not exclusively) affected Microsoft operating system products, most of which crash with the notorious blue screen of death (BSOD) appearing. Fortunately, patches that fix this problem are now routinely available and are usually incorporated into operating system products that were vulnerable only a few years ago.

- **Land attack.** A land attack capitalizes on the fact that properties of packets usually adhere to certain constraints. Normally, for example, SYN packets do not have the same source and destination IP addresses, nor are the source and destination ports normally the same. If an attacker sends SYN packets that have these or other characteristics in a land attack, the receiving host might go into some kind of abnormal state, causing it to crash.

- **WinNuke attack.** A WinNuke attack capitalizes on a weakness in the TCP/IP implementation in certain versions of Windows NT. In this attack, a perpetrator sends out of range input (that is, input with parameters that are not within the range the receiving host expects) to a victim host through a connection established on TCP port 139. Massive over-allocation of CPU in dealing with this abnormal condition causes the victim host to crash. The problem, which is fixed in Windows NT 4.0 Service Pack 3 and higher, is due to a failure to check whether input is within an expected range.

- **Distributed denial-of-service (DDoS) attacks.** Although similar in many respects to conventional denial-of-service attacks, DDoS attacks are different primarily in that they require taking over hosts that are then assigned various roles in the impending DDoS attack(s) through installation of special, malicious software. Note also, however, that DDoS attacks can be initiated from one's own systems, too. DDoS attacks involve master, handler, and zombie hosts:

  - Zombies are agents that actually release a flood of packets that bring down hosts and also being the network to a standstill. Zombies do not act on their own, however; they release a packet flood only if instructed to do so by another host, namely a handler (see next bullet).

  - Handlers are really nothing more than intermediate machines that neither initiate an attack nor release the packets that flood the victim network. They instead perform tasks such as confirming that agent software has been installed in hosts (zombies) throughout the network and that it is ready to work. Handlers thus query the zombies at designated intervals.

Handlers also receive a signal from the master, another host typically not placed within the network in which the DDoS attack is to occur, to initiate a DDoS attack to the agents, as shown in Figure 2.1. (See step 1 in this figure; the handler is the host with the circle around it). The handler in turn then sends a signal (see step 2 in Figure 2.1) to the zombies (all other hosts shown in the left side of Figure 2.1) to release a barrage of packets.

- The third accomplice in a DDoS attack is the master. The master is the host that is usually directly under the attacker's control. It is used to direct any handlers to send the command to release a flood of packets to the zombies.

DDoS attacks in 1999 and 2000 caused major financial loss and/or disruption for a number of institutions, including the University of Minnesota, ZDnet, eBay, E-Trust, Amazon.com, and others. The major threat is of a prolonged outage, although the cost of investigating hosts for evidence of compromise by DDoS tools and restoring the integrity of these systems can also be very high. Many types of DDoS attack tools have been identified. One, Shaft, even builds in its own detection mechanisms, enabling it to avoid being detected by intrusion-detection programs. Additional DDoS tools that have been identified include Trin00, Tribe Flood Network (TFN), TFN2K, Slice3, Stacheldracht, and others.

Web Defacement

Web defacement refers to unauthorized altering of the content of one or more web pages at a web site. Web defacement, in and of itself, is a significant threat in that an altered web page can lead to the following consequences:

- Embarrassment[1] for the organization that has experienced the web page defacement.

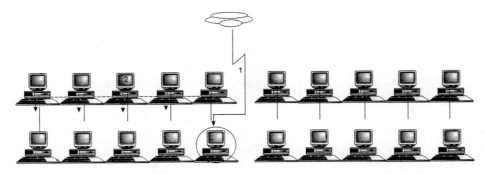

Figure 2.1 Initiating a DDoS attack to the agents.

---

1. See www.alldas.org or www.antionline.org for reports of web defacements. The sheer number of such reports is likely to startle anyone who has not visited these sites before.

- Denial of service. Customers cannot connect to an organization's web site to order products, services, and so forth during times when systems and network devices are down or network routes are flooded.

- Dissemination of erroneous information (including pricing information, information about corporate policies, and so on) that can result in one or more negative outcomes (such as lawsuits, a negative image, and so on).

Another important but often overlooked facet of web defacements is that they are often only the *beginning of things to come*. Many web defacements are followed by full-scale attacks on hosts within an organization. Web defacements should thus also be viewed as a kind of advance warning about impending attacks.

Virus and Worm Attacks

Viruses are self-reproducing programs that typically spread through user actions (such as attaching infected macros, sharing infected disks, and so forth). Worms are similar to viruses in that they are self-reproducing, but worms typically are transmitted over networks independently of user actions. Here is some more information about each:

- **Viruses.** Viruses generally infect system files, applications, or macro executables in programs such as Microsoft Excel or Word. Viruses use a variety of mechanisms to cause themselves to become executed as well as to reproduce themselves. For example, many macro viruses cause the application that uses macro routines to execute a rogue Save As that results in the virus becoming executed. All things considered, viruses are not very glamorous, but they constitute one of the greatest security-related threats in today's computing environments. Antivirus vendors such as Symantec, Network Associates, and Finjan have estimated that there are currently more than 50,000 viruses in the wild today. Virus infections can rapidly become widespread, causing catastrophic consequences such as loss of hard drives and corruption of system or data files.

- **Worms.** Worms are like viruses in that they are self-reproducing programs, but unlike viruses, worms can spread independently of user actions. In one sense, worms can be viewed as programmed cracker attacks. The best-known worm is probably the Internet Worm, which in 1988 infected thousands of UNIX systems that were connected to the Internet. Many worms with far more destructive and disruptive effects have surfaced since then, however. The Adore Worm, for example, has infected tens of thousands of Linux systems. Worms constitute a special level of threat because they work independently of human intervention. By the time people realize that worms have been reproducing over a network, hundreds of systems might be infected, causing data deletion, the need to restore systems, and many other undesirable outcomes.

Viruses and Worms

The distinction between viruses and worms, while still useful to some degree, is becoming less meaningful. This is because self-reproducing codes now often use a variety of mechanisms to spread themselves. Consider, for example, the W32FunLove.4099 worm, malicious code that infects systems such as Windows 98, Windows NT, and Windows 2000. This worm can spread when a user hits a web site, something that is dependent on user actions (like a virus) but that can also spread independently (like a worm) by finding unprotected shares. Shares are mechanisms for remotely reaching file systems in Windows systems.

Malicious Active Content

Another serious and ever-growing threat is the threat of *malicious active content* (also called *mobile code* and *executable content languages*). Active content comes in many flavors: ActiveX, Java applets, JavaScript (not to be confused with Java), VBScript, and others. Active content was developed with the intent of expanding web functionality; animation, sound effects, and so forth are all the product of active content.

Active content is downloaded into a machine that has connected to a web site and then is executed on that machine. Most of the existing implementations of active content are safe, but some are malicious, causing outcomes such as system crashes, halting of the execution of other active content executables running at the same time, a proliferation of windows on the desktop, capturing sensitive data and sending it to the address of a perpetrator, and so forth (see the following sidebar). The problem is especially serious with ActiveX. ActiveX controls, unfortunately, have almost no built-in execution constraints, enabling them to reach files on the system on which they run and even to initiate network connections after they are downloaded into a system. The only real security constraints in ActiveX are as follows:

- The creation of *zones* (sites from which ActiveX controls are allowed to be downloaded) within browsers such as Internet Explorer.
- *Authenticode*, a feature that allows the recipient of an ActiveX control to examine a certificate that accompanies the control to determine who the author of the control is. Authenticode might sound desirable from a security perspective, but in reality, it is less than desirable in that it is entirely post-hoc in nature. In an extreme scenario, a user could download a malicious ActiveX control that causes all kinds of mischief, only to find that the alleged author's identity is spoofed. In fact, at the time this chapter was written, a Microsoft employee's identity was spoofed in a Verisign certificate; this attests to the potential problem of tracing a user's identity.

Malicious Active Content Executables

Malicious active content executables are not just some theory or "proof of concept." Here are some examples of some of the many types of malicious Java applets:

- **Applet Killer.** Kills any other applets that might be running in the same browser

- **AttackThread.** Fills up the screen with more and more black windows

- **DemonDialer.** Initiates an outgoing phone call

- **DiskHog.** Fills up the hard drive with garbage

- **Known file.** Copies any file on a target system

- **Pickpocket.** Steals information from the Java Wallet

- **Wasteful.** Causes excessive CPU consumption

Several malicious ActiveX controls are out in the wild, too, although they are outnumbered by malicious Java applets. The following are some malicious ActiveX controls:

- **RadioActiveX.** Tricks Quicken into sending a check from a user's banking account

- **Exploder.** A fully signed control that causes the W9X system that downloads it to shut down

The good news is that, to date, not too many incidents have resulted from downloading malicious active content executables. Many organizations block active content at their external gateways, greatly reducing the risk that active content can introduce. The bad news is that we are probably only at the tip of the iceberg as far as malicious active content executables go. Because of the immense popularity of the Web, perpetrators know that web browsers provide one of the best ways to introduce malicious code into a remote network.

Back Doors or Remote Control Programs

Back doors (sometimes also referred to as *trap doors*) are methods (often in the form of programs, although not necessarily) set up in victim systems that allow attackers to readily regain access to those systems when the attackers want to do so. A simple type of back door is an illegitimate account that an attacker creates. This account often is given an innocuous name that system administrators are not likely to notice as they look through the names of user accounts. An example of a back-door program is the previously discussed Ramen toolkit. Another is /tmp/bob in UNIX and Linux, which is functionally nothing more than an inetd[2] configuration file that contains one line that opens up a remote root shell when the line is sent to inetd. This allows anyone to log in via the telnet program by connecting to a predesignated port. Especially dangerous back-door programs that give an attacker superuser access (using encrypted sessions) to compromised systems also exist in Windows 9X, Windows NT, and (to a lesser degree) Windows 2000. The names of some of these programs include BackOrifice, BackOrifice2000 (BO2K), SubSeven, and NetBus.

---

2. The inet (Internet) daemon. In UNIX and Linux, a *daemon* is a program that runs in the background and "wakes up" when it receives network input through designated ports.

Spoofing Attacks

IP spoofing is a type of network attack that can be directed against any host that deals with IP traffic. The goal of an IP spoofing attack is to establish a connection with a client unknown to a server by making that client appear to be a legitimate client, and then to exploit the relationship between the server and the bogus client to gain unauthorized access. Here is a well-known way to perpetrate an IP spoofing attack:

1. Make the legitimate client unable to respond to the target server (see step 1 in Figure 2.2). This can be accomplished through limited SYN flooding, making the service or daemon that receives input from each port wait for input that will never come, thereby making the machine unresponsive to other inputs (such as connection request acknowledgements from other servers). This step is necessary because if the legitimate client were able to respond to the target server, the bogus client would not be able to "break in" to their communication.

2. Send a SYN packet from the bogus client to the target server to request that a connection be opened (see step 2 in Figure 2.2). This packet must indicate that the connection request is from the legitimate client (for example, it must bear the IP address of the legitimate client), even though in reality the packet must originate from the bogus client. The bogus client's request packet includes the initial packet sequence number (PSN) for that client.

3. The target server sends a SYN packet to the legitimate client containing data such as the server's PSN and the client's PSN incremented by one (see step 3 in Figure 2.2). The legitimate client has been SYN flooded, however, so the legitimate client will never respond to this packet.

4. The connection request is allowed if the client increments both PSNs (that is, for both the client and the server) in a manner that the server expects (see step 4 in Figure 2.2). The software running on the bogus client must then send a reply SYN packet containing the source address of the legitimate client with appropriate PSNs (one for the client and one for the server) incremented by one.

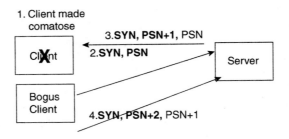

Figure 2.2 The sequence of events in an IP spoofing attack
(the server's PSN is shown in dark letters).

Deriving the client's PSN is easy; this PSN is an arbitrary number of which the server is not initially aware. The challenge is guessing the target server's PSN. The best clue concerning the value of the PSN that the server sent to the legitimate client in the first place is within the contents of already captured network traffic; packet dumps can reveal the previous PSNs for the server's connections to other systems. If the target server's PSN for a connection request from an entirely different client began with 24080 a few seconds previously, and if the PSN is always incremented by one for any new connection request, the next PSN for a new connection is likely to be 24081 if the initial PSN is not random. IP spoofing software that returns a PSN of 24082 from the bogus client to the server would therefore be very likely to correctly anticipate the appropriate PSN.

If the bogus client sends the correctly incremented value of both PSNs to the server, the attacker will have established a connection between the two. The attacker can then attempt to exploit the relationship between the two machines to gain unauthorized access to the target server. UNIX and Linux, for example, support the rlogin command that allows trusted access from one host to another. In many flavors of this system, by default, no password needs to be entered to obtain this level of access. For several years, IP spoofing was one of the most frequently observed types of attacks on the Internet. Although not used as frequently today as it was several years ago, IP spoofing still is a potentially serious threat to organizations. The availability of so many automated IP spoofing tools also greatly exacerbates the threat.

In the past, UNIX systems based on Berkeley Standard Distribution (BSD) UNIX and Windows NT systems were more vulnerable to IP spoofing attacks than were other types of operating systems. The solution at the operating system level is to program a server that gets an IP connection attempt to generate a truly random PSN in the SYN packet it returns to the client that has initiated the connection attempt.

Session Tampering Attacks

In *session tampering attacks*, an attacker (or, more often, a program that runs on behalf of an attacker) does something that allows the attacker to modify the characteristics of an already established session. In this next section, we will consider two types of session tampering attacks: session hijacking and session replay attacks.

Session Hijacking Attacks

In *session hijacking attacks*, an attacker takes over an already existing session. As discussed earlier, every time a client and server communicate with each other using IP-based communication methods, their packets bear a PSN. In a session hijacking attack, the attacker must gain access to a host that is between the legitimate client and server on the network. The attacker must then capture traffic going over the network to find an existing session and determine the PSN of the packet(s) that the server last sent to the client (as shown in the top part of Figure 2.3).

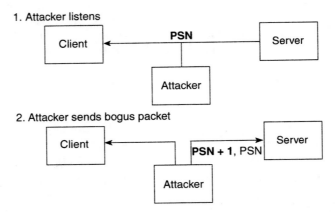

Figure 2.3 A session hijacking attack (the server's PSN is shown in bold letters).

The attacker must now beat the client in replying back to the server. The attacker (or, again, more properly the program that runs on behalf of the attacker) sends a packet with the correct PSN of the server incremented by one (see the lower part of Figure 2.3). The server continues the session, but this time with the attacking host. The session with the legitimate client is now dropped. The attacker can do anything that the person who was the legitimate client can do. The problem is especially serious if the session is a superuser session because the perpetrator gains the highest possible level of access to the victim system. Encrypted sessions or shared signatures between the client and server help prevent this type of attack.

Session Replay Attacks

Session replay attacks are another way to tamper with existing sessions. The attacker must again gain unauthorized access to a host located between two other hosts. This time, however, the attacker captures the packets sent between both hosts. When a session is established, the attacker can intervene by transmitting packets that have already gone across the network to one of the hosts. One of a number of outcomes can then occur. If one of the original hosts is an authentication server, replaying the original packets might enable the attacker to authenticate to that server. Alternatively, if one of the servers is an e-business server, the attacker might be able to do things such as gain access to databases that hold sensitive information, initiate business transactions, and change data without authorization. Fortunately, session replay attacks are not commonplace. The bad news is that many, if not most, applications do not have built-in protections against session replay attacks. Fortunately, session replay attacks are more difficult

3. Kerberos provides strong network authentication by issuing and using credentials called *tickets* to users. Version 5 of Kerberos also builds in protection against session replay attacks.

to accomplish than might be apparent. They depend on factors such as the context of a particular network connection. Additionally, recent versions of protocols such as the Kerberos[3] protocol generally incorporate mechanisms that help prevent these attacks.

The Ever-Broadening Nature of Security-Related Incidents

"Experts" keep telling us that the goals of information security are CIA: confidentiality, integrity, and availability. You have already seen in Chapter 1, "An Introduction to Incident Response," that other considerations such as nonrepudiation and the need for accountability do not fit into this nice, neat little way of thinking. New, emerging trends in incidents also show how far off the mark it is to think of security purely in terms of CIA. Cyber harassment (using electronic means to scare, intimidate, or embarrass someone else), for example, is growing rapidly as a type of security-related incident. Transporting and storing pornography (including child pornography) is another, as is defamation of character and posting negative characterizations of companies and other organizations. The use of computers in a variety of ways by organized crime also does not fit the nice little CIA mold. In short, the nature of security-related incidents is changing rapidly and now includes types of incidents that few people envisioned even a decade ago. With this change comes the need to characterize the goals of information security less simplistically.

Obtaining Data About Security-Related Incidents

What about determining the specific kinds of security-related incidents that are most likely to transpire in a particular organization? This is by no means an easy task. The next part of this chapter explores some approaches to this problem.

Data About Incidents Within One's Own Organization

One of the most readily available sources of information for an organization is data about incidents that have occurred in the past. To at least some degree, incidents that have already occurred serve as a predictor of incidents that are likely to occur in the future. An organization that has had a rash of break-ins over the last few years, for example, is likely to continue to see the same pattern, at least in the near future.

Successfully gathering incident data of this nature generally requires that there be a policy concerning whether incidents must be reported to a central group or function. Mandatory rather than voluntary reporting results in both more data and better quality data. Additionally, standardizing reporting in terms of the type of data to be reported is generally more useful in producing the kind of information that is likely to be helpful: the total number of incidents, types of incidents, the duration and severity, and so forth. Chapter 3, "A Methodology for Incident Response," deals with the specific types of information that are critical when incidents occur.

Firewall and system logs are a good source of data pertaining to incidents that occur within one's own organization. Firewall logs are particularly valuable in that they can capture all traffic coming in to and going out of a network. The problem, of course, is the voluminous amount of information that both firewall and system logs are likely to capture. Additionally, the format of these logs is often far less than optimal from a human usability viewpoint. Another good way to collect incident data is to deploy intrusion detection systems (IDSs). IDSs declare certain events they detect to be incidents or, alternatively, at least anomalous.

Data About Incidents Collected by Other Organizations

A number of incident response teams make information about incidents and potential incidents publicly available. CERT/CC, for example, releases summaries of current incident activity.[4] CERT/CC's quarterly summaries of the kinds of incidents that have been reported to this center, in addition to its advisories that describe new attack trends, can provide extremely valuable information about previous incidents and threats. Additionally, certain agencies and organizations within the U.S. Government (such as the National Infrastructure Protection Center [NIPC]) furnish threat update information at various times through electronic advisories and/or web pages.

Web sites such as alldas.org[5] and antionline.com[6] can also be sources of extremely worthwhile information about incidents that have occurred as well as hosts and sites that might be currently targeted. Although no statistics are ever immune from at least some form of criticism, these teams' and web sites' statistics can serve as an excellent source of at least a general understanding of incidents (including their relative prevalence), something that can be readily translated into risk estimates.

Vulnerability Analysis

Vulnerability analysis can also provide data about risk. Vulnerability analysis involves finding out how the security of systems, network devices, applications, and databases can be breached; how easy or difficult it would be to exploit each weakness that has been identified; the particular systems, network devices, applications, and data that are vulnerable; and the kinds of impact each breach would have. Note that vulnerability analysis is most effective when it is paired with penetration testing, which can provide tangible evidence not only of the presence of vulnerabilities but of the degree of difficulty in exploiting each.

4. www.cert.org/current/current_activity.html
5. www.alldas.org
6. www.antionline.com

Vulnerability Detection

The value of vulnerability analysis is by no means limited to risk identification and assessment. Finding vulnerabilities before they are posted on newsgroups and then cooperating with vendors to address the vulnerabilities that have been discovered, for example, constitutes one of the most productive and proactive activities in the entire information security arena.

Determining that most vulnerabilities (and all potentially high-impact vulnerabilities) have been patched in nearly every system and application throughout an enterprise, for example, would translate to a much lower estimate of risk than if the vulnerabilities were not addressed. Or, alternatively, perhaps some types of systems (such as AIX or AS400 systems) have many unpatched vulnerabilities, but others (such as NetWare and Solaris systems) have few. In this latter case, the magnitude of estimated risk would be considerably lower than in the former case.

The Importance of Risk Analysis in Incident Response

Why has the majority of this chapter been devoted to risk analysis when this book is supposed to cover incident response? Let's put together everything that has been covered so far. Chapter 1 already introduced the major types of incidents. These included breaches of confidentiality, compromised integrity, disrupted availability, repudiation, harassment attempts, extortion attempts, pornography trafficking, computer misuse that involves organized crime, subversion, and hoaxes. We also have presented data showing that cyberattacks and system misuse are causing substantial financial loss for companies and organizations. Now, most recently, we have gone over major categories of risk and their potential impact.

Knowing about the major types of incidents that occur (or that are likely to occur) in greater frequency and their associated risks is important in helping those who are part of an incident response effort to prepare for the types of incidents that occur. A critical requirement in responding to incidents is being prepared to respond before each incident occurs. (Chapter 3 covers this topic in considerably more detail.) *Knowing the incidents that are most likely to result in the greatest amount of loss and/or destruction or other undesirable outcomes in your organization so that you can devote more attention and resources to such incidents should they occur is essential.* To say this another way, certain kinds of incidents are potentially much more catastrophic than others and thus merit considerably more advance planning and preparation for incident response. This is where at least some level of risk analysis can greatly help incident response efforts.

A Few Caveats About Risk Analysis

The term "risk analysis" is well ingrained in the minds of most information security professionals. If you work at a bank, stock brokerage, or government agency, your organization probably devotes a disproportionate amount of time and resources to risk analysis. The risk analysis performed by these organizations, however, is not exactly the type of risk analysis that has been advocated and discussed in this chapter. What we are referring to in this chapter is a kind of risk analysis that identifies the areas in which incident response is most likely to be needed. This requires a level of effort that is usually considerably lower than in a more formal risk analysis. It is important, too, to understand that risk analysis has some extremely significant inherent limitations, as follows:

- Although risk analysis can help information security professionals better understand and deal with major risks, risk analysis is still a very subjective, imprecise art. For this reason, some professionals reject risk analysis altogether.

- *Even the best risk analysis estimates risk at only a particular point in time.* New risks emerge perpetually, and what was a major risk yesterday might be a relatively minor one several days later.

- Security controls (for example, third-party authentication devices) can reduce risk, but they never eliminate it. Even if security controls reduce risk substantially, a determined attacker will sooner or later be able to compromise the security of any system or network device. What controls really provide, therefore, is time—a delay in an attacker's efforts.

Given these important caveats, a reasonable strategy within the entire information security arena would be to rely less on risk analysis and rely more on threat assessment and intrusion detection. A significant vigilance component should be present within operational environments. Chapter 3 builds on this theme.

Consider this example. Suppose a petroleum company's greatest assets are its data regarding where crude oil deposits are located. Suppose also that this data is located in databases on servers dispersed throughout various subnets throughout the company's network. Perhaps, too, measures that fix vulnerabilities in these systems are in effect, but in reality, patching systems is a slow and disjointed process. To make matters worse, assume that several of these vulnerabilities are being frequently exploited in systems connected to the Internet. A good incident response strategy is to first learn as much as possible about the systems in question, including ways in which their security could be compromised. Determining how any incidents that might occur in these systems could be dealt with in a manner that minimizes the possibility of information loss or integrity compromise would then be a good next step.

Risk is dynamic. New threats constantly emerge, and older ones often diminish in magnitude and potential impact. Risk analysis, if done correctly, is dynamic. Keeping up with new threats and new developments is thus imperative in a successful incident response effort.

Summary

This chapter has focused on risk analysis and its relationship to incident response. Professionals within the field of computer and information security do not universally agree on the exact meaning of "risk analysis," but at the most basic level, risk analysis means determining the expected amount of loss associated with each source or cause of loss in computing systems and networks. Both quantitative (in which the results are represented numerically) and qualitative risk analysis can be performed. Major types of risk include break-ins, execution of rogue programs, privilege escalation, exploitation of common gateway interface (CGI) scripts in web servers, denial of service, web defacement, viruses and worms, malicious active content, back doors or remote control programs planted in victim systems, spoofing attacks, and session tampering. Each of these major types of risk has been discussed in some detail.

Data about risks is available from a number of sources. Organizations, for example, might have data concerning security-related incidents within their own computing system and networks. Outside organizations such as CERT/CC and NIPC also make data publicly available. Vulnerability analysis—identifying vulnerabilities in systems, network devices, applications, databases, and so on as well as the potential impact—can also produce data about threats. Risk analysis is important in responding to incidents in that it can help identify areas for which incident response should be assigned the highest priority. This, in turn, will help those involved in incident response to be most prepared to deal with incidents involving these areas.

3

A Methodology for Incident Response

W E HAVE NOW ESTABLISHED THAT INCIDENT RESPONSE is extremely important in today's cybercomputing world and that security-related incidents pose high levels of threat to organizations. With this background in mind, we will now move on to the *process* of responding to incidents. Specifically, this chapter describes a methodology and framework for responding to incidents. It also presents important considerations surrounding the use of this methodology. We will start by considering why it is important to use an incident response methodology in the first place.

Rationale for Using an Incident Response Methodology

Is it important to use an incident response methodology? Both of this book's authors, longtime veterans of the incident response arena, are confident that the answer is a resounding "yes." Reasons are discussed in the following sections.

Structure and Organization

It would be nice if security-related incidents generally occurred in a slow and orderly fashion. In this hypothetical scenario, staff charged with the responsibility of dealing with such incidents would have the luxury of being able to "dabble" with the incidents, turning their attention to events at hand as their whims dictated. Anyone who has been involved with security-related incidents, however, knows that in real world, dealing with incidents in this manner would be ludicrous. In reality, pandemonium can and does occur very quickly when security-related incidents happen. Worse yet, in real-life settings, incidents tend to occur in anything but a serial fashion. Simultaneous incidents are more the rule than anything else, especially in larger organizations with massive computing infrastructures. Using a methodology for responding to incidents helps impose structure and organization in situations that can otherwise get out of control very quickly.

Efficiency

Security-related incidents are often costly in terms of financial costs as well as the toll on human beings and organizations. The longer incidents last, the higher the probability that the cost and disruption they cause will escalate. Using a sound methodology entails using processes and procedures that have proven value and worth in resolving incidents with greater efficiency.

Facilitating the Process of Responding to Incidents

Following a methodology for responding to incidents facilitates the *process* of responding to incidents. By this we mean that a suitable methodology breaks incidents into distinct stages and defines suitable procedures and methods for dealing with each stage. Additionally, a suitable methodology helps those who are responding to incidents recognize when one particular phase of an incident has ended, necessitating a shift in response strategy to deal with the next phase. (For example, at first, an incident response team might try to identify the source of an attack and the identity of an attacker. Over time, however, they might discover that while they are conducting tracing activity, the attacker is damaging other systems. A shift in response strategy would be necessary.) Finally, a good methodology actually incorporates mechanisms for *improving* the process of responding to incidents. The discussion in the "Follow-Up" section later in this chapter explains this notion in greater detail.

Unexpected Benefits: Dealing with the Unexpected

Another significant benefit of using a methodology for responding to incidents is that it tends to help those who use it to better understand the process of dealing with incidents. A good methodology incorporates a thorough understanding of the process of dealing effectively with incidents. As staff members follow this methodology, they develop a mental framework for effective incident response that can be extrapolated into novel situations for which no procedures exist at the time they are needed. Following an incident response methodology can thus help those who respond to incidents to deal with the unexpected.

Legal Considerations

One of the recurrent themes in Chapter 7, "Legal Issues," is that whatever happens when people and automated processes respond to incidents has strong legal repercussions. In many countries (and especially in the United States), someone can file a lawsuit for almost any reason. If an incident gets out of control, becoming increasingly costly and complicated, someone might have strong grounds for a lawsuit, especially if the escalation of the incident can be linked in a court of law to incompetent decisions and actions made in responding to the incident. We have already seen, however, that following a sound incident response methodology lessens the likelihood that incompetent and inefficient actions will occur if a proven framework and methodology guide the process of responding to an incident. In many respects, adopting and following a widely accepted incident response methodology constitutes the practice of "due care"—adopting a reasonable and responsible set of measures to guard against harm. Legal considerations thus constitute still another reason for following an accepted incident response methodology.

RFC 2196: Incident Management

RFC 2196 (see `ftp://ftp.isi.edu/in-notes/rfc2196.txt`) provides incident management guidelines for minimizing the adverse potential impact of incidents. Some of the guidance in this RFC includes to avoid providing too many technical details when informing employees of security-related incidents, working with law enforcement agencies in gathering evidence, and having the public relations office handle contacts with the media. The provisions of this RFC are described in Appendix A, "RFC-2196."

A Six-Stage Methodology for Incident Response

Now that the reasons for following an incident response methodology are clear, it is time to become acquainted with the methodology advocated in this chapter. The particular methodology presented here is by no means the only one that has ever been invented, but it is certainly the oldest[1] and most time-honored methodology in the incident response arena. It consists of six stages: preparation, detection, containment, eradication, recovery, and follow-up. (The acronym PDFCERF embodies the first letters of all six stages; see Figure 3.1.) The next sections cover each of these stages in detail.

---

1. The six-step methodology presented in this part of the book was created at the Invitational Workshop on Incident Response at the Software Engineering Institute in Pittsburgh, Pennsylvania, in July of 1989 by approximately one dozen workshop participants, the first author of this book included.

Figure 3.1   The PDCERF incident response methodology.

Preparation

The first stage is preparation, which means being ready to respond before an incident actually occurs. This stage is extremely important because so many of today's incidents are so complex and time consuming that preparation is a necessity, not a luxury. Here are the basic notions behind preparation:

- Setting up a reasonable set of defenses/controls based on the threat that presents itself
- Creating a set of procedures to deal with incidents as efficiently as possible
- Obtaining the resources and personnel necessary to deal with the problem
- Establishing an infrastructure to support incident response activity

We will now examine all four of these considerations in more detail.

Setting up Defenses/Controls

Setting up appropriate defenses/controls is one of the most important steps in establishing an effective incident response capability. Having wide-open systems that are completely vulnerable to attack but having a strong incident response capability is, to put it bluntly, downright stupid. On the other hand, having strong controls without any incident response capability is naive. It is thus important to achieve a balance between these two extremes. The trick is to allocate sufficient resources to achieve at least a baseline of security in systems, network devices, applications, databases, and so forth, so that incidents (particularly in areas in which risk is very high) are not likely to become commonplace. An appropriate part of the resources, however, also needs to be devoted to the *operational* side of security—to what we have previously called the "vigilance" function—in case the defenses that are in place are breached.

There is another side to setting up defenses and controls. Too often, people forget to ensure that the systems and applications used in handling incidents are themselves resistant to attack. An attacker could access the intrusion-detection tool you use, for example, and alter its parameters, rendering it useless. The potential consequences in terms of damage, destruction, and corruption, as well as the potential legal impact,[2] are frightening. You and others with whom you work on incident response efforts might, for example, have downloaded instances of what you believe to be malicious code into a particular server belonging to your organization. Now, just before you start to analyze this code, suddenly everything you have downloaded disappears and the system logs are erased. You now have nothing to analyze. The point here is that you also have to secure the systems and applications that are going to be used in dealing with incidents.

Procedures

Chapter 5, "Organizing for Incident Response," covers incident response procedures in detail. Suffice it to say here that procedures should cover the following at a minimum:

- Specific steps to be taken by those involved in incident response and under what circumstances
- Whom should be contacted and under what circumstances
- Types of information that can and cannot be shared outside of your immediate organization
- Priorities in response activity
- Division of labor—what roles will be assigned to each of the people who participate in an incident response effort
- Acceptable risk limits and what kinds of activities, events, communications with others, and so forth must be documented (and how)

Obtaining Resources and Personnel

It goes without saying that resources and personnel are necessary if any incident response effort is to be successful. Resources are needed to pay the cost of labor, but resources are also needed for hardware, software, and training. An incident response effort almost invariably requires dedicated hardware platforms that can be used for purposes such as analysis and forensics. Hardware, such as personal digital assistants (PDAs), dictaphones, and locking combination safes or vaults, is also likely to be necessary. Sharing these sensitive platforms with other organizations is, for all practical purposes, out of the question.

---

2. Chapter 7, "Legal Issues," covers this issue in much greater detail.

Software such as intrusion detection software, reverse engineering tools (used to determine how an executable works when the source code is not available), forensics analysis software, and database server software is often also needed. Also, whoever is part of an incident response effort will need periodic training to ensure that each person has more than enough knowledge and skills to bring to each new situation. Forensics training in particular is becoming increasingly necessary in the world of incident response. The manager in charge of an incident response effort must ensure that sufficient attention is paid to obtaining the proper level of resources and personnel.

Building an Infrastructure to Support Incident Response

Ultimately, the process of responding to incidents works best if an infrastructure within an organization is established to support this process. An infrastructure provides a uniform, coherent way of organizing each element of the incident response process. In short, the business of incident response dictates that an organization should make incident response part of its overall business. To do this requires buy-in from senior management, which must ensure the following:

- Suitable management oversight has been devised and put in place, including establishing lines of accountability, defining roles and delegation of authority, creating processes for evaluating the effectiveness of the incident response effort, and so forth.
- Appropriate defenses/controls are chosen and implemented in systems, network devices, applications, databases, and so forth.
- A set of procedures for incident handling is written, well distributed, and followed.
- Appropriate tasks are assigned to each person in each incident response effort.
- Resources are available to ensure that necessary hardware and software tools and technical personnel are available. Lack of funding is, all things considered, the biggest obstacle that an incident response capability is likely to face. The best solution is to prove (in terms of dollar figures) just how much this capability is being used and (again, in terms of dollar figures[3]) how much money it has saved.
- Contact lists (for staff involved in incident response, cognizant managers, law enforcement, points of contact for other response teams, and so forth) are created and updated as needed (see the next sidebar).
- Any evidence gathered during the course of an incident is adequately preserved.
- Legal considerations are being adequately addressed.

---

3. The latter is potentially extremely helpful in obtaining and maintaining funding, but unfortunately, it is often also very difficult to calculate meaningfully.

The Importance of Contact Lists

Little things that are too easily overlooked can make the difference between success and failure in an incident response effort. Contact lists are a good example. A new incident response team was being put in place a number of years ago, when suddenly a massive worm attack was discovered during the early part of an evening. Management tried to call team members in to work, only to discover that some of the key team members had unlisted phone numbers or their home numbers had changed. Consequently, by the next morning, only a small portion of the team had been assembled.

Fortunately, this team learned from this experience. The solution was to create a laminated card with proper contact information—including work phone, home phone, mobile phone, pager number, and other contact information—for each primary and secondary team member. This card was the same size as the employee badge and could be hung on a badge holder; when each team member picked up the badge to go to work, he or she now also had the contact information. The team manager also ensured that contact information was reviewed regularly so that any changes could be quickly incorporated.

Much of the burden of preparation actually falls on system administrators. Implementing system security measures, for example, is the responsibility of system administrators, who need to do the following:

- Ensure that the password policy is implemented through password filters (that reject weak passwords when users try to enter them) and/or password cracking tools[4]
- Ensure that dormant and default accounts are removed or disabled
- Install and maintain the appropriate security tools (for example, intrusion-detection tools, forensics tools, a secure email program, and others)
- Run and regularly examine system logging/auditing
- Install patches and fixes (after their integrity and functionality have been tested)
- Check system files for integrity
- Back up each system as needed (including during incidents)
- Investigate suspicious occurrences (no one knows what is "normal" and "abnormal" in any system better than the system administrator)

---

4. npasswd, a free UNIX password filter, is available at ftp://cerias.purdue.edu/tools/unix/ or http://www.utexas.edu/cc/unix/software/npasswd, and most flavors of Linux offer password filtering through PAM, the built-in Pluggable Authentication Module. StrongPass, a free Windows NT password filter, is available at www.ntsecurity.nu. John the Ripper (available from http://packetstormsecurity.org) is a free UNIX and Linux password cracker (although John the Ripper will not work against Linux systems if MD-5 is used for password hashing in lieu of DES encryption). l0phtcrack (available from www.atstake.com) is the most popular password cracker for Windows NT and lc3 will crack Windows 2000 systems.

Detection

The second stage in the PDCERA methodology is detection. This section discusses the many considerations related to this stage.

About Detection

As far as incident response goes, detection and intrusion detection are *not* synonymous. *Detection* means determining whether malicious code is present, files or directories have been altered, or other symptoms of an incident are present and, if they are, what the problem as well as its magnitude is. *Intrusion detection*, in its most typical connotation, means determining whether unauthorized access to a system has transpired and (in a more complete definition) whether misuse[5] has occurred. A virus infection can be found using detection but not intrusion-detection software, for instance. Detection thus embraces a potentially much wider range of incidents than does intrusion detection.

From an operational standpoint, all actions that transpire as part of the incident response process depend on detection. To be blunt, without detection, there is no meaningful incident response; detection triggers incident response. This elevates the relative importance of detection among the other five stages considerably.

Intrusion-Detection Systems (IDSs)

Many books have now been written about IDSs. For this reason, as well as the fact that the types of incidents discussed in this book are far broader than break-ins, this book does not cover IDSs in much detail. A quick summary, however, of the most important considerations will be helpful in understanding the second stage of the PDCERF methodology better.

Two basic types of IDSs, host-based and network-based IDSs, exist. *Host-based IDSs* must be installed on every system on which intrusion-detection capability is desired. Although much better suited to picking up attacks such as insider attacks, host-based IDSs can be quite expensive and can tie up system performance substantially. The alternative is *network-based IDSs*, which gather data from sensors and systems and process this data on a central host. Network-based IDSs tend to be less costly and do not affect system performance appreciably, but they generally are not as good as host-based IDSs in detecting attacks on systems. They also can be defeated by setting up encrypted links from victim machines to attacking machines and are more subject to denial-of-service attacks. The debate concerning host- or network-based IDSs will continue to rage, but a growing number of experts in the field of intrusion detection are simply advocating the use of both.

---

5. Misuse can be defined as a violation of security policy. See Tuglular, T., and Spafford, E.H. "A framework for characterization of insider computer misuse." Unpublished paper, Purdue University, 1997; a white paper available at http://cerias.purdue.edu.

Most current IDSs base their recognition capability on *signatures*, characteristic patterns of attack. In Windows NT, for example, sending

```
net use \\<IP address>\IPC$
```

to a Windows NT host is very suspicious in that the sender is setting up a null session on behalf of the anonymous user. Although signatures constitute a very intuitive approach to intrusion detection, critics argue that signatures are always post-hoc and are thus not capable of detecting new attacks when they first surface. A few IDSs also analyze the nature of protocol connections to determine whether or not they are normal.

Detection Software

Given the sophistication of so many of today's attacks, detection software (such as virus detection software, IDS software, integrity-checking software, and so on) might, for all practical purposes, be necessary if an incident response effort is to be successful. For example, widely available vendor software can rapidly detect viruses in desktop systems and mail servers. This software usually can also detect worm infections and whether backdoor trojan horse programs (such as NetBus, Back Orifice 2000, and SubSeven) have been covertly installed in Windows systems. But buying and installing this type of software and then doing nothing more has few benefits; the software must also be regularly updated to include the latest signatures. It is also important to systematically assess the applications you use. An application (such as intrusion-detection software) that was effective three years ago might now be ineffective. Incorporating provisions for frequent updates of virus-protection software and regular evaluations of all applications you use in handling incidents as part of the incident response effort is thus another essential consideration.

Some kinds of incidents do not require detection software, however, because certain symptoms of incidents are rather obvious. Sources of information such as system and firewall logs might, in these cases, be sufficient. Some of the more obvious symptoms are as follows:

- **Failed login attempts.** These are one of the most obvious symptoms that an attack has occurred.

- **Logins into dormant and default accounts.** Dormant and default accounts (as well as orphan accounts, accounts that are not maintained) should be viewed suspiciously, especially if the system administrator knows that the user of any of these accounts has not been able to log in for some time.

- **Activity during nonworking hours.** In and of itself, activity such as logins or connections to services during off hours does not prove that an intrusion has occurred, but the fact that attackers prefer to gain unauthorized access at times when system administrators and users are least likely to notice their presence is well established.

- **Presence of new accounts not created by the system administrator.** One of the best examples was when an attacker from the Netherlands broke into systems, escalated privileges, and then created a new superuser account named "rgb" on each compromised system several years ago.

- **Unfamiliar files or programs.** Often these files or programs are back-door programs, and they are given innocuous names such as /tmp/bob, /etc/inet.d/ bootd, or even "..".[6]

- **Unexplained changes in file and directory permissions.** File and directory permissions could be changed to give an intruder back-door access, or a program that an attacker has run could also have changed these permissions.

- **Unexplained elevation or use of privileges.** As mentioned previously, one of the goals of many attackers is to gain superuser privileges.

- **An altered home page or other page(s) on a Web server.** This is one of the most obvious signs of an attack on a Web server.

- **Presence of pornographic images on a system.**

- **Use of commands or functions not normally associated with a user's job.** A good real-life example is when logs in a UNIX system indicated that an administrative assistant's account, used only to read email until then, had been used to compile programs.

- **Presence of cracking utilities.** When cracking utilities are found on a system, this usually means either that an attacker has planted them or that a legitimate user has downloaded them (knowingly or unknowingly).

- **Gaps in or erasure of system logs.** This is one of the prime indications that a system has been compromised, given the prevalence of "rootkit" tools that masquerade the presence of the attacker.

- **Changes in DNS tables or router or firewall rules that cannot be accounted for.**

- **Unusually slow system performance.** Be careful about concluding that a security breach has occurred whenever system performance is sluggish, but problems such as the presence of rogue programs can cause unusually slow system performance.

- **System crashes.** These could be due to deliberate DoS attacks, or an attacker might have broken into a system and performed some actions or executed some routines that did not work as expected, causing the system to crash.

---

6. In UNIX and Linux systems, entering the ls command produces a file and directory listing that displays "." first and then "..". Many, if not most, system administrators and users are not likely to notice the inclusion of a second, innocuous entry such as ".." (which in reality is dot-dot-space or space-dot-dot).

- **Social engineering attempts.** Reports of social engineering attempts usually mean that a concerted attempt to break the security of an organization's systems and/or networks is underway and that almost certainly one or more of these attempts has been successful. Figure 3.2 shows real-life indications from the UNIX process accounting log (usually in the /var/adm/pacct path in UNIX systems and /var/log/pacct in Linux systems) that an attack on a UNIX system is occurring. In this case, the system administrator was already on the system, but someone attempted to log in directly as root at the same time.

Figure 3.3 shows accounting logs from a VMS system that indicate that a security-related incident has occurred. In this case, MAILER, which is the mail program, is running with All Privileges, the highest level of privileges (see the third entry in this log). Someone has almost certainly gained access to the MAILER account and then escalated privilege in this system.

Figure 3.4 captures the Windows NT Event Log entries for a series of brute force attacks. One of the administrator accounts was targeted in these attacks. You can view the Security Log by going to Start, Programs, Administrative Tools, Event Viewer. If the Security Log is not displayed right away, pull down the Log menu in the upper-left corner to Security Log. Note that Event Code 529 in Windows NT means an unsuccessful logon attempt. If the system administrator double-clicks on the highlighted entry in the Security Log, an Event Detail screen that provides some additional information is displayed (see Figure 3.5).

COMMAND NAME	USER	TTYNAME	START TIME	END TIME	REAL (SECS)	CPU (SECS)	MEAN SIZE
#acctcom	root	?	14:54:01	14:54:46	0.03	0.03	24.88
sh	root	?	14:54:01	14:54:40	0.02	0.02	22.25
login	root	?	14:54:01	14:54:29	0.04	0.04	23.77

Figure 3.2   Process accounting data showing an attempted attack on a UNIX system.

```
***********
21 Mark Clark              CLARK   [450,4763]  XBY        Normal  4  USER1:[CLARK
***********
21 Mary Berry             BERRY    [450,4763]  XBY        All     4  USER1:[BERRY]
***********
156 WIN/TCP Mailer MAILER          [776,776]   OVERHEAD   All     4  TWG$TCP:[NETDIST.MAILER]
***********
156 WIN/TCP Mailer MAILER          [776,776]   OVERHEAD   System  4  TWG$TCP:[NETDIST.MAILER]
***********
***********
```

Figure 3.3   Accounting entries showing an attack on a VMS system.

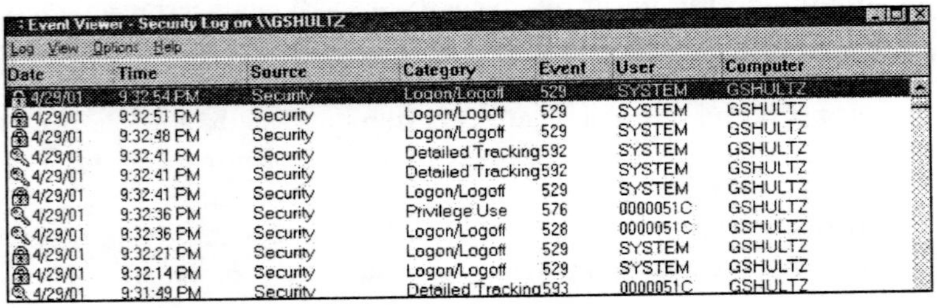

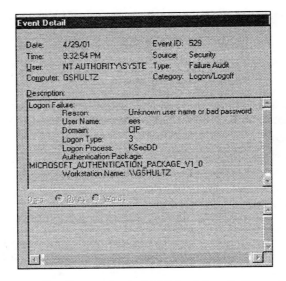

Figure 3.4   Security Log entries showing brute force attacks on a Windows NT system.

Figure 3.5   An Event Detail screen for the highlighted Security Log entry in Figure 3.4.

Figure 3.6 shows Windows 2000 Event Log entries for a several brute force attacks (Event Code 677[7]), followed by a successful logon to the Administrator account (Event Code 680), followed by a change in the password of another account (Event Code 577). You can view the Security Log by going to Start, Programs, Administrative Tools, Event Viewer. If the Security Log is not displayed right away, pull down the Log menu in the upper-left corner to Security Log.

---

7. For an explanation of event codes, see Schultz, E., *Windows NT/2000 Network Security.* Indianapolis: New Riders, 2000.

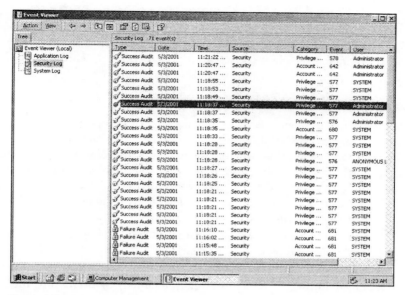

Figure 3.6   Security Log entries showing an attack on a Windows 2000 system.

It is important to realize that of all the suspicious indications that manifest themselves in real-life settings, a relatively small proportion will turn out to be security-related incidents. Being cautious about the meaning of a single suspicious symptom, such as multiple login failures, is thus a wise strategy. Multiple login failures, for example, are frequently caused by a user who has had to change a password but who cannot remember what the new password is. Alternatively, the user's Caps Lock key on the keyboard might have been accidentally pressed, causing the user to enter all capital letters during each logon attempt.

Suspicious events, such as multiple connection attempts to file systems, often end up being due to problems such as a misconfigured application. Remember, too, that many times, "obvious" symptoms of attacks (for example, repeated system crashes) are not good indicators, but small, multiple indicators (resulting from something such as perpetrators failing to completely cover their tracks) can be the best indicators. Clifford Stoll, in his now legendary book, *Cuckoo's Egg*,[8] points out that a 75-cent discrepancy between computed charges for computer usage by a single user led to an investigation that led to the identification of four Germans who were paid by another country's intelligence service to glean information from U.S. computers.

8. Stoll, C. *The Cuckoo's Egg*. New York: Doubleday, 1989.

Having a team of the best technical personnel you can find (and also that you can afford) is one of the best solutions to the challenge of identifying incidents, despite that fact that symptoms might be very non-obvious. Chapter 4, "Forming and Managing a Response Team," greatly expands on this theme.

Initial Actions and Reactions

If a security-related incident appears to have occurred, it is important to avoid panicking. It is also important to avoid causing panic in others. Granted, the incident could be very serious and potentially costly, but human error costs organizations far more than security-related incidents do. Gathering your wits and thinking carefully about your next course of action is the best strategy in almost every case.

The following are some of the actions that tend to have the highest payoff during the detection stage of dealing with incidents:

- **Taking the time to analyze *all* anomalies.** As mentioned earlier, sometimes very small symptoms indicate that an incident is in progress, so analyzing every anomaly that can be found is a very good measure.

- **Enabling auditing (if it is not already enabled) or increasing the amount of audit information capture.** If auditing on the possible victim system is not enabled, during the time you or others notice a possible incident would be a good time to enable it; if a small amount of auditing is currently being captured, increasing the amount of auditing would be wise.

- **Promptly obtaining a full backup of the system in which the incident has apparently occurred and gathering a copy of any compromised files/bogus code for analysis.** This is a "showstopper action item" because if you don't take this action right away, an attacker might be able to erase or corrupt evidence that can be used for analysis as well as for legal purposes later.

- **Starting to document everything that happens.** It is also extremely critical for every person involved in the possible incident to write down virtually everything that is at least marginally relevant to an incident (including names, phone numbers, and email addresses of everyone with whom you communicate). You and the others will not immediately know what information will ultimately be important and useful and what will not, so recording everything is essential.

Case Study: Making A UNIX Backup for Incident Response Purposes

Making a full backup of the victim system right away when it appears that an incident has occurred is an important thing to do. In some operating systems, however, some types of full backups are better than others. UNIX (and also Linux), for example, supports three types of backups: tar (tape archive), dump (the primary backup program), and dd (device-to-device copy). Because dd reads the files that are input to it on a block-by-block basis, it can capture data (such as deleted blocks of data) in a backup that tar and dump cannot. dd is thus most suitable for forensics analysis.

To run tar, enter the following:

```
tar -<flags> <device> <file system to be dumped>
e.g., tar -cvf /dev/rmt0 /home
```

To run the dump command, enter the following:

```
dump -<flags> <device> <file system to be dumped>
e.g., dump -f /dev/rmt0  /home (where f is the device name)
```

To run dd, enter the following:

```
dd if=<input file> <output file>
dd if=/dev/hd01 of=/dev/rmt0
```

To find out more about these commands, check the man pages of your UNIX or Linux system. (Note that in most Linux systems, a dash (-) does not appear before any flag[s]).

Estimating the Scope of the Incident

After an incident has been detected, it is important to promptly determine the scope of the incident. This not only helps in determining what to do during the next stage, containment, it also can help management and technical staff assign a priority to handling this incident. Here are some of the considerations:

- How many hosts have been compromised? The more that have been compromised, the wider the scope. Different intervention methods are generally required as the scope of the incident increases.

- How many networks are involved? As in the case of systems, the more networks involved, the broader the scope and the greater the need for urgent action.

- How far into the internal network did the attackers get? If they have attacked only a host or a host outside of the security perimeter, the implications are radically different than if the attackers have gotten well within the internal network.

- What level of privileges did the attacker(s) gain? Unauthorized superuser privileges greatly escalate the scope of an incident.

- What is at risk? How critical are compromised machines to an organization's business/operations? Are valuable applications and/or data highly at risk? The more critical the compromised machines and the more valuable the applications and data, the wider the scope of the incident.

- How many avenues of attack are being used? If the attacker is using the Internet, dialing in through the public phone system, and using PBX routes, the scope is much wider than if the attacker is using only one attack avenue.

- Who knows about the incident, and how or to what extent can that knowledge make the damage from the incident worse? Customers gaining knowledge about an attack might have serious business repercussions, for example.

- How widespread is the vulnerability that the attacker(s) exploited? Are many machines vulnerable to the same kind of attack to which other systems have succumbed?

The Reporting Process

Notification of the appropriate authorities when an incident is first identified is also a crucial component of the detection phase. Incident response efforts in which critical information does not get to those who need it are seldom successful because most incidents are not limited to a single host within one network. Incidents are truly international in origin nowadays. Timely reporting to staff and organizations that need to know about incidents to be able to fulfill their role in the overall incident response infrastructure is thus imperative.

Unfortunately, the reality is that people do not distribute information to those who need it nearly as much as they should. Creating and enforcing provisions for mandatory reporting in an organization's information security policy is the solution if incident reporting is to occur. Policy provisions should include the following at a minimum:

- Types of information to be reported
- To whom this information must be reported
- How quickly it must be reported
- The type of method (for example, secure email, hard copy, and so forth) to be used
- The consequences of violating the policy provisions

Requiring that the Chief Information Security Officer (CISO) be notified is, in most cases, also a minimal requirement. Other notifications that might be required include the following:

- Personnel (in situations such as insider attack or misuse)
- Public affairs (because of the possibility of adverse publicity due to security-related incidents)
- A incident response team (such as AFCERT in the U.S. Air Force[9])
- A government agency's chief of information security and/or the head of classified computing for the agency
- The legal department (Chapter 7 will greatly expand on this and other considerations)

---

9. See Schultz, E.E., et. al. "What Do People Really Need to Know about Computer Security Incidents?" In *Proceedings of 16th Department of Energy Computer Security Group Training Conference*, Denver, Colorado, 1994.

What Type of Information about Incidents Needs to Be Reported?

When incidents occur, the need to communicate information from one person or organization to another almost invariably presents itself. What kind of information is most needed by others? Many variables affect the answer to this question—more data would, for example, be appropriate if a massive set of intrusions occurred than if a single system were infected by a virus. Nevertheless, the following guidelines for reporting (derived from an empirical study on this issue) may be useful in determining what needs to be reported:

- Basic information about the incident, including the type of attack, the attacker's apparent purpose, the type of operating system and version of the victim system, the particular networks/subnets involved, commands that the attacker has entered, the particular account(s) that have been compromised, and any information about the identity and characteristics of the attacker and/or any malicious programs

- Information concerning the origin of the attack—the attacking host(s), type of connection to the victim(s), and any known route(s) across the network used in the attack

- The consequences of the attack—whether the attacker has gotten superuser privileges, what particular data (if any) have been accessed without authorization, any integrity changes that have been made in the victim system, and so forth

- Threat—how widespread the attack is, the other systems that have been compromised, how sensitive any compromised systems and data are, and the likelihood that damage and/or disruption will escalate

- Status—the current status of the incident and when the incident is likely to be resolved

- Critical personnel contacts (for the victim and source systems, networks, as well as for the incident response staff)

Other kinds of information, such as vulnerabilities that have been exploited and audit log data, may also be helpful. Creating a form that includes fields that correspond to each of the above bullets and making this form widely available is a good way to help ensure that information that needs to be reported is actually reported.

Containment

The purpose of the third stage of incident handling, containment, is to limit the extent of an attack and thus the potential for damage or loss. Containment-related activity should, of course, occur only if the indications observed during the second stage conclusively show that an incident is occurring.

The Logic of Containment

After an incident has been confirmed, whoever is handling the incident should quickly determine reasonable ways to contain the incident and then decide on the one that appears to be best. Containment-related measures can, in some cases, be relatively simple and quick. If several bad login attempts against a single account have occurred, for example, a reasonable containment measure would be to disable that account (at least temporarily). On the other hand, if an intruder has gained superuser access to multiple hosts, containment will almost certainly be more extensive.

It is important to never take containment lightly because so many incidents can get out of hand so quickly. A good example is a worm infection; it is important to limit the spread of a worm within a network as quickly as possible.[10] Port scanning and vulnerability scanning attacks, even though they occur so much that they have become commonplace, also constitute a potentially significant threat in that they are often harbingers of determined attacks. Similarly, the discovery of zombie or handler software in one or more hosts should elevate the priority of containment-related activity substantially, given the potential amount of damage that has resulted from DDoS attacks in the past. The same principle applies to Web defacements, which are often followed by all-out attacks.

The Role of Users When Incidents Occur

Users are in many ways a "two-edged sword" as far as security-related incidents go. Users are often the first to notice security breaches and anomalies that need to be investigated. On the other hand, users often attempt to eradicate incidents (or more often, *perceived* incidents) that do not turn out to be bona fide incidents), often doing more damage to their systems and files than an attacker could ever have done. In general, providing users with the following instructions results in a reduction in damage and/or disruption:

- Do not shut down your system or disconnect from network without first consulting authorities.

- Follow your organization's reporting procedures—report any suspicious occurrences to your security point of contact.

- Continue to monitor and document suspicious occurrences until help arrives.

- Do not modify system or application software.

- Do not talk to the media without prior management approval.

---

10. The way to do this depends on how the worm in question functions. If, like the Internet Worm of 1988, a worm spreads through password attacks, access to mail-forwarding files, and vulnerabilities in service programs such as sendmail, stopping the spread of this type of worm can be relatively difficult. One possible technique is to "inoculate" every system with the signature the worm looks for in determining whether it will infect a system. The Internet Worm (like so many others that have surfaced since) attempted to avoid multiple infections of any single system.

Possible Containment Strategies

An essential part of containment is decision making, (that is, what to do to minimize the spread of damage and/or disruption). Possible decisions include any or all of the following:

- Shutting a system down altogether (a drastic, but sometimes very advisable, decision to prevent further loss and/or disruption).

- Disconnecting from a network. This at least allows local users to obtain some level of services, although it will prove disruptive.

- Changing the filtering rules of any firewalls and routers to exclude traffic from hosts that appear to be launching the attacks.

- Disabling or deleting login accounts that have been compromised.

- Increasing the level of monitoring of system and/or network activity.

- Setting traps such as decoy servers, as discussed in Chapter 12, "Traps and Deceptive Measures."

- Disabling services, such as file transfer services, if vulnerabilities in services are being exploited.

- Striking back at the attacker's system(s), although you should in general avoid doing this and should never do this without the explicit approval of top-level management.

Sometimes this decision is trivial; shutting down a compromised system if the system, its data, and/or its applications are classified, sensitive, or proprietary is an obvious thing to do. The same applies to a compromised system that holds proprietary information or applications. In other cases, it is worthwhile to risk a certain amount of damage to the compromised system if keeping the system up might enable you to identify an intruder.

Other Considerations

Other considerations during the containment stage are also extremely important. In general, we recommend the following:

- Adhering to well-defined and detailed containment procedures. This helps maximize the probability of successful incident containment.

- Continuing to record in a notebook, dictaphone, PDA, or other means virtually everything that occurs during the course of the incident, what those who are dealing with the incident have done and how much time each action has required, and other important details.

- Defining acceptable risk limits in dealing with an incident well in advance. After all, making decisions such as leaving compromised systems running and connected to the network involves elevated risk.

- Advising users of the status of an attacked system that they use if there is prolonged disruption, if data are destroyed, and so forth. Sooner or later they will figure out that something is wrong, but at least you will be able to control false rumors (and also possibly the panic) that are likely to spread.

- Continuing to report (through secure channels such as secure email) any significant updates to appropriate organizations and people mentioned in the previous section of this chapter.

- Following an organization's policy regarding contact with the media (see the following sidebar).

Dealing with the Press

Part of the containment process includes containment of possible public relations damage that a security-related incident can cause. One thing is certain—if an incident has a large impact and/or if it involves many hosts from many different organizations, at least one reporter will learn of it, then subsequently probe for details. Chapter 4, "Forming and Managing an Incident Response Team," covers how to deal with the press when a security-related incident occurs.

One of the fundamental parts of containing an incident is finding out whether attackers and/or malicious programs have installed any back-door programs that enable unauthorized reentry to compromised hosts and network devices. If any back doors have been installed, removing them is usually the best course of action. There might be exceptions—such as when those involved in an incident response effort are trying to gather evidence to be used in a legal prosecution effort—but when the back doors allow immediate superuser access, there is really little debate concerning what to do with them. Similarly, if someone has gained unauthorized superuser access to a host or has obtained a copy of the password file, it is also typically prudent to change all passwords as soon as possible (because the attacker might have cracked or reset passwords).

Eradication

The fourth stage in the PDCERF methodology is eradication. After the incident has been contained, it is now time to eradicate the cause of the incident.

The Logic of Eradication

The goal is to eliminate the *cause* of the incident. Software might be available to help you in this effort. For example, eradication software is available to eliminate most viruses that infect small systems (and often even larger ones). If any Trojan horse programs (other than back-door programs or ones that could cause an incident to spread), which should have already been eradicated during the containment stage, remain in the system at this time, it is now time to delete them. In the case of infections by extremely malicious and dangerous programs, it is probably best at this time to clean and reformat any hard drives containing the infected files. Finally, ensure that all back-ups are clean. Many systems infected with viruses become periodically reinfected simply because people do not systematically eradicate the virus from backups.

If a classified system has been infected by a virus, a worm, or some other kind of malicious executable, it is essential to follow guidance issued by the department or agency that has jurisdiction over classified computing. We also strongly advise that, in this case, a low-level format be performed to ensure that whatever has caused the incident is fully eradicated. In classified environments, however, the department or agency with jurisdiction over classified computing might instead require destruction of media.

Eradication Procedures

As in virtually all the stages of the PDCERF model, preparing detailed procedures and then following them is critical in the eradication stage. Procedures are exceptionally important in the eradication stage because it is so easy to overlook a critical detail or two in the heat of battle. Overlooking any detail could result in undesirable outcomes such as another flare-up of the incident or destruction or tainting of forensics evidence. We will now examine some of the procedures that can be used to eradicate the cause of UNIX (and Linux) and Windows NT incidents:

Eradication in a UNIX System

The following steps constitute a sound basic set of minimal eradication procedures for compromised UNIX systems:

1. Ensure that no unauthorized entries exist in .forward files.

2. Use **ps** (with appropriate flags such as **-elf** in System V UNIX systems) to look for stray processes running.

3. Ensure that the following files are not modified:

   /etc/dfs/dfstab (or /etc/exports)
   .login
   .logout
   .profile
   /etc/profile
   .cshrc
   All files in the /etc/rc path
   .rhosts
   /etc/hosts.equiv
   at

4. Also examine the following for unauthorized changes:

```
netstat
ls
sum
find
diff
/etc/nsswitch.conf
/etc/resolv.conf
/var/spool/cron
/var/spool/cron/crontabs
kerb.conf
```

5. To discover the real modification time for files, enter **ls -lac**.

6. To discover suid programs enter the following:

   find / -type f -perm -4000 -ls

   or

   find / -type f -perm -4000 -print

7. Ensure that there are no modifications of the following:

   ```
   -/etc/passwd
   the shadow password file
   -/etc/group
   -yppasswd
   ```

8. Ensure that no unauthorized entries exist in .rhosts files and /etc/hosts.equiv. Enter the following:

   find / -name .rhosts -ls -o -name .forward -ls

   or

   find / -name .rhosts -print -o -name .forward -print

9. Inspect the following to ensure that no unauthorized services are running:

   ```
   -/etc/inetd.conf
   -/etc/inittab
   -/etc/services
   -/etc/hosts.allow
   -/etc/hosts.deny
   ```

10. Search for all files created during the time you think the attack(s) occurred by entering

    find / -ctime -1 -ls or **find / -ctime -1 -print** and eradicate as necessary.

11. Search for all files modified during the time you think the attack(s) occurred by entering

    find / -mtime -1 -ls or **find / -mtime -1 -print** and take the action you deem appropriate.

12. Use the `strings` command to inspect binaries because even though the binary might look like nonsense, cleartext strings within in might give some indication of what a modified binary is doing (for example, setting up an encrypted session using OpenSSH)

Eradication in a Linux System

In most flavors of Linux, the commands and associated functions are generally the same as in UNIX. Note, however, that in most flavors of Linux, flags used with commands are not preceded by a dash (-).

Eradication in a Windows NT System

We recommend that you use the following basic procedures for eradication in compromised Windows NT systems:

- Ensure that the following have not been modified:
    - The Security Accounts Manager (SAM) database[11]
    - Services (check by going to the Control Panel and then double-clicking on the Services icon)
    - All .dll files (especially MSGINA.DLL, which is the graphics interface for user logons)
    - Dial-in settings (especially the RAS.PBK[12] file) at (or, in SP5 and up, the Task Scheduler)
    - User Manager for Domains settings, particularly Account Policy, Audit Policy (remember that attackers love to disable auditing) and Trust Relationships settings
    - All logon scripts
    - The integrity (including ownership) of all Registry keys and values below HKLM\Software\Microsoft\WindowsNT\CurrentVersion\Winlogon and HKLM\System\CurrentControlSet\Control\LSA
    - HKLM\Software\Microsoft\Windows\CurrentVersion\Run and HKLM\Software\Microsoft\Windows\CurrentVersion\Run (and RunOnce and RunOnceEx)
    - Membership in all privileged groups but especially the Domain Administrators and Local Administrators groups
    - System and user profiles

11. Using a tool such as Tripwire for NT (see www.tripwiresecurity.com) is one of the best ways to check the integrity of any file in Windows NT. Be sure, however, to guard the integrity of any program that checks file integrity. One trick of attackers is to corrupt integrity-checking programs so that they always display the same results, no matter the contents of the files they check. Tripwire for UNIX is also a great tool to check the integrity of most UNIX flavors.

12. This is the RAS phonebook, which contains the names of users allowed to dial in.

Eradication in a Windows 2000 System

We recommend that you use the following basic procedures for eradication in compromised Windows 2000 systems:

- Ensure that the following have not been modified:
  - The Security Accounts Manager (SAM) database (in mixed mode[13]) or the ntds.dit file[14] (in native mode)
  - Services (check by going to the appropriate policy that controls services)
  - All .dll files (especially MSGINA.DLL, which is the graphics interface for user logons)
  - Scheduler entries (go to the Scheduler icon in the Control Panel)
  - Policy settings (particularly Password Policy, Account Lockout Policy, Kerberos Policy, Audit Policy, Dial-in Policy, and Trust Relationships) as well as the order of Group Policy Objects (GPOs)
  - All logon scripts
  - All Security Option settings
  - All permissions for Active Directory
  - Active Directory schemas
  - All DNS settings
  - The integrity (including ownership) of all Registry keys and values below HKLM\Software\Microsoft\WindowsNT\CurrentVersion\Winlogon and HKLM\System\CurrentControlSet\Control\LSA HKLM\Software\Microsoft\Windows\CurrentVersion\Run and HKLM\Software\Microsoft\Windows\CurrentVersion\Run (and RunOnce and RunOnceEx)
  - Membership in all privileged groups but especially the Enterprise Administrators, Schema Administrators, Domain Administrators and Local Administrators groups
  - Permissions and ownerships in \%systemroot%\ntds and \%systemroot%\SYSVOL\sysvol and below

Other Considerations

Other considerations during the eradication stage are also extremely important. In general, we recommend the following:

- Adhering to eradication procedures such as the ones recently described for UNIX and Windows NT systems

---

13. In mixed mode, domain controllers are both Windows NT and Windows 2000. In native mode, all domain controllers are Windows 2000.

14. This is the password file in Windows 2000 native mode.

- Continuing to record everything that occurs
- Continuing to keep users advised of the status of any compromised systems that they use (if appropriate)
- Continuing to report any major updates to appropriate people and organizations
- Continuing to follow any applicable policy requirements concerning contact with the media

Recovery

The fifth stage in the PDCERF incident response methodology is recovery. After the cause of an incident has been eradicated, the recovery phase defines the next stage of action. The goal of recovery is to return any compromised system and network device completely back to its normal mission status.

Recovery Procedures

Following detailed technical procedures for system recovery is every bit as important during the recovery stage as in any other PDCERF stage. Procedures almost without question will vary across organizations; different organizations need different levels of assurance concerning the certainty regarding any compromised systems' complete integrity. Additionally, procedures for recovery will necessarily differ from one operating system to the next.

When it comes to recovery, one of the surefire recovery methods is to perform a full system restore from known good media. This might be difficult and time consuming, especially if many systems have been compromised, but provided that the media used to restore compromised systems have been adequately safeguarded at all times, this strategy can provide a high level of assurance that systems and network components have been returned to their normal operational status. Note that a full restore, including changes to every password, should be mandatory if an attacker has gained superuser access to a system.

Data recovery can be tricky. One reasonably safe (albeit less than perfect) method is to restore data from the most recent full backup (or incremental backup, provided that there have been data changes since the time of the last full backup). Another is to use fault tolerance system hardware such as a redundant array of independent drives (RAID) to recover mirrored or striped data that resides on the redundant hard drives. We are assuming, of course, that these files and data have not also been compromised. Recovery in classified computing systems is generally very detailed and time consuming, well outside the scope of this book. The agency or organization that has jurisdiction over classified computing will provide guidance concerning recovery in these systems.

Other Considerations

As in the other stages, other considerations during the recovery stage are critical to a successful outcome. You should continue to do the following:

- Record everything that occurs (including the time required for each person working on incident response to perform each recovery-related task).
- Keep users aware of the status of any compromised systems that they use (if appropriate). In particular, after recovery efforts are complete, it might be best to assure users that everything is back to normal.
- Advise appropriate people and organizations of any major developments that might affect them.
- Adhere to any applicable policy requirements concerning contact with the media.
- Continue to log system and activity, but in general, return logging to a more normal level.
- In the case of a network-based attack, install patches for any operating system, firewall, or router vulnerability that was exploited. Patches should be installed in both compromised and other systems.

Finally, during the recovery stage, it is also important to remove any interim (stop gap) defensive measures that have been deployed as short-term containment measures. To stop a series of remote FTP attacks, for example, network administrators might block all incoming traffic bound for TCP ports 20 and 21. During the recovery stage it would be appropriate to go back to the original filtering rules for FTP traffic (or perhaps even to tighten these rules somewhat but not block all FTP traffic anymore).

Follow-Up

The final stage in the PDCERF methodology is follow-up. The overall goal is to review and integrate information related to an incident that has occurred. Follow-up is, unfortunately, the most likely stage to be overlooked (partially because resources are usually limited and personnel are often exhausted by the time recovery from an incident is complete). This stage is extremely critical, however, so critical that it is hard to envision a successful incident response effort if it is omitted.

The Importance of Following Up

Conducting follow-up activity after recovery is essential for several reasons:

- It helps those involved in handling an incident develop a set of "lessons learned" to improve their skills and learning in future situations.
- This stage also provides information (including metrics) that can help justify an organization's incident response effort to management, "proof" that the team has been very active and achieving its purpose.

- Any lessons learned can serve as training material for new team members. A collection of previous "lessons learned" reports can acquaint new team members with the mistakes that can be made, the kinds of actions that do and do not work in a variety of situations, and so forth.
- It can serve as a basis for team building.
- It can yield information that might be useful in legal proceedings.

The Nature of Follow-Up Activity

The most important element of the follow-up stage is performing a postmortem analysis on each significant incident. Exactly what happened and at what times? How well did the staff involved in dealing with the incident do? What kind of information did the staff need sooner, and how could they have gotten that information sooner? What would the staff do differently next time? Did management prove to be part of the problem or part of the solution? Why?

A follow-up report should also provide information that can be used for reference if other, similar incidents occur. Constructing a timeline of events (including observed events as well as actions taken to mitigate them) is also important for learning as well as legal reasons. Similarly, rapidly obtaining a monetary estimate of the total damages resulting from the incident is critical. Monetary damage and its implications will be discussed in greater detail in Chapter 7, but for the time being, we can define monetary damage in terms of destruction of, damage to, or unauthorized copying or possession of software, data files, and/or hardware damage, as well as labor and travel costs incurred in responding to the incident. The estimate of monetary damage can serve as the basis for prosecution efforts aimed at convicting perpetrators and recouping damages.

Another important part of the follow-up stage is reevaluation and modification of an organization's incident response procedures on the basis of the lessons learned. This is one of the more strategic (as opposed to tactical) benefits of this stage. Personnel who follow their organization's incident response procedures will invariably identify some gaps in the procedures. Certain steps might even cause problems that waste time and effort.

A good example of a procedures gap occurred a few years ago. Someone called a response team to report that the human genome database at a certain site had been broken into. The person who handled the phone call reported this to the team leader, who asked for more information. The team member reported that he had no information regarding how to contact the person who had originally called. As things turned out, the person who handled the phone call had followed the incident response procedures properly, but the procedures did not specify that everyone who comes in contact with someone who reports an incident should immediately record the phone number and email address of that person. This gap in the procedures was a topic of discussion at a follow-up meeting later; the organization's procedures were modified accordingly soon afterwards.

Another important part of follow-up activity is the process of having people involved in incident response interact with each other to improve the way they go about their business. This is potentially a very valuable activity in that it can promote team building. It can also sensitize management to the problems and challenges that people who deal with security-related incidents face.

Caveats

After reading this chapter, you might be tempted to think that if you use the PDCERF methodology to respond to incidents, things will somehow simply go better. Additionally, you might assume that you will do what is required to address the issues in one stage and then close these issues, moving on to the next.

Unfortunately, the real world does not work this way. Many security-related incidents do not unfold themselves in a serial manner. Just when you think that you have eradicated the cause of an incident, something else might happen that causes you to realize that whatever has caused the incident has surfaced again. You might have just done your best to contain an incident when another just like it occurs.

Several caveats will help you apply the PDCERF methodology better:

1. It takes time to use a methodology like PDCERF. The learning curve is not too steep, but nevertheless there is a learning curve. An effective remedy is to practice responding to mock scenarios—simulated incidents—when there are no real incidents to handle, as covered in Chapter 4, "Forming and Managing an Incident Response Team."

2. As mentioned in the examples presented earlier, few incidents follow the linear progression depicted in Figure 3.1. Furthermore, there might at best be a fuzzy distinction between the resolution of one stage and the beginning of the next.

3. A methodology works only if it is custom tailored to the organization in which it is deployed. A bank, for example, is likely to treat containment differently than a university would. A DoS attack on a billing system has vastly different consequences than a DoS attack on a network used primarily by students.

4. Even the most skilled and experienced handlers of security-related incidents have to deal with incidents for which there is no precedent whatsoever and for which few if any distinct stages actually exist. Insider attacks, covered in Chapter 10, "Responding to Insider Attacks," provide one of the best examples of attacks in which often those who deal with them might have great difficulty determining what to do at any point.

5. A methodology will work better if follow-up activity occurs than if this stage is neglected. Feedback, review, and analysis of mistakes made are all key components of an effective incident response effort.

All things considered, however, and for reasons explained earlier in this chapter, it is far better to use a methodology such as PDCERF than to not use one. The incident response arena is very often on the brink of pandemonium. Use of a sound methodology provides some degree of sanity in an otherwise insane world.

Chapter 4 covers how to start and sustain an incident response team effort.

Summary

This chapter started by making a case for using an incident response methodology. Deploying this kind of methodology can impose structure and organization, result in greater efficiency, facilitate an understanding of the process of responding to incidents, enable those who use a methodology to better respond to unexpected events, and help in dealing with legal issues.

This chapter has presented the PDCERF methodology, one of several possible methodologies, but one that is very time proven and well accepted. The first stage is preparation for dealing with an incident. The second is detection—identifying that an incident has occurred or is occurring. The third is containment—limiting the potential that an incident will spread. The fourth stage is eradication of the cause of the incident, and the fifth stage is recovery, returning any compromised systems, applications, databases, and so forth back to their normal mission status. The sixth and final stage involves follow-up activity, including reviewing the incident, deriving lessons learned, and gathering loss statistics for management and law enforcement purposes. Using an incident response methodology does not guarantee success, and incidents seldom go by the book. A methodology works only if it is customized according to an organization's needs.

4

Forming and Managing an Incident Response Team

F ROM TIME TO TIME, WE'VE MENTIONED THE word "team" in the process of covering various topics related to incident response. This chapter delves into forming and managing an incident response team—what a response team is, the rationale for forming an incident response team, major issues that must be addressed, and special management considerations. These topics are particularly important. Many incident response efforts fail or flounder because of mistakes made in forming and/or managing a response team. This chapter again presents the authors' perspectives and real-life experiences in dealing with the many issues related to this area. We will begin by considering the most fundamental part of an "incident response team"—the meaning of the term itself.

What Is an Incident Response Team?

In many contexts, you will see "incident response" equated with "incident response team." Equating these two constructs might superficially appear logical, but doing so often constitutes a departure from reality. Why? People who know little or nothing about the process of incident response often become involved in dealing with security-related incidents. Users are a classic example.

Suppose a worm infects numerous systems. Users might collaborate to analyze what has happened and to combat the worm, yet they can hardly be called an incident response team. The reason is that an incident response team is a capability responsible for dealing with potential or real information security incidents. A team is assigned a set of duties related to bringing each security-related incident to a conclusion, ideally in accordance with the goals of the organization it serves. *The difference, therefore, between individuals who are dealing with an incident and an incident response team is the mission—in terms of job-related responsibilities—assigned to each.* Individuals might sometimes become involved in dealing with incidents, but an incident response team is assigned the responsibility of dealing with incidents as part or all of the job descriptions of the individuals involved.

How many individuals must be involved in an incident response effort for them to collectively be considered a team? A team consists of one or more individuals. You might ask how a team can consist of one individual when one person is not, in most situations, sufficient to deal adequately with most incidents. The answer is that one individual can effectively serve as the coordinator of efforts by a number of people. When incident handling efforts are finished, the others involved in the incident are released from any responsibilities they might have had in dealing with incident. But the team member has the ongoing, day-to-day responsibility of handling incidents and will have to deal with the next incident that occurs.

Many incident response teams have many team members, each with a specialized role. Consider, for example, the Computer Emergency Response Team Coordination Center (CERT/CC). Some of the many members of this team are engaged in daily operations, receiving reports of incidents and attempting to identify the type, source, impact, and other facets of security-related incidents that are reported. Others attempt to deal with vendors to close known vulnerabilities in operating systems, applications, and so forth. Still others examine data to identify and project incident trends, something that is more related to research.

Outsourcing Incident Response Efforts

Should an organization have its own incident response effort, or should it contract with a consultancy or contractor to provide incident response support? The answer in most cases is that it depends on a number of basic factors. Let's consider the alternatives.

Hiring a Contractor or Consultancy. One of the many advantages of contracting with a commercial incident response team is that the overall cost of dealing with security-related incidents is likely to be lower. Why? Incident response personnel—contractors or consultants—need to deal only with incidents that occur. Unless there is a plethora of incidents, there is no need to keep regular personnel around to wait for incidents to occur. Additionally, contractors or consultancies usually offer special kinds of expertise that are often not available within any particular organization. Be careful, however. Many consultancies and service providers offer incident response services, some of which are far superior to others. Be sure to ask for references, preferably from current and ex-customers, before signing any contract for incident response services with any consultancy or service provider.

Using In-House Capability. The major rationale for developing an in-house incident response capability is to handle incidents in accordance with the policy and cultural/political needs of an organization. Security-related incidents are potentially very sensitive and political; an in-house capability is likely to deal with them in a manner that is most advantageous to the organization (provided, of course, that the individuals within this capability understand the culture and politics of the organization).

Why Form an Incident Response Team?

Why might some organizations want to form an incident response team? This section focuses on some possible reasons.

Ability to Coordinate

In general, it is easier to coordinate the efforts of individuals who are on an incident response team because they generally report to the team leader, who can direct them to become involved in one particular activity or another.

Expertise

Information security incidents are becoming increasingly complex; *incident handling experts* are thus becoming increasingly necessary. Technical gurus always come in handy when incidents occur, but pure technical expertise is not enough when it comes to many incidents. Having helped with many previous incidents, knowing what policies to consider and procedures to follow, and so forth are just as critical, if not more critical, than pure technical skills. One of the best ways to build expertise is to serve on a dedicated incident response function.

Efficiency

A team builds a collective knowledge that often leads to increased efficiency. An isolated individual can easily go astray in dealing with an incident, but collective wisdom accrued within a team can help incident response efforts get back on track. Additionally, a team (as opposed to any individual or a few independent individuals) is more likely to develop and follow procedures for incident response, something that boosts efficiency.

Ability to Work Proactively

Being proactive (that is, adopting measures that address incident response needs before incidents actually occur) is one of the keys to a successful incident response effort. Training users and system administrators to recognize the symptoms of incidents and what to do (as well as what *not* to do) is a good example of a proactive effort. Although it is possible for any number of individuals to engage in proactive efforts, having a team increases the likelihood that proactive efforts will occur. Having a team allows the luxury of having different persons specialize in different functions, especially in proactive activity. Additionally, successful proactive efforts are often the byproduct of successful collaboration by teams; individuals are not as likely to think of and carry out successful proactive activity.

Ability to Meet Agency or Corporate Requirements

Another advantage of having an incident response team is that a team is generally better suited to meeting agency or corporate requirements. The main reason is that a team has individuals who are geared toward the same mission. Note that some government agencies and corporations go one step further in that they *require* (through a management directive or a policy statement) that an incident response team be formed.

Serving a Liaison Function

Response teams are better suited to serving a liaison function than are individuals because outside entities are not likely to learn of and/or be motivated to deal with individuals. Having a team identity provides extra external visibility as well as credibility, both of which are more suited to the liaison function. Furthermore, a "team," in many respects, commands a certain degree of legitimacy within internal and external organizations.

Ability to Deal with Institutional Barriers

Institutional politics invariably affect virtually any effort that occurs within an institution. Incident response teams (or at least incident response teams sanctioned by senior management), however, provide at least some degree of immunity from politics that provide barriers to incident response efforts. The main reason is that these teams are likely to have more authority to take action—such as shutting down systems that have been compromised at the superuser level—than individuals. Additionally, teams often involve individuals from a cross-section of organizations and groups, making them more politically palatable within a range of an organization's divisions and groups.

Issues in Forming a Response Team

Forming an incident response team generally is not as easy as it superficially might appear. The individual(s) charged with this responsibility must deal with many key issues, including policy, whether or not a team is really necessary, defining and communicating with a constituency, defining functional requirements, defining the role of the incident response team, staffing the team appropriately, and creating and updating operational procedures. This section discusses these issues.

Policy

The most important issue in forming and managing an incident response team, all things considered, is policy. Any incident response team must always operate within the constraints of the policy of the organization to which it belongs or that it serves. Suppose, for example, an organization requires that no employee make contact with or answer questions from the press unless that person obtains written approval from the head of the public relations department. Another organizational policy provision might be that no system being attacked can stay connected to the network if it holds extremely valuable resources (such as proprietary data, proprietary source code, and so forth).

Additionally, an incident response team might impose its own policy provisions on its own operations. A policy provision of this nature might be that no team member can spread information about any incident outside of the immediate team without the direct permission of the team leader. Failure to conform to existing policy spells catastrophe for an incident response team; consequences can range from embarrassment to termination of employment or even to dissolution of the team itself.

Is a Team Really Necessary?

Another extremely important issue is whether an incident response team is really necessary. Some of the advantages of forming a response team have been presented earlier in this chapter, but it is not always advantageous to create such a team. An alternative is to have individuals who are not part of an incident response team but who are available (usually on the basis of a matrix agreement[1] between organizations) when incidents occur. Here are some possible advantages of adopting this alternative approach:

- **Smaller organizations generally do not need a team.** A smaller organization, such as a small startup company, does not usually need an incident response team per se. This kind of company is not likely to have very much internal structure; creating policy and procedures, in many cases, is something that must be placed on the proverbial backburner while more immediately pressing issues (survival of the business) are addressed. Forming an incident response team would constitute overkill.

- **Few resources might be available.** One of the major reasons for *not* forming an incident response team is lack of resources, particularly personnel resources. Although not a particularly good reason from a security viewpoint, lack of resources is too often a problem for information security efforts in general.

---

1. An agreement of this nature typically specifies, at a minimum, how many hours per time period (week, month, or year) an individual from one organization is available to incident response activities. It also guarantees that the individual devoted to these activities will be paid by a cognizant manager, often the designated incident manager. An agreement of this nature might take the form of a service-level agreement.

- **Incident response might work better as a distributed effort.** In some organizations, incident response works better as a distributed effort. Different individuals from different divisions or groups can be called in whenever an incident of sufficient magnitude or impact occurs. Having this kind of arrangement can make these divisions or groups feel that they have some kind of direct control over the incident response process; some of their own staff members will be involved in handling their own incidents. Additionally, a distributed effort can help ensure that people who know and understand how individual units work, how the systems and networks are configured and maintained, how the applications work, and so forth will be involved in handling incidents. This can lead to better insight into what should and should not be done to resolve each incident satisfactorily.

What if You Don't Have a Response Team Per Se?

The authors of this book feel that, all things considered, it is better to have a response team to deal with security-related incidents than to call on individuals when incidents occur. Many readers of this book will never be part of an incident response team, however. If it is not possible to have such a team, you can adopt measures that will increase the likelihood of success in your efforts to handle incidents. Consider the following suggestions:

- Identify key personnel (especially technical personnel), people you feel are qualified to deal with incidents and obtain contact and other information.

- Establish some kind of ground rules or agreements concerning the availability of people who are likely to be needed in dealing with incidents. Try to get a commitment from management that guarantees a minimum number of hours of participation (per week, month, or year) from each individual who might be involved. Try to obtain assurance that even more hours of support will be available in the case of a severe incident.

- Be wise in your dealings with organizations that provide individuals who are available for incident response support. In many cases, having these individuals participate in incident handling detracts from their own mainstream missions. Avoid being overly demanding and be prepared for a "no" answer. Sometimes an organization might refuse to allow someone from that organization to deal with an incident due to a pressing need such as meeting a major project milestone. Having a long list of potential incident support personnel—so that if one person is not available, you can turn to another—is thus essential.

- Provide some kind of training and orientation to everyone who is likely to help in dealing with incidents. Ensure that everyone has at least a minimum level of knowledge about responding to incidents and that everyone understands the importance of cooperation and teamwork.

- To the maximum possible extent, solve leadership and authority issues in advance. In many (if not most) incidents, having someone in charge is essential to success. Conversely, having several people think they are in charge is extremely counterproductive.

- Do not call on the individuals who are available for incident response support unless they are genuinely needed. You are disrupting some other business unit or group's work each time you call on such individuals. You will wear out your welcome if you call on these individuals too much or if you call them into too many false alarms.

- Organize a committee or board that oversees incident response activities. Have this entity analyze critical aspects such as difficulty in obtaining support personnel, efficiency of incident response activity, and others. This entity might be instrumental in pointing out to management things that need to be improved (such as resource levels) and might prove to be instrumental in helping you form a team in time.

What Are the Functional Requirements and Roles?

If you have ever taken a course in software engineering, you have learned that defining requirements right up front is crucial to the success of the project. Incident response teams are no exception to this principle; functional requirements and the role for this team need to be defined as early in the life of the team as possible.

Basic Requirements

The most fundamental requirement for an incident response team is providing incident response support to a constituency. In providing incident response support, a response team can serve several potential roles:

- A team can assume full control over an incident and any computing and data resources involved. The extreme version of this role is to go to a site or area within a facility and take over all incident response efforts.[2] In most settings, however, this approach does not work too well in that it alienates others, particularly the owners of the computing resources and data, causing territory wars. If mandated by senior management, however, this approach can be viable in that it establishes a clear line of authority during incidents.

- Another, less extreme approach is control sharing—both the incident response team and operations or business unit staff. This generally causes less friction, but questions concerning who is in charge at any time are likely to arise.

- Still another possibility is providing direct (hands-on) incident response support but limiting this support to a purely advisory role. This means that an incident response team will do something only when its constituency requests that it do so. This role ruffles fewer feathers but typically also greatly limits the role and effectiveness of the people who serve on the incident response team.

---

2. A good example of a successful use of this approach comes from the well-known Citibank incident in 1994. Two Russians were breaking into several Citibank computers and initiating bogus money transfers. Citibank personnel promptly noticed what was happening and assigned an incident manager, who was given a high level of authority in dealing with the incident.

- A final potential role for a response team is providing indirect rather than direct support in the form of advice but nothing more. This role is the most limiting for team members. However, it also tends to alienate others the least of any role.

Additional Requirements

In many circumstances, simply providing incident response support is not sufficient to keep management happy. Management too often views an incident response team as individuals who sometimes are busy but at other times have absolutely nothing to do. Management might, therefore, demand more of the team. In other cases, the individuals who attempt to create a response team can see the need for the team to perform other activities related to incident response support. Here are some additional potential types of requirements for a response team:

- **Interagency/corporation coordination/liaison.** The response team might, for example, provide a liaison function with other response teams, an organization's business continuity organization, law enforcement agencies, or some other entity.

- **Serving as a clearinghouse.** A clearinghouse serves as a central repository for information, patches, tools, and so forth. Although almost every response team in some way serves as a clearinghouse for information about incidents and vulnerabilities, serving as a clearinghouse for patches and tools has quite a few additional risks. What if the team provides the wrong patch, resulting in an unexpected incident or system failure? The same applies to tools. The point here is that serving as a clearinghouse for patches and tools often (but not always) poses more risk than potential benefit.

- **Contingency planning and business continuity services.** In some organizations, an incident response team also engages in contingency planning and business continuity functions. This is potentially a good idea in that incident response personnel generally become very proficient in recognizing and dealing with emergencies. All things considered, however, the best way to meet this kind of requirement is to have one or more individuals from a business continuity team closely work with or even join an incident response team. Business continuity staff members generally know things that incident response people need to know, such as what to do to protect business interests in the case of a prolonged outage. This kind of knowledge can be well applied to security-related incidents such as massive distributed denial-of-service attacks.

- **Information security tool development.** Another possible requirement is for the incident response staff to develop information security tools in their spare time. This kind of requirement can result in the availability of useful tools for a team's constituency. The downside is that tool development sidetracks team members from the team's main focus, namely handling incidents. A division within the team—incident handlers versus developers—might even develop.

- **Incident response planning and analysis.** A few teams have a requirement to analyze trends and plan for incident response and security needs of the future. Although most teams are not funded sufficiently to engage in efforts of this nature, incident response planning and analysis is one of the most proactive and potentially valuable activities in which a response team can engage.

- **Training and awareness.** We will discuss training and awareness in more detail later in this chapter. Suffice it to say, at this point, that training and awareness is one of the most proactive activities in which a response team can engage. Response team members will learn about many developments and trends—such as new types of malicious programs, new types of attacks, new countermeasures, and so forth— that are potentially of great value to the team's constituency. Training and awareness activities are a good outlet for disseminating this kind of information.

Who is the Constituency?

An essential issue in incident response is determining exactly whom you are supporting. In other words, you need to find out who your constituency is. The reason this is so important is that an incident response effort that does not meet the needs of those it serves is doomed to failure. If you can determine whom your constituency is, you can communicate with that constituency to learn the needs that exist. You also will know how to better focus your efforts.

If, for example, you discover that your constituency consists largely of system administrators, your approach to providing incident response support will be substantially different than if you have mostly users as customers. In the first case, you will probably need to be more technical in your approach. Your communications with system administrators will, in all likelihood, be of a technical nature. In the second case, you will almost certainly take a much less technical approach, emphasizing instead things that users need and can understand. Motivating users to engage in sound computing practices—such as updating antivirus software on desktop systems and helping users whose systems have virus or worm infections by advising them to avoid dealing with these incidents directly[3]—would in this case be more appropriate.

A response team's relationship with its constituency will make or break an incident response effort. Providing quality help to the right people will eventually result in positive feedback to both the team and its management or sponsor. Many teams (some of which are still in existence, others of which are not), however, have failed primarily because they have neither understood who their constituency is nor served their constituency's needs very well. The following sidebar describes some of the many mistakes that some incident response teams have made.

---

3. As stated in Chapter 2, "Risk Analysis," human error causes far more loss than do sources of security-related issues (such as crackers). Damage inflicted by panicked users is right at the top of the list of reasons for loss.

Case Studies: Failing to Adequately Serve a Constituency

Several incident response teams have lost most or all credibility within their constituent communities for a variety of reasons. Consider the following mistakes that these teams have made:

- **Failing to get back to someone who contacts a response team to report an incident or new vulnerability.** Some incident response teams send an automated reply containing an incident number but do nothing more. In the perception of a constituency, this is as bad as not replying at all. Several teams have thus deservedly earned the reputation of being a black hole. People who can be an excellent source of information about new incidents and vulnerabilities often quit contacting their incident response team after just one case of failing to follow up a report of an incident.

- **Spreading misinformation.** Recently an incident response team informed someone at the site at which the senior author of this book works that multiple systems at the site were infected by a worm. After hours of investigation, no evidence of any worm could be found in any of the four allegedly infected machines. The individuals who performed the investigation developed negative feelings toward the response team for not getting its facts straight and for wasting their time.

- **Becoming too intrusive.** One incident response team for a government agency became intensely disliked within its constituency because it initiated a project to monitor network traffic at the external gateways at each site without the consent of management at each site. People at the sites felt that the incident response team was eavesdropping on them.

- **Causing embarrassment or leaking information without authorization.** Another incident response team was hired to perform a security evaluation at one of its constituent sites. After finishing the evaluation (in which a considerable number of vulnerabilities were found), the response team reported the results to the head of security within the government agency that oversaw both the site and the response team. Management at that site had expected that the results would be confidential.

- **Betrayal.** Under the edict of Congress, a certain U.S. government contractor launched a set of network attacks against several U.S. government sites. The attacks were very vigorous; the attackers not surprisingly achieved more than a minimal level of success. Not knowing the source of the attacks, those who noticed the resulting security breaches in victim systems frequently turned to their agency's response team.

  As the attacks progressed, people at some of the sites within one government agency noticed a strange phenomenon: After the identity of a victim system had been reported to the agency's response team, that system was never attacked again. After several weeks, the attacks ceased entirely. Soon afterward, the nature of the "white hat" penetration tests started to become common knowledge. Along with the news of the nature and purpose of the tests came the news that one response team was working in full cooperation with those who were launching the attacks. When a site detected an intrusion into a system and reported it to the response team, that response team forwarded the information to the attackers, who quit accessing the system in favor of launching new attacks against others. Since all this happened, virtually no one at any site has wanted to deal with this response team any more.

Communicating with a Constituency

After a response team's constituency is defined, establishing communication channels is essential. One-way communication, in which the response team keeps sending information to its constituency without communication being initiated by the constituency, generally does not work. An effective response team needs to obtain information about what is actually occurring within its constituency. It is possible, for example, for a response team to be unaware that a worm is circulating within part of its constituency's networks. Learning that this is happening would enable the response team to be able to better serve its constituency.

The bottom line here is that an effective incident response team establishes two-way communication. It shares information about vulnerabilities and types of incidents that are occurring within its constituency. As the saying goes, "You have to give information to get information." If the response team's constituency does not share information with the response team, the response team is not likely to have much worthwhile information to share with its constituency.

A response team can use any or all of the following avenues of communication:

- **Telephone.** One of the most simple and direct avenues of communication is the telephone. Calling someone can inject a personal touch into communications with a constituency. The fact that telephone conversations are in real time is also an important advantage of this means of communication. The downside is that people do not always speak and/or listen as well as they should; misunderstandings and miscommunication can occur. Another downside is that telephone communications are subject to eavesdropping, especially with cordless telephones based on radio frequency transmission and wireless telephones.[4]

  Secure telephones solve the eavesdropping threat in that they encrypt voice transmissions from one secure telephone to another. An example of an encrypting telephone is an STU-4—something that the U.S. government uses for transmitting classified information via telephone. A limitation is that not everyone can have access to a secure telephone when it is needed. Additionally, secure telephones can prove financially costly.

- **Email.** Email is another potentially advantageous means of communicating with a constituency because of its efficiency. You can send a message to someone else in another part of the world in only a few seconds. Furthermore, the person to whom you send the message does not have to be monitoring email at that particular moment in time. Additionally, you can create mail *exploders* to which you send a message that is subsequently sent to an entire distribution list of email addresses. As pointed out in Chapter 3, "A Methodology for Incident Response," however, email is extremely prone to eavesdropping. Email can also easily be spoofed, and incident response team members are also sometimes spammed by attackers.

---

4. Protocols that secure wireless communications currently exist, but they are not widely used because they tend to interfere with performance.

A better solution is secure email, which encrypts email messages sent from one system to another. Various freeware and commercial packages that deliver email encryption are available. They provide a good solution for the eavesdropping problem but tend to be plagued with problems related to using encryption—particularly key distribution and key recovery.

- **Fax.** Sending faxes is an often overlooked but potentially effective means of communicating with a constituency. A nice feature of faxes is that they generally result in an easy-to-read hard copy. Additionally, faxes can be sent when one's network or mail server is down. Some types of fax machines can even explode a single fax message to hundreds of fax numbers in only a few minutes.

  Faxes, like anything else, are hardly a panacea, however. One of the greatest limitations is that they do not work when the destination fax number is busy or out of order. Faxing messages can also be unduly labor intensive because it takes a while to set up a fax transmission, undo any paper clogs at both ends of the transmission, replace empty paper bins, and so forth. Additionally, fax transmissions are potentially subject to eavesdropping. Secure faxes solve this eavesdropping problem, but they tend to be more expensive. Because of all the potential complications associated with fax communications, our recommendation is to use this method of communication as a *backup* rather than as a primary method.

- **Bulletins/notices.** Bulletins and notices provide an excellent way not only to communicate important information to a constituency but also to gain credibility. CERT/CC, vendors, and others already publish more than enough bulletins; ensuring that there is added value is thus an important consideration. An incident response team might, for example, publish alerts describing only the vulnerabilities currently being exploited most frequently. Alternatively, bulletins might describe new types of countermeasures.

  One of the keys to using bulletins and notices effectively is creating, and then constantly updating, an accurate distribution list. Doing so, however, is likely to be more labor intensive than one might imagine. Additionally, there are many potential pitfalls. Neglecting to add the email address of a key person from within one's constituency (or worse yet, accidentally or intentionally deleting that person's address) is a potentially major mistake. If bulletins are sensitive or proprietary but continue to be sent to employees who leave a company or organization, trouble can also occur.

To Pay or Not to Pay, That Is the Question

In the spring of 2001, CERT/CC announced that its advisories would no longer be available for free and that organizations would have to pay a yearly fee of up to $70,000 to obtain these advisories. A negative reaction within part of the Internet community resulted. Critics pointed out that CERT/CC's capabilities were developed at U.S. taxpayers' expense and that to start charging for CERT/CC advisories was unfair. Since CERT/CC made this announcement, other organizations that create bulletins describing new vulnerabilities have announced that they, too, are considering charging a fee for their bulletins. Even if CERT/CC does charge a fee for its bulletins, there is no need for panic. Many other teams and organizations produce bulletins of such high quality that there will be no shortage of information about vulnerabilities and incident trends.

- **A web site.** One of the most effective ways to share information with a constituency is to create and maintain a web site. Given the current popularity of the World Wide Web, it is now virtually mandatory for an incident response team to have its own web site. The web site should disseminate a variety of useful information, including bulletins and notices, how to contact the response team, and so forth. A response team might even use its web site to distribute patches and/or software tools if it chooses to perform this clearinghouse function.

  A key consideration related to running a web site is the security of the site. A break-in or defacement can cause all kinds of trouble, not only in terms of loss of face for the response team but also for that team's constituency. Without sufficient web site security, users might obtain bogus information or might download malicious programs. Another possibility is that the web site might not be available due to a prolonged outage because of a denial-of-service attack. The distributed denial-of-service (DDoS) attack on CERT/CC in the spring of 2001 is one of the best-known attacks of this nature.

- **Conferences.** Participating in a conference or actually holding a special conference can provide an effective way to communicate with a response team's constituents. Talks and panel presentations can disseminate useful information to a team's constituents. Additionally, having response team members participate as speakers and panelists can enhance the reputation of the team and help it gain more visibility within its constituency.

- **Courses and workshops.** Courses and workshops provide still another potentially useful way to communicate with a constituency. If of sufficient quality, courses and workshops can impart a considerable amount of information to those who need it. They can also enhance the reputation and credibility of team members who teach a course or workshop. Best yet, courses and workshops represent proactive efforts at their best. No incident response team will ever be able to help everyone within a constituency when incidents occur, but courses and workshops can teach users, system and network administrators, and managers enough to be able to deal adequately with most incidents that occur.

  A word of caution is appropriate here. Note that the preceding paragraph included the phrase: "If of sufficient quality . . . " If a course or workshop is not of sufficient quality, the team that develops and presents it can quickly become despised within its own constituency. The availability of so many outstanding security-related courses nowadays has raised the proverbial bar for security training. Getting help from training specialists, possibly from a consultancy, is often a wise move.

- **Media interviews.** Media interviews can also help in the process of communicating with a constituency. If done correctly, these interviews can enhance a response team's reputation and visibility. The following sidebar describes some basic principles in dealing with the media.

Dealing with the Media

Dealing with the media is often an important part of responding to incidents. Much of the damage from many incidents is in terms of loss of reputation or confidence in an organization due to one or more catastrophic incidents. Your organization should have a policy dictating that all contacts with the media be approved in advance by management. In fact, in the ideal scenario, a public relations department should handle all contacts with the media. (You might, in turn, be called upon to furnish technical information.) The following are time-proven methods for dealing with the media:

- Learn as much about the interview in which you are going to participate as early as possible and prepare accordingly.

- Outline the major points you want to get across.

- Anticipate a wide range of difficult questions and prepare answers in advance.

- Establish rapport with your interviewer as soon as possible.

- Use brief sentences.

- Provide simple explanations of each technical point you make.

- Every time you speak, steer your communication to some *point you want to get across* (take the initiative to do this!).

- Don't get intimidated.

- Turn negatives into positives.

- Be diplomatic, but always tell the truth.

- When you don't know the answer, admit you don't know (and perhaps offer to find out).

- Be liberal in giving credit but stingy in assigning blame.

- Dress appropriately.

- Avoid image-damaging nonverbal communication, such as avoiding eye contact or slouching as you sit.

- After the interview, ask to review any written materials for inaccuracies.

- You, the interviewee, have rights. Feel free to terminate the interview at any time if your rights are not respected!

The following are some questions you are most likely to be asked:

- What happened?

- What was the result/damage?

- What was the cause?

- What did you do about it?

- Is what happened likely to reoccur?

- What can people do to avoid what happened?

- There are, of course, no guarantees of success when you deal with the media, but following these principles listed can go a long way toward achieving a desirable outcome.

- **Videotapes.** A final method of communicating with a response team's constituency is videotapes. Videotapes can convey important information such as why having a response team is important, how to contact the response team, the kinds of incidents that are mostly likely to occur, and what to do if an incident actually occurs. If produced professionally, a videotape can have great impact on those who watch it. A videotape can also be shown multiple times with what usually amounts to little effort on a response team's part.

The security group in one organization developed a very short but effective videotape titled "30 Seconds for Handling Security Incidents." This videotape presented a few major types of incidents and what to do about each if any should occur. The video played continuously in the organization's cafeteria; employees going in and out of the cafeteria were likely to catch at least some of the videotape as they were hanging their coats up or putting them back on.

Like anything else, videotapes have limitations. Producing them through an in-house effort can be frustrating, time consuming, and financially costly. Yet a videotape produced by the team itself will almost certainly at least be tailored to the specific needs of the organization.

Requirements for Communicating with a Constituency

Because communications with a constituency are so critical to an incident response team's success, trying to meet all of the following goals is extremely important:

- Relevance. A response team must provide information that is relevant to whomever it serves. If the constituency has mostly UNIX and Linux systems, providing bulletins about the latest vulnerabilities in mainframes will, if anything, antagonize individuals from within the constituency.

- Timeliness. The information that a response team provides must be current. This means that if a new vulnerability that is being widely exploited by freely available cracking tools has been discovered, an effective response team will get this information to its constituency soon afterward. Additionally, this means that if other response teams have written and distributed bulletins about a new vulnerability, a response team cannot afford to lose face within its own constituency by waiting several days after the others have issued their bulletins to issue its own bulletin.

continues

continued

- **Accuracy.** Information provided by a response team must be accurate. Few things destroy a response team's credibility as quickly as disseminating inaccurate information. At a minimum, every sentence of every bulletin or notice should be reviewed (preferably by experts outside the team) for accuracy before the bulletin or notice is sent. At the same time, however, it is important to realize that not all the information that will eventually be available might be available at the time one's constituency needs to hear about some new vulnerability or pattern of incidents. What superficially appears to be true might not turn out to be true over time. Being prepared to issue revised bulletins and notices, therefore, is critical. The same basic principles apply to training materials, press interviews, and so forth.

- **Originality.** First-rate response teams write their own bulletins and notices. Copying or appending other teams' bulletins and notices is generally a bad idea. (An exception is when a very small incident response team has too few people to expend the level of effort needed to create original bulletins). Constituencies generally do not hold teams that merely copy other teams' bulletins in very high regard.

- **Understandability.** Information that a response team disseminates must be readily understandable by those who receive it. Given that part of one's constituency is likely to be management and another part will be technical staff, this is a potentially difficult issue. Sometimes writing an executive summary at the start of a bulletin that is primarily technical in nature solves this problem. In other cases, producing two bulletins on each issue—one for management, one for technical personnel—works.

- **Reliable distribution.** The information needs to get to those who need it—without exception.

Developing Out-of-Band Communications

At some time during the life of an incident response team, conventional communications channels will not be available. It is therefore important to develop out-of-band communications capabilities. A few alternative channels are wireless networks, text pagers, fax communications, and email delivery via a postal service. The first two of these alternative channels, in particular, require advance arrangements and coordination within a response team's constituency. It is expedient to analyze current communication channels and then develop out-of-band communications capabilities for plausible primary communications outage scenarios. You should ensure that each communication channel meets some kind of minimum security standards, and you should regularly test each communication channel to ensure that it works as expected. New developments show that HAM radios are becoming a popular mode for emergency communications.

Case Study: A Lesson Learned in Establishing Communication Channels

Early in the existence of the Computer Incident Advisory Capability (CIAC), the incident response team for the U.S. Department of Energy (DOE), the main avenue of communication between this team and its constituent sites was via fax. At this time, the Internet was not like it is today. The ARPAnet, in fact, had been split into the Milnet and the NSFnet (the Internet) less than a year before an interesting development occurred. The CIAC team was based in the East Bay of the San Francisco area. In October 1989, a massive earthquake struck the area, causing widespread power and telephone outages. Although the CIAC team did not experience any power outages, telephone service was interrupted. At the time of the earthquake, a worm called WANK/OILZ was infecting VMS systems around the world, including many systems within DOE sites. Attempts by CIAC team members to warn DOE sites of new developments and countermeasures for this worm were halted while team members attempted to contact individuals at these sites via other means. Numerous individuals at these sites had email, but the earthquake also disrupted CIAC's email services. The stoppage of telephone and email services lasted for approximately two days; during this time, CIAC was virtually unable to communicate with its constituency.

This episode provided important "lessons learned" for this team. Soon afterward, the team worked on developing better out-of-band communications capabilities through use of more cellular telephones and emergency procedures for contacting key individuals at sites.

Staffing Issues

So far, we have described many difficult issues that need to be addressed, but no issue is more difficult than dealing with staffing. Addressing staffing-related considerations such as team size, prerequisite skills, and location of team members is critical. A discussion of these considerations follows.

Team Size

The size of your team will undoubtedly be dictated by available funding. This is particularly true during the early stages of your team's existence. At a minimum, you will initially want to have someone to manage the team and, if funding permits, someone with the technical skills necessary to deal with the problems that are most likely to surface within your constituency.[5] You can then add staff to broaden the range of expertise as funding allows.

---

5. Recall the importance of gauging risks, as discussed in Chapter 2.

Team Skills

This section presents the kinds of skills that are generally required in an effective incident response team.

- **Management skills.** Proficiency in management is almost without question the single most important skill. Without effective management, even the most technically proficient team will falter. The manager of an incident response team must be able to ensure that the team has the appropriate skill sets; organize and coordinate the team's activities; keep team members motivated and on track; ensure that the team has sufficient resources and that the resource burn rate is within acceptable limits; ensure that proper priorities, procedures, and policies are in place and are revised as necessary; prepare reports for senior management; monitor how well the team is meeting its requirements; intervene if and when conflict occurs; and play politics well enough to both shield team members from them and keep management supportive of the team.

  The team manager does not have to be technically proficient (and, if fact, probably should not be too technically proficient to avoid the temptation of getting involved in technical issues at the expense of performing critical management responsibilities). At the same time, however, the team manager needs to know enough about technical matters to be able to make good judgments about priorities and to avoid hurting the team's reputation when the manager deals with the constituency, vendors, and others.

- **Technical skills.** Technical skills are extremely essential to a response team's effectiveness. Many incidents require a high degree of technical proficiency in analyzing what is wrong and dealing with the situation. Additionally, unless team members earn a large degree of respect for their technical prowess within a team's constituency, no one will contact them for help, nor will they heed their warnings and advice. Technical skills in operating systems (UNIX, Linux, Windows NT and Windows 2000, NetWare, OS390, and so forth) and network security are particularly critical.

  Programming experience, particularly in system programming, can help considerably when a response team needs to reverse-engineer malicious programs such as worms and back doors. There is no substitute for real-world troubleshooting experience such as dealing with operational outages. Computer crisis coordination capabilities are constantly in crisis mode; previous relevant experience has great payoff.

  Not every team member needs to be a top-notch technical expert, however. Exceptionally strong technical personnel are rare. Furthermore, they generally command top salaries. Funding realities will generally limit how many gurus can be hired. A key to having sufficient technical expertise, therefore, is to hire one technically accomplished staff member to anchor each key technology area in which the team needs to become involved. The guru in each area can then advise and mentor less technically accomplished team members.

- **People skills.** Nowhere are people skills more important than in the incident response arena. Harmony within the team is critical to the team's efficiency and effectiveness. Being able to get along well with individuals within the team's constituency is also very important. Technical gurus often have the reputation of being hard to get along with, so the challenge of hiring team members with good people skills is a difficult one. Periodic training in interpersonal skills can also have a high payoff.

- **Teamwork skills.** Teamwork skills are somewhat different from people skills in that they involve different types of knowledge, abilities, and perspectives. Teamwork skills are related to having a common vision, effectively dividing responsibilities, effectively estimating task completion time, knowing when to start new tasks, knowing how to get out of other team members' way when doing so is appropriate, obtaining feedback concerning each team member's progress, and so forth. Strong management skills are once again the key ingredient; good managers promote and build team skills. We also recommend participating in periodic team skills training.

- **Communication skills.** Communication skills go hand-in-hand with both interpersonal skills and team skills. Special kinds of communication skills, particularly writing and speaking skills, can be exceptionally valuable. Many incident response teams hire a technical writer for the specific purpose of producing accurate, understandable bulletins and notices. Additionally, speaking skills are very useful for conference and workshop presentations, filming videotapes, and so on.

Location of Staff

Where should team members be geographically located? If an organization and its constituency are all within a single geographical area, the answer is obvious. But what if the constituency is spread out among several different locations, possibly even on different continents? Should all team members reside at one location, or should the team be divided so that each part of the team's constituency is served by team members located where they are needed?

The answer to this question depends on a number of factors. Some advantages of having all team members at a single location include a better ability to coordinate the team, greater ease of communication within the team, facilitation of team building among team members, and (generally) a lower financial cost because only one physical facility, one telecommunications provider, one document custodian, and so forth will be necessary. Additionally, separating a team into different parts residing in different geographical locations often results in undesirable divisions and negative politics within the team itself. In this case, it is not unusual to find that each piece of the team develops an "us versus them" mentality.

Advantages of having multiple locations are generally related to providing a higher quality of service to one's constituency. If part of the constituency is in central Europe, for example, and part is in the central United States, the difference in time of seven hours might prove to be an overwhelming obstacle if all members of a response team are in the central United States. If someone in central Europe arrives at work at 8 a.m. Monday morning and discovers an incident, that person would likely have to wait approximately seven hours before being able to talk to someone from the response team. It would probably be better, in this case, to have part of the team reside in central Europe.

Should you have full-time or part-time team members? The answer to this question is simple; in general, it is better to have full-time team members. Having full-time team members means more personnel resources will be available when they are needed. This is particularly important when high-impact incidents occur or when a multiple-points-of-presence attack (in which multiple attacks are launched against sites in different geographical locations) is launched. On the other hand, funding realities might dictate that part-time team members be hired. Alternatively, perhaps some gurus are available only on a part-time basis. In these cases, part-time involvement is better than no involvement at all.

Creating Operating Procedures

The topic of procedures is potentially very complex. Entire books on effective information security–related procedures have been written. Previous chapters of this book have touched on this topic, especially regarding the necessity of having well-written, well-distributed procedures for incident response. Additionally, procedures must constantly be revised if they are to be effective in guiding the incident response team and others to appropriate actions.

You cannot really simply copy some other team's procedures and then use them. You must instead create procedures that are appropriate to your particular team and the requirements that team must fulfill. The following, however, are issues that any set of procedures must address if they are to be effective:

- What the purpose of the procedures is
- To whom or what the procedures apply and under what conditions (if at all)
- Lines of authority within the incident response team and the organization(s) it serves
- Restrictions on the kinds of actions in which team members can and cannot engage (including actions such as counterattacking sites known to launch attacks)
- How information and evidence must be documented
- Who can contact outside entities (such as the media, law enforcement agencies, and so forth) and under what conditions
- Priorities in response efforts (for example, protecting the lives of humans, keeping systems and networks operational, and so forth)

- What to do in case of incidents in highly valuable, sensitive, proprietary, or classified systems and/or networks
- Kinds of information that can and cannot be disseminated outside of the immediate group or division in which the incident response team belongs
- Management's role with respect to the response team and its activities
- When and how the procedures must be changed
- How the procedures are to be distributed

Procedures should in every respect be a living document. Every time your incident response team engages in the follow-up stage of the PDCERF methodology (or whatever methodology your team creates), it should evaluate existing procedures to determine whether they actually worked. You should then revise your procedures as needed.

About Managing an Incident Response Effort

Now that we have covered the many considerations involved in forming an incident response team, let's next turn our attention to how to manage such a team. We will consider management style, coordinating with other entities, how to develop and use metrics of effectiveness, maintaining the desired level of proficiency, preparing reports, and how to gauge where a response team is in terms of the stages of the life cycle for incident response teams to adjust one's management strategy.

Management Style

Incident handling is often a stressful, difficult activity if it is done correctly. It is thus important for the team manager to convey a positive, supportive management style. Failing to do this can seriously undermine the morale of an incident response team. In addition, we offer the following suggestions:

- **Avoid micromanagement.**[6] Unless you see trouble, adopt a hands-off philosophy. Micromanagement can ruin an incident response effort by causing loss of morale, a high turnover rate, conflict, and so forth.
- **Learn to handle visibility.** A manager of an incident response team will almost certainly gain elevated visibility. Conferences and the media are likely to become very interested in getting that manager to participate; the manager, after all, will know about incidents that are likely to fascinate audiences, readers, and viewers. Take this visibility with a proverbial grain of salt; don't let it change your opinion of yourself and how you relate to others (particularly your other team members). Learn to use whatever visibility you gain to the benefit of the team—to give greater recognition to other team members, to obtain more funding and support, and so forth.

6. *Micromanagement* means managing minute details of subordinates' jobs (that is, telling others exactly what to do at any point in time).

- **Obtain written evaluation/feedback of your managerial performance from team members and adjust your management style accordingly.** Doing this once every three months or so can help you become a better manager and be better accepted by fellow team members.

- **Take feedback in the form of "flames" seriously.** Consider revising your procedures, attitudes, and so forth accordingly.

- **Help keep team members' efforts on track.** Team members might become confused about a next course of action or might be so burned out after dealing with a complex incident that all they want to do for the next few days is web loafing. Dealing with web loafing is particularly challenging. Intervening and telling that person to quit web loafing usually amounts only to micromanagement, something that usually results only in resentment on that person's part. Ultimately, the answer lies in assigning a reasonable set of tasks with reasonable deliverables and unambiguous due dates for each. If a team member wants to web loaf, that's fine, but whatever is due will nevertheless be due by the assigned date. If that person does not get the job done on time, it is time for that person to deal with the consequences.

- **Be decisive about dealing with baggage and loose cannons on your response team.** In general, weed them out. Incident response generally is as much political as it is technical. It has been said that "loose lips sink ships." Similarly, one or two loose cannons on an incident response team can completely undermine the credibility of that team.

Coordinating with Others

"No team is an island." You need to develop channels of communication and cooperation accordingly. Focus your attention on groups such as business units within your organization; your human relations, legal, and public relations offices; other incident response teams; vendors; law enforcement agencies (if your management so directs); and others. You will also need to develop relationships with other departments and divisions within your organization that have experts whom you might need from time to time. Expertise needed might include information security, information technology, business continuity, and law.

Suggested Action Items for Incident Response Team Managers

- Ensure that your team's existing policies and procedures are current and appropriate. Update and expand them as necessary.

- Perform, review, or update the risk analysis for your team.

- Have an objective evaluation of your incident response team's charter, efforts, and procedures performed by someone outside of your team.

- Have your policies and procedures reviewed by legal and human relations professionals.

- Evaluate your team's expertise and capabilities; bring in new team members (or reassign some existing team members) as appropriate.

- Evaluate your team's communications capabilities and make changes as appropriate.

- Participate in FIRST (Forum of Incident Response and Security Teams; see www.first.org). FIRST works only if teams participate and contribute.

Success Metrics

As far as information security goes, success in many respects means having no incidents whatsoever. Having no incidents, however, will almost certainly spell doom for an incident response team. It makes it even more difficult to rationalize spending resources on your incident response effort. In an odd sense, therefore, success in incident handling requires that incidents transpire. Most significantly, however, actions taken to deal with incidents must be successful. This is where the difficulty begins—what constitutes success in incident response activity?

One of the best ways in information security to communicate results to management is to develop and use metrics. A number of possible metrics for incident response exist:

- How many incidents the incident response team has dealt with in a given time period[7]

- Whether the number and/or percentage of incidents handled in which the estimated financial loss is below a criterion value

- Self-evaluation measures[8] such as questionnaires

- Written or verbal reports of success or failure with people within a response team's constituency

- Average time and manpower needed to resolve each incident plotted against the apparent complexity of each incident

- Documentation by team members of the actions taken to deal with each incident

- Awards presented by organizations and other forms of external recognition[9]

Unfortunately, none of these measures is all that adequate, nor is any combination of them very satisfactory. You should thus view these potential metrics as a start, a proverbial "straw man" for developing your own set of metrics.

7. This metric is not particularly good, however, in that someone might contact an incident response team without the team ever bothering to respond. Some response teams even proudly count (and report to their sponsors) the number of vulnerability scans reported to them as if they were incidents handled, even though the team took no action.

8. Be careful here, too. This measure smacks of a fox guarding the hen house!

9. Also be wary of this measure. Some agencies and organizations have been known to bestow some form of recognition on their own response team to bolster a sagging incident response effort in the eyes of the user community.

Maintaining Proficiency Levels

Forming a response team is not the only major challenge associated with an incident response team. When expertise within the team is established, it is also a formidable challenge to maintain this expertise. Both the credibility and proficiency of an incident response team are directly related to the managerial and technical expertise within the team. Turnover of team members—managers and technical staff—is a constant problem. Additionally, the technical staff needs to expand its skill base and learn of new technology developments. How then can an incident response team maintain its current level of proficiency?

- Ensure that there is ample funding for training of all team members, managers, and technical staff. They should be able to attend several training sessions every year.

- Make sure that relevant books, journals, and papers that expand the managerial and technical skills and perspectives of team managers are freely available to them.

- Ensure that junior team members are paired with your team's experts to help the junior team members in their effort to master the learning curve.

- Every once in a while, have a member of your team visit another response team[10] or organization that excels in areas that you value to learn what they do and how they do it.

- Invite outside experts to visit your team, give presentations, and so forth.

- Encourage team members to take university courses in operating systems, networking, cryptography, information security, and other areas related to incident response.

Preparing Reports and Management Updates

Any effort, such as an incident response team effort, is accountable for its activities to management. Traditionally, an effort will prepare reports to management to relate the activities in which the team has been involved, successes (and possibly failures), the resource burn rate, and other matters of interest to management. In the incident response arena, preparing such reports is particularly important. Remember that incident response is generally an overhead activity, something of which management tends to be suspicious in the first place. Providing carefully prepared reports to management can be potentially advantageous to a response team in that they can provide evidence that the team is on track with expectations.

---

10. Ensure first, however, that the other response team is an effective one. Participating in the activities of a deficient response team could actually lower the proficiency level of your team members.

How often should the team manager prepare such reports? The answer depends on the particular organization. Some organizations require monthly reports. Others require quarterly reports, and still others require yearly reports. Regardless of the required frequency of reporting, an incident response team manager would do well to submit frequent reports to management to update them as to the team's efforts and accomplishments. The downside is that sometimes incident response activity becomes so intense that finding time to prepare reports becomes impossible.

Reports should contain the types of information that management expects. If management expects metrics of incident response success, the team manager (or whoever prepares the report) must engage in best-effort attempts to create and use metrics. Be aware that technical jargon turns management off; write in the language that management uses and understands. Be sure to include an executive summary and always remember that these reports comprise an outstanding effort to sell what you are doing to management, thus possibly enabling your response team to obtain greater levels of funding and support. Finally, be sure to properly archive the reports. They can be used as another source of lessons learned as well as analyzing trends and the growth of your incident response effort.

Life Cycle Stages of an Incident Response Team

At the time this book was written, information security incident response teams had been in existence for nearly 15 years. Some incident response teams have flourished. Others have fared poorly. In more than a few cases, an organization or government agency has replaced every member of an existing response team, often turning to a completely different source of manpower (such as a different contractor). One thing we have noticed is that incident response teams seem to go through a cycle of stages as they grow from their initial inception to a certain point in their existence (see Figure 4.1). The following is a model to represent these stages.

The Stages

- **Initial.** The initial stage is what the name implies—the incident response team is just getting started. Normally, someone has submitted a proposal to form an incident response team; management or a sponsoring agency or organization has approved this proposal. Someone (usually the person who will eventually serve as the team manager) tries to get the initial aspects of the response team in existence, perhaps by starting to define the constituency and getting some level of funding in place. At this stage, the effort is by no means even close to being operational (that is, of use to any constituency). Most people have not heard of the emerging team.

- **Critical.** The critical stage is the one in which the incident response team is being formed. It is during this stage that requirements are formalized and then approved by management, a team infrastructure is established, initial procedures are written, communications methods are implemented, and reporting methods and procedures are put in place. If sufficient funding exists, new staff members are added to the team. Additionally, the constituency that the team is to serve is usually finalized at this point. Most people still have not heard of the fledgling team, but someone, usually the team manager, begins actively promoting the team to the constituency. The team becomes capable of limited operations, handling inquiries from users and perhaps giving advice or directly intervening in incidents that the team is qualified to handle.

  This stage is called the critical stage because many things have to be done correctly at this stage if an incident response team is going to experience at least some measure of success. The future of the team is still uncertain. Failing to correctly define requirements, failing to get management's full approval of the requirements, writing deficient procedures (or failing to follow them), being unable to adequately staff the team, or something else can cause the team to falter. Conversely, successfully resolving the many issues that must be addressed during this stage can effectively move the effort to the next stage.

- **Established.** During the established stage, the incident response team achieves a stable level of existence. The team establishes effective operations and fulfills its charter by efficiently dealing with incidents that occur. Management (or possibly a sponsoring agency or client organization) appreciates the job that the response team does. Other agencies and groups recognize the team as the legitimate body for dealing with incidents.

  The team's constituency turns to the response team when it needs help, or if the response team has the authority to assume control when incidents occur, the response team comes to a site and effectively deals with the incident and then returns to its normal location. Other response teams look up to the established team as a model of effective incident response. During the established stage, it becomes clear that the response team's existence is indefinite, that the team will in all likelihood exist in its present form for years to come.

- **Postestablished.** During the postestablished stage, a response team expands its operations to include requirements and operations that were not part of any of the previous stages. Activities are increasingly proactive and now include an increasing amount of analysis and research efforts. Usually, the basis for this expansion is success at the previous stages. Additional team members are added; this in turn expands the range of expertise within the team.

An example of a team in the postestablished stage is CERT/CC. CERT/CC is now engaged in many activities other than incident response operations per se. Part of this team analyzes trends; CERT/CC also has a large and successful research capability. Additionally, CERT/CC was able to obtain funding for a systems survivability center. Finally, virtually the entire Internet community is aware of CERT/CC's existence, and CERT/CC bulletins have had a very positive impact on this community in that these bulletins have enabled system administrators and others to become aware of, and then fix, known vulnerabilities that are related to security incidents.

The Value of This Model

This model incorporates elements that characterize the status and sophistication of an incident response team. This model enables incident response team managers (as well as managers who oversee incident response efforts) to monitor the progress of their teams on the basis of the characteristics of each stage of what amounts to a maturity model. The goal, of course, is to bring the teams to the highest possible stage of maturity. This model provides a benchmark against which the activities and progress of each team can be measured. A team that is still in the initial stage after one year, for example, desperately needs to progress to subsequent stages. Ultimately, a team needs to progress at least to the established stage if it is to be viable.

The progression from one stage to the next is not necessarily in a forward direction, however. It is possible, for example, for a team that has progressed to the established stage to fall backward to the critical stage due to a number of factors such as massive changes in management and technical staff. A team that in the past has functioned well and that was well accepted by its constituency can deteriorate to the point that it is dysfunctional and no longer is well accepted by its constituency.

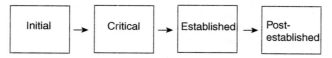

Figure 4.1   The stages of a response team's life cycle.

Summary

This chapter began with a definition of the term "incident response team." An incident response team is one or more individuals with the mission of dealing with security-related incidents. Why should one form an incident response team? Major reasons include expertise, efficiency, having a proactive emphasis, meeting requirements, establishing a liaison with other teams and organizations, and others.

Forming a response team is not always necessary; in some situations, a response team can actually be detrimental to an organization. Above all else, you have to figure out what role you need to perform and what your basic requirements are. Then you have to identify your constituency and determine how to communicate with them. Staffing, procedures, and other considerations are other critical issues that need to be resolved.

Managing an incident response team presents a set of extremely difficult challenges. Issues such as exuding a positive management style, setting up communications with others, developing and using a reasonable set of metrics, and establishing suitable reporting methods are all critical to response teams. Response team maturity can be characterized in terms of four stages: initial, critical, established, and postestablished. Getting a response team to the established stage or further is an important goal of incident response team managers and their management.

5

Organizing for Incident Response

Chapter 4, "Forming and Managing an Incident Response Team," discussed establishing an incident response team. Unfortunately, this is often as far as some organizations go. All too often, a company will go through a major project to design, establish, and train an incident response team. After this is accomplished, the company forgets about it. Team members go back to other jobs, the team never meets or communicates, and when an incident occurs, the team is unprepared to react.

Forming a team is only the first step in the process. Regardless of whether the team is composed of full-time or part-time members, they must continue to coordinate and communicate. The team should be the primary point of contact within a company, not only for incident response *per se* but also for the formulation of policies associated with it.

The team also requires periodic training. The field of incident response changes rapidly as new technology is introduced. Many skills are perishable and require constant practice (or at least refamiliarization). When virtual teams are used, the members might be intimately familiar with their normal operations but might have forgotten that operations during an incident are anything but normal.

Virtual Teams—Ensuring Availability

One major problem with virtual teams is that team members might not be available when required. If their daily responsibility is operations, it might be difficult to pull them when needed (especially if the affected system in an incident is one for which they are responsible).

The policy that establishes the incident response team should clearly articulate the requirements for availability. Senior management sponsors should affirm the policy that incident response duties must take precedence over normal operational responsibilities. If this is not clearly stated to line managers, they might be unwilling to release team members when they are required. Because team members will eventually go back to reporting to that line manager, they will obviously be reluctant to alienate him or her.

Another major consideration is defining what the actual availability requirements are. For example, do some team members need to be available in real time, or can they contribute on a different schedule? Team members with critical technical skills might still be able to contribute if, for example, they are sent data to analyze and are given a deadline to complete the work. This analysis does not necessarily need to be done concurrently with other response work.

The incident response hotline might need to be staffed around the clock, or maybe a help desk can fill in during normal working hours. In many cases, the help desk is the user's first contact, so the person staffing it needs to understand the basics of recording incident information and reporting it to the team. Team contacts might be available via cell phone or pager at other times.

Real-time availability is preferable, however. External coordination with other agencies (law enforcement, service providers, other victims, and so on) requires real-time contact—especially if the data is extremely time sensitive—and communications lags can be damaging. For example, if the intruder is still connected, the intrusion is best traced immediately. If the attacker has left the system, it is likely that logs might be overwritten or destroyed unless immediate action is taken to preserve them. Incidents also can have an extremely short duration. If the incident response team is not immediately reachable, constituents might go elsewhere for support or might not receive any support at all until it is too late.

Collection of data might be time sensitive, but analysis of that data might be much less so. Preparatory activities such as analysis of vulnerabilities and preliminary coordination with other operational units within the organization and with external agencies can also be performed on a more relaxed time schedule.

Unfortunately, good incident response team members are probably also good operations personnel. The same character traits that make a system administrator invaluable can quickly burn him or her out when reacting to an incident. One solution is a revolving duty roster. Team members would be responsible for initial response (including answering the hotline and email or wearing a pager) for a set period of time. After that on-call period, they would rotate to a reduced alert status. Although still available for support, the initial steps (including the midnight phone calls) would go to the next person on the list.

Training the Team

One of the major advantages of a virtual team is that members stay current on technology through their normal operations jobs. A full-time team, if there aren't sufficient incidents (or the incidents do not impact certain systems or applications), can become out of touch as new technology is deployed within the company. No incident response team member can possibly know a system as well as the people responsible for maintaining it on a daily basis.

If the focus of the team members is on daily operations, however, they might not consider that many things change during an incident. For example, a systems administrator will think nothing of logging in as root to investigate a malfunctioning server. If the server has been compromised, however, logging on directly can destroy evidence or trigger logic bombs installed by the attacker.

The team will, as a minimum, require periodic training in evidence-handling procedures. This is perhaps the most dramatic difference between normal operations and incident response. Team members must be aware of the proper steps to take when securing digital evidence. If a team member is also the administrator for those systems, the problem is even greater. He or she must be reminded that his or her responsibilities change after an incident is formally declared. It might even be preferable to have another team member collect the evidence as a check and to prevent the appearance of impropriety or a conflict of interest.

If the team consists of full-time members, they must constantly strive to remain current and technically competent. Some teams do this by having team members conduct training or by issuing technical advisories. Although this might be a good method for maintaining proficiency, it is even more vital that the members be accurate. Issuing a technical advisory to operational units that contains errors will quickly undermine the credibility of the team and its members. Technical inaccuracy during training and awareness sessions will do the same.

Unfortunately, there are no easy answers to these issues. However, some practices have proven valuable in other organizations. As covered in Chapter 4, "Forming and Managing an Incident Response Team," training in the form of attendance at technical conferences, bringing in outside speakers and resources, making technical journals and books available, and having staff engage in operations with other incident response teams are well established types of training. However, as you organize for incident response, you might find that these types of training are insufficient for the variety of training needs that exist. Thus, the following types of training might also be appropriate:

- Establish a mentoring program. Senior staff can assist in training (both formally and informally) junior, less experienced team members. Senior full-time staff can also mentor virtual members.

- Encourage self-study and ensure that appropriate technical references are available. Individuals should subscribe to free trade magazines. The company should consider subscribing to periodicals that are not free. An incident response library, including technical references, legal documents, and information about the specific processes (such as forensics), can be invaluable during an incident.

- Full-time team members, especially if they are on call all the time, should be given some time off from incident handling. This is not the same as vacation (they will probably get called while on vacation anyway), but it gives them some time away from the pressures of incident response to explore appropriate technical issues. This might include Internet research, testing new tools, or simply doing research and hands-on familiarization with new technologies.

- Have team members periodically review the post-mortem reports that have been written. As mentioned in Chapter 3, "A Methodology for Incident Response," these provide one of the best ways to convey lessons learned to team members, especially newer ones.

- Involve team members in incident simulations. The next section of this chapter discusses this idea in detail.

Testing the Team

Training is only an initial step. After the team is formed and initial training has occurred, the team should be tested. Testing can consist of scheduled events of which the team is aware ahead of time or no-notice tests in which only key personnel know that an incident is actually a test.

It is difficult to realistically simulate a security incident and is virtually impossible to test all aspects of the incident response process. For this reason, it is best to concentrate on critical pieces of the process when designing a test. Team leaders and senior managers should assess the perceived strengths and weaknesses of the team in the context of the corporate culture and decide what portions are most likely to need remedial attention.

The first point to test is probably the notification process. The system by which a user notifies the incident response team can be simulated simply by identifying a typical user, presenting that user with a situation, and observing the results. Did the user know whom to call or contact, how to contact that person (phone, email), and if not, where to get that information (from the intranet, phone listing, employee handbook)?

After the initial contact has been made, is there a process in place to contact individual team members? Are the phone numbers (including, when appropriate, home, cell, and pager numbers) correct? Do team members know what to do or where to go when they are contacted?

After the notification process has been tested, management might choose to expand the testing process. Again, it is difficult to accurately simulate an incident, especially if the team has operations members. There are, however, ways to test the response process without impacting mission-critical applications.

The team can be assembled and a scenario presented. This is probably best done by an outsider (or at least not a team member). The scenario would present an initial problem, and members would be asked to describe their actions in response. As they continue, more details would be provided.

For example, the scenario might be that a critical server has started malfunctioning. The team might state that it would review logs, both on the server and on associated machines.[1] The facilitator would then provide more information such as the contents of the logs. Based on that data, the team would be asked to expand its answers and provide details about follow-up steps.

This scenario-based approach can also be valuable as a training aid for the team and management. Senior managers, incident response team members, and operational managers can be pulled into the scenario. Each constituency can be asked what it recommends as response steps and to defend its actions. The difference in perspective between line managers (who probably want to get the system back online quickly), incident response personnel (who want to find out who attacked it), and operations personnel (who want to find out what happened and fix it) can be extremely enlightening to everyone involved.

Finally, it is sometimes possible to actually simulate an incident, provided that proper safeguards are in place to ensure that neither the simulation nor the response actually damages production systems. For example, an external attack can be launched at the web server to test whether the intrusion-detection software catches the attack and whether the notification and response procedures are properly implemented.

It is almost certainly better to employ outside facilitators to conduct team testing. It is unlikely in all but the largest organizations that trained incident response personnel exist with the qualifications to assess the team (unless they are already team members). Bringing in outside facilitators can also help reduce advance knowledge of the test to assist in gaining a more accurate perspective of the actual situation within the team.

Outsiders can range from paid consultants to peers from other organizations. For example, if persons in the company have personal relationships with other incident response teams, members of those teams can be invited in to facilitate and observe the testing. Professional organizations such as HTCIA might be sources of such contacts. Law enforcement might be willing to provide assistance (but keep in mind that law enforcement personnel have their own interests and those interests might not directly coincide with the company's).

There are no easy answers regarding whom to select as facilitators and how to judge their qualifications. Much depends on reputation as well as technical skills. The target audience must be considered as well. If, for example, the team (or the portion of the team being evaluated) consists of highly technical personnel, the facilitators must have technical personnel as well. A group of generalists will probably not be taken seriously by technical specialists. Conversely, if the focus of the test is to demonstrate policy shortcomings to senior management, management consultants with a knowledge of security might be better suited to discuss the business impact of the problems as opposed to the technical details.

---

1. Note: This is intended as an example only, and the information in this scenario is not intended to be the right or wrong answer as to what actions to take in such a situation.

A good start for selecting facilitators might be an organization with which the team already has a relationship. This could be the consulting arm of a product vendor or consultants who have previously performed engagements for the organization.

Demonstrating Interteam Communications

One major challenge with incident response is accommodating multiple, often widely varied expectations. Technical personnel tend to focus on the technical side of the problem. Businesspeople tend to ignore the technical realities and focus on the business issues. Other key personnel, such as legal or human resources, might also find it difficult to view the entire incident.

One suggestion for demonstrating the difficulties inherent in such a multidisciplinary approach is to conduct a training scenario specifically designed to illustrate these issues.

Team members (including nontechnical personnel) and other constituents are assembled in separate rooms. The facilitator presents each group with the same scenario. When a group develops a course of action, that information is then presented to the other groups by the facilitator.

The role of the facilitator in this scenario is to present each group's recommendations and explain the rationale behind its decisions. Other groups might have come up with dramatically different ideas as to how to proceed because they approach the problem from a different perspective.

If done properly, all participants will emerge from this training with a new appreciation for all the considerations that go into a holistic and complete understanding of a major incident.

Barriers to Success

Even after the team is formed, training has begun, and the team is managing incidents, there are still obstacles to overcome en route. The success or failure of the team and the incident response process depends on dealing with these obstacles. Some might be impossible to overcome, but the team (and its stakeholders) must, as a minimum, address the problems and develop strategies for coping with them.

The most effective way to overcome the following obstacles is through a competent, efficient, and timely incident response process. Dealing with incidents promptly and effectively will go further in selling the team to stakeholders and defusing potential conflicts than will anything else. Conversely, a poorly managed incident will cause harm to the team and its reputation, harm that no amount of good will or good intentions can fix.

Budget

Lack of funding is typically the major obstacle. A team might be formed as a response to an incident. The company might have good intentions, might acquire excellent people, and might give them the time, training, and equipment they need. Unfortunately, security all too often is one of the first items reduced in the budget process, and the team might be an attractive target.

The team's own success often works against it. An incident response team might mitigate the impact of several small incidents. When the budget is reviewed, management might simply feel that there have been no incidents to speak of, so there is money to be saved in this area.

Security is inherently hard to quantify. One of the major problems in information technology as a whole is to define cost savings or improved productivity. Whereas the impact of a new machine on the shop floor might be obvious, adding email connectivity to all managers might be much less so. The cost savings for information technology tend to be soft, and productivity typically tends to be seen in terms of jobs changing function as opposed to workers producing more direct output.

In the same way, security does not directly produce revenue. Although it might save large amounts in the long run, these savings are extremely hard to define. Cost savings typically come in the form of avoiding large payments as opposed to actual reductions in operating costs. For example, good security might help shield the company from lawsuits or might reduce the amount of recovery costs incurred after an incident. It might even include such unquantifiable items such as opportunity costs. When distributed denial-of-service attacks hit an e-commerce site, to what extent does good security allow the site to remain operational for customers to continue to come (or did poor security allow customers to visit other sites instead)?

Good record keeping during incidents is valuable not only to quantify the cost of the incident for potential litigation, but also to help develop data on cost savings. The incident response team should address costs and potential savings early in its formulation and should develop a process to track these items (within the corporate accounting system) for use in later budget cycles.

Management Reluctance

Unfortunately, incident response is viewed as simply another overhead function. Managers might be unlikely to support another source of overhead when revenue centers might be competing for the same resources. As in the budget process, managers might believe that incidents do not happen or only happen to others.

Users might be reluctant to call on the incident response team if they are unfamiliar with its capabilities or charter. They might fear the perceived consequences of admitting that there is a problem more than the actual consequences involved in the issue.

This is primarily an awareness issue. Team leaders must meet with line unit managers and discuss the team's capabilities and what it has to offer the business as a whole. Real incidents that have happened recently to the business or to peers can be used to illustrate the severity of the problem. The team, however, must be viewed as firefighters rather than auditors. Managers and users should see them as the people to call when things go wrong, not as people who will come in looking to place blame.

Organizational Resistance

Resistance to a new computer incident response capability might come as other organizations feel threatened. There are almost certainly rival organizations within the company that could feel that incident response should fall within their purview. If the team gets additional resources, other groups might see it as a threat.

Not only will the team find itself competing for critical resources with these other groups, it might also find itself not getting the coordinated assistance required to properly manage an incident.

In Chapter 10, "Responding to Insider Attacks," the importance of coordinating with physical security is discussed. The physical security organization typically controls all physical access to the facility and might have the data needed to place a person at the keyboard. They might also have trained investigators that can be invaluable in providing support such as interviewing witnesses, interfacing with law enforcement, or securing physical evidence.

IT operations might also feel threatened. They might see the incident response function as a specific criticism of their ability to secure their systems. The team will require extensive support from operations during the course of an incident but must be careful not to alienate them during the investigation.

One-on-one coordination between peers can be extremely helpful in allaying these fears. Managers should meet, discuss their capabilities, and develop methods of providing mutual support during both incidents and normal operations. Peers at the engineering level should ideally do the same. For example, a UNIX security engineer can meet with other systems administrators and discuss common UNIX security problems. He or she might find that the other administrators are unaware of many of these. He or she might also find that some security measures cannot be implemented in the current environment. It is far better to be aware of potential risks ahead of time and to understand the logic that went into accepting those risks than to be surprised during an actual incident. Administrators might also find that some of the security measures might make their jobs easier as well.

Incident response can also assist the physical security people by providing forensics support. If, for example, a person is accused of physical theft of equipment, a forensics examination of the equipment might provide additional evidence. If a person is accused of theft of trade secrets (even if that theft doesn't involve digital data), an examination of the person's computer might yield either more evidence or at least more information regarding where and what to investigate.

Politics

It would be wonderful if businesses and organizations had no internal politics. The team, regardless of its skills or capabilities, can become a pawn in a political game. For example, if the team is funded by the information security organization and traditional ill will exists between security and IT operations, it is unlikely that the team will ever be accepted. If the team is formed out of internal audit, line managers might feel threatened.

There are no easy answers to this problem and certainly no "one size fits all." The only secret to dealing with political issues is to consider them carefully during the formation of the team and address them early. Management and user buy-in are critical to the success.

User Awareness

User training is often viewed as a panacea for security. It is true that many incidents are, in fact, noticed early in their life, but users are often unaware of what they are seeing. Users must be knowledgeable not only about basic security practices such as password choice, but also about what constitutes an anomaly or what might be an incident in the making. For example, many UNIX systems display the last time the user logged on. When the user logs on, if the time displayed is not the same as he or she remembers it (if, for example, the last logon was during the weekend or when the user was out of the office), this information does no good unless the user reports the inconsistent data to someone.

There are many ways to spread the information about the incident response team. The first step is to educate the help desk. These people will field most end user questions first and must be able to recognize the difference between a simple password reset request ("I've forgotten my password") and one that could be caused by an intrusion ("My password doesn't work anymore").

The next step is to get the word out to end users. Logon banners can help, but users tend to ignore them over time. Mouse pads or stickers on the monitor are also ways to spread contact information. The team should have an internal web site with an easily remembered URL (such as `security.company.com`). It should have a central telephone number, again something easy to remember. The number, web site, and team email (perhaps `security@company.com`) should all be at the front of the corporate phone directory. A team that is not called is every bit as useless as one with no skills.

External Coordination

An incident response team cannot exist in a vacuum. Several of the other chapters in this book discuss issues related to dealing with other company organizations. It bears repeating that the team must involve other company personnel to effectively manage the incident.

The systems affected in a security incident do not belong to the response team. They exist for the sole purpose of filling a business requirement. There is no difference in availability between a system compromised by an intruder and a system taken offline waiting for examination.

Coordinating with organizations outside the company might also be within the purview of the incident response team. The team might coordinate directly or might go through other company personnel. Regardless, the team must develop and maintain communications with external organizations.

Law Enforcement Agencies

Early in the life of an incident, management needs to address the issue of whether to pursue legal action against the person responsible for the incident. Chapter 7, "Legal Issues," discusses this at some length. When the decision is made, the appropriate law enforcement agencies should be contacted in a timely and professional manner. This is much easier if the incident response team has already developed a working relationship with local agencies (and representatives of national ones).

A number of forums can be used to develop such relationships. Local professional groups such as the ISSA or HTCIA can allow team members to meet and speak with law enforcement personnel in a neutral setting. Other groups within the company might already have contacts. Physical security organizations typically have ex-law enforcement personnel on staff and normally interface with the police on a regular basis.

When the time comes to notify law enforcement, a designated contact within the team should make the call. Only that team member should be authorized to contact law enforcement personnel. That person could be the team leader or could be a virtual member of the team such as a representative from physical security or legal. The importance of this cannot be overstated. After the call has been made, it cannot be unmade. The existence of the incident, and possibly the details of it, will probably become public. The company has, to a large extent, relinquished management of the incident.[2]

Media

Negative media exposure can be more damaging than any actual loss of availability or data. As an example, consider defacements of government web sites. Most of these sites contain no sensitive data. However, a defacement does damage the reputation of the agency.

The System Administrators and Network Security (SANS) web site (www.sans.org) was defaced in mid-2001. The impact to the reputation of a security organization cannot be overstated. On the other hand, skillful management of the public relations battle can help minimize this damage. Although the damage cannot be undone, perhaps the public perception can be influenced by emphasizing positive actions and minimizing the negative aspects of the incident.

Consider, for example, a hack against Microsoft that occurred in late 2000. It appeared that an attacker placed (or found) a trojan program on the home computer of a Microsoft employee. The attacker then used this program to connect to Microsoft's internal network using its own virtual private network solution.[3]

---

2. This is, by no means, meant to imply that companies should not report security incidents. See Chapter 7 for a discussion of this decision.

3. Microsoft's press release on the incident is available at www.microsoft.com/presspass/features/2000/oct00/10-27security.asp.

This was an extremely serious compromise. Depending on the permissions of the remote user, the attacker could potentially have accessed anything on the internal Microsoft network. Microsoft responded by contacting the FBI and then publicly announcing that it had done so. The company issued a press release stating that it had been compromised and that an investigation was ongoing. Regardless of the seriousness of the incident, skillful handling of the public relations piece allowed the company to downplay the effects.

If the benefits of coordination are clear (as well as the drawbacks of failing to coordinate), the question of who should contact or talk to the media is not. There are a number of possibilities. The announcement can come from an external organization such as law enforcement. However, after the announcement is made, the company will certainly be contacted by the press. It's better to make the announcement in the first place.

As mentioned in Chapter 4, incident response personnel often have the option to deal directly with the media. This generally is not the best idea for several reasons. The team is normally too busy working on other issues to have the time to speak to the press. Second, technical members might not be the best choice to explain the issue to an unsophisticated audience. A formal policy dealing with media relations should be part of the team's charter. It should state that any unauthorized contact with the media or release of any incident information to an outside party is strictly forbidden.

In most cases, it is better to rely on the company's public relations staff to brief the press. If necessary, a member of the team can be present to field specific questions (of course, with the caveat to not reveal information that can compromise either the investigation or further security). If there is the slightest possibility that knowledge about an incident could leak, public relations personnel must be briefed immediately, even if the company chooses not to make a statement. It can be extremely damaging when the company spokesperson is asked a question during a press conference but has no knowledge of the incident.

Other Incident Response Teams

The team might also want to coordinate with other teams during the investigation. For example, it might be necessary to exchange information with service providers to detect the source of an incident or to block traffic. Peer (or competitor) organizations might be experiencing similar attacks.

An excellent model for this coordination exists in the area of financial fraud. Banks and financial institutions can be very aggressive competitors. When threatened by fraud, however, they cooperate extremely well. That same level of cooperation should be available during an incident.

Because the security industry is still relatively small, members might know each other from professional organizations or previous jobs. A great deal of behind-the-scenes coordination is possible using these personal contacts. It can be extremely valuable during an attack, for example, to know whether you are the only target or your competitors are being hit as well. This information can go a long way in helping to evaluate the motivations and intent of the attacker.

On a more formal level, members of incident response teams can contact information-sharing agencies. The FBI runs a program called Infragard through its local field offices. The program is billed as an information-sharing forum. However, even if data is not provided directly to Infragard, contacts made there with other local teams can be used to exchange data.

Infragard

Infragard is a joint partnership between FBI field offices and private companies. At its most basic, it is a forum to allow members to exchange data about security incidents.

The FBI, in coordination with the National Infrastructure Protection Center (NIPC) runs the program. They provide information and training about infrastructure protection issues and security bulletins about current threats and vulnerabilities.

Infragard has been criticized on several fronts. The data submitted is not anonymous, and the FBI reserves the right to open an investigation on any data received from a member. Vulnerability alerts have been criticized for both timeliness and technical accuracy.

The program does allow local members to meet each other and law enforcement personnel in a neutral setting, however, and does facilitate some communications between the parties.

More information on Infragard is available at www.infragard.net.

The Forum of Incident Response Teams (discussed in Chapter 13, "Future Directions,") also provides members with a forum to discuss details and request assistance with security incidents.

Managing Incidents

The actual management of incidents is covered throughout this book. There are, however, some issues that should be addressed early in the organization phase of the team's life cycle.

Obviously, the first step in managing and responding to an incident is to assemble the team. This might be either physical or virtual. Ideally, a core team can meet quickly in person and discuss the incident. It can then either meet with or call the affected persons and gather information quickly to formulate a response strategy.

Chapter 1, "An Introduction to Incident Response," defines incident response as the "actions taken to deal with an incident that occurs. These actions normally represent some form of intervention to negate or minimize the impact of the incident." The incident response team must develop a plan to contain and eradicate the incident as quickly and efficiently as possible.

The team might have specific objectives as well, including the following:[4]

- The preservation and protection of human life. Most organizations specifically address this as the highest priority in their incident response policy.
- The preservation of evidence for litigation or prosecution.
- The preservation or recovery of business data.
- Resumption of computing and network services.
- Containing and preventing escalation of the incident, including preventing the incident from spreading to other, unaffected computers or networks.
- Cooperation with law enforcement, regulatory, or investigative agencies (including internal agencies such as internal audit).
- Avoiding or minimizing damage to the company's reputation.

These priorities should be discussed during the initial team meeting. Some of them (for example, collection and preservation of evidence) might dictate many of the follow-up actions and might require that certain steps occur. It is always easier to gather the evidence early in the process and choose later not to use it; it is usually impossible to go back and try to collect usable (or admissible) evidence later.

This is also the time to begin assigning resources to the incident. The incident should be prioritized in relation to other incidents that might be occurring (and to other requirements such as training or operations support). When possible, key personnel should not be assigned to minor incidents; they should be saved for the major problems. This might not be an option in some teams, but the team leaders must be able to reassign personnel quickly if another incident breaks.

Surviving the Long Haul

There is a danger when managing large incidents that team members might burn out early in the process. It is natural to work extremely hard when the incident is first discovered. Members might work around the clock for several days. This is fine, provided the incident is of a relatively short duration. If the incident drags on, however, those key personnel might not be able to keep up the pace.

Team members must plan (and leaders must enforce) an arrangement to sustain the incident management effort over time. Critical team members might find themselves neglecting other duties, home life, rest, and meals when working on the incident. This must not be allowed to continue over an extended period of time. The person will likely burn out and not be able to continue. Performance will certainly suffer, invariably at a time when critical decisions are required.

---

4. Other than the first bullet about the protection of human life, these are not in any suggested priority. Each organization must examine its own information assets, risks, and culture to establish priorities.

The team operating procedures should address this contingency and should have a procedure for assigning long-term tasks and managing the resources required to sustain them. For example, early in the incident, the team might be meeting twice a day. As the incident drags on for months (not unheard of in the event of large incidents involving prosecution), the meetings might drop to once a week.

Strategies for Sustained Operations

One organization discovered that team members were skipping meals to work on the incident. The company started furnishing breakfasts (coffee, donuts, and bagels) as soon as the workers arrived as well as lunch and dinner (typically fast food such as pizza or fried chicken) throughout the day. This was extremely helpful during the early phases of the incident, but it became unsupportable as the effort moved into the second and third months.

In this same organization, one key team member was working extremely long hours and even sleeping in his office to avoid the commute. The team leader recognized that this member would probably not scale back his efforts, even if told to do so. The company furnished the employee with a computer so that he could work from home. This allowed the employee to continue his efforts without completely neglecting his health or his family.

Assigning Incident Ownership

Another important consideration in organizing for incident response is ensuring that there is an owner for every significant incident (every incident in which severity ratings produce a score indicating elevated risk to an organization). An "owner" is a person assigned the responsibility of bringing the incident to as successful a conclusion as possible. Without ownership, incidents often "slip through the cracks," and when someone within an incident response team's constituency complains about the team's lack of action, a simple investigation usually reveals that lack of ownership is the reason. Persons assigned specific responsibilities are personally accountable for fulfilling those responsibilities and are usually thus motivated to do so.

We recommend assigning the roles of team lead and alternate lead for every significant incident. The team lead is the primary owner, and is responsible for day-to-day progress in dealing with the incident until its resolution. This person also normally serves as the main point of contact with the person who has reported the incident as well as the incident response team manager. If insufficient manpower or technical expertise is available, the team lead should promptly inform the incident response team manager accordingly. The team lead should also keep the team manager and other key players (including other team members working on the incident as well as people within the response team's constituency) informed of progress and developments. The alternate lead is, in effect, the secondary owner. This person should be prepared to fill in for the team lead in case the team lead must go on travel, becomes sick, becomes assigned to another, higher priority incident, and so forth. The alternate lead can also serve as a member of the team that is dealing with the incident.

Assigning the right person the role of team lead and alternate lead is critical. If a significant incident involving a Unix system occurs, a person with technical expertise in Unix is the logical candidate for the team lead. The same applies to the alternate lead. At times, however, your team's expertise will be stretched thin. You may, in these cases, have to temporarily assign someone the team lead role even though that person has little relevant expertise. Later, someone with the relevant expertise can replace the temporary team lead, who then might be moved to the role of alternate lead. As mentioned in Chapter 4, sometimes the best course of action is to bring in outside expertise. In some of these cases it may be prudent to assign the consultant or contractor the team lead or alternate lead role.

Tracking Charts

When the team is managing multiple incidents, some form of tracking is essential. As new incidents occur, the details of the earlier ones might be forgotten and required actions fail to occur.

Ideally, the team will have some sort of a "War Room" where it can conduct face-to-face meetings or teleconference with off-site personnel. Status charts on the walls allow the team leaders to quickly review the current status of any open incidents.

These charts can supplement an automated tracking system. Although automated systems are useful, especially in preparing reports to management, they are themselves a vulnerability. Because no one can predict ahead of time what systems might be compromised, there should always be a manual backup to any incident tracking and reporting system.

One chart that has proven useful in the past is illustrated in Figure 5.1. The format can, of course, be modified to fit the specific requirements of the organization, especially if the company already has incident tracking or priority criteria.

- **Incident Number.** This field can contain any useful tracking number. If the company has an accounting system that allows charge backs, the charge number could be used. This is especially useful when gathering data about the costs of incidents.

- **Type.** This is used to indicate information about the incident (virus, network penetration, internal investigation, and so on). The types of incidents outlined in the checklist in Appendix A, "RFC-2196," can be used, or the team can develop other categories.

- **Location.** This could be physical (Singapore), logical (Internet banking), or both.

- **Point of Contact.** This is the primary operations point of contact, often the system owner or manager of the affected business area.

- **Phone.** The team's phone numbers, including work, home, pager, mobile, and email.

- **Priority.** This is the priority assigned to the incident. Priorities and severity models are addressed in the next section.

- **Status.** This is the current status of the incident. This field can contain as much or as little information as the team desires. It can also contain notes about upcoming status meetings, required reports, and outstanding actions.
- **Last Update.** This is the date and time the information on the chart was last changed.
- **Team Lead.** This is the team member currently managing the incident.
- **Alternate Lead.** This is the person responsible for assisting the team lead and/or picking up responsibility if the team's lead cannot, for any reason, continue to manage the incident.

Prioritization

Not every incident is a major priority. A minor virus outbreak that merely requires that a couple of PCs be disinfected is not the same as a major worm spreading through the company's mail servers. A few "script kiddie" probes against the web server that are detected and blocked automatically are not the same as a major denial-of-service attack against the same server.

It is not possible to design a "one size fits all" solution to prioritization and severity. The relative importance of an incident depends on the platforms and systems affected, in the context of the business. For example, it is common in many government organizations to take servers offline in response to a virus outbreak. Arguably, the self-inflicted denial of service caused by taking the servers offline might be greater than that caused by the virus. However, this might be an acceptable solution if those servers are simply used to provide information to the public. The "company" can afford to make its "customers" wait for a day to get the address of the local tax office, for example.

If, however, the organization is a commercial enterprise, the server is conducting real-time e-commerce, and there are competitors for the customers. Taking the system down for a day might not be a viable solution because it causes the company to lose hundreds of thousand of dollars a day in revenue. The web server, in that case, becomes a critical business asset, and incidents involving it gain a much higher priority.

As part of the risk analysis, companies should develop some idea of their information assets and the relative values of those assets. This is the first step in developing a prioritization plan. High-value targets must be assigned a high priority.

Incident Operations Status									
Incident Number	Type	Location	Point of Contact	Contact Info	Priority	Status	Last Update	Team Lead	Alt Lead

Figure 5.1   A sample incident operations tracking chart.

The severity and scope of the incident should also fit into the methodology. A virus or worm infecting one PC is different than one that has spread throughout the organization. A virus that merely spreads is less dangerous than one that also destroys data or emails files to random addresses.

For example, the organization could define a four-level severity model.

1. The first level is an event that affects only one location (physical or virtual) and that has a relatively low impact. Examples would include a small virus incident that does not damage or destroy data and the unauthorized use of an account on a local file server.

2. The second level would be a local event that has a major impact on operations. An example would be the compromise of a privileged account or the physical theft of critical equipment.

3. The third level would be an event that affects two or more locations (again, defined either physically or logically) but that has a minor impact. Examples might include the proliferation of a nondestructive computer virus on the network or spamming of the email system.

4. The fourth level would be a high-impact event that affects multiple sites. This would require major intervention and the highest priority. An example might be an intrusion into a critical global application.

Other models might be tied in with studies done by other organizations. For example, physical security might have already prioritized physical assets and assigned values to them. They also might have a severity model that can be modified to fit information assets. If the company has a working business continuity or disaster recovery plan, it might also have already assigned priorities to systems for the purposes of recovery. A model that is already in use and accepted by management might be better than introducing a new one.

Obviously, it is impossible to fully quantify the impact of an incident. In the earlier example, compromise of the web server might fit into the severity model as a Level 2 but might warrant a higher priority based on the potential impact on the business. A model will help the team develop a framework for prioritizing resources when responding to multiple incidents.

Summary

Organizing and running an incident response team is an ongoing effort that requires continuous attention. It is not sufficient to pay consultants to come in, design a team, deliver a document, and walk away. The formation and design are only the first steps.

The acceptance of the team depends on its perceived capabilities, its ability to coordinate with other organizations, and the expertise and professionalism it displays when working with actual incidents. The team will not be successful until the other stakeholders in the company view it as an important ally in the protection and preservation of their data.

To gain that acceptance, the team must demonstrate that it is not a threat to other (perhaps rival) organizations but that it can provide them with support when needed and can assist them in their operations as well. Second, users must know about the team and must be willing to call on it when required.

The incident response coordination capability derives its authority from the company policies that establish it. This is not, in itself, sufficient. The team might be established by senior management and might report directly to the CIO. When established, however, the team must then begin the process of coordinating with other constituents. It must begin an ongoing training program to ensure technical expertise. It must establish, from the beginning, the highest standards of excellence when dealing with actual incidents. Anything less will doom the team to failure.

6

Tracing Network Attacks

THE TWO PRECEDING CHAPTERS IN THIS BOOK, Chapter 4, "Forming and Managing a
Response Team," and Chapter 5, "Organizing for Incident Response," covered the content that their titles indicate. One of the major themes advanced is that because security-
related incidents can cause such havoc and because humans and organizations must deal
with incidents, ensuring that there is an appropriate structure and process for keeping
people, activities, paperwork, and so on organized and well functioning is imperative.
Now that these issues have been covered, let's next turn our attention to a more specialized and technical issue: how to trace attacks. You will explore what tracing network
attacks means, how to put this kind of activity in perspective for incident response, what
some methods of tracing network attacks are, and how to construct an attack path.

What Does Tracing Network Attacks Mean?

"Tracing network attacks" can have different meanings, depending on the context in
which this term is used. At a minimum, it means discovering the origin of incidents
that occur. In most (but not all) cases, this minimally implies finding the IP address, the
media access control (MAC) address,[1] or the hostname from which the unauthorized

---

1. The media access control address is the physical address of a host. The MAC address is put
into each network interface card.

activity originated. At the other extreme, it means determining the identity of the attacker(s). This chapter focuses on determining the origin in terms of address or hostname. Chapter 11, "The Human Side of Incident Response," focuses on pinpointing the identity of perpetrators.

In the case of insider attacks in which a perpetrator has gained physical assess to a particular system or network device or hardware component, tracing the attack to its origin is not nearly as much of a challenge as identifying the perpetrator. Insiders often leave some kind of physical evidence (such as fingerprints, their appearance captured by cameras, hair strands, and so on) that indicates they have physically accessed one or more systems or network devices, or at least the physical area in which the systems and/or network devices have been placed. Insiders might also leave virtual evidence, of course, such as log entries, file permission changes, and so forth. By "virtual evidence," we mean evidence related to processing activities, memory contents, system configuration, packet data, and other nonphysical indications of computing and networking activities. A major difference between tracing internal and external attacks, however, is the fact that virtual evidence typically is the only evidence available when network attacks occur. The necessity of dealing with virtual evidence instead of physical evidence is, in fact, one of the greatest challenges of tracing network attacks.

Another important consideration in tracing network attacks is the fact that IP addresses are *virtual addresses*, not physical addresses. Media Access Control (MAC) addresses are physical addresses that are stamped into network interface cards (NICs), but IP addresses are not. Network services such as DNS translate IP addresses into hostnames (and vice versa), but IP addresses are not "locked into"[2] Internet-connected hosts. As such, these addresses can readily be spoofed. Furthermore, the use of Dynamic Host Configuration Protocol (DHCP) and dynamic ISP addresses results in the assignment of different IP addresses to the same machine at different times, making determining the origin of a network attack on the basis of IP address even more difficult.

Putting Attack Tracing in Context

Attack tracing is often a misunderstood and misused concept. This section explores what attack tracing is, the costs versus benefits, and reasons for wanting to trace attacks.

Attack Tracing Versus Intrusion Tracing

Sometimes attack tracing is erroneously equated to intrusion tracing. As mentioned in Chapter 1, "An Introduction to Incident Response," however, an intrusion is just one of many types of security-related incidents. Suppose, for example, that a DDoS attack occurred recently. A victim organization might want to determine where this attack

---

2. Assuming you have sufficient privileges, try entering `ifconfig` in UNIX and Linux systems, `ipconfig` in Windows NT and 2000 systems, and `winipcfg` in Windows 9X systems. You can specify the IP address for a host. Note also that for nonlocal IP addresses, the MAC address will be the router's IP address.

originated. The only intrusions *per se* that might have occurred are ones in which zombies and handlers have been installed in systems, although many of today's attack techniques do not require any kind of actual break-in to result in the introduction of Trojan horse programs in victim systems. Exploiting bugs in NFS, the network file system, to write-mount a volume and then transfer malicious programs to the victim system is a good example.

Tracing vulnerability scans is a special problem. In most network environments, vulnerability scans occur almost constantly. Tracing scans cannot realistically be considered a type of intrusion tracing *per se*. The term "attack tracing" fits better (see the following sidebar), but perhaps "scan tracing" is the most appropriate term. Most importantly, however, tracing the source of scans is likely to be extremely unproductive because a large number of scans are initiated from legitimate hosts that have been compromised by attacks. Furthermore, the sheer number of scans that occur every day makes the prospect of tracing the origin extremely unrealistic. Although it is wise to pay attention to the problem of scans, tracing their origin is, in most cases, not a good use of time and resources.

Vulnerability Scans: Intrusions, Attacks, or ???

Vulnerability scans, unfortunately, occur almost incessantly. Users who have a cable modem or DSL connection to their ISP and who use a personal firewall usually discover that their systems are first scanned only a few minutes after they log in. What are scans, anyway? Are they a type of intrusion, simply an attack, or what? This issue is a matter of debate. Scans are usually not considered intrusions, yet some scan tools actually attempt to gain shell access to systems, at least in the process of testing for vulnerabilities in certain services such as FTP. Many information security professionals do not consider scans to be attacks, but rather simply a form of information gathering (parallel in many respects to using a search engine on the Internet). Others (the authors of this book included) consider scans to be attacks but very low-level ones. Regardless of how scans are labeled, their constant occurrence constitutes a clear and present danger. Well-configured external firewalls and commitment to promptly installing patches for known vulnerabilities are two good countermeasures.

Relationship to the PDCERF Methodology

Chapter 3, "A Methodology for Incident Response," covered the PDCERF methodology. How is attack tracing related to this methodology, and to what particular stage(s) is attack tracing most related? The answer is that it is most closely tied in with the detection, containment, and eradication stages. Let's consider why.

Detection

Attack tracing is related to detection because, many times, tracing an event to a particular IP address will help incident response personnel conclude that a connection or flow of packets across the network is not legitimate. Consider, for example, the meaning of a network connection (such as a telnet connection) from a known hostile address. If there is no possible legitimate purpose for such a connection, there is really no logical conclusion other than this connection represents a security-related incident.

Containment

Attack tracing is also related to containment in that knowing the source of an incident can help those involved in handling the incident take corrective measures to limit the spread of an incident. Knowing that an attack on hosts within one's internal network has originated from a particular IP address enables incident response staff or automated mechanisms to change router or firewall filtering rules to block traffic from that address. This course of action can slow down or halt an attack.

Eradication

Knowing the source of an attack can also help eradication efforts. Attackers might, for example, include bogus entries in critical files such as `.rhost` or `/etc/hosts.equiv` files in UNIX and Linux hosts, enabling them to gain back-door entrance to victim hosts. Discovering and then deleting these entries can eliminate the access avenue(s) used by attackers.

Considering Costs Versus Benefits

Weighing costs versus benefits is integral to everything done in the practice of computer and information security. Tracing network intrusions is no exception. An organization with extensive computing resources and with extensive connectivity to the outside will experience many hundreds, sometimes thousands, of attacks every day. It is not practical to respond to every attack let alone trace the source of the attack. Tracing the source involves even a greater level of effort and resources. It is important, therefore, to have a policy that specifies when intrusions must (or at least *may*) be traced or, perhaps more realistically, to assign priorities related to the need to trace each incident and then trace attacks that have the highest priority when many attacks occur simultaneously. Perhaps tracing lower priority attacks should be attempted when only a few attacks occur simultaneously, or perhaps lower priority attacks do not need to be traced at all. Again, an organization's policy concerning whether attacks should be traced—and, if so, to what extent—is the key.

Motivation for Tracing Attacks

A few organizations have a policy that specifies that attacks must not (except perhaps in extraordinary circumstances) be traced. The normal rationale for such a policy is one (or all) of the following:

- Tracing attacks could result in leakage of information about the incident, something that could potentially embarrass or disrupt the organization.

- Tracing attacks requires more time and resources than are available because the organization in question has a plethora of attacks.

- Tracing attacks represents a violation of the organization's security policy. The policy is to simply close off attacks and get back to normal as soon as possible (see the following sidebar).

Do No Evil, See No Evil?

As just mentioned, certain organizations have adapted the approach that when security-related incidents occur, staff members must not attempt to trace the origin of the attack. When the attack is shut off or discontinued, victim systems and network devices are rebuilt, and any potentially compromised data are restored. This approach is the "Do No Evil, See No Evil" approach.

Although relatively few organizations have such a policy, it is important to understand that one option for dealing with the possibility of tracing attacks is to squelch tracing attacks altogether. Although an often-used approach in the past, the majority of organizations today do not adopt this approach. One major reason is that organizations that adhere to this philosophy do not really learn anything useful from attacks that occur. In most circumstances, it is profitable to at least understand where attacks originate so that firewall and/or filtering rules can be modified. Additionally, this approach virtually precludes efforts to discover the nature of the threat to an organization's systems and networks. This approach also precludes cooperation with law enforcement agencies.

Tracing Methods

Several tracing methods can be used to attempt to pinpoint (or at least guess) the source of an attack. This section describes some of the most useful of these methods.

Search Engines

The first tracing method covered here, using search engines, is a bit "shaky" from a technical perspective. It is nevertheless potentially very useful. The basic notion is that people who do bad things to computing systems and networks often have big mouths. You might remember the old military slogan, "Loose lips sink ships." The same applies to security-related attacks that occur. Perpetrators often brag about their exploits. In so doing, they often reveal information both about the source of any attacks they have launched and even about their identity.

If one or more of your organization's web pages has been defaced or some other type of web-related breach has occurred, good places to initially check include alldas.org and www.antionline.org. Both of these sites report alleged web deface-ments. Although perpetrators do not reveal their identities when they report web-related breaches of web-site security, visiting these sites can help incident handlers obtain additional information about an incident, enabling them to be able to conduct a more extensive subsequent search for the source IP address. A posting on either of these two sites can, for example, enable you to determine the possible attack technique as well as other information such as the time and date that the attack occurred.

The next level of using a search engine is performing a search on a particular word. Suppose the victim machine is in a particular domain, such as domain.com. You can use a search engine such as Google (www.google.com) to determine whether there are any postings related to attacks on domain.com. Additionally, entering **+link:domain name** shows every web page with a cross-link to the victim domain listed on every web page that contains information about the attack(s) that occurred.

Searching not only for the domain but also the specific hostname and IP address of the victim(s) can be useful. If you search for an IP address, be sure to put quotes around the address. You can also include Boolean operators such as "and denial of service." If the perpetrator uses a handle (such as Darkest Doom Godzilla), as so many crackers do, and you discover this handle, you can also search by entering the handle. Again, using a Boolean operator such as "<domain name> and <cracker handle>" can produce extremely useful results. Also try typing the search term **+host:domain <source domain> and hack*.** to determine the web links of potential perpetrators who have launched attacks from the domain name you have specified. You can substitute words such as "warez" or "mp3" to find information relevant to warez or mp3 dealers. If you click on "View original posting," you might be able to discover the identity of the original server on which each message was posted. Use sites such as www.anonymizer.com or www.the-cloak.com if it is important to remain anonymous while you are doing web searches.[3]

You can often use the aforementioned methods at a minimum to learn of other compromised hosts/IP addresses, enabling you to possibly contact the system administrator of these systems. The system administrator might be able to provide data (such as an apparent source address) that you might otherwise be unable to obtain directly. Additionally, although perpetrators typically spoof source addresses when they make public postings, they occasionally get careless. You might, therefore, be able to find a possible source address by examining postings by suspected perpetrators.

The reason we have labeled using search engines as "shaky" is that no guarantee of the integrity or source of network postings exist. A malicious user could even implicate a completely innocent user or an arbitrary host in a posting. Using a search engine nevertheless can sometimes be very useful, especially if the search engine is used in connection with other methods described next.

3. These sites shield your IP address from other sites to which you connect. At the same time, however, it is important to realize that any privacy site you use will have your IP address; you thus must trust the privacy site to not misuse this address or other information about you.

The *netstat* Command

You can obtain apparent source addresses by entering `netstat -(flag or switch)` from the command line of many types of operating systems. In Windows 9X, Windows NT, Windows 2000, and most UNIX systems, for example, you can enter the following:

```
netstat -a -n
```

The `-a` switch displays all connections and listening ports. The `-n` switch displays addresses and port numbers in numerical format. Table 6.1 displays the type of output that results from running the `netstat` command on a Windows 9X system.

Table 6.1 **Output of the *netstat* Command in Windows Systems**

Active Connections			
Proto	Local Address	Foreign Address	State
TCP	198.128.4.231:2178	128.3.41.19:143	ESTABLISHED
TCP	198.128.4.231:2180	128.3.41.19:143	ESTABLISHED
UDP	198.128.4.231:137	*:*	
UDP	198.128.4.231:138	*:*	

One of the limitations of the `netstat` command is that it produces data only for the time during which this command is run. In other words, `netstat` records current connections and nothing more. If you enter the `netstat` command once every day, you will miss possible connections at all other times. One possible remedy is to set up a scheduled job using `cron` in UNIX and Linux systems or the Scheduler in Windows NT and Windows 2000 systems. You can schedule this command to run every few minutes (or perhaps every hour), dumping the output into a file using the following format:

```
netstat >> textfile
```

Log Data

Log data from systems can provide informative data concerning potential source addresses. Log data includes system audit data, firewall log data, and data from monitoring and/or intrusion-detection tools. System audit data can, for example, reveal information such as the following:

- The start and end time of access
- The port number used to access system
- The name of the task executed or command entered
- Attempts to change permissions
- Files accessed
- The baud rate of the connection

Next you'll look at logging in some of the major operating systems used today.

UNIX and Linux Logging

Table 6.2 lists commands that can be used to display log data in the UNIX and Linux operating systems and the information that each provides. Please note that the lastcom and sa commands are available only in certain flavors of UNIX and Linux (these commands originated in Berkeley Standard Distribution [BSD] UNIX).

Table 6.2 **UNIX and Linux Commands to Display Log Data**

Command	Data Displayed
who	Usernames, ports used, login times
last	Last logins by users, terminals
ps	Current processes
acctcom	Commands executed, start/end, CPU usage
lastcomm	Commands executed (displayed in reverse order)
sa	Login accounting information

Commands such as who (which shows each login ID's login and logout times), last (which displays the time of each login ID's last login) and pacct (process accounting, which displays commands entered and the time of each command entry) generally provide a ttyname (terminal name) or source IP address for each entry. Remember, however, that the apparent source might not be the actual source.

Most perpetrators utilize methods that remove the intruder's activity from UNIX and Linux logs. Furthermore, UDP and X-Windows-based activity often does not show up in these logs. Running a wrapper tool that logs incoming service requests and taking measures that record all activity such as NFS-related activity (for example, using NFS Watch) is thus extremely useful if you want to obtain information about the source of an attack.

Windows NT and Windows 2000 Logging

In Windows NT and Windows 2000 systems, entering eventvwr in the Run menu (or going to Start, Programs, Administrative Tools, Event Viewer) brings up a display of one of the event logs (System Log, Security Log, or Application Log). Going to the Log menu bar and pulling down to the selection that corresponds to the particular log you want to view enables you to access any of these three logs. Of the three types of logs, only the Security Log contains security-related data such as the account name and time of failed logons, changes in accounts and groups, access to files and directories, and so forth. The data available depend on how the Security Log is configured.

Unfortunately, however, the Security Log in Windows NT and Windows 2000 does not contain the source of recorded events; the event logger does not record the source IP address. One solution is obtaining and installing a packet filter such as the Nuke Nabber tool (www.dynamsol.com) that records attempted connections on specified ports. Another is buying a third-party tool that yields more complete audit data.

NetWare Logging

NetWare auditing is done by the AUDITCON.EXE utility located in the SYS:PUBLIC directory of each file server. The administrator can configure auditing, but anyone (regardless of assigned privilege level) can access the audit logs and control various auditing functions by entering the appropriate password. Events related to the NetWare directory services (NDS) and file system events are audited independently of each other.

To read audit reports for directory services, select Audit directory services from the AUDITCON main menu. The Audit directory services menu is displayed. Select Change session context in the Audit directory services menu to go directly to a container. Otherwise, you can select Audit directory tree to go through the NDS tree structure to locate a container of interest. The currently selected container is shown at the top. Choose the container you want from the Audit directory tree screen and then press F10. The Available audit options menu is displayed. Select Auditor container login, type in the password, and then press Enter. The Available audit options menu will now be displayed. Finally, select Auditing reports. The particular audit data displayed will depend on how you have configured directory services auditing.

To view NetWare audit reports for volume auditing, enter **AUDITCON** and then select Change current server to choose the appropriate service. From the AUDITCON main menu, select Change current volume to specify the volume of interest. Next, select Auditor volume login from the AUDITCON main menu. The Enter volume password input box will be displayed. Type in the auditing password for the volume you have chosen, press Enter, and then select Auditing reports, a selection within the Available audit options menu that will be displayed. As in the case of directory services auditing, the particular audit data displayed will depend on the configuration of volume auditing.

VMS Logging

VMS commands to access log data are shown in Table 6.3. VMS not only allows incident handlers to quickly discover the apparent source addresses of attacks, it also yields other extremely useful information such as logon times and privilege level.

Table 6.3 **VMS Commands to Display Audit Data**

Command	Information Displayed
SHOW USERS	Names of users who are currently logged in
SHOW SYSTEM	Current processes and process IDs (PIDs)
SHOW PROCESS	A specific process (of your choice)
SHOW	Current users' logon times, privilege level, and so on
ANALYZE/AUDIT/EVENT=name	Failed logins, modification of system authorization function, and so on
ACCOUNTING/FULL	All activity on system

Data from firewalls are often the most useful when incident handlers are trying to determine the source of an attack. This topic will be explored next.

Firewall Logs

Most commercial firewall products include logging capabilities that capture information such as the type of service requested, the source and destination IP address, and so on. Some firewall logging capabilities are much better than others, however. Some simply capture a greater amount of information; some display data in a more human-usable format.

When all is said and done, firewall logs generally provide the best source of information about apparent source IP addresses of attacks. Although firewalls, like hosts that reside in internal networks, are vulnerable to attacks, they are usually more difficult to tamper with than other hosts. In their "bastion host" role, they need to be more secure. As such, the information they capture is likely to be complete and unaltered, at least as compared to information gleaned from individual systems. Additionally, external firewalls gather data from a central point—the external gateway. Investigators can conveniently access the firewall to obtain information about source addresses and other parameters related to a variety of attacks that might have occurred within their internal network.

Unfortunately, we live in an imperfect world. Firewall logs can be altered or deleted by attackers. (For this reason, running a Tripwire tool that checks the integrity of firewall logs [as well as system logs] is a good thing to do.) Attackers can also flood firewalls with so much traffic that examining logs can become unmanageable. Finally, attackers can launch DoS attacks on firewalls, causing them to crash or at least slow down so much that they become functionally "brain dead."

Intrusion Detection System Alarms and Data

Intrusion detection systems (IDSs) also produce alarms and data that contain apparent IP addresses. This book does not cover IDSs, however. More information on this subject is available in books such as Stephen Northcutt's *Network Intrusion Detection: An Analyst's Handbook*.[4]

Raw Packet Data

Another method that can be used to determine the source of an attack is implementing a tool such as TCP Dump or Snort that records the apparent source IP address. Typically, this means putting some kind of device that captures packets as part of a configuration designed to gather raw packet data. Raw packet dumps contain, among other things, the source IP address.

---

4. Northcutt, Stephen. *Network Intrusion Detection: An Analyst's Handbook*. Indianapolis: New Riders, 1999.

Examining Raw Packet Dumps

The IP header in packets contains information that is potentially useful in tracing the origin of an attack.[5] Table 6.4 below shows a data dump from an IP header.

Table 6.4 **A Data Dump from an IP Header**

```
0x0000 45c0 005c c562 0000 1d06 4f81 8003 09f0
0x0010 d2dd 054a 0203 4b44 0000 0000 4500 002c
0x0020 79a4 0000 1c06 4a88 5804 004a d09b d9bf
0x0030 7443 0011 6a55 c3d1 0000 0000 6002 00a4
0x0040 44c3 0000 0106 005a 3220 6907 0000 0000
0x0050 0000 0000 0000 0000 0000 0000
```

The hexadecimal values in this header dump have been converted from binary values by a packet analysis tool. You can convert each value to decimal by multiplying the right-most number by $16^{**}0$ (or 1), then multiplying the next number to the left by $16^{**}1$ (or 16), then multiplying the next number to the left by $16^{**}2$ (or 256), and so on.

The first column of numbers (starting with 0x0000 at the top left side) corresponds to the row. Table 6.5 shows the format.

Table 6.5 **Fields and Field Lengths in the IP Packet Header**

Field[6]	Length (Bits)
Version	4
Header length	4
Type of service	8
Total length	16
Identification	16
Flags	3
Fragment offset	13
TTL (time to live)	8
Protocol	8
Header checksum	16
Source address	32
Destination address	32
Options	24
Padding	8

5. For additional information, see RFC-791 at www.ietf.org.
6. Starting at bit position (offset) zero.

In Table 6.4, you'll see that the values in the first line start with 45c0. The 4 means that the version is 4; in other words, this is an IPv4 packet. The header length is 5. The type of service is c0 or 192. Skipping ahead a little bit, note also that the value 8003 09f0 appears at the end of the first line. In this example, this is the source IP address. 0x80 is decimal 128, 0x03 is decimal 3, 0x09 is decimal 9, and 0xf0 is decimal 240, so the source IP address is 128.3.9.240.

How to Capture Packet Data

Myth, not fact, predominates when it comes to methods of capturing packet data. Legend has it, for example, that it is impossible to capture packets in a switched network environment, but this is simply not true. It is true, however, that it is *more difficult* to capture packets in a switched environment, but this is because of fundamental differences between hubs and switches. Hubs do not support connections, and as such, they echo every packet to every port on the hub except for the source port. Switches, on the other hand, support connections. Switches thus form a temporary connection when a packet arrives; packets are forwarded to the destination port.

These properties of hubs and switches make a big difference when it comes to capturing packet data. The fact that hubs do not support connections enables someone to install a packet capture device that captures virtually all traffic that passes through. Switches, on the other hand, are not so versatile when it comes to capturing packets. To put it bluntly, they can miss packets if specific solutions are not put in place to ensure that a packet capture device picks up traffic that goes through the switch.

The major solution for capturing packets in a switched environment is a port called a "spanning port." A spanning port can be configured in a manner that causes a switch to behave like a hub for a particular port. Figure 6.1 illustrates how this can be done. The connection between the switch and a particular host can be monitored using a spanning port that dumps packet contents to a machine used specifically for capturing packet data. This does not, of course, guarantee that all packet data will be recorded. Additionally, one of the limitations of switches is that only one port can be spanned at any point in time. This greatly complicates simultaneously capturing packets from more than one host. Finally, the sheer throughput of a switch makes collection and processing of packets quite challenging. Of course, any form of packet encryption—such a packets transmitted via a VPN—defeats successful analysis of collected packets.

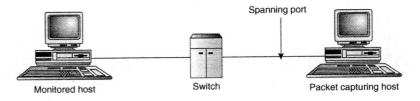

Figure 6.1   A typical configuration for using a spanning port.

Another alternative is to put a hub or a network tap device (hereafter called a "tap") between the switches, between a router and a switch, or between a monitored host and a switch. Figure 6.2 illustrates the last of these three possibilities. A hub between the resource machine and the switch is, in this case, copying packet data that pass between the switch and the monitored host. The hub then shunts the copies of the network traffic off to a host that stores the data.

The use of a hub or other device in the manner shown in Figure 6.2 is also less than optimal; it can be used only for monitoring single hosts. Placing more than one host on the hub also causes a number of networking complications that are beyond the scope of this chapter. Still another complication is that for all practical purposes, a fault-tolerant hub must be purchased. Fault tolerant hubs, however, are generally expensive to buy.

Still another deployment option is to deploy a tap, a device that connects directly to network media, instead of a hub in the configuration shown in Figure 6.2. Most taps have built-in fault-tolerance capabilities yet have a more reasonable purchase price. In this deployment, it is important to ensure that traffic flow to the data storage host is one-way to avoid the possibility of obtaining a considerable amount of data from hosts for which you already know the source IP address. It can also, in some cases, reduce the probability of a denial-of-service attack from excessive traffic. Commercial products that support one-way traffic flow are available.

A final caveat is appropriate before moving on. By now, it should be apparent that there is a lot more to capturing packets than meets the eye. Careful planning, particularly in the preparation stage, is thus a prerequisite. You will also need to ensure that the host you use to store the captured data has sufficient storage capacity. It is not difficult to fill a 20GB or 30GB hard drive with packet data in a relatively short period of time, assuming high network throughput rate at the point where data are being captured. Because of this, some organizations use optical media (such as worm drives) with many terabytes of storage capacity for recording packet data.

We will next consider what to do if you should happen to obtain one or more source addresses.

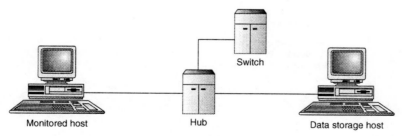

Figure 6.2   A hub sending data passing between a monitored host and switch.

Next Steps

Finding the source address of one or more attacking hosts might require considerable effort. Remember, too, that the majority of people who engage in unauthorized network activities exercise great care in covering their tracks. Assuming that you have discovered one or more source addresses, however, what are some logical next steps? This portion of the chapter explains possible subsequent courses of action.

Sending Email to *abuse@*

One course of action is to send email to abuse@<domainname> or possibly root@<domain name>. For example, if you discover that a particular IP address is within the aol.com domain, you can try to send mail to abuse@aol.com. Your message is likely to be received by someone who administers security in the domain in which the apparent offending host resides. You will, in most cases, receive some kind of autoreply (see Figure 6.3). The reply you get, however, is not nearly as important as the fact that you have now helped someone investigate whether the apparent offending host has been compromised or misused.

Subject: Re: Unauthorized connection from 128.3.9.240
Date: Friday, 25 May 2001 09:51:27-0930(EDT)
From: Judy Brown<sbrown@somedomain.net>
  To: I.M.Violated@someothernet.net

Thank you for alerting us of this incident. We have begun investigating the cause of the problem.

The IP address to which you refer is assigned to one of the systems in an open computing area within our institution. A copy of this response is being sent to the security liaison for this area, Mr. Robert Smith. His address is rsmith@somedomain.net.

Should other incidents of this nature occur within your network, please do not hesitate to contact us.

Judy Brown
========================
Judy Brown
Security Coordinator
Somedomain Computing Corporation
jbrown@somedomain.com
(999) 999-9999
========================

Figure 6.3   A sample autoreply message.

Sending email to an "abuse address" is, unfortunately, a less-than-perfect strategy. First, the source address you obtained might simply not be the correct one. Second, you might not be able to get any information back, or if you do, it might be the kind of information shown in Figure 6.3 instead of more meaningful information. Finally, the attackers might have control of the `abuse@` or `root@` accounts. At a minimum, you might now have tipped them off that you have discovered their activities. They might now attempt to remove all traces of their presence on your systems before you can start forensics procedures. They also might now attempt to have a little bit of fun with you (as unethical as this might be) by doing something such as sending you bogus information that sends you on a wild goose chase.

All things considered, the benefits of sending email to `abuse@` or `root@` often outweigh the disadvantages. Many if not most attacks simply go unnoticed, giving a huge advantage to those who perpetrate them. Attempting to send email to those who are responsible for security in systems from which attacks have apparently originated at least allows a chance for those who need to intervene to do so.

Tracking Down a Suspected Source IP Address

At some point in the process of responding to an incident or set of incidents, the true identity of the attacking host(s) might become evident. This often is because multiple attempts to pinpoint the source address keep resulting in the discovery of a single address or possibly a small group of addresses. A number of commands can now be of great value. These include `dig/nslookup`, `whois`, `ping`, `traceroute`, and possibly others.

dig/nslookup

A sound next step is to reverse map the identified source IP address into a domain name. The `"dig -x ip"` *NIX command accomplishes this goal by doing a reverse lookup on an IP address of interest using its domain name server. Entering the `-x` flag with the `dig` command is a wise move because it guarantees that all DNS table records (for example, which name servers and email servers are used, the host-resolved name, and so forth) regarding the host of interest will be sent.

Another good strategy is to enter the `nslookup` command for all the addresses in the network to which the offender's machine is connected. The `nslookup` command maps the relationship between a hostname and IP address. Simply enter the following:

```
nslookup <hostname or IP address>
```

If the offender appears to have originated an attack from 12.34.56.78, you can do an nslookup for 12.34.56.1 through 12.34.56.254. You can often find information that an nslookup on a single address might not yield. Note that this strategy is feasible with a class C network (which has 254 addresses) but not with class A or class B networks (which have a larger address space).

whois

Using the whois command to find out to whom the offending IP is registered is another good next step. This involves using the resolved name to attempt to identify the country of the particular IP address in question. Different whois gateways are available for this purpose. The main gateway in the United States is ARIN (for "American Registry") at whois.arin.net. RIPE (whois.ripe.net) is the main European gateway, and APNIC (whois.apnic.net) is the primary Asian Pacific gateway. Enter **telnet whois.arin.net** (or another address as previously shown) to connect to the appropriate gateway. Then enter whois. After the special prompt appears enter one of the following:

»host attacker.corp.com (to attempt to find the name and phone number of the system administrator as well as the IP address of the connecting machine)

or

»net 128.115 (to attempt to find the name and phone number of the network coordinator)

or

»finger@<address> (to attempt to find out who is logged in to the suspected source machine)

Attempts to use whois might or might not work. Sometimes the whois data does not correspond to the resolved name. Furthermore, whois databases tend to be updated too slowly, resulting in out-of-date information. If initial whois attempts with the gateways introduced earlier fail, another possible course of action is to reach country-specific whois databases to attempt to identify the registered owner. You can find these country-specific databases at www.allwhois.com.

ping

The ping command can sometimes be useful in that it can tell you whether a host you suspect has been used to launch an attack is alive and on the network. Enter the following:

ping <address>

One drawback of using ping, however, is that because it uses the ICMP protocol, it might not reach the target address. Firewalls and screening routers often (wisely) filter out all incoming ICMP traffic, so if a ping attempt fails, the meaning of the outcome might be unclear. The host you suspect of launching an attack might not be alive and on the network, or a firewall or screening router might have blocked your `ping` attempt. Yet another limitation is that even if you successfully `ping` the suspected host, this does not show that the host attacked you.

traceroute

You can also enter the following:

```
traceroute <address>
```

The `traceroute` command (or its equivalent in Windows systems, `tracert`) shows intermediate hops between the host on which this command is entered and a target host. If you enter `traceroute` soon after you find suspicious activity from a particular host, you are likely to discover the route through which traffic between your host and the suspected host traveled at the time the activity occurred.[7] This is potentially very helpful because if the IP address you obtain for the suspected host does not resolve, you can possibly get some clues about that host. You might, for example, be able to determine the ISP for the suspected host. Similarly, you might be able to determine the particular part of the world from which the activity originated by examining the path over which the packets traveled.

Should You Scan a Host that May Have Attacked You?

A number of net postings and conference papers advocate scanning a host that has apparently attacked one of your hosts. Scanning can enable you to determine which ports are open. It can also help you determine whether a host is being used as a relay host. Relay hosts typically run services such as Internet relay chat (IRC), Remote Procedure Calls (RPC), and Virtual Network Controller (VNC). With tools such as NMAP and Nessus in the public domain, virtually anyone who wants to can engage in such activity.

There also is a danger, however. What if the host you are scanning has *not* been involved in an attack? How will the system administrator respond? Might the system administrator retaliate? Furthermore, conducting such scans without explicit management approval is against many organizations' policies. Finally, there is an important ethical question: Is it acceptable to do what attackers do when you have been attacked? The resolution of this issue thus depends on many issues. In general, we, the authors of this book, would like to discourage anyone from scanning other machines in response to an attack, primarily for ethical reasons. Being attacked does not constitute license for attacking others.

7. Note that because IP finds its own best route, routing might change from time to time. This will affect the output of the **traceroute** command.

You can also use the `traceroute` command in another way. If you can successfully run the `traceroute` command shortly after a host is attacked, you can count the number of hops over which packets travel. If you have also captured packets on the network segment to which the victim host is connected, you can now count the TTL (time to live) value[8] of the packet (see Figure 6.4 to find out more about the TTL field within an IP header). If you see that an IP packet header has a TTL value of, say, 99, but a `traceroute` indicates that the suspected IP address is only three hops away over the network, something is wrong. TTL values are typically either 64 or 128. You might accordingly conclude that the source address has been spoofed.

The limitations of `traceroute` are the same as with `ping`. `traceroute` is based on the ICMP protocol and thus might be blocked by one or more firewalls or screening routers. Additionally, a successful execution of the `traceroute` command does not prove that the target host attacked you.

Constructing an "Attack Path"

You have now considered many methods of obtaining information about a host that might have launched an attack. So what? The next and final section of this chapter deals with piecing together all the information you obtain to construct an "attack path."

What Is an Attack Path?

An attack path is a model of the network or possibly the telecommunications route used to launch an attack. In other words, if during the time of a certain attack a certain victim host had a connection with another host to which another host was connected, the trail of the attack could be constructed.

Constructing an Attack Path

After someone has a reasonable amount of information about the nature of the attacks and the potential source IP address(es) of the attacks, it is possible to construct an attack path. As mentioned many times previously in this book, a competent incident response effort documents all information it receives. This information can be used as the basis of constructing an attack path.

Pinpointing the Source

How does somebody construct an attack path? The answer lies in piecing together all information gathered from using methods described in this chapter: the type of protocol used (or perhaps "misused" is the better word), the source address, the desti-

---

8. TTL values are important because a packet with a TTL value of 0 will be dropped by the device that receives it.

nation address, intermediate addresses involved, and more. Now the fun begins. Commonality is the key. If over half of the attacks involve misuse of the FTP protocol from only one or two potential source IP addresses, data commonality narrows the source of attacks considerably.

The Direct Trace Method

In the direct trace method, you determine the source of an attack while the attack is underway and then contact the system or security administrator of the other (source) system (labeled System 1 in Figure 6.4). The system or security administrator of System 1 looks at current connections to verify the connection from System 1 to your system and then determines the source of the connection to System 1. You then contact the system or security administrator of System 2, the source of the connection to System 1, and so on, until you identify what is apparently the true source host (see Figure 6.4). In an ideal scenario, you call in law enforcement, which catches the perpetrator(s) in the act.

Cliff Stoll[9], and others who cooperated with him, used this method to track down the Hanover Hacker. Stoll contacted staff members from organizations with intermediate hosts in the attack path to eventually pinpoint the source of the attacks. This method is the most direct, logical way to trace an attack, but remember that the apparent source address might not be the real source. Unless only IPsec connections to hosts are allowed, packet header information can easily be spoofed. Additionally, wide-scale cooperation is not easy to obtain. Determining the immediate source of a connection often means you will contact someone from an organization that has a "see no evil, do no evil" policy. In addition, an organization with a host in the attack path you constructed might be a competitor of yours.

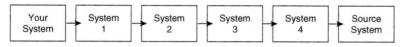

Figure 6.4   A hypothetical attack path.

9. Stoll, C., *The Cuckoo's Egg*. New York: Doubleday, 1989.

The Indirect Trace Method

The indirect trace method is similar to the direct trace method except there is no real-time element. The attack path is constructed from accounting and other data that indicates that particular types of connections occurred as well as the times of usage from one part of the attack path to the next. Because there is no real-time element, each party involved in using the indirect trace method does not have to be focused on reacting quickly. This potentially allows a slower, more careful analysis of a wider range of data. The main limitations, on the other hand, include systems that do not have any logging enabled (an all-too-common problem) and logging failures (such as when attackers plant rootkit-type tools). The result is the inability to trace an attack beyond a certain point in the trail.

Other Clues

As you construct a path of attack, you will find that other sources of information can also be useful in this effort. Names of accounts created by an attacker, command usage patterns, typical types of errors (such as misspellings of certain commands), the baud rate of connections, and other "signatures" can help fill in missing pieces of data necessary to construct the path of attack. Knowing, for example, that a particular attacker always creates a new account named "abc" in systems to which this person obtains unauthorized access can help you pinpoint the source of an attack. Knowing that a series of hosts now have accounts named "abc" could lead you to hypothesize that many or all of these hosts are part of one or at least a few attack paths. Using attacker "signatures," however, requires at least one previous determination of the source of the attack. Additionally, copycat attacks in which someone who is junior to an attacker within a hacking group copies the actions of a more experienced attacker can be very misleading. Still, the more information you obtain, the more likely it is that you'll be able to locate where attacks originated.

Final Caveats

Those who are experienced in attack tracing know that tracing the source of attacks is by no means easy. Attackers usually do everything in their power to cover their tracks. One time-proven method they use is to "leapfrog" from one host to another to another. By the time an attack goes through six or seven intermediate hosts, it is very difficult to use the direct trace method let alone the indirect trace method. The reason we raise this point is not to discourage you, but rather to once again remind you that when you are dealing with attacks, you must usually make a large number of decisions.

First and foremost, adhere to your organization's policy concerning attack tracing. If the policy dictates that attacks must not be traced without prior approval from senior management, failure to adhere to the policy will be career limiting for you. If your organization's policy allows for tracing attacks, be careful to avoid wasting a lot of time pursuing every attack that occurs. Carefully analyze the costs and benefits first, remembering that the likelihood of success in an attack with multiple intermediate hosts is not great.

The information in this chapter could possibly motivate the would-be cybercop to devote even greater levels of effort in fighting cybercrime—to nail every cybercriminal. We've seen plenty of speakers at information security conferences who posture themselves as cybercops, but in reality, unless someone works for an agency such as the FBI or Interpol, the cybercop mentality is likely to accomplish nothing more than annoying others, hindering cooperation between organizations, and resulting in foolish mistakes. Tracing attacks is not about being a cybercop; rather, it is something that one does from time to time as needs (and policy) dictate.

Finally, there is a big difference between responding to an incident and conducting an investigation (an examination of wrongdoing on the part of one or more employees). In general, organizations that have an incident response capability do not authorize incident response personnel to also conduct investigations. Taking the liberty to conduct an investigation is likely to have all kinds of negative fallout, including legal implications (as discussed more fully in Chapter 7, "Legal Issues.") In short, understand your organization's policy as well as what you are and are not expected and authorized to do when you respond to incidents. And never forget to use good old-fashioned common sense.

Good luck!

What do you do if you conclusively pinpoint the source of an attack or attacks? We will now move on to a discussion of this and other legal issues in the next chapter.

Summary

This chapter covered important issues related to tracing incidents. We delved into what tracing network attacks means and involves, namely finding the source (usually in terms of the identity of a host or IP address) of an attack. Tracing network attacks is *not* synonymous with tracing network intrusions; many attacks other than intrusions occur. It is important to put attack tracing in proper perspective, paying particular attention to issues such as what your organization's policy is regarding tracing attacks. A number of organizations have a policy that specifies that attacks must not (except perhaps in extraordinary circumstances) be traced. Considering other issues such as costs versus benefits, available resources, the number of ongoing attacks and the priority of dealing with each, and so forth is essential.

Various methods are available to trace the source of attacks. These methods include search engines (to try to find postings that contain information about attacks that have occurred), the `netstat` command (which shows current connections), log data (particularly from systems and firewalls), data from intrusion detection systems, and raw packet data. After you obtain a candidate source IP address, you can send email to `abuse@<address>` or possibly `root@<address>`, although the attackers might get your messages instead if they have obtained superuser-level access. Use `dig/nslookup` to reverse map the identified source IP address into a domain name, `whois` to discover to whom a machine is registered (as well as possibly other information), `ping` to determine whether a host is alive, and `traceroute` or `tracert` to identify intermediate hops over which traffic travels between the victim host and the possible source of the attack.

Attack paths can be constructed using either the direct trace method (a real-time or near-real-time method to trace connections back to their source) or the indirect trace method (which has no real-time or near-real-time element). Attacker signatures (such as the particular tools installed, keystroke errors, and so forth) can also be useful in filling in missing pieces of information. Tracing attacks is usually difficult and time consuming, especially when the attacker's route includes multiple intermediate hosts, so it is important to make wise decisions and always keep what you are trying to do in proper perspective. Adhering to your organization's policy concerning attack tracing and investigations is essential.

7

Legal Issues

INCIDENT RESPONSE, OF ALL THE COMPUTER security disciplines, is probably the most affected by legal considerations. Many, if not most, incidents involve some sort of crime. Those that do not almost certainly involve some sort of policy violation. An organization might want to prosecute an offender, in which case it must consider the legal implications of the incident and must assist law enforcement in preparing the case (or at least ensure that the incident response team's actions do not impede the investigation and prosecution). An organization might choose not to prosecute but to instead take some kind of administrative action against an employee (such as suspension or termination). In this case, employment statutes might limit the company's actions. In either situation, the company, its officers, and the incident response team could be liable for violations of laws or regulations during the conduct of the investigation.

This chapter will discuss U.S. and international laws that might affect or impact the incident response process. It will also discuss the importance of developing policies that support incident response efforts and investigations.

The law has been criticized for its slowness to adapt to the Internet and the legal problems associated with it. International and interjurisdictional cooperation is difficult at best. What constitutes a crime in one area might not, in fact, be illegal in another. This would not normally be a problem in more conventional situations because the jurisdiction in which the crime was committed is straightforward in most other crimes. For example, if a person from Russia robs a New York resident at gunpoint in

Manhattan, that person has committed a felony in the city and county of New York (regardless of his origin). If, however, a person from Russia accesses computers located in New York (and to make it more difficult, suppose the company's headquarters are in London), there is some question as to whether the crime was committed in New York, London, or Russia. Even if the police can make a case in New York against the suspect, it might not be illegal in Russia to break into the system.

In such cases, there are usually three options:

1. Ignore the problem, fix the vulnerability, and move on. Although not particularly attractive, it might be easier than attempting to conduct an international investigation and prosecution.

2. Prosecute the offender in his or her own country. This assumes that the crime is, in fact, illegal and that local law enforcement agencies perceive that they have a case and can successfully prosecute it.

3. Apply for extradition and prosecute the offender in the country where the computers are located (or perhaps where the company headquarters are located). Unfortunately, this option requires the assistance of agencies in both the home country and the foreign jurisdiction.

In some situations, it is possible to conduct a variation of the third option. For example, Vladimar Levin, the convicted intruder in the 1994 Citibank incident, was persuaded by law enforcement agencies to come to the United Kingdom. There he was arrested by British police and extradited to the United States. This alternative actually works (and has worked several times) against high-profile criminals, although we should probably assume that there are many more who are smart enough not to put themselves in this kind of situation.

Experienced attackers might choose to route their attacks through multiple locations and often choose countries that might be unwilling (or unable) to cooperate in the investigation. When multiple jurisdictions are involved and some of them might not be friendly or sympathetic to the victim, the law can be extremely complex.

U.S. Computer Crime Statutes

The U.S. Federal Bureau of Investigation makes a distinction between crimes against computers and crimes involving computers. A crime *against* a computer, for example, is when an unauthorized person accesses a computer. A crime *involving* a computer might be a case of cyberstalking, in which the computer was only the tool used to commit the crime.

This is a valuable distinction when discussing legal aspects of computer crime. Many of the crimes people hear about are not crimes against computers at all. These typically are processed under other statutes such as fraud or theft. It is also possible for a crime to be a combination of the two. For example, if a hacker breaks into an e-commerce site and steals credit card information, he or she might have violated some computer crime statutes in the original break-in. Using the credit card numbers would then be a violation of other federal and state laws.

The Computer Fraud and Abuse Act

The standard statute covering computer crime *per se* in the United States is the Computer Fraud and Abuse Act of 1986 (updated in 1996). This act, Title 18, Section 1030, covers crimes against computers. The act is concerned with what it calls "federal interest computers." A federal interest computer is defined as a computer used by any financial institution or the U.S. government or one used in interstate or foreign commerce or *communication* (author's italics). This is an extremely loose definition and, given the widespread use of email, could technically apply to virtually any networked computer. Almost any business computer could be covered under one or more of the definitions in the code.

The act prohibits the intentional, unauthorized access of any protected computer if the attacker gains any government information. In addition, financial information (including credit card data) is specifically protected. Any information about the computer or the network is protected under the code if the computer is used in interstate or foreign commerce.

The 1996 revision added provisions against the damaging of computers. In particular, the law prohibits the transmission of programs specifically designed to damage computers or data. This section was specifically designed to deal with viruses. Unfortunately, denial-of-service attacks are not specifically covered (although other laws might apply).

The threshold of damage for invoking the Computer Fraud and Abuse Act is $5,000. Any violation with damages greater than $5,000 can be prosecuted under the act. Chapter 3, "A Methodology for Incident Response," discusses the importance of capturing all the data and costs associated with an incident. The costs of the investigation and recovery can be included in this calculation. Under these rules, establishing damages greater than $5,000 should be relatively simple. As part of the incident response program, a cost-tracking system should be in place to account for direct costs (such as hardware, software, and consultants), indirect labor costs (such as overtime for incident response personnel), and opportunity costs (the downtime during the incident and recovery period).

As a matter of fact, however, most federal prosecutors will not be interested in pursuing a crime with damages of only $5,000. If the crime is especially egregious or involves large losses to one or more companies, the federal law enforcement agencies might be more willing to investigate. Small crimes are more likely to be handled either administratively by an organization or by local law enforcement.

Space obviously does not allow a complete discussion of local and state laws. Many states have enacted legislation that essentially mirrors the federal statutes, while others have even stricter regulations. In addition, other state laws might apply depending on the specifics. For example, illegally accessing a computer over a modem might violate some state telecommunications or wiretap laws.

Crimes involving computers are prosecuted under conventional statutes. For example, a person who breaks into a web server and steals credit card numbers can be prosecuted under the federal act because it specifically addresses credit card information. The person could also be prosecuted under fraud statutes if the card information is used to steal goods or services. Other laws prohibit money laundering or embezzling, regardless of the tools used.

Similarly, items such as copyright laws protect information that can be disseminated (or stolen) in digital form, such as books, music, or software. Many of these laws have been updated to address the challenges of digital piracy.

The U.S. fraud statutes (Title 18, section 1029) also cover the use of counterfeit access devices. These are defined as cards, codes, account numbers, passwords, personal identification numbers (PINs), or any other identifying instrument or information that can be used to obtain money or anything else of value. Trafficking in stolen passwords or password-stealing programs is therefore illegal under this section.[1]

Other laws protect data during transmission. The Electronic Communications Privacy Act prohibits the interception and disclosure of wire, oral, or electronic communications. There are, however, important exceptions to this law. First, the term "communication" under this statute covers aural (meaning sound) communications only. Voice over IP is probably covered, but email is not. For law enforcement to capture traffic, a warrant is required. A service provider can capture and monitor traffic, provided it is done for the purpose of improving or maintaining service quality only.

New Laws

Several industries have new regulations that might require additional or increased vigilance. For example, in 1996, the U.S. government enacted the Health Industry Portability and Accountability Act (usually referred to as HIPAA). The major focus of this act was to provide for portability of health insurance if employees change jobs. However, there are additional requirements on health care providers in the statute that are of interest to incident response teams.

Near the end of the HIPAA is a section describing safeguards required for health care information. The act requires all persons with access to this information to take reasonable care to protect the integrity and confidentiality of patient data. Full compliance with this section was to be phased in over time and is required in 2003. This section has been interpreted as requiring health care providers to implement appropriate security standards. Because it is included in an administrative section of the bill, the standards are not explicitly defined. Most insurers, however, are now implementing security postures, including risk assessments and security testing, to ensure the privacy of patients.

In a similar fashion, a law designed "to enhance competition in the financial services industry"[2] was passed in 1999. This law, known as the Gramm-Leach-Bliley Act after its sponsors, streamlined several processes and allowed more competition from insurance agencies, brokers, and banks.

1. This law was used in the prosecution of Robert T. Morris (see Chapter 13, "Future Directions," for more discussion of this subject).
2. Public Law 106–102, title.

As with HIPAA, near the end of the law is a short section concerned with privacy. This section states that Congress has a responsibility to ensure that financial institutions are taking proper steps to safeguard private customer information. It includes prohibitions against the release of any customer data without the prior consent of the customer.

Of more interest, the act also requires financial services institutions to protect customer data from unauthorized access. These include administrative, technical, and physical safeguards. Again, the details and specific requirements are not explicitly defined, but the language of the act does clearly place a new privacy obligation on financial services institutions.

As privacy becomes more important, it is likely that additional legislation on the protection and disclosure of personal data will occur. Especially considering constraints placed on U.S. companies doing business abroad (discussed in the next section), the pressure to implement privacy legislation is growing. One fundamental problem with privacy legislation is that the details are extremely difficult to reconcile. Most current privacy regulations in the United States protect the rights of the individual against government intrusiveness. Data held by companies is, for the most part, unregulated. In much of the rest of the world, however, privacy regulations cover data held by companies and private organizations, while governments are all but unregulated. The United States has chosen to regulate privacy by industry. For example, health care information, financial services information, and even what videos a person views is protected, but general customer data including name, address, telephone number, and buying habits is not.

Incident Response under HIPAA and G–L–B

The total impact of HIPAA and Gramm-Leach-Bliley on incident response is still unclear. Although the laws do impose new requirements for the security and confidentiality of personal data, there are no test cases to define what these requirements might mean in the context of an investigation.

For example, under HIPAA, patient personal data must be protected. Does this mean that the priority during an investigation into an incident involving medical systems should focus on the protection of privacy over other priorities (such as the apprehension and prosecution of the intruder)?

Similarly, the rules for releasing personal information are also uncertain. Can outside consultants do forensics on machines containing patient data? Can backup tapes that contain system logs but also personal information be released to law enforcement?

These issues should be addressed and policies developed to deal with them. Obviously, legal counsel should be involved in the discussion, and the incident response team and management should carefully review the potential conclusions of any policy decision.

International Statutes

Each country has its own statutes covering computer crime. These can vary widely and might range from extremely draconian (such as China's execution of persons convicted of hacking into banks) to virtually none at all. The accused author of the Love Bug worm was released when it was determined that the Philippines had no statute prohibiting the authoring and release of a computer virus.

A major challenge in investigating and prosecuting computer crimes is the issue of multiple laws in multiple jurisdictions. It is difficult enough to get a warrant for records in one country; when the incident involves multiple countries, it can be almost impossible. Resolving (or at least reducing) this problem has been a major initiative in recent years.

The COE Treaty

One of the most recent and promising proposals to improve international cooperation is the Council on Europe draft Convention on Cybercrime. The council approved the treaty in June of 2001, but it still must be ratified by individual European states. The Council of Europe was founded in 1949 and represents 43 individual European countries. Other countries, including the United States, Japan, Canada, Mexico, and the Vatican, have observer status. If the convention is ratified by the members, these observer countries will be allowed to ratify it as well.

The U.S. Department of Justice was active as an advisor during the negotiations. Officially, the department has made no comment as to whether the United States is expected to ratify the treaty if and when it comes up for review.

The full text of the draft treaty is available at the Council on Europe web site (`http://conventions.coe.int`). The treaty is too large to include here, but several of the items in the document bear discussion. The convention requires signatories to adopt legislation or regulations to comply with each of the titles in the document.

Title 1: Offenses Against the Confidentiality, Integrity, and Availability of Computer Data and Systems

This section of the convention addresses crimes that could typically be described as crimes against computers. Specifically, the section prohibits the illegal access of systems, illegal interception of communications (computer data only, presumably voice is addressed under other rules), modification or deletion of data, and interference with systems (denial of service).

In addition, the title also prohibits the sale, use, distribution, import, or possession of any device (including software) designed to commit any of the preceding offenses. Unauthorized possession of passwords is specifically prohibited. This item has been criticized by many in the security community as prohibiting legitimate research into system security. For example, some people have argued that the research that went into a tool such as L0phtcrack and the possession of such a tool would be impeded by this regulation. The convention, however, only prohibits these items when they are intended to be used to commit the preceding offenses. Research and the legitimate use of such tools by security professionals appear to be excluded.[3]

Title 2: Computer–Related Offenses

This section addresses crimes that could best be described as crimes involving computers. It expands the definitions of fraud and forgery to include the modification or deletion of computer data with the intent to defraud.

Title 3: Content–Related Offenses

Content-related offenses, in the context of the convention, are a metaphor for child pornography. Laws against child pornography vary widely, even within Europe. The age of consent ranges from 16 to 18. The convention states that each signatory must implement laws or regulations against measures that are illegal under its domestic laws. A minor is defined as a person under the age of 18, but countries have the option to choose the lower age of 16.

Specifically, if a given image or item is judged to be illegal under one country's laws, then the production, distribution, offering, and possession of that item on a computer system are also illegal. This section essentially ensures that existing child pornography laws are modified to accommodate computer-related issues.

Virtual Pornography

The convention specifically prohibits three actions in the definitions section. It defines child pornography as the depiction of the following:

1. A minor engaged in sexually explicit conduct

2. A person appearing to be a minor engaged in sexually explicit conduct

3. Realistic images representing a minor engaged in sexually explicit conduct

All three items are also illegal under U.S. law. However, the third item has been challenged in appeals court and the outcome is uncertain. Countries have the option of not applying the second and third items.

Title 4: Offenses Related to Infringements of Copyright and Related Rights

This section addresses the problem of digital copyrighted material. It specifically refers to earlier agreements, including World Intellectual Property Organization (WIPO) treaties. Signatories are required to uphold the obligations in these treaties through either criminal or administrative sanctions.

---

3. As always, legal disclaimers apply. Consult with a legal professional when in doubt.

The WIPO copyright treaty received a lot of publicity and discussion when it was adopted. The critical measure in this treaty is a general prohibition against any measure or device designed to circumvent copyright protection. Under this treaty, for example, it is illegal to reverse-engineer the encryption algorithm used to prevent illegal copying or distribution of DVD movies.

Intellectual Property

Intellectual property rights and protections have received a lot of attention in recent years. Content publishers (including book publishers, musicians, and movie studios) are increasingly concerned about digital piracy. As more content moves into the digital arena, it becomes easier to make and distribute illegal copies.

A number of high-profile legal cases are still defining the laws. Napster was finally prohibited from sharing music files unless it could prevent the downloading of copyrighted material. In this case, the legal opinion stated that Napster was, in effect, condoning and supporting the illegal copying of copyrighted material by providing the forum. 2600 (www.2600.com, publishers of a hacker magazine) was prevented from publishing the source code used to copy-protect DVD movies. Most recently, a person was arrested at the 2001 DefCon conference after giving a presentation about defeating the encryption protection in electronic books.

The implication to major corporations with large intellectual property concerns is obvious. However, even smaller organizations might have risks. It is not inconceivable for a company to be held liable if its employees are trafficking in copyrighted material. Acceptable-use policies (defined later in this chapter) should specifically address this issue and make it clear that the company has the right to search for such information and punish any offenders.

Title 5: Ancillary Liability and Sanctions

This last section states that aiding any organization or individual in the commission of any of the preceding offenses is itself an offense. Corporations are also held liable under the provisions of the treaty. Signatories are explicitly warned that they must, when appropriate, be able to hold individuals within a corporation accountable for the actions of the organization.

The remainder of the treaty is concerned with procedures, but part of these procedures includes search and seizure and the interception of data. The convention requires signatories, within the context of their own laws and constitutions, to adopt policies for the search and seizure of computers and computer-related equipment. Agencies must be able to intercept communications data, including compelling a service provider to collect that data.

The treaty ends with a long section about international cooperation—arguably the major impact of this agreement. The convention binds its members to extradition in the event of computer-related crimes. The convention requires each member to set up a contact network, available on a 24 × 7 basis, to facilitate cooperation. It also acts as a multilateral agreement for cooperation for those states that do not have an agreement in place already. So, for example, if the United States and France did not already have an agreement in place to facilitate law enforcement cooperation, this treaty would act as one.

The EU Privacy Act

The European Union has adopted a number of strict privacy regulations dating from 1995 to 2001.[4] These regulations require EU members to set up a privacy commission to oversee the collection, storage, and dissemination of personal data (that is, data on any individual). Members are prohibited from sharing this data with any country that does not have similar protections in place.

This has been a major point of contention with the United States. The United States has no overarching privacy regulation. Although some data is protected (for example, it is illegal to share information about the videos an individual rents), other information can be freely exchanged.

The U.S. proposed a "Safe Harbor" provision to the EU. This is a provision in which organizations can either join or create privacy programs designed to protect personal data. At the time of this writing, however, the EU had rejected the Safe Harbor provision, alleging that organizations cannot successfully self-regulate.

Under the EU rules, a multinational company could be prohibited from transferring customer data from one of its organizations within the EU to another organization outside. This has extremely grave consequences to large corporations, which might process data in several countries. It will be all but impossible to ensure that no personal information about customers or employees is transferred inadvertently to a noncomplying country.

The impact of these regulations is still unknown at this time. The privacy regulations adopted in 1995 are to be phased in over time. They are scheduled to go into full effect this year. No one has been punished for noncompliance yet, although many European companies (and international companies with a European presence) are concerned that the privacy commissioners might look for a test case.

Search, Seizure, and Monitoring

Search and seizure of employee computers is a sensitive subject. Although employees might be told that their computers are for work purposes only, most people will have some personal data, whether it's email, phone numbers, or personal documents.

---

4. The specific text of these regulations is available on the EU web site at `www.europa.eu.int`.

There are a number of misconceptions about search and seizure. Within the United States, people are protected by the Fourth Amendment, which prohibits "unreasonable search and seizure." However, that prohibition only applies to searches by agents of the government. As a general rule, employers can search the work areas (including computers) of their employees without any special requirements and even without cause. Some of the rules change if the employer is a government agency or contractor, but essentially private employers have few restrictions.

Some local jurisdictions have adopted tougher limitations on employee searches and monitoring. As always, you should *always* consult with proper legal authority prior to conducting a search.

Employee monitoring is especially sensitive. Employees can be monitored directly or by video surveillance, and most people, if they are informed, generally accept such monitoring as long as it is not intrusive (for example, cameras in the bathrooms). Monitoring of computer traffic, however, might be perceived differently. Even if employees are told that the company might monitor email, web traffic, or computer activity, many employees still expect those activities to be private. Policies addressing this monitoring will be discussed later in this chapter, but the human cost of intrusive monitoring might be great, even if there are no legal barriers.

Monitoring of employee activities might also be technically difficult. For example, in most configurations, it is not possible to monitor web content if the employee connects to a secure (SSL) site. Most corporations content themselves with monitoring the connection only in that case. In a similar situation, an employee can send an encrypted email that the company will not be able to read.

Search and Wiretap Warrants

Search warrants can be used by law enforcement to seize and search computer systems. A qualified law enforcement agent can obtain a search warrant by presenting probable cause to a judge. The Electronic Communications Privacy Act, however, protects data in transit (as opposed to data stored on the computer). If the agent wants to intercept communications, he or she must obtain a wiretap order, which is much harder to obtain.

At the time of this writing, there is an organized crime case pending in New Jersey. Federal agents, using a search warrant, raided premises they believed were being used by organized crime and seized personal computers. One of the computers had files encrypted with the PGP (Pretty Good Privacy) program.

Using another search warrant, the agents placed a keystroke logger on the PCs to capture the user's pass phrase. When it was obtained, the encrypted files were used to obtain an indictment.

The defense is arguing that the keystroke logger, by its nature, intercepted data in transit because it did not (presumably) distinguish between keystrokes to files on the computer and keystrokes to, for example, email. If true, the agents would have required a wiretap order instead of a search warrant to emplace the logger.

The U.S. government has so far refused to discuss the technical details of the keystroke logger. The defendant is being supported by privacy advocates who are worried about the precedent that might be set, and the outcome of the case is being closely watched.

A number of technologies are available to monitor an employee's use of his or her computer. These products are available both in hardware and software. Companies can buy specialized monitoring tools or can use freely available tools (including trojan programs such as Back Orifice). Again, the technology and legal implications are fairly clear-cut, but the human impact might be much more subtle.

Encryption is generally treated by law enforcement as a locked container. If the agency has the legal authority to search an area (for example, a house) and finds a locked file box in the area, they can compel the owner to open the box. In the same way, if law enforcement has the right to search a computer and finds encrypted files, it can compel the owner to provide the keys.

Policies

Acceptable-use policies for employees are the starting point for managing insider risk. The company must define what constitutes the acceptable use of corporate computer resources, and employees must be made aware of these policies (and ideally should acknowledge that they have been made aware).

Policies provide a framework for investigations by defining what actions can be investigated. They can provide consent to search and monitoring (depending, of course, on other applicable laws).

Without policies in place, the organization might find it impossible to punish or terminate an employee. The employee can successfully argue that there was no explicit rule prohibiting a certain conduct, and absent that, the organization has no right to punish him or her for those actions.

Acceptable-Use Policies

Acceptable-use policies should cover obviously illegal activities such as the circulation of copyrighted or obscene material. By stating explicitly that the company will not tolerate the illegal use of its computers, it allows the company to distance itself from a single employee's misconduct.

The policy should also cover activities that might not be illegal *per se* but that might expose the company to liability. For example, the policy should cover threatening or harassing emails. There have been cases in which a company was held liable for sexual harassment when an employee either displayed sexual material in an office or cubicle (such as a calendar) or downloaded such material in a public area. Some courts have ruled that allowing such conduct was instrumental in creating a hostile environment and that the company was responsible for creating that environment because it did not immediately act to prevent such conduct when it was made aware of it.

On the other hand, the policy should *not* state that everything on an organization's computer is the property of the company. If an employee does have illegal or harassing materials on his or her computer, the organization does not want to acknowledge ownership of that material.

There is a question as to whether the policies should state that the equipment is to be used for official use only or that occasional personal use is permitted. If the company chooses to prohibit all personal use, it might find the following:

1. Employees will ignore the prohibition.

2. The policy might be held to be worthless if the company is aware that employees are ignoring it.

It might be useful in this context to view computer equipment as similar to telephones. Most companies allow occasional use of company telephones for personal business (for example, to call a daycare center or to make dinner reservations). When told that the phones are primarily to be used for business purposes and that any personal use cannot interfere with business, employees are more willing to accept such a policy.

Some corporations have adopted severe measures regarding personal use of computers, especially the use of web browsers. There are a number of reasons why a company might want to restrict web access:

1. The company does not want its name linked to certain web sites. When an employee visits an inappropriate site, the IP address might be recorded, and the company might not feel it is in its best interest from a public relations point of view to have its name linked to that site.

2. A site might be labeled as inappropriate for some reason. The company might feel that there is no legitimate business reason for an employee to visit that site during business hours.

Acceptable-Use Policies

Generalizations in policies can sometimes backfire because there often are exceptions. In a previous job, one of the authors managed a service that did Internet monitoring. A new employee was being briefed concerning the corporation's standards of conduct overview and was briefed on the company's acceptable-use policies. During the briefing, the company official stated, "You are free to visit or view any Internet site, provided there is a business reason to do so. However, there is no contract at [this company] that requires anyone here to ever visit playboy.com." The employee raised his hand and asked about his job, which involved investigating sites that other people might have visited. The official quickly stated, "I forgot about you guys, but there's no other contract that requires anyone else here to ever visit playboy.com."

One of the downsides of this particular policy is that the company chose to enforce it by blocking certain web sites at the proxy server. Employees who did have a legitimate reason to visit certain sites had to use dedicated computers that bypassed the company network and firewall. Although blocking software might be appropriate, the full impact should be considered prior to implementation.

3. The company might be concerned about productivity and lost time and might not want employees engaging in certain activities (including gambling, online trading, or buying personal articles) during business hours.

A policy should address these items. Some companies employ filtering software to help monitor and block certain sites; others leave it up to local managers. As previously stated, absent these policies, the incident response team might be severely hamstrung when it is called on to conduct an investigation into these actions.

Email Usage

Another part of the acceptable-use policy is the use of corporate email. Again, like a telephone, a company can choose to restrict email to business use only or can allow occasional personal use.

The policy should, however, address activities that are strictly prohibited, such as the sending of threatening or harassing emails. Circulation of chain letters and jokes might be prohibited if an organization feels they waste either time or bandwidth. If the organization is concerned about potential liability, the incident response process should be prepared to conduct an investigation and should know how and where to look to collect evidence and information.

Encryption

Every organization should also have an explicit policy dealing with the use of encryption. If the company provides encryption products for business use (probably a good idea, especially for people traveling with laptops), the policy should state that the keys are the property of the company and that the individual can be forced to provide them if necessary. The policy should also express the company's right to search encrypted files and volumes at any time.

Any other encryption, provided by the employee, should be prohibited. The encryption policy should prohibit the use of unauthorized encryption and should state that the employee can be forced to provide the keys. Failure to provide encryption keys or the use of unauthorized encryption products could result in termination. This topic is discussed in more detail in Chapter 9, "Forensics II." Without an explicit policy addressing the use of encryption, the team might find it impossible to collect evidence or to compel the employee to provide the keys.

Searches and Monitoring

Under U.S. law, a number of conditions can legitimize a search. For example, law enforcement can obtain a search warrant. Certain officials are permitted to search in limited circumstances to remove a threat to the public (for example, firefighters can break down a door if there is smoke coming from a room to which the door provides access). Regardless, individual can always give their consent to a search.

As part of a company's policy, the employees should be told that the organization for which they work has the authority to conduct searches (overt or covert) of their computer equipment at any time. The employees must consent to this search as a condition of employment. By obtaining consent to search at the time of employment, the individuals are aware that they can be searched and thus will have no expectation of privacy.

In a similar fashion, employees should be told that the organization for which they work has the right to monitor any and all computer activity and communications. As with searches, there are a limited set of circumstances in which communications can be monitored. Service providers are allowed to monitor communications for the purpose of maintaining and improving service. It is unlikely that monitoring web content fits under this distinction. However, by obtaining advance consent, the issue becomes moot.

The policy should state that the company might monitor any and all communications but is not obligated to do so. This will protect (or at least *help* protect) the company if unauthorized activities occur on the network and the company fails to detect them. The condition in which the company is aware of the activities and fails to address them is discussed in the liability section later in this chapter.

Unauthorized Activities

Finally, the acceptable-use policy should cover network and computer activities that are unauthorized. These might include actions that might introduce vulnerabilities into the infrastructure. For example, sharing of passwords or logins should be prohibited. This section should also address password choices. Not only will this help users in choosing and using strong passwords, it also will help in investigations. If a particular activity can be tied back to a login, for example, it is far more difficult for the user to deny the activity if the alternative is to admit to giving out his or her password.

The policy should also address the use and installation of unapproved applications and software. There are two major issues at hand. First, unapproved software can introduce technical vulnerabilities into the system. It could be infected by a trojan or could modify the network in some way (say, for example, by opening a particular port) that increases the vulnerability of the local computer or network to internal or external attack. Second, this software might be unlicensed. If there are licensing issues and the company fails to address them, it could be held liable for the unauthorized use.

The policy should also prohibit activities such as attempting to access other computers (both within the network and outside), port scanning, network mapping, and so forth. In conjunction with good intrusion-detection software around critical servers, this policy can help mitigate insider risk. If it has been explicitly banned, then any detection of scans or multiple login attempts on the network can trigger an immediate alarm and investigation. In addition, the company has enormous liability if its systems are used to illegally access outside networks. The use (and possibly possession) of hacker tools by anyone in the company (except people in the security organization) should be proscribed and should be grounds for disciplinary action.

Login Banners

Login banners should be a major ingredient in any company's use policies. These banners can remind users that the system is to be used for business purposes only and that accessing the system constitutes consent to monitoring.

There is some doubt as to the actual effectiveness of login banners as an awareness measure. Because users see them every day, they might come to ignore them. If the banners are made more intrusive (for example, a pop-up box that requires the user to clear it before proceeding), it can become even more routine. Unauthorized access might bypass the login entirely. However, a login banner that explicitly states that the system is for official use only and that use of the system implies consent to monitoring greatly increases the organization's ability to assert that a given user exceeded his or her authorization by accessing the system.

There is at least one case in which a Welsh cracker claimed he was unaware that access to the system was prohibited because there was not explicit warning given on entry. The judge, in that case, ruled against the defendant, but this line of defense could be invoked by future attackers because there are no clear precedents.[5]

There is a story that frequently circulates in security forums and at conferences concerning the wording of login banners. In the early 1980s, VMS systems announced "Welcome to . . . ." The story goes that a cracker penetrated the system and protested that he was authorized because the login "welcomed" him. Supposedly, the charges were dismissed. Variations of this story abound, but details are scarce. The author has it on good authority that this is simply an urban legend.

Liability

As stated many times in the preceding paragraphs, the potential for liability to a company is huge. A company might incur liability if it fails to prevent or react to certain conditions *and it is aware that they are occurring*. These might include the possession or dissemination of illegal or copyrighted materials, the distribution of harassing emails or documents, and the use of corporate computers for illegal activities.

To be held liable, the company must be aware that these activities are taking place. However, knowledge by one or more officers of an organization is probably sufficient to establish knowledge. Going back to the policy on monitoring, it is important to distinguish between the right to monitor and the responsibility to monitor. If the company has a policy in place that allows it to monitor activities, it could be held that the company should have known about certain activities on the network.

5. www.cnn.com/2001/TECH/internet/07/06/hacker.fbi/index.html

Best practices in security are extremely hard to define. An organization is at risk, in litigation, of being accused of not following best practices. For example, the organization could state that it does not use intrusion-detection software and was therefore unaware that certain attacks were occurring. However, if the majority of the organization's peers are using IDSs, it could be construed that the company was negligent in not employing certain control measures. It could even be interpreted that, had the company been complying with best practices, it should have known about the activity.

Unfortunately, the net effect is that a company can be liable whether or not it knew about an activity. The only advice is to attempt to mirror security practices among peer industries and to ensure that appropriate policies are in place and enforced.

Appropriate monitoring and search policies, including consent by employees to monitoring and searches, can go a long way in preventing employee lawsuits during an investigation. Although the rules of evidence are different for private organizations and in administrative proceedings, the consequences are also different. Instead of having evidence thrown out as inadmissible, an organization can be sued by the employee or union or can be prosecuted by local authorities for violating employment laws.

Proper legal counsel should always be consulted early in any incident investigation. As previously discussed, laws are changing constantly, and the precedents are unclear at best. All the legal statements in this chapter (and, in fact, in this book) are general by nature. Laws and statements are subject to change and interpretation by authorities.

Corporate legal counsel (or qualified external counsel) is a critical part of the incident response team. The counsel's objective is to protect the company by providing qualified advice about the legal issues in the incident. This includes, where appropriate, advice about the legal rights of the accused (if only to ensure that evidence is not excluded in later proceedings).

There are other potential dangers in addition to improper searches. A poorly conducted investigation, especially if the incident response team has already formed a theory, could result in punishing the wrong employee. If this happens, the company can face wrongful termination lawsuits. Even if the company has no intention of prosecuting the offender, consultation with an organization's legal and human resources can ensure that all the proper steps are taken during the investigation and subsequent administrative or disciplinary actions.

Not only can an organization be liable for the actions of employees, it also can be liable for failing to properly prevent external attacks. New regulations might require certain industries to maintain adequate safeguards of personal data; failure to do so can result in civil or criminal penalties against the organization. In addition, if personal data is compromised, the individual can always sue the organization directly.

If a high-profile attack occurs that impacts the company's earnings or reputation, shareholders can sue the company or its officers and directors and assert that the company failed to maintain fiscal responsibility by not implementing adequate defenses.

To Prosecute or Not?

One of the classic conflicts in incident response in private organizations is related to the decision of whether to prosecute or not. (In government and quasi-government organizations, the decision is usually much simpler. These organizations have much less leeway, and the decision to prosecute is probably made by a law enforcement agency, an officer of the court, or a senior officer of the agency such as the inspector general.) The decision and the decision-making process have been criticized by both industry organizations and law enforcement agencies.

Law enforcement is often viewed by industry as too quick to prosecute. It is seen as being more interested in completing a high-profile case than in assisting the company in recovering its systems, its data, or its money. Many corporations are afraid that an agency will show up, ask which systems were affected, and seize them for examination, even if they are mission-critical.

Second, an investigation means that knowledge of the incident will become public. Companies are nervous that embarrassing details about a sensitive incident might leak (or even be released by a zealous prosecutor) and might influence public opinion (and therefore market position).

On the other hand, it is a popular view among many the government and law enforcement agencies that corporations are deliberately hiding security-related incidents, even if regulations or statute require them to be reported. Some authorities have stated that large corporations often hire outside investigators and contract the work through the corporate general counsel in an attempt to protect the knowledge of the incident. If subpoenaed, the corporation and the outside team can both claim attorney-client privilege and refuse to discuss the details of the incident.

The actual truth is somewhere in between. Many senior law enforcement officials will acknowledge that they have a reputation as being heavy-handed in their conduct of investigations and that they traditionally have not been overly concerned with the business interests of the victim. In many cases, it is possible now to conduct most of the investigation without revealing the name of the affected company. Many agencies will allow the company to release the initial details or will conduct a joint press release.

Critical servers are seldom seized for a number of reasons. The investigators realize the importance of the computers to the operation of the business. Investigators might not have the knowledge to properly examine the systems (either online or off) and might ask for assistance from the company. The systems might be so large (for example, a RAID array on a transaction processing system) that it is not feasible to examine them offline. Legal precedents have evolved to the point that backups and copies of the affected systems (or even part of the systems) meet the "best evidence" criteria and are admissible.[6] Some of these issues are discussed in Chapters 8 and 9.

6. See Chapter 9 for more discussion about performing forensics on large servers.

Although the original evidence is clearly preferred, when it is unavailable, a copy is often sufficient. Corporations are also realizing the value of law enforcement assistance. In a major incident (especially one large enough to damage the company's reputation), it is likely that the details will eventually leak out. It might be preferable to release the details in a controlled fashion and to make a point that the incident is under investigation (especially if it looks like an arrest and prosecution are likely).

It might also be appropriate to prosecute offenders to make an example of them. Although the legal and social theory of criminal prosecution is to punish the criminal, companies might also view it as deterrence. If a company has a reputation for tenaciously pursuing people who commit computer crimes, the criminals might choose either to not attack the system or to attack another company instead. For example, it might be a standard, if unwritten, policy for a bank to aggressively pursue and prosecute armed robbers without considering the amount of the crime. In response, in most areas of the world, armed robbery against large corporations is relatively uncommon, and most similar organizations have similar "best practices" of protection (for example, teller cages and alarm systems).

Conclusion

Again, nothing in this chapter or book is a substitute for proper legal advice, preferably prior to the fact. A representative from the general counsel should be available to the incident response team, if not an actual member. If the corporate counsel is not well versed in the intricacies of employment law, criminal statutes, intellectual property issues, and computer crime, outside counsel might be warranted. It will be much more difficult later when dealing with law enforcement agencies to say that the team was unaware of the specific steps to follow in collecting and safeguarding evidence. It will be even more difficult later when the company is sued for failing to maintain adequate safeguards.

8

Forensics I

C OMPUTER FORENSICS, SOMETIMES REFERRED TO as cyber-forensics, is the detailed examination of computer systems in an investigation. It normally deals with storage media (such as hard and floppy disks), but it is sometimes used to refer to the examination and analysis of network logs as well. The word comes from the adjective used to describe certain legal evidence:

forensic   *adj.* Pertaining to, connected with, or used in courts of law; suitable or analogous to pleadings in court.

forensic medicine   *n.* Medicine in its relations to law; medical jurisprudence.[1]

Forensics is generally now used to refer to any systematic or scientific examination of evidence in the investigation of a crime. Network analysis is discussed elsewhere in this book; this chapter and the next will generally deal with examinations on single computers only (although those examinations might include the analysis of logs contained on the computer).

---

1. *The Oxford English Dictionary*, 2nd Edition, Oxford, Clarendon Press, 1989.

Forensics is arguably the most repeatable and scientific of the incident response disciplines. There is a certain set of rules that, if followed exactly, will make the investigation straightforward and will preserve the integrity of the evidence. The methodology of a forensics examination will not change dramatically from one investigation to the next, even when the scope of the investigation or the technology changes.

Important Note

This chapter (and the next) is not designed to make anyone a forensics expert. Incident response personnel who anticipate a requirement for computer forensics are strongly urged to get proper training before undertaking any forensics task. Improperly trained personnel can, as a minimum, destroy vital data or compromise the chain of evidence such that the information is inadmissible. They can also be held liable in civil or criminal actions if the search and seizure were improperly conducted.

Incident response personnel should be trained in the immediate steps required to secure the evidence scene until properly trained and equipped personnel arrive to conduct the investigation.

Forensics is an extremely valuable tool in the investigation of computer security incidents. It can provide the investigator with direct evidence of the incident. The evidence is difficult (but not impossible) to counterfeit, allowing for a greater confidence in its authenticity. There are, of course, certain kinds of incidents that lend themselves more readily to forensic examinations.

At the risk of stating the obvious, an incident response team can only conduct forensics on those computer systems to which it has legal access. In most corporate settings, these are limited to company-owned systems. If an insider is suspected of violating acceptable-use policies, his or her corporate workstation can be examined for evidence of those violations. If the company does not own the system, law enforcement assistance (and probable cause) is required to search the home computer. In these cases, the law enforcement agency will probably do the seizure and the forensics examination.

Acceptable-use violations are especially well suited to forensics investigations. The investigator only needs to find evidence that the policy was violated. This can be as simple as an Internet cache file or the remains of an email message. Finding evidence that a computer was used to access other systems, for example, is much more difficult.

Forensics also has certain limitations. Most importantly, a forensics examination can, at best, identify the *computer* involved in an incident. Without additional evidence (such as eyewitnesses or physical security logs), placing a specific person at that computer is an entirely different question. This issue cannot be overstated. A forensics examination that does not also involve other corroborating evidence sources cannot be conclusive.

Although it is possible to recover some deleted files from computers, tools exist to securely delete files. A skilled attacker can clean the computer of evidence. The absence of incriminating evidence on a computer does not necessarily mean it was not involved in the incident. In some cases, the complete lack of any evidence, however, might indicate that these tools were used and might justify further examinations.

Even without the use of these tools, the evidence might be overwritten through normal usage. Internet browsers retain a history of sites they have visited for a finite period of time (typically two to three weeks). After that time, the history files are overwritten and might not be recoverable. Cache files are overwritten as needed. Windows swap files are overwritten during normal usage, and items written to memory in the swap file might not be available for examination, especially if the computer has been rebooted.

Disk and Data Structures

Disk drives are made up of platters covered in a magnetic media. A hard drive has one or more platters, arranged in a stack. The platters spin at a high rate, on the order of 7,200 to 10,000rpm. There are small sensors that read and write the data to the drive. These "heads" float on a tiny cushion of air above the platters. Hard drives are extremely sensitive to dust or shock. If the heads touch the spinning platters, it causes a "head crash" that can destroy the data on the disk. For this reason, a forensics investigator should never attempt to open or examine a hard disk without the proper tools and environment.

When the disk is formatted, the operating system divides the disk into logical, pie-shaped units known as *sectors*. Sectors contain a number of units called *clusters*. The size of a cluster is defined by the overall size of the disk and the operating system. Data is stored in these clusters. When a file is created, the operating system writes the data to the disk. It also writes the location or address of the data clusters to a special table. This table is generically called a *file allocation table (FAT)*. When data is written, the operating system allocates clusters to the data. A cluster could, for example, be 512 bytes in size. If a 1024-byte file is created, it will use two complete clusters. If, however, a 1032-byte file is created, it will use three complete clusters, even though that will leave unused data space in the third cluster. This unused space is known as *file slack*.

When files are deleted, the data is not overwritten. Instead, the file system simply marks the clusters as available. The next time the system needs to create a file, it can use these clusters (or any other available clusters). Therefore, when files are deleted, the data might still be present on the disk and be recoverable by forensics tools unless it has been overwritten. Even if it has been partially overwritten, the new file might not fully use the file slack from the old file, so some fragments of data might still be present. So-called *secure delete programs* work by overwriting the files multiple times with random data.

The longer a disk is in use, however, the more likely it is that deleted files will be overwritten. Even the act of booting the machine might create temporary files that can destroy critical evidence. Preservation of the evidence requires that it be seized and protected from modification or damage as quickly as possible following the incident.

Finally, without a clear understanding of the incident and the desired outcome, it is extremely difficult to conduct a forensics examination. The investigators need to clearly understand the scope of the investigation and plan the examination clearly. For example, a user might be accused of posting insider information to a public stock forum (such as RagingBull or Yahoo!). As part of the investigation, the computer might be examined for items in the browser history that show that the user visited the site *at the date and time of the posting.* This could help corroborate other evidence, but the user could simply claim that he was looking at a publicly available stock forum. Unless the URLs in the history clearly delineate between the forum itself and the pages used to post or reply to messages, the evidence is inconclusive. Furthermore, the dates and times on the history files are based on the local system, while those on the posting are based on the web server. If the computer clock has been reset, no correlation is possible. The forensics examiner must plan the investigation carefully in coordination with the rest of the incident response team to narrow the search to an acceptable scope and to define what constitutes a successful (or unsuccessful) conclusion.

All this assumes, of course, that the investigator is dealing with a relatively unsophisticated user. A suspect is certainly capable of modifying or deleting log, cache, and history files. He or she can also modify the MAC (Modify, Access, Create) dates on any files. Although it might be possible to use data-recovery tools to retrieve some of these deleted files, they can be overwritten or deleted beyond recovery by a skillful user.

Guiding Principles

There are two major categories of principles in the conduct of computer forensics. Both are designed to protect the investigator, the evidence, and the rights of the accused.

Ethics

First, the investigator must have the authority to seize and search the computer. In corporate settings, this is normally granted by policy. The company acceptable-use policy should state that the company has the right to conduct a search on any or all company equipment, at any time, for any reason. (Note: Government agencies and contractors working for government agencies might have different requirements. IRT personnel should consult with their legal counsel prior to drafting policies.)

Second, the search should have clearly defined goals. "Fishing expeditions," in which a computer is searched for any evidence of any wrongdoing, have the potential to dramatically impact employee morale. Although the company probably has the legal right to randomly search company assets at any time, this will likely be perceived by employees as an unreasonable invasion of privacy.

Legal Statements in this Chapter

All legal statements in this chapter are generalizations based on best practices in the forensics field and U.S. law. All statements are subject to interpretation and modification by local authorities. Second, as in most areas of computer crime, the legal precedents are unclear and constantly changing. Always consult with legal counsel before undertaking any forensics examination.

Conduct of the Examination

There are basic rules to be followed in the conduct of any forensics examination. Although sometimes the specific situation might require an exception to these rules (some exceptions are covered in Chapter 11, "The Human Side of Incident Response"), following these rules will make any eventual legal proceeding much more likely to succeed.

When computer forensics was first introduced, investigators found themselves defending their actions during the course of the examination. In the same way that the defense attempted (and succeeded) to cast doubt on the purity of the DNA evidence in the O.J. Simpson trial, an attorney might attempt to convince the court that the computer evidence has been tampered with or tainted by the investigation. The following rules are designed to make it more difficult to tamper with evidence:

1. The examination should never be performed on the original media. An exact copy is made of the media, the original is then secured as evidence, and all examinations are performed on the copy.

2. The copy is made onto forensically sterile media. This means that the target media either is new and still in the shrink-wrap or has been cleaned of all old data. Given the relatively low cost of storage today, new media should always be used if available.

3. The copy of the evidence must be an exact, bit-by-bit copy. A simple DOS copy is not sufficient because it will not include deleted files, file slack, and other information.

4. The computer and the data on it must be protected during the acquisition of the media to ensure that the data is not modified. This includes ensuring that the computer operating system does not access the evidence disk at any point in the examination. Specific requirements for media acquisition are provided in the section "Media Acquisition Tools," later in this chapter, but the computer must never be allowed to boot up using the evidence drive.

5. The examination must be conducted in such a way as to prevent any modification of the evidence. Simply viewing a file will change the attributes of that file. When it is not possible to prevent data modifications, it is even more important to perform the examination on a copy of the media.

6. The chain of custody of all evidence must be clearly maintained to provide an audit log of who might have accessed the evidence and at what time.

Fortunately, there are checklists and guidelines that provide assistance in maintaining these rules. Some of the forensics software described later in this chapter is specifically designed, for example, to protect the original files from modification.

Forensics Hardware

If an incident response team anticipates conducting forensics examinations, it should acquire a dedicated forensics platform. This computer does not need to be particularly powerful; in most cases, the limiting factor in conducting an investigation is I/O speed, not processor power. The computer should be set up to accommodate most likely configurations; specialized equipment can be added as needed.

Standard Corporate Desktop

Most of this section (and indeed, most of this chapter) assumes that the standard corporate desktop is an Intel or compatible clone, running some version of Microsoft Windows. UNIX investigations will be discussed further in Chapter 9, "Forensics II," although most of the basic techniques in this chapter are applicable to UNIX desktop systems. If the company has Macintosh systems, it will require a dedicated Macintosh forensics platform.

- **CPU.** With Moore's Law showing no signs of slowing, it is difficult to state the minimum or appropriate CPU speed. However, a CPU similar to the standard desktop configuration in the company should be sufficient. The CPU needs to be able to run the operating system and forensics software, so consulting those manufacturers for compatibility is recommended. It might also need to run some desktop software. If the company has high-end or proprietary applications (for example, graphics or CAD), the machine should be capable of running these applications as required to view data files.

- **Motherboard.** Because the system might be modified as needed by adding other components, the main board should have several available slots. The BIOS needs to be as current as possible to recognize large storage devices. It might be preferable to custom-build the forensics computer to ensure that the system has as open an architecture as possible.

- **Case and cables.** The computer should have a case design that allows for easy access to the drive bays and expansion slots. A tower configuration, with multiple vacant drive bays and sides that remove completely, is preferred. The computer should have extra power cables available to add additional storage devices or peripherals and multiple IDE or SCSI control cables.

- **Storage.** The computer needs a primary disk drive capable of storing the operating systems and the software. More important than the primary disk is the capability to add multiple secondary disk drives. One or more of these secondary drives will be used for the storage of evidence as it is processed. Other drives might be the evidence drives themselves (more on this later). SCSI drives are recommended for their I/O speed, but the computer must be able to mount IDE drives as well.

- **Floppy drives.** The computer needs the capability to read from floppy drives during the course of the investigation. Typically these will be 3.5″ high-density drives, but if the company uses other removable media such as ZIP disks or 3.5″ super drives, the computer should have one of these drives mounted as well. Although 5.25″ drives have all but disappeared from the corporate environment, it might be wise to procure a 5.25″ drive while they are still available and mount it in the forensics computer just in case an investigation turns up older floppies.

- **CD writer.** A CD writer can be used to read in evidence from CD-ROMs as needed. It can also be used to record evidence during the investigation. If the CDs are closed at the end of the writing process, they can be used to demonstrate that the evidence was not modified during the period between the investigation and the eventual legal or administrative hearing. This is not a substitute for proper evidence handling and storage, but it is valuable as an additional demonstration of the authenticity of the evidence.

- **Tape drives.** If the company uses tape drives for backup, a compatible drive is useful. If the population of tape drives in the company is small or varied, a drive can be added later if an investigation requires it.

- **Network card or modem.** It might be useful to be able to transfer files or data from the forensics computer to other systems. It is also useful to be able to access the Internet for system and software updates. However, these benefits must be weighed against the risk that a networked computer is inherently more vulnerable to unauthorized access. Even if the system is properly secured, the perception that an unauthorized person might have accessed the system and modified the data might be harmful when attempting to demonstrate proper evidence safeguards. If the system is networked, it is recommended that networking be disabled at any time during an actual examination of the evidence.

- **Operating system.** The computer must be capable of reading any media or file system likely to be collected. The most common Windows file systems are FAT, FAT32, and NTFS. At the present time, only Windows 2000 is capable of reading all these systems. As an alternative, the forensics computer can be set up to dual-boot to both Windows 95/98 and NT. If other files systems such as Linux are in common usage, the system should be set up to boot to them as well. Some of the forensics packages discussed later in this chapter provide the investigator with the capability to overcome these limitations. For example, data could be imaged from an NTFS drive using EnCase and then be viewed and examined using EnCase under Windows 98. If, however, the drive is restored, an NT or 2000 system will be required to read the drive.

It is also possible to buy dedicated forensics machines from vendors. A quick Internet search on computer forensics will provide several links if the response team wants to buy a ready-made machine instead of building one from scratch.

Forensics Software

Specialized tools are available for the acquisition of the forensics media, the recovery of data from that media, and the searching and cataloging of that data. An investigation team should be trained in the use of a standard suite but should be familiar with other tools as well. Case law on the admissibility of software is mixed. At one time, the investigator would be asked to personally validate the source code of the tools used. Many of the tools discussed in this chapter do not provide their source code. However, the vendors might be willing to provide expert testimony if requested or might be able to provide other information (such as case precedents) if this is an issue. Some forensics training courses and texts refer to "generally accepted forensics tools." However, there does not seem to be a consensus in the investigative community (at least at the time of this writing) as to what those generally accepted tools are. The best advice is to use commercially available tools that have a track record of successful use in litigation and prosecution, and to not rely on custom or internally developed techniques unless the investigator is prepared to personally testify as to their effectiveness and reliability.

Product Information

Nothing in this section or chapter is intended to act as an endorsement of any particular product. Information on these products is current as of the time of writing, is provided for informational purposes only, and is not intended to be exhaustive. Other competing products might also be available, and product specifications are subject to change without notice.

Media Acquisition Tools

When acquiring the media for examination, there are two major considerations. First, the software must make an exact, bit-by-bit copy. Without this, any evidence in deleted files will be lost. It will also be extremely difficult to defend the evidence in any proceedings unless an exact copy is obtained. Second, the software must not modify the original data in any way. Most media-acquisition tools accomplish both objectives by loading a trusted operating system that is used to copy the data from the original disk to a destination drive or drives.

- **Hardware-copying devices.** Although it is possible to use a dedicated drive-copying machine, these generally are not recommended. They usually are limited as to the size or characteristics of the disks they can clone, so they are not as flexible as software-copying tools. However, if an organization has such a machine (possibly used for building and distributing desktop PC configurations), it could be used to make a copy.

- **Disk-cloning software.** A number of readily available tools can clone a hard disk, or a partition, from one disk to another. These are generally sold not as forensics tools but as tools used when upgrading or replacing a disk drive. For example, DriveCopy by PowerQuest (www.powerquest.com) "can easily copy the entire contents of your old hard drive to your new one. DriveCopy copies every setting, preference, and byte of data, including hidden files. No more guessing or worrying if everything was copied."[2] The issue with tools like this is that they might not make an exact, bit-by-bit copy. This can make it difficult to defend the sanctity of the evidence. However, they can be useful in certain circumstances (for example, if the evidence disk needs to be replaced so that the suspect can continue working).

- **SafeBack.** SafeBack (www.forensics-intl.com) was developed specifically to make exact imaged copies for forensics purposes. It enables the investigator to copy the drive to another drive or to removable storage (such as ZIP disks or tape). The image then can be either examined directly using some search tools or restored to a target hard disk for examination. The tool can image any file system, provided the drive is running on (or can be mounted on) an X86-based system because the tool addresses the drive at the partition level, not the file system. SafeBack certifies that the copy it makes is an exact, bit-by-bit copy of the original. The tool streams the data from the source drive to the target. This bit stream can then be restored to another drive (provided, of course, that the target is at least as large as the original).

Search Tools

Searching the evidence requires both a capable search tool and a careful plan on what to search for. File viewers are invaluable during the search phase. File viewers include those bundled as part of other suites (such as Norton Utilities) as well as dedicated viewers such as QuickView Plus.

Disk editors can also be useful during search and analysis. Norton Disk Editor has been the de facto standard for years. Hex editors are useful to examine file fragments for text strings.

Some other software tools can be used during the search phase as well. For example, the file search capability within Windows can be used to find files containing text strings. The *grep* utility (available in UNIX and NT) also provides this capability.

Any tool that examines the drive at the operating system level, however, will modify the data. This means, for example, that a tool can be used to find certain files and examine them, but the date and time stamps will not be reliable after the files have been viewed.

---

2. DriveCopy Product Specification Sheet, http://a480.g.akamai.net/7/480/2667/6d12701a048fb0/www.powerquest.com/drivecopy/DC3_EI_spec.pdf.

Some specialized search tools have been developed for law enforcement use to search and categorize images. These are generally used to search for pornography on seized systems. They are not available to the general public, but the investigator might see them if assisting a law enforcement agency.

- **DiskSearch Pro.** DiskSearch (www.forensics-intl.com) is a text search program used to search evidence drives for strings of text embedded within files. It also provides the capability to search both deleted files and file slack. DiskSearch supports all types of FAT file systems.

Integrated Suites

A number of integrated software suites provide the capability to acquire data, perform searches, and produce reports.

- **Byte Back.** Byte Back (www.toolsthatwork.com) provides the capability to write-protect the evidence media during acquisition. It also provides analysis of the physical and logical structure of the disk. It enables the analyst to do rudimentary searches of the evidence for certain data and enables files to be viewed as either HEX or ASCII. Byte Back supports FAT16, FAT32, and NTFS drives. (Note: Most, if not all, of these suites can acquire data from other file systems but cannot do analysis on those systems.)

- **DriveSpy.** DriveSpy (www.digitalintel.com) also provides the capability to block any writes to the evidence disk during acquisition. The tool calculates an MD5 hash of the disk to verify that the final copy is exactly the same as the original evidence. The software also provides some search capabilities, both at the physical and the logical layers. DriveSpy supports FAT disks only.

- **EnCase.** EnCase (www.guidancesoftware.com) is arguably the most widely used forensics software suite, at least for Windows. The tool enables the investigator to copy the original disks (which are write-protected during the process) to multiple files using a proprietary compression algorithm. These files can then be either analyzed directly using the tool or used to create a clone of the original disk. Each file is hashed during creation, and the hash is verified during the analysis portion. The tool has extensive keyword searching capabilities and also allows for certain file viewing plug-ins (for example, to view graphics files). EnCase supports FAT16, FAT32, NTFS, Linux (EXT2), and Macintosh (HFS and HFS+). The tool also has an extensive reporting capability.

- **Expert Witness.** Expert Witness (www.asrdata.com) enables the investigator to make an exact, bit-by-bit copy of the original evidence. The tool supports multiple file systems for Macintosh, including HFS, HFS+, FAT12, FAT16, UFS, ISO9660, and EXT2. It accesses the drives at a level below the file system.

Acquiring Evidence

The most commonly accepted principles for seizing computer systems are defined in the U.S. Justice Department's guidelines for search and seizure of electronic evidence. The most recent of version of these guidelines, however, seems to concentrate almost entirely on obtaining and executing search warrants and much less on the physical seizure of equipment and data. The complete document, called *Searching and Seizing Computers and Obtaining Electronic Evidence*, is available on the department's web site at www.usdoj.gov/criminal/cybercrime/searchmanual.htm. Earlier versions might still be archived on the Web and provide extensive technical details about searches.

The basic rules are to (1) document everything that the investigator does and (2) take all appropriate steps to ensure that the evidence itself is not compromised in any way (or in the least way possible) during the acquisition. In most situations, the evidence is copied and then the actual evidence disk itself is secured. All analysis is performed on the copy. There are situations in which the evidence might be modified or the examination must be performed on the actual media. These situations are covered in more detail in the next chapter.

Acquiring the data generally consists of securing the system, conducting an examination of the system and its surroundings, copying the media, and securing the evidence. In most configurations, the following steps will preserve the evidence and provide the investigator with any data he might require later (see Figure 8.1 and following list):

1. **Secure the physical area.** Take photographs of the system, including monitor and the back of the case, showing all the cable connections. Take photographs of any papers, disks, or peripherals in the immediate area. Inventory and collect any papers or disks that might be involved or might contain evidence.

2. **Shut down the system.** Unplug the machine from its power supply. *Do not* touch the keyboard, use the power button on the machine, or otherwise tell the system to do a graceful shutdown. Shutting down the operating system might trigger logic bombs designed to destroy evidence. It will definitely modify or destroy data in virtual memory.

3. **Secure the system.** If the computer is to be seized intact, it should be sealed before it is moved to the examination area. Insert a blank, write-protected floppy disk or a floppy-size piece of cardboard into the floppy drives. Label all cables and connectors prior to disconnecting any. Place evidence tape across the floppy drive, the power button, and all cable connectors.

4. **Prepare the system.** If the computer is not seized, or when the system is examined later in the laboratory, open the case. Take photographs of the inside of the computer prior to disconnecting any cables. Disconnect the power leads from all hard drives. Start the system and go to the setup menu.

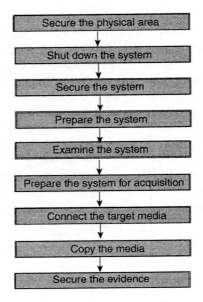

Figure 8.1   Steps taken to secure the system.

5. **Examine the system.** Check the Setup menu for the current system date and time. Record the date and time, comparing it against a known standard. This is important later in correlating file timestamps to other evidence.

Entering the Setup Menu

The command to enter the setup menu varies depending on the particular hardware and BIOS. For example, IBM laptops enter setup by depressing the F1 key and holding it down while the system is powered up. Other systems use the Delete key, the F2 key, or some combination of keys such as Ctrl+Alt+Insert. If the investigator is not familiar with the system, the manufacturer's documentation (probably available on the manufacturer's web site) should be consulted prior to the examination. Because a boot from the hard disk will irretrievably modify the data, it is extremely important that the hard disk power leads be disconnected prior to this first boot.

6. **Prepare the system for acquisition.** Change the boot sequence in the BIOS to boot from the floppy drive. If possible, the system should boot from the floppy only. If this is not offered as an option, the sequence should be floppy and then hard drive.

7. **Connect the target media.** Place a forensically clean drive into the system to use as a target disk. If possible, this disk should be set as Disk 1, with the original drive as Disk 2. This will also help prevent the system from booting to the original disk. Place a forensics boot disk containing the acquisition software in the floppy drive. Boot the system and make sure it does boot to the floppy and that it recognizes the target disk. Power the system down and reconnect the original drive power leads.

8. **Copy the media.** Boot the system again, using the forensics floppy. Use the software on this floppy to copy the original drive to the target. If time permits, it is always a good idea to make a second copy at this time as well.

9. **Secure the evidence.** Remove all drives from the system, place them into anti-static bags (never use plastic zip-lock bags), and seal them with evidence tape. Date and sign the evidence tape and secure the drives in a locked container.

Examination of the Evidence

The acquisition of the media, although tedious, is generally clear-cut. A trained investigator, following a set of rules, can be reasonably certain that the data was acquired properly and is not tainted. Examining the evidence to find proof of wrong-doing, however, can be anything but straightforward.

Planning the Search

The most important step in the examination is to plan what items to search for. A poorly designed search will result in either no results at all or so many results that they are unusable. A well-designed search consists of unique items that are unlikely to occur outside the scope of the investigation but that are also likely to be present in any incriminating evidence. This might be a simple task, but it is often anything but. The examples in the sidebar are useful to illustrate this.

Search Examples

Misuse of company resources: The suspect is accused of using the company computer and Internet connection to visit adult web sites and download images. In this case, the search criterion is simple. The investigator needs only to demonstrate that the suspect did visit these sites. Any unique image or fragment of an image might be sufficient to establish this. One of the simplest things the investigator might search for is image files, including files in the browser cache (and deleted files). The investigator can also search the history and bookmark files for URLs, cookies from the sites, and the Windows Registry for connection data. Any items found are probably conclusive to demonstrate that the computer, at least, was used to visit those sites. Placing the person at the computer might involve several additional steps. For example, network logon records, physical security records, or eyewitness accounts can be used to correlate to the date stamps on the recovered files.

continues

continued

Harassing or inappropriate email: The suspect is accused of sending harassing emails to other persons. A search of the mail server logs might be inconclusive or inconvenient. A direct search of the user's computer is always valuable in any event to provide corroborating evidence. The first place the investigator might choose to look would be the actual mail client files. Many of these are encrypted or use some proprietary format that cannot be read without the proper software. The investigator might have to copy the mail files to the forensics machine and open them using the mail client to view old messages. If this is unsuccessful, a possible next step would be to search the computer (first all the files and then all the deleted files and slack space) for text fragments that correspond to the offending emails. The keywords for the text search must be refined to provide a complete search without returning an overly large (and unmanageable) number of "hits." Each successful search must then be manually examined, in the context of the surrounding file fragments, to determine whether it provides a match to a pattern from the email or is simply a false positive.

File Recovery

As part of the examination, data might be found in file fragments or file slack. To examine this data in context, it is often necessary to recover the deleted files. Most of the forensics suites described in this chapter provide a recovery capability. File recovery is often a hit or miss proposition, however. File header information might be missing and contain vital information. For example, the text of a word processing document could be recovered in its entirety, but the header information that contains data (such as the name of the creator and "Undo" information) might be unavailable.

Image files are especially difficult to reconstruct because they are often highly compressed. Fragments missing from image files might make it impossible to decode the compression and view the file.

In any case, viewing the recovered file can provide a clearer picture of the evidence, along with surrounding data. Some of the forensics tools can provide date and time information for deleted files, including a created, modified, and deleted date (which might be useful in establishing a pattern during the investigation).

Operating System Files

Certain operating system files might contain crucial evidence. The Windows Registry, for example, might contain information such as recently accessed files, system usernames and passwords, and network connections. Some files can be viewed or examined on other systems. For example, Windows NT stores some logging information in event log files with an .evt extension. Any NT machine can open and examine those files.

Other information, however, is not so readily accessible. The Registry is the best example of this. Much of the information in the Windows Registry cannot be accessed unless the operating system is running. In this case, it is necessary to restore the entire evidence drive to a backup copy and then use this copy to boot up a machine for examination. This copy will be irreversibly altered by the boot process.

However, the investigator should be able to demonstrate empirically that the copy produces the same Registry information every time and that the specific data recovered is not modified by the boot and examination process.

Conclusions

Computer forensics is a vital tool in incident response. It has the potential to provide conclusive evidence in an investigation and to assist in corroborating other evidence. It is, however, a discipline for the trained professional only. Well-meaning amateurs can cause irreparable damage to the evidence and should not be allowed to conduct an investigation without the proper training.

Fingerprints on the Floppy

There was a suspected case of sabotage at a U.S. government site. All the Macintosh file servers had the contents of their hard drives erased. During the investigation, a floppy disk labeled "OOPS BOOM" was discovered in an adjacent room. One of the investigators ran the program on a test machine and found that it erased the contents of the hard drive. Never examine or test the actual evidence.

Based on the location of the floppy and access to the file servers, the team suspected a summer intern. They contacted the FBI to conduct the investigation. When the FBI agents arrived and attempted to test the floppy disk for fingerprints, they found that so many people had handled the disk by that point that any fingerprints were unusable. Furthermore, the disk had been handled and tested by so many people without any controls that its contents also could not be verified. Preservation of the evidence is paramount. Investigation kits should contain latex gloves and evidence bags for the acquisition and storage of evidence.

It also has the potential to be an enormous task. When computers had small (or even no) hard drives, it was feasible to conduct a sector-by-sector search. When computers were relatively uncommon, it was feasible to seize a company computer and search it. When an entire team has computers, and each of those computers has a very large hard drive, the search task can become overwhelming. If the incident is not particularly serious, if the range of suspects cannot be constrained to a manageable number, or if the amount of data cannot be reduced to a controllable amount, management should ask whether it is an effective use of resources (internal or external) to conduct an in-depth investigation on potentially terabytes of data.

The fundamental limitation of forensics cannot be overstated. Computer forensics can, at best, identify that a specific computer might have been involved. At that point, the forensics investigator must then look for other sources of evidence to place the person at that computer at the time of the incident.

The forensics examination can provide the incident response team with additional evidence. This evidence, even if inconclusive *per se*, can be valuable when interviewing potential suspects or when viewed in the context of a complete investigation including physical security logs, network logs, eye witnesses, and other factors.

9

Forensics II

ALTHOUGH A FORENSICS EXAMINATION MIGHT BE TEDIOUS, it is generally a straightforward process. A trained investigator can, by following a standard set of rules, be reasonably assured that most of the incriminating data in the media will be found and the evidence will be admissible. However, there are special cases in which the standard guidelines cannot be followed without variation or the situation presents unique considerations.

For example, the investigator might be asked to conduct a search without alerting the suspect or suspects that the search was occurring. In such a case, the team is not able to seize the computer without the subject's knowledge. The team might also be asked to investigate systems that cannot, for one reason or another, be taken offline.

Companies might also have legacy systems or applications that might be involved in an incident. Although conventional forensics might be able to recover some data, if the data is in some sort of proprietary format, recovery alone is insufficient. It is possible that the only system capable of reading or interpreting the data is the system under investigation. Even the hardware might be proprietary or obsolete. In one incident, some evidence data was stored on 5.25-inch floppy disks. However, the forensics equipment had no 5.25-inch floppy drives available. An older PC, destined for the trash heap, had to be cannibalized to provide a method of recovering the data.

Covert Searches

A company might be able to narrow down the range of suspects to a small group. For example, network logs might indicate that harassing emails came from a specific subnet, but logs might be unavailable to further refine the specific client. Access logs might implicate a certain group of administrators, all of whom had a common administrator account. The company could choose to call in all of the suspects, advise them of the situation, and seize their computers for examination. The company could also decide to examine the computers covertly without the employees' knowledge. A company can also choose to covertly examine a computer if it doesn't want to directly confront the employee until it has more evidence.

In such a covert search, there are two major considerations (neither of which is related to forensics). First, the company must have the authority to conduct such a search. In most cases, if the system is owned by the company, it has this authority and does not require the explicit consent of the employee.[1] Second, the company should carefully consider the human implications of conducting an unannounced, covert search on its employees. It is likely that employees will eventually discover that such a search occurred. Those employees who were searched might feel that the company violated their trust, and there might be significant human costs to such an action.

There are two major ways to conduct a covert search. The first, and most invasive, is to make an exact copy of the computer's hard drive and place that replacement copy back into the computer. The original drive is then preserved as evidence and is used to make further copies for forensics examination. Other than the fact that a replacement drive is provided and the actual replacement occurs without the user's knowledge, this is essentially a standard forensics search.

The second option is to make a copy of the disk for examination while leaving the original disk in the computer. Although this does not preserve the evidence on the original drive, it could be used to conduct an initial examination to determine which computer or computers warrants further investigation. The disk can be removed for copying and then replaced, or tools can be used to make imaged copies via an external cable (such as a parallel cable). SafeBack and EnCase (discussed in the preceding chapter) both support this method. Note, however, that imaging a large disk over a null modem cable takes an extremely long time (on the order of one to two hours per gigabyte), so this method might be difficult if the time window is small.

It is also possible, using some tools, to make an imaged copy of the computer over a network connection. Given that the target computer will be running at the time, it is unlikely that this image will be an exact copy. The admissibility of such a copy has yet to be challenged, but it is probable that a skilled attorney, using expert witnesses, can cast significant doubt as to its accuracy. However, if this copy is used for an initial search, a true image can be made later (using more conventional methods) for the formal investigation.

---

1. Again, the disclaimer about legal advice applies. Consult with competent legal counsel before undertaking any action involving search or seizure.

Prior to conducting a covert search, the company must develop a cover story. The story should explain the presence of people in the facility during nonworking hours and any minor changes or disturbances they cause that might be noticed by employees. For example, if a user shuts down his computer, it is a simple task to remove the hard drive for examination. If, however, he locks the workstation, it must first be shut down. When the imaging task is complete, the workstation could be rebooted but will not display the Locked Workstation screen. The employee might wonder why his computer was rebooted during the night. The company could advise all employees that facility maintenance personnel are making modifications to the power equipment and that all power will be shut off for a brief period. Employees would be told to shut down all computers prior to leaving for the evening. It is highly recommended that, after the examination is complete, the power actually be cycled to reset all clocks and any computers not examined (otherwise, the employees might wonder why nothing else was reset).

Advanced Searches

Even if the search does not require covert access, there might be cases in which the basic techniques described in the preceding chapter might not be feasible. For example, the machine in question might have had a hardware failure, or it might have some nonstandard storage configuration that prevents a direct disk-to-disk copy.

Hardware Recovery

Occasionally, an investigator might be asked to recover data from damaged media. The media might be physically damaged (either intentionally or unintentionally) or might have suffered some logical damage such as the deletion of files or a reformat. Most of the forensics tools discussed in the preceding chapter offer the capability to recover deleted files and data from file slack. If a drive was repartitioned, it might be possible to recover some or most of the data using forensics techniques.

Recovering physically damaged media is beyond the scope of both this book and most forensics investigators. There are stories about investigators, for example, taking a damaged floppy disk and gluing it to a blank disk for recovery. However, the chances of further damaging the data on the drive are extremely high. Hard disks are extremely sensitive to damage from dust, and a well-intentioned but poorly equipped recovery that does not have the proper environment will certainly damage the disk further.

If an investigator is tasked with data recovery from a damaged disk, it is recommended that qualified data-recovery specialists be consulted. The recovery rate of these services is extremely high, and some of them offer a forensics option in which they will handle the media and recovery process according to the federal rules of evidence. The incident response team, if it anticipates a requirement for data recovery, should coordinate with a service in advance. The IT operations or business continuity planning organizations might already have an arrangement with such a service.

Laptops

Until recently, portable computers were uncommon in the corporate environment. However, with a mobile workforce and a tendency toward telecommuting, more companies are issuing notebook computers as the corporate standard configuration. These computers might include docking stations, external keyboards and monitors, and even external storage such as additional hard drives. Although desktop computers have a generally standard hardware configuration, notebooks tend toward proprietary components. A desktop hard drive will almost certainly use a standard IDE or SCSI interface and can be imaged on the suspect machine or placed into the forensics computer for copying and examination. Notebook computer drives are much smaller and have non-standard pin configurations. Most notebook drives use a single connector for both the IDE controller and the power supply, whereas standard IDE has a 40-pin cable for the controller and a separate 5-pin power cable.

In some situations, it is possible to adapt a notebook drive to a standard IDE cable. Cables N Mor (`www.cablesnmor.com`) offers an adaptor for 44-pin, 2.5-inch notebook drives that will allow the investigator to connect a standard IDE drive cable. Figure 9.1 shows a picture of this device in use.

Figure 9.1   A notebook IDE adapter[2].

2. Picture courtesy of Cables N Mor, `http://cablesnmor.com/f26500.html`.

The IBM ThinkPad series also has a 44-pin connector, but the pin-out is different. However, IBM offers a docking station that includes spare IDE bays. The notebook can simply be placed in the docking station with the target disk in one of the spare drive bays for imaging.

Another alternative is to copy the data to an alternate source using a parallel or serial port. SafeBack and EnCase (discussed in the preceding chapter) both allow the investigator to connect peripherals such as ZIP drives to the computer and copy the data to the external peripheral. EnCase also supports what it calls a "client-server mode," in which the source computer is connected with a parallel or serial null modem cable to the forensics machine and the data is copied over the cable. As previously discussed, however, both of these techniques take an extremely long time to run because of the limited data transfer speed through the ports. A direct connection using an adapter is preferable from a speed standpoint. It also might be more defendable if the accuracy of the copy becomes an issue. Again, if this is perceived to be an issue, the incident response team might want to consult the software vendor for assistance, including expert testimony if required.

Another issue with laptops might be the problem of a power supply. If the laptop drive cannot be mounted to another system using one of the aforementioned adapters, the data must be copied using the laptop itself. If the power supply is unavailable, however, the investigator must be able to provide an alternate. If the team perceives that it might be called on to perform laptop forensics, it can provide power supplies to the forensics lab. An adjustable power supply with multiple adapters is one alternative. Care must be taken, however, to ensure that the output power has the correct voltage and polarity to avoid damaging the laptop (and evidence). Another alternative is to procure a universal power supply designed for multiple systems. Computer supply vendors often carry such systems for business travelers, and a universal system with multiple adapter plugs can be obtained for less than $150.

Older Systems

It is possible that an investigator might be called on to perform forensics on older legacy systems. For example, a company might be using older systems as thin clients, or it might have legacy applications that only run on certain platforms. Specific requirements for imaging and searching legacy systems will vary widely. It might be as simple as finding a drive capable of reading the disks, or it might be as complex as a file system incompatible with the forensics machine.

If the data is stored on a media that can be recognized by an x86-based system, imaging the data is simply a matter of mounting the media onto a forensics box and using imaging software. If, however, the medium is in some proprietary format, imaging might be difficult or impossible. The vendor, if still in business, might be able to help with conversion or connection software or hardware. Some data-recovery services also have the capability to extract data from legacy hardware.

If the data can be successfully imaged but uses a file system not recognized by the forensics software, an investigation is still possible using a disk editor. By accessing the disk structure directly, the investigator can search for ASCII text fragments. A more detailed search is probably not possible without building a custom machine running the same operating system as the target.

Personal Digital Assistants

Personal digital assistants (PDAs) are becoming more popular in the corporate environment. If the corporation provides the device, it should have the authority to search it (with, of course, the usual disclaimers). If, however, the user has provided the device and has connected it to his or her work computer, the issue is much less clear. As always, competent legal counsel should be consulted. Arguably, the data (or some of it) might belong to the company if, for example, the PDA is downloading corporate email for offline reading. The admissibility of a forensics search of a PDA has not, as of the time of this writing, been challenged, so the legal precedents as to issues such as bit-by-bit copies are still unclear.

PDAs can be standalone devices without the capability to connect to a computer. More often, however, they share and synchronize data with a desktop machine. Some might include removable storage or networking capabilities. Most store data in flash memory as opposed to conventional disks (although IBM makes a hard drive capable of fitting in a Compact Flash slot).

The investigator has two alternatives when searching a PDA. The device can be synchronized or backed up to the forensics computer and the data examined there, or the device can be examined on its own. In practice, both alternatives are recommended. Any removable data store should be removed and imaged separately. For example, a Compact Flash card can be removed and mounted using either a PCMCIA card or an external adaptor. It can then be imaged using forensics software and examined like any other disk image.

The device should then be connected and a full backup made. This backup can be examined using a hex editor. Depending on the format, ASCII text might be visible within the backup file. If not, it can be restored to a clean PDA for examination offline. There are shareware programs available that directly access various PDA database files. Although this might yield valuable evidence, it should be confirmed by other sources (such as a search of the user's computer or an interview with the subject) because the admissibility of this evidence might be suspect.

Finally, the PDA itself should be searched. Some models (for example, models running versions of Microsoft Windows) can be mounted to the forensics machine as a virtual device and examined using the forensics software. Others must be searched manually by using the email, text editor, and other programs supplied on the device.

Encryption

Strong encryption systems using sophisticated algorithms are readily available as both free downloads and commercial products. The company might choose to use its own encryption to protect sensitive data (for example, laptops that are vulnerable to theft). Office automation programs, such as email and word processing, provide some encryption capabilities within the application.

As a general rule, law enforcement and the legal profession tend to treat encrypted files as locked containers. If the investigator has the authority to search the device, he has the authority to compel the owner to provide the encryption keys. In the corporate environment, the acceptable-use policy should address the use of encryption products (both authorized and unauthorized) on corporate systems. Encryption keys and pass phrases for corporate systems (including email and encrypted file systems) are the property of the company, and the policy should explicitly state that the company can require the user to provide the key or pass phrase. Failure to provide the keys can result in termination.

Unauthorized encryption should also be explicitly addressed in the policy. As a general recommendation, the policy should state that any encryption programs or files not provided by the company are unauthorized and that the company, again, has the authority to compel the user to provide the keys.

Some commonly available encryption schemes provide little protection. The PKZIP format provides the capability to encrypt archives. This format, however, is vulnerable to certain types of attack, and programs can be downloaded to extract the files. Microsoft Office programs also use a weak encryption scheme, and programs and services to defeat the encryption are available either free or commercially. Bokler Corporation, a company that makes strong encryption tools for developers, has an excellent page on the weakness of some of these products and offers links to password-recovery services at `www.bokler.com/bokler/bsw_crak.html`. Some of these services include Access Data (`www.accessdata.com`), Crak Software (`www.crak.com`), and Passware (`www.lostpassword.com`).

If the user chooses a strong encryption algorithm, it is probably not feasible to defeat the encryption. For all the talk about the weakness of 56-bit DES, it is almost certainly not cost-effective to attempt a brute force attack. However, a major weakness of PC-based encryption is that the plain text must exist on the computer at some point. A search for deleted files and file fragments might reveal, for example, the temporary files used by the word-processing program when the file was created. A search of the temporary directories (including browser cache) and the virtual memory file might also yield results. A recent thread on the BugTraq vulnerability forum addressed the Windows 2000 Encrypted File System. In some configurations, plain text files are written to disk when used and might not be completely purged.[3]

3. More information on this is available at `www.securityfocus.com/frames/?content=/vdb/bottom.html%3Fvid%3D2243`.

Steganography

Steganography, from the Greek *steganos* (hidden) and *graphy* (writing), is a method of concealing information within other files. Computer files contain redundant or insignificant bits of data within their file structure. Steganography works by replacing those data bits with content. The file appears unchanged to the casual viewer, but the hidden data can be extracted through the use of a key. Steganogaphy can be viewed as the digital equivalent of invisible ink.

Free and shareware programs are available to hide files or content and to detect it as well. The security of a steganographic algorithm is, like any form of encryption, dependent on both the algorithm and the key. Better programs use robust keys, similar to DES or Triple-DES. Poor programs use either known algorithms or short keys.

Steganography is also used in digital watermarking. An identifying piece of content can be inserted within an image or multimedia file. The content does not discernibly change the file and would be unnoticed by an observer. With the proper key, however, the "watermark" can be recovered to demonstrate the original ownership of the file.

The major problem with steganography as an alternative to more conventional forms of cryptography is that the amount of hidden content has to be small in comparison to the size of the file exchanged. Although it could be used, for example, to hide a pass phrase or some critical piece of information about the company, large documents would require an extremely large file to conceal it.

Some shareware tools can detect hidden content, depending on the algorithm used. These might be valuable to the investigator. More information and links to some of the tools are maintained at a web site called www.stegoarchive.com.

In addition, if the original file can be obtained, it can be compared through the use of a hash algorithm to detect whether it was modified in any way. For example, a person might take an MP3 audio file and conceal a small image file within it. The hash of the original audio file would be different from the one containing the image, however, and further investigation might be warranted at that point.

Home Use Systems

The practice of telecommuting is growing. Whether this involves an employee who works from home full or part-time or employees who simply have the capability to access their mail and files remotely, this introduces new risks into the environment.

If the home computer is provided by the company, the company probably has the authority to search the computer. This almost certainly does not extend to the authority to seize the computer. The employee must provide the system for examination. If the employee refuses, this is grounds for either separation or prosecution.

The problem with this is obvious. The employee knows that an investigation is underway and has the time and opportunity to clean incriminating evidence from the computer prior to turning it over. It might be possible to craft a cover story ("Turn in your home computer so we can upgrade the email software"), but it is likely that the employee will suspect something.

If the system belongs to the employee, the company has no inherent authority to search. The only recourse in this case is to seek the assistance of law enforcement. If the company can make a convincing case for prosecution and can provide sufficient probable cause for a search, the law enforcement authorities can seize the computer with a warrant. In this case, the authorities will almost certainly conduct the forensics examination as well. The incident response team might be asked to assist (and should volunteer to do so) by providing specific information on which to search. There is a risk to this option because a search of the computer by law enforcement might discover other information unrelated to the original incident. This information could carry liability to the company. Examples include copies of pirated software or pornography if it is determined that the company was aware of its presence and failed to act on this knowledge.

UNIX and Server Forensics

Until this point, the assumption has been that the target computer is some sort of PC or workstation, probably running a version of Microsoft Windows. Regardless of the version, PC forensics is generally the same whether the computer runs DOS, Windows NT, or Windows 95. UNIX, however, offers some significant challenges to the investigator.

UNIX has both advantages and disadvantages for power users. It is a simpler operating system than Windows in that it has fewer layers between the hardware and the end user. Configuration files tend to be text-based as opposed to some sort of binary. There are literally no restrictions on the power of the superuser account. These same advantages can make UNIX both more difficult and easier to conduct forensics.

UNIX is Different

One of the fundamental differences between UNIX and PC operating systems is the general simplicity of the system. Because UNIX is an open system, internal operations of binaries, libraries, and networking protocols are well documented. The disadvantage of this is that many tools exist to modify system binaries to allow remote access, hide network traces, and conceal evidence of intrusions.

On the other hand, UNIX offers some advantages to the investigator. A drive or partition can be mounted read-only for analysis. If a trusted version of the operating system is used, the investigator has complete control over the media, including the capability to view and analyze hidden and system files.

Imaging UNIX Workstations

In some cases, imaging a workstation is no different from imaging a PC. If the workstation is x86-based, the investigator can simply insert a blank drive, boot from the forensics floppy, and use one of the tools in Chapter 8, "Forensics I," to make an image of the disk for later analysis. If the workstation has a different processor but has a disk drive that can be mounted in the forensics computer (for example, a SCSI disk), the investigator can still make an imaged copy.

UNIX Forensics Workstations

If the incident response team anticipates a requirement for UNIX forensics, it might be worthwhile to build or procure a dedicated workstation. This can be either a normal workstation (perhaps with additional tape drives or spare drive bays) or a custom-built machine.

If the company has a standard configuration and most of the likely target systems are similar, using a standard workstation is recommended. This will allow compromised drives to be examined using the same operating system and will allow direct comparisons of system binaries.

If the company is running multiple versions of UNIX, however, a custom forensics machine might be in order. Linux is recommended as the operating system because it supports multiple file systems. The file system types currently supported are listed in linux/fs/filesystems.c: adfs, affs, autofs, coda, qnx4, romfs, smbfs, sysv, udf, ufs, umsdos, vfat, xenix, and xiafs.[4]

The hardware requirements for a PC forensics workstation (as discussed in Chapter 8) are sufficient, although a SCSI card and tape drives will probably be required as well.

This copy can be examined to some extent by using the forensics software to search the disk at the hardware level for text fragments. More detailed examination, however, will not be possible without an operating system that can read the file system. The first imaged copy can be used to make multiple backup copies that can then be analyzed on another platform.

If it is not feasible to make an image this way, the investigator can use native UNIX utilities. The best utility for copying UNIX partitions is the dd command, which makes a complete copy (including deleted files and slack space). This copy can be then restored to a clean partition on the forensics machine or can be examined directly (see the sidebar about Linux loopback devices).

Linux Loopback Devices

LINUX supports the use of loopback devices, in which a file system can be contained inside a file. This is extremely useful when examining backups. A dd copy can be made of the target computer. That file can then be mounted in a Linux machine as a virtual file system. If the copy of the root partition from a Solaris system is contained in a file called c0t3d0s0.dd, the image can be mounted (read-only):

```
mount -o ro,loop,ufstype=sun -t ufs c0t3d0s0.dd /mnt
```

This will yield a complete copy—protected from modification because it is read-only—of the root partition under /mnt on the Linux system. Because Linux can read the Solaris file system, the Linux machine can then be used to examine the data. The Linux copy would, of course, contain its own binaries that are trusted for the purposes of the examination, so trojans in the Solaris binaries can by bypassed.

---

4. From the Linux man pages for *mount*.

The rule of thumb when shutting down a personal computer is to simply pull the power cord. This is also the simplest, and probably safest, technique with a UNIX workstation as well. It does, however, have some drawbacks:

- Any data that has not yet been flushed to disk will be lost.
- Running processes will be lost.
- Current network state information will not be available.

The investigator might choose to cautiously examine the machine prior to shutdown to find out information such as last logon, processes running, active network connections, and open file handles. However, the risks to a graceful shutdown are also high:

- The attacker might have inserted trojans into the shutdown command to delete logs or other evidence.
- The /tmp directory will be flushed.
- Common commands might also have been modified to either destroy evidence or provide incorrect information.

The investigator must assess the benefits of securing this information prior to the shutdown and weigh this against the suspected skill of the attacker. When in doubt, a crash shutdown by pulling the plug is less likely to destroy evidence than a graceful shutdown.

In some cases, a dd copy might not be feasible. Backup copies using tar or cpio might be alternatives, understanding that significant evidence such as file slack will not be preserved. It is also possible to remove the disk drive and mount it as a separate read-only device in another machine. This is not recommended because any error by the investigator can result in the destruction of the original evidence. It is far safer to make an imaged copy and perform all analysis on the copy. If the drive can be successfully moved from one machine to another, it should be possible to make a copy as well.

UNIX Analysis

Most analysis of UNIX systems is performed using native UNIX utilities. Disks can be examined using a disk editor regardless of the operating system or file system, and it might be prudent to use one of the forensics tools from the preceding chapter for this portion of the search, if only to be able to state that the tools used were commonly accepted in the field of forensics.

Binary Files

The fundamental rule of forensics is to never examine a drive using its own operating system. With a Windows machine, this is done to prevent two major issues:

1. The very act of using the machine will modify the disk and data in unpredictable ways.
2. The operating system on a compromised machine might have been modified so that it either will not reveal data or will destroy it.

These two problems exist in UNIX as well, although the relative severity of the two is probably reversed. RootKit tools exist for all major UNIX variants. These tools allow an attacker to do the following:

- Hide his or her login and command history
- Hide any processes running under his or her control
- Hide any files and directories owned by the attacker
- Hide open network sockets
- Log in at any time with an unknown name and password

These tools work by replacing such system binaries as `login`, `ps`, and `ls`. For this reason, all the binaries in a compromised system must be assumed to be untrusted and must not be used in the examination.

The simplest way to conduct this examination is to mount the disk (the copy, of course, not the original) as a separate read-only file system on a separate machine. Ideally, this separate machine should have the same operating system (and the same patch level) as the suspect machine so that binaries and configuration files can be compared for possible modifications. In practice, this is usually not possible.

One of the basic steps in the examination of UNIX systems is to look for compromised or modified system files. The simplest way to do this is to use a tool such as Tripwire that makes a cryptographic hash of all the critical files. If the current hash is different, the file has been modified. Obviously, this supposes that Tripwire was installed on the machine prior to the compromise.

Failing that, the second choice is a direct comparison with known files. Again, this supposes that a machine with the same configuration and operating system is available (with exactly the same patch level). This might also be impossible. Sun is developing a database of MD5 checksums for all standard releases of Solaris at various patch levels, but this tool is not yet available.

The final option is to manually inspect the system binaries. This is generally done by using the `strings` command to search for ASCII text within the binary. For example, the `/bin/login` command has no readable text within it. If the `strings` command provides any output, the program has been compromised. Even if an exact copy of the binary cannot be found, the strings output between a clean and a compromised copy will be similar. However, it is trivial for a sophisticated attacker to disguise the text within a binary. The absence of output should not be considered conclusive.

Configuration Files and Logs

The next step is to look at logs and configuration files on the target machine. These include system logs such as `sulog`, files that control services such as `inetd.conf`, and system text files such as `/etc/passwd`. If an examination of any of these logs reveals a suspicious user account, its home directory should be carefully searched for hidden files, `.rhosts`, or shell history files. Any odd or unusual binary files should be examined with the `strings` command as well.

One potential problem with using another machine to examine the system is that all file ownership information comes from the trusted machine, not the imaged disk. The investigator must manually compare user IDs and group IDs to determine the actual owner of the files. The Coroner's Toolkit, discussed in the following sidebar, provides a way to directly determine the ownership of the files.

The Coroner's Toolkit

The Coroner's Toolkit (TCT) was developed by Dan Farmer and Wietse Venema. It provides tools for the search and investigation of UNIX file systems. The three major tools are as follows:

- **grave-robber.** This tool scans the file system for i-node information, which is then used by the other tools.

- **unrm and lazarus.** These tools can recover deleted file space and search it for data. Unlike the forensics tools discussed in Chapter 8, these tools do not allow the investigator to preview the data. They simply recover all deleted data to an available file system.

- **mactime.** This program traverses the file system and produces a listing of all files based on the modification, access, and change timestamps from the i-node information. It accepts the target system's password file as input, so it will yield the true owner of the files.

The kit is available as source code with instructions. The current version as of May 2001 is 1.06. TCT can be downloaded from www.fish.com/tct/.

System files that have been modified or that show strange ownership permissions are immediately suspect. A well-documented change-management program can be invaluable in this task. If the system documentation can enumerate all authorized changes, including the dates, the investigator's task is much simpler.

A good business continuity plan with periodic backups is also important. The standard procedure for restoring a compromised system is either to restore from a known, clean backup or to rebuild the system from clean media. Neither is possible unless backups are current and the system configuration is documented.

Servers and Server Farms

When the incident involves a large server that cannot be taken offline or that has so much storage that it cannot be successfully imaged (or that has RAID, so an image is technically not feasible), the investigator has no choice but to perform the analysis online. The best option is still to perform some sort of backup, at least of the suspected files and logs, and analyze them offline. A tape backup will not include all the information such as file slack, but this might be the only alternative.

Working on a compromised machine, especially if it is still online, is a high-risk proposition. Because none of the system binaries can be trusted and because the attacker might have planted tools to destroy evidence, the investigator must proceed very carefully. Documentation is extremely important, if only to record what happened during the investigation as a protection from future liability.

The specific steps in analyzing a mission-critical system are beyond the scope of this book. The most important step, however, is a frank discussion of the potential risks with the business managers. The system owners must be aware of all the potential dangers inherent in this action, and they must be willing to accept the risks. System owners might be under pressure to keep critical servers online. If this is the decision, it is the responsibility of the incident response team to provide management with enough information to make an informed decision. The final determination lies with business management, not with the incident response team. The following are some possible risks:

- Unrecoverable damage to the server operating system or data
- Loss of evidence
- Alerting the attacker to the investigation

On the other hand, the system might be so critical that taking it offline will cause the company a greater loss (either in lost revenues or in public embarrassment). The final decision must lie with the affected business owners.

Conclusions

Although computer forensics might be a technically simple task, the exact steps can be difficult to follow in every case. The "best evidence" rule must be considered when the situation prevents the investigator from exactly following the standard steps. In most cases, if the investigator takes a certain degree of care to protect the evidence from modification and tampering and can demonstrate why certain steps were omitted, the evidence will probably still be admissible.

Advanced forensics, however, should also be considered the realm of the properly trained expert, not the well-intentioned amateur. The risk of destroying evidence, damaging critical machines, and exposing the company to liability is high. When in doubt, the incident response team should limit itself to securing the area and the evidence and should rely on expert outside assistance in the actual investigation.

Again, where large volumes of data are available or where the incident response team does not have specific expertise on the suspect machine, outside assistance might be invaluable. In other cases, IT operations might have the only available knowledge of proprietary applications or legacy systems. Assuming that there are no reasons to exclude operations personnel (that is, they are not suspects), these administrators can be vital in the conduct of the investigation. When they must be excluded, the incident response team must accept (and inform management) that it might not be possible to completely examine all the data.

10

Responding to Insider Attacks

INSIDER ATTACKS CONSTITUTE A SPECIAL, CHALLENGING situation for an incident response team. Insiders already have access to sensitive systems, access that might include a high degree of privilege. These people are, at least nominally, trusted. The attacks are often difficult to detect. Intrusion detection systems might be unable to distinguish an attack from a normal pattern of behavior. In fact, the theft and removal of data might not even qualify as an attack in the technical sense. Everyone who investigates might be a potential suspect.

An insider attack can be defined as the intentional misuse of computer systems by users who are authorized to access those systems and networks. It is often difficult to distinguish intentional misuse from simple human error. Insiders might be employees, contractors, temporary help, or even customers or business partners. This definition ignores attacks by ex-employees or by employees who are not specifically authorized to access systems, but those attacks share some characteristics with more classic insider attacks as well.

This chapter will discuss the specific challenges of preparing for and responding to insider attacks, along with measures that might mitigate their impact. It will present various types of insiders and attacks and will discuss legal considerations that should be discussed when preparing a response.

Early statistics on computer security incidents stated that insider attacks accounted for the majority of incidents. In recent years, this has apparently declined. The 2000 Computer Security Institute study stated, "Survey results illustrate that computer crime threats to large corporations and government agencies come from both inside and outside their electronic perimeters, confirming the trend in previous years. Seventy-one percent of respondents detected unauthorized access by insiders. But for the third year in a row, more respondents (59%) cited their Internet connection as a frequent point of attack than cited their internal systems as a frequent point of attack (38%)."[1] There is some question as to whether this is due to an increase in external attacks or simply better detection. In any case, insiders can still cause the greatest damage. The same survey reported that the most serious cases involved the theft of proprietary information (66 respondents reported $66,708,000).[2]

Statistics on insider attacks are poor. There has been almost no research on the characteristics of the insider problem. To complicate this, information sharing among victims is extremely rare, so most data is anecdotal at best.

Types of Insiders

There are as many motivations for insider attacks as for external attackers. Traditional insider attacks are often perpetrated by disgruntled employees. Employees might feel threatened by management changes, mergers or acquisitions, downsizing, promotions (or lack thereof), evaluations, personal conflicts with other employees, or almost anything that causes stress in the workplace. A threatened employee is in the perfect position to attack the company from within. These attacks can range from the destruction of systems or data to the theft or sale of confidential information.

Security personnel, including the incident response team, are not immune to these feelings. These personnel are especially dangerous because they have access to the most sensitive systems and are in a position to detect and block any investigation. In the same way that Robert Hanssen was able to hide for 15 years as a spy in the FBI, a security administrator knows the techniques, personnel, and policies that can be used in an investigation.

Rogue System Administrators

A system administrator can be perhaps the most dangerous of insiders. The administrator has privileged access to the critical systems. He or she often is a member of the incident response team or at least has knowledge of ongoing investigations and procedures.

System administrators are subject to the same motivations as any employee. They can be passed over for promotions or be downsized. In addition, skilled administrators often have a disdain for people who are less technically proficient. If another employee, who might be perceived as less technically qualified, receives a promotion or pay raise, the administrator might feel slighted.

1. Computer Security Institute, *Computer Crime and Security Survey*, March 22, 2000, www.gocsi.com/prelea_000321.htm.
   2. *Ibid.*

Administrators often have a God-like complex. This is especially true in companies in which the technology is not well understood by the average employee or manager. The administrator might believe that he alone possess the necessary skills to keep the company running. He might feel a sense of ownership of company systems and networks. Although these motivations are not necessarily bad in most settings and can, in fact, contribute to a strong work ethic, they can also create a feeling that any actions the administrator might take are justified because the systems "belong" to him.

This is true whether the administrator is acting to "protect" the systems from other users or is taking some sort of revenge against the company. Administrators might, for example, change system passwords if they feel other users or administrators are not qualified. They might also plant logic bombs or destroy systems or data if they feel threatened. They might bypass controls or policies simply to "get the job done," especially if they believe those controls either do not apply to them (because of their superior technical skill) or are impairing the smooth functioning of the systems.

Investigating an administrator is especially challenging. Administrators can monitor and frustrate the investigation:

- Skilled administrators can detect monitoring efforts and thwart them.

- They can modify or delete logs.

- They can enlist the aid of other technical personnel to act as allies. This might include technical members of the incident response team.

It is often wise to bring in outside expertise when investigating a system administrator. This expertise can ensure that the administrator and other members of the operations group (and the incident response team) are not aware that an investigation is occurring. These outsiders can also serve as an outside audit of the investigation. This is useful in demonstrating due care during and following the investigation. It might be prudent to relieve the administrator of privileged access during the course of the investigation. Of course, if access is removed or restricted, the person will know that something is going on. In this case, he or she should be briefed that an investigation is ongoing and that access will be restored upon completion.

Interviewing a system administrator can be a difficult task. The administrator might have a low tolerance for people perceived as technically unqualified. Physical security personnel, especially if they have a law enforcement background, can be viewed with contempt. The administrator might refuse to cooperate. He also might lie, especially about his technical actions. The interviewer might not be able to detect these lies. Human resources personnel, although often trained in interviewing techniques, might suffer the same shortcomings if they are perceived as technically clueless. An interview team should include both people skilled in the techniques of talking to subjects and people with the technical skills to understand the answers. Another administrator can often establish a dialogue or a relationship with the subject. However, this administrator must be completely trusted. It might be wise to rely on external assistance in this case.

If an employee has been terminated, the danger is not over. Oftentimes, employees who either leave or are fired can still access corporate systems. This might be because their accounts are not cancelled when they leave or because they either install a "back door" into the systems or work with a person still inside the company to gain access.

A back door can be as simple as the installation of a trojan such as Back Orifice or NetBus on a system. It can also involve the compromise of remote access servers or the installation of unauthorized modems.

If another employee is assisting, an outsider can gain access in any number of ways. Any kind of network traffic can be tunneled through legitimate ports such as mail (25) or web (80). To the network IDS, this traffic appears to be legitimate and will be neither detected nor blocked. However, the intruder can remotely control computers inside the corporate firewall or transfer data at will.

Employees might also be motivated simply by financial considerations. An employee might be providing data to competitors and might also be providing remote access. The outside organization could be a competitor, a government agency, or an organized crime syndicate. In certain areas of the world, companies receive economic intelligence from their country's intelligence services. These services are not above using traditional spying methods (such as insiders) to provide them with data. There are apocryphal stories about Russian organized crime breaking into financial institutions to steal money. There are also stories about the syndicates transferring money *into* the institution to launder it.

There are three classic indicators of an insider attack. The attacker often spends more time on the job than average. He might also have a lower than average salary and might display overt signs of dissatisfaction. These people often are introverted and have poor social skills. They might, however, have high technical skills. Some of the characteristics of potential attackers are often shared by dedicated developers and system administrators. If the attack is conducted with a degree of stealth, it is impossible to distinguish a skilled attack by an administrator from the normal performance of his job.

Types of Attacks

Insider attacks can manifest themselves in all the same forms as external attacks, as well as some additional variations. An insider is perfectly placed to cause a massive denial of service to other users. This can take the form of traditional network-based denial-of-service attacks such as SYN floods. These are extremely simple to detect, however, and router and network logs will quickly pinpoint the attacker.

An insider can also deny service by launching other attacks. Some operating system vulnerabilities can only be exploited by a user with a valid logon to the system; others might normally be blocked at the corporate firewall. For example, there is a vulnerability in Windows 2000 in which a user can send a malformed Remote Procedure Call (RPC) packet to a critical server and cause it to stop responding to requests for service. Under normal configurations, this would not be a major vulnerability because the RPC port would normally be blocked by the corporate firewall. If the attacker is already located behind the firewall, however, the attack can cripple a corporate network until the server is restarted.[3]

---

3. Microsoft Corporation, *Microsoft Security Bulletin (MS00-066), Patch Available for "Malformed RPC Packet" Vulnerability*, `www.microsoft.com/technet/security/bulletin/MS00-066.asp`, September 11, 2000.

An attacker can even cause a major slowdown in service by simply using a large amount of network resources, such as copying large files to a network drive or sending large email attachments to everyone in the company. Insider denial-of-service attacks are extremely easy to detect (assuming, of course, that the company has IDSs or network-monitoring tools on the network). The attacker could download a virus such as Melissa and purposely infect himself to disrupt network services. It is probably easier to divert suspicion by performing an act that can reasonably be viewed as negligent as opposed to criminal.

A rogue system administrator could change system passwords or delete critical system files. He could delete or withhold encryption keys. In one incident, a system administrator coded a shell script to clean up temporary log files each day. The script ran automatically and recursively deleted all the files in the log directory. The script failed to check the current directory before running and caused several critical servers to fail when it was run from the root directory. An administrator with root access could easily set up such a script and cause it to run either on a schedule or when a certain condition occurs (for example, when a person's supervisor logs in).

Like external attacks, insiders can also steal or misuse computer resources. This can range from inappropriate use of corporate computers to actual theft of hardware and software. Clearly defined and well-understood policies on appropriate and inappropriate usage will help mitigate the business risks and provide a framework for the appropriate disciplinary action if required.

Some employees have gone so far as to run a business on their company computers. Although an employee keeping a spreadsheet for his home-based business on a company computer might not carry a lot of risk, employees running web-based gambling sites or on-the-side consulting practices can consume corporate resources (not the least of which is employee time). They can also carry liability for the company if a customer or legal authority decides that hosting the employee's "other job" constitutes an endorsement of the service or product.

Other improper use of computing resources can consist of visiting inappropriate web sites, downloading data (including copyrighted or illegal material), or sending threatening emails. Downloading illegal material (such as child pornography or pirated software or music) can result in both civil and criminal actions against the company, especially if it is determined that the company was aware of the actions and failed to act on them. Companies can choose to block unauthorized sites (such as adult or hacker sites) at the web proxy server. They can also monitor web traffic and warn users who visit these sites.

Users who post to Internet bulletin boards should be cautioned against using company computers to post because it might tie the company name to the posting. System administrators and developers might post comments to technical bulletin boards or newsgroups. Often developers might ask a technical group for assistance with a particular problem. In doing so, however, they reveal sensitive configuration information about company systems that can be later used by an attacker. They might also respond to postings by other persons and provide answers or assistance (even including code fragments). If this code is found to be faulty, the company can bear some liability for the employee's actions.

Threatening or inappropriate emails can carry liability for the company. Employees should be cautioned against posting or sending nonbusiness-related emails from company systems. It is hard to enforce a policy that strictly states that any personal use of company email systems is prohibited, but a reasonable compromise might be a policy that states that the systems are for business use primarily and that personal use should be only occasional. The policy should also enumerate what constitutes inappropriate usage of email systems, such as the spreading of viruses, sending chain letters, posting offensive content, and so on. The policy should *not* state that all data and messages on company systems are the property of the company. Doing so could make an organization liable for employee misconduct if, for example, an employee sends harassing emails to an external party. The company, in this case, would not want to claim ownership of the offending messages.

Employees can also use company computers as platforms to launch attacks. These attacks can be against either company computers or external systems. Attacks against other computers on the internal network might be motivated by a desire for revenge, simple curiosity, or a drive to gain information for personal gain. System administrators, because of their privileged status, are able to monitor network traffic, map users' drives, and read their email. Care should be taken when conducting sensitive discussions such as salary negotiations, potential reorganization or downsizing, or business planning unless participants are confident that administrators are not reading them.

Systems are also vulnerable to physical theft. Employees can steal laptops, disk drives, monitors, and other peripherals. Theft of memory chips is especially common in many high-tech companies. The chips might be taken home for personal use, or the employee might simply be "upgrading" his company system at the expense of others.

The theft of proprietary or sensitive company data is perhaps the greatest threat that an insider can pose. The employee might have legitimate access to the data or might gain access either by hacking into other computers or by stealing paper documents from printers, copiers, fax machines, or wastebaskets. If an employee is determined to send data out of the company, there is virtually nothing that can be done to stop it. The employee can email the data directly to a competitor. If email is monitored, the person can use a web-based email service such as Hotmail. If email is monitored for content, he can change the names and extensions of files, add files to zip archives, or encrypt files prior to transmission.

Encryption poses a special challenge because it can restrict the company's capability to search for sensitive data or evidence of abuse. Companies should address the use of personal encryption products in their usage policies so that employees know that unauthorized encryption will not be tolerated. Authorized encryption products can be a strong safeguard, especially for a traveling work force with laptops. However, the company must have a key recovery or escrow policy in case the employee is terminated or forgets the password. In some jurisdictions, the presence of encryption tools might open up the company to criminal liability. Some European and Asian countries, for example, do not allow any encryption products to be brought into the country unless the encryption keys are provided to authorities.

Employees can also remove data from the premises without using the network. They can copy it to floppies, CD-ROMs, or high-capacity disks such as JAZ or ZIP. With the advent of personal data assistants, it is now possible to copy large quantities of data (over 256MB at the time of this writing) to removable data storage on a PDA. With the right setup, this can even be done via infrared transfer without any wiring or direct connection. The data can be stored on a small card less than 2 inches square.

Data, even if it is not provided directly to competitors, can be extremely embarrassing or damaging to a company's reputation. Internal documents about potential mergers or downsizing have been posted to stock bulletin boards, resulting in a loss of stock value. Forged documents have also been posted. Even if the documents are not true, the company might be forced to respond to them, and the reputation or stock value might still suffer.

Employees can also pose as external attackers. At the time of this writing, there had been an increase in the number of extortion attempts against companies. Attackers would break into the systems, extract some data, and then threaten to either release the data or repeat the break-in unless the company paid them. In one incident, an insider removed sensitive data and then posed as an external attacker in an extortion attempt. The data could only have been obtained by someone with access to the computer systems, so the company was forced to take the threat seriously. An audit of the affected systems, however, indicated that it was extremely unlikely that the attack had occurred from outside the network. The investigation was shifted to concentrate on insiders who had access to the data.

Preparing for Insider Attacks

Good preparation is the key in responding to an insider attack. The most critical preparation step is the development and implementation of policies. These policies should spell out acceptable and unacceptable behavior by employees. They should explicitly address system administrators and others with elevated privileges. The policies should have senior management buy-in. They might, for example, be signed by either the CEO or a direct report.

The policies must be distributed to all employees, who should then acknowledge receipt of them. For example, the policies could be distributed during employee orientation, and employees could be required to sign a statement confirming that they have received, read, and understood the policies. These policies should cover the rights and authorities of the company with respect to monitoring and ownership of critical data. They should state that the company has the right to conduct electronic monitoring of network traffic and company-owned computer systems. They should not state that the company necessarily *will* monitor all traffic, but that it has the right to do so.

Appropriate prescreening of employees, including background and credit checks or contacting references and former employers, might be helpful in identifying potential attackers. Obviously, procedures for this must be in place beforehand, and appropriate input from the human resources and legal departments is critical in defining what screening is appropriate (and legal) in the context. Periodic rescreening is also helpful to identify employees who might have developed problems during their employment. This is not infallible, as in the cases of Aldrich Ames and Robert Hanssen, both of whom were able to circumvent or evade periodic rescreening over several years.

The appropriate hardware and software to conduct monitoring should be installed, and procedures to review the data should be implemented. If periodic reviews are a normal business practice, the data gathered by those reviews is much more likely to be admissible if the company chooses to prosecute or litigate later.

Physical access to critical systems should be controlled. Many serious vulnerabilities require some level of physical access. For example, a person with console access can use readily available hacker tools to change the administrator password on a Windows NT server. It is a fundamental principal of security that no system is secure if unrestricted physical access is allowed. Physical access to network hardware is also critical. An attacker could plug a laptop into a vacant network port and conceal it behind furniture to sniff network traffic. The wiring closet and switch room should be guarded as closely as the server rooms or data center.

Detecting Insider Attacks

Detection of insider attacks is extremely difficult. A skilled and patient insider can develop and execute an attack that is indistinguishable from either human error or normal patterns of behavior. Intrusion-detection systems might not be able to determine that a very slow probe is, in fact, an attack.

Network IDSs are generally designed to detect (and possibly block) conventional, external, network-based attacks. IDSs might require extensive modification to the rule sets to detect a stealthy probe. They should be placed at critical junctures around sensitive servers. Even if they are not successful in detecting and preventing an internal attack, the logs produced can be invaluable during a later investigation, especially if the IDS is a separate, standalone system that a potential attacker (even with root or administrator privileges on the network) cannot access or modify.

System IDSs to detect changes in critical data or system files should also be in place. This can consist of specific products that periodically hash system files to detect changes to binaries (the best-known of these is probably Tripwire). It can also consist of data-logging tools such as the data access and auditing facilities included in database management systems or email servers. Again, these tools are not always useful in detecting an ongoing incident, but they can be invaluable in providing evidence during the investigation stage.

Host-Based Intrusion Detection
Host-based IDSs consist of tools designed to detect changes to systems. The best known of these is probably Tripwire. Tripwire is designed for UNIX systems, but similar products (both free and commercial) exist for Windows systems as well.

These systems examine critical system files and construct a cryptographic hash of the files. The hashes are stored offline. Investigators can compare the hashes of the files on the system with this baseline set to determine whether an attacker has modified any files on the system.

Security of the baseline hash set is paramount because an attacker could simply create new hashes of the modified files. The hash set should be copied on removable media and physically secured in a locked container.

If the company is using network-based IDSs to detect insiders, these systems should also be secured. When possible, the engines should communicate to the IDS console on a secured link, outside of the normal network infrastructure. These systems are vulnerable to an attacker who either wants to conceal his or her actions or might want to use the system to gather intelligence about the network.

Unusual access, access during nonworking times, or access by system or unused accounts is often indicative of insider attacks. System accounts that have no normal user associated with them should be heavily logged and monitored. Accounting logs that have been disabled or logs that have unexplained time gaps are also indicators of an attack.

As a challenge, most suspicious occurrences will not be attacks. A previous example was a shell script used to clean up temporary files. When this script ran from the wrong directory and crashed several critical servers simultaneously, the first assumption was that it had to be an insider attack because of the nature of the servers.

Human detection is often the most reliable indicator of an insider attack. Employees should be trained to detect indicators of an attack, including technical indicators such as changed passwords or the last login message that displays when they access their accounts. They should be aware of their work environment and alert to signs of discontent. Correlating technical indicators with the real-life work environment is critical, but it is often extremely hard to implement.

Responding to Insider Attacks

Although the methods used in responding to an external attack are still valuable, some special techniques are especially useful in insider attacks. Computer forensics is possibly the most specialized of these. Forensics is discussed further in other chapters, but it has special applicability to insider attacks. First, the computer used in an attack probably belongs to the company, so there is generally no issue about search and seizure. The company might have physical control of the computer (less so when the computer is a laptop). If the investigation is to be conducted without the subject's knowledge, the company can arrange a "black bag" job in which the drive is imaged during the night or weekend and the forensics conducted offsite. The important thing to remember about forensics is that they can be extremely time consuming and often produce circumstantial evidence but not a "smoking gun." They are useful, however, in providing information to be used later in an interview with the subject, even if conclusive evidence is not discovered. Because it might not be clear who is involved (or who might be involved) in an incident, proper evidence handling is especially critical. (This is discussed in more detail in the forensics chapters.) Offsite storage might be wise, especially if the company cannot guarantee a secure evidence-storage facility.

Interviews are also unique to insider attacks; the suspect can be questioned about his actions. Human resources and the legal department should be consulted prior to questioning because the employee might have certain rights under an employment agreement. The choice of interviewers is not a simple one. For example, physical security personnel might be skilled in interviewing most subjects but might not have the technical skills to establish a rapport with a system administrator. If the interview becomes too accusatory or hostile, it is unlikely to produce results. If the incident response team does not have access to a skilled interviewer, bringing in outside assets is probably wise.

Profiling of attacks can be a valuable tool in assisting the investigation. Profiling is discussed in more detail in Chapter 11, "The Human Side of Incident Response," but some dangers are inherent in the profiling process, especially in insider investigations. The people involved might have preconceived notions that might impair their judgment. Because they are closely involved with the investigation and know the people, they might be quick to form opinions that might later turn out to be faulty. Here are some other concerns about profiling:

1. Believing that there is one "hacker" profile and suspecting the insider that most resembles the popular stereotype

2. Coming to a conclusion too quickly and blaming the wrong employee, which can lead to a wrongful termination

3. Constructing the profile without technical input and cooperation

Physical security personnel and physical access logs can be vital tools in the conduct of the investigation. Physical access logs are critical in taking an investigation to the last step—that of placing the person at the computer at the time of the incident. Computer forensics might be capable of identifying the "guilty" computer but cannot, by itself, pinpoint the person.

Depending on the particular composition of the incident response team and the corporate culture, an insider attack might require the team to work closely with operations personnel. Both management and operations will have to be consulted, for example, before taking a critical server offline to conduct forensics. Operations might already have hardware or software in place or might have access to resources that can be vital in the investigation. This includes both trained personnel (who are intimately familiar with the operating environment) and access to the hardware and systems required to conduct monitoring of network traffic. Obviously, if a member of the operations group is suspected, the coordination becomes much more difficult. It might require, for example, that a single trusted person within operations provide access to logs or network traffic. The difficulties of conducting a technical investigation on a live system in which the administrator is suspected cannot be overstated. This person can, at the very least, detect the investigation and delete or modify logs. At worst, the person can retaliate by destroying or corrupting evidence to implicate a third party or even destroying the system under investigation.

Monitoring of employees is a sensitive subject, but an insider attack lends itself to increased monitoring. This can be monitoring of network access, emails, keystroke logging, or even videotaping or actual surveillance by other personnel. Again, both human resources and the legal department should be consulted prior to any extensive monitoring.

Incident response teams should develop (and practice) out-of-band communications. If the network is unavailable because of an attack or if an administrator is suspected in an insider attack, the primary means of communication about the attack should not be email. Even if the administrator is not a suspect, it is important to remember that the person could still monitor the email traffic and tip off the suspect (either wittingly or unwittingly). Company phones might be subject to monitoring by telecommunications personnel. During the conduct of the investigation, team members should consider whether communications methods are secure before passing any sensitive information.

As a general rule, investigating insider incidents requires the incident response team to be much more circumspect during the investigation. An insider investigation is intrusive by its very nature. It will require the team to limit the sharing of information outside and perhaps even within the team. Initial hypotheses about the incident should be very closely held. They might be wrong and might cause misunderstanding. They might alert the attacker, especially if the initial theory is incomplete or inaccurate. They might have legal implications if the wrong suspect is investigated. The fundamental difference between investigating an insider attack and an external attack is that it is never clear who can be trusted during the investigation.

The analysis of network logs (routers, switches, servers, and so on) in insider attacks is similar to that of external attacks, except that the company has more access to the logs and they are generally more reliable. Although some attacks, for example, can spoof IP addresses, the router logs will still show the MAC address. It is much more difficult for an employee to launch a network attack and remain undetected. There are three major considerations in network log analysis:

- First, the logs are essentially useless unless they are time synchronized. When tracing an attack back from one hop to the next, the only common factor is often the time stamp. Companies should use an internal time synchronization server to set the time on all network devices (including workstations, servers, and personal computers).

- Second, the use of dynamic IP addresses within corporate networks is increasing. Often, however, the network logs only identify the subject by IP address. If the DHCP server does not maintain logs of IP leases and those logs are not periodically archived, it might be impossible to determine which workstation was involved.

- Third, a determined and skilled attacker can delete or modify logs. If a system administrator is under suspicion, all logs must be viewed with some degree of skepticism unless it can be verified that the administrator had no access to the system. UNIX logs are especially easy to modify because they consist of simple text files. There are now tools available to modify NT logs, including the deletion and insertion of single records in the log files.

Special Considerations

Insider attacks require the assistance of other players in the company. The human resources department is a key player in the incident response process. It can advise the incident response team regarding employee rights and responsibilities and the disciplinary or termination process. The department probably has people skilled in interviews that could be useful when confronting suspects, victims, or witnesses. HR should be informed as soon as an investigation indicates the potential involvement of an employee.

The corporate legal team is also a key player. This team can provide legal advice on searches and employee privacy issues. It also can represent the company's interests when matters of potential liability are discussed. If the company is deciding whether or not to investigate an incident, for example, the legal department can advise senior management as to the corporate and personal liability if the incident escalates. Many corporate legal counsels are not well versed in computer law. In this case, contacting a cyberlaw expert is highly advisable before proceeding with an investigation. Illegal searches not only can result in the evidence being unusable, they also can result in civil or criminal penalties against the company, its officers, or the incident response team.

The physical security organization can also be crucial in an investigation. As previously discussed, these people can provide corroborating evidence to place the person at the computer. Physical security personnel might also be skilled in personal interviews, especially if they have a law enforcement background. They might have contacts in law enforcement and are often experienced in conducting investigations. Even if they are not particularly computer literate, their experience can be useful in the overall conduct of the incident response effort. In fact, they might bring insights to the process that a purely technical response might overlook.

Public relations should also be kept informed if there is any chance that knowledge of the incident might become known. If the employee is terminated or if the decision is made to prosecute the employee, public relations personnel should prepare a statement for the press. The statement does not necessarily have to be released, but timely preparation can prevent a hasty reaction later when the details of the incident have leaked. Managing the public details of the incident can be even more crucial to a company's reputation than managing the technical details.

Special Situations

Certain situations are ripe for the onset of an insider attack. One of the most dangerous situations for a company to handle is the termination of key employees. When senior managers are terminated, the prospect that intellectual capital might be removed is extremely threatening to a company's reputation and viability. Obviously, both HR and the legal department should be involved from the beginning when a senior manager is removed for cause (or leaves to join a competitor). The person's network and physical access should be terminated, preferably while the employee is in an exit interview. The employee should then be allowed to remove any personal items from his or her office while under the supervision of another trusted person. A complete audit of any items or data that the employee might have had access to might be required.

Even more dangerous from a computer security point of view is the termination of either a system administrator or a member of the security team. Because these personnel have the technical knowledge to evade detection, a thorough audit is required. This audit should focus on what information the employee might have removed and what access the employee might have to company systems. It should also look for any signs that the employee can access the systems after his or her termination. If the employee is a member of the incident response team, care must be taken to ensure that the personnel conducting the audit and investigation are trusted and that they are not conspiring with the ex-employee. Even if their reliability is above reproach, it might still be wise to have an external audit by a trusted third party, if only to demonstrate due diligence. This might also serve as a deterrent to future employees and a demonstration that the company takes security seriously, especially when a security person is involved.

Terminate or Prosecute?

The ultimate decision in the investigation of an insider attack is whether to discipline the employee, terminate the person, prosecute the person, or some combination of these. This is not a simple decision, and it should be raised (at least in general terms) early in the investigation. Senior management should be briefed and must make the decision. This is a business decision, not a security one.

A number of factors should be considered in this decision:

- What is required to terminate an employee? In the United States, if an employee was hired at-will, it is probably easy to terminate the employee for cause or even for no reason at all. If the employee is unionized or has an employment contract, it might be more difficult. If the investigation has to be sufficient to fire a contracted employee, it might be just as easy to prosecute the person at the same time.

- What is the nature of the offense, and is it likely that law enforcement will be interested? The offense might not be illegal. It might also not be great enough for a prosecutor (whether federal or local) to pursue a case. This might also depend on the relationship the incident response team has with local law enforcement and the standing of the company in the community.

continues

continued

- What is the reputational danger to the company if (when) knowledge of the incident becomes public? If the employee is prosecuted, full details of the incident will be released to the public. It might be possible, however, in an embarrassing incident to keep the details private, especially if the employee is disciplined and not terminated.

An employee should not be terminated until the investigation is complete. Placing an employee on administrative leave protects the company from wrongful-termination lawsuits. In addition, it can be used to gain the employee's cooperation. For example, the employee could be told that the company will not press charges provided the employee provides all details of the attack. The employee also could be provided immunity if he or she agrees not to release information about the attack. The employee can even be offered a severance package, subject to certain conditions.

Legal Issues

A number of legal issues surround the investigation of an insider attack. Company liability has been briefly discussed. The company might be liable if the investigation is not complete or if the employee was involved in illegal activity and the company did nothing about it. Pirated software and child pornography are obvious examples of material that might result in corporate liability if the offense is not properly handled. In addition, if the incident is mismanaged and it affects the company's profits or value, shareholder lawsuits could result. Corporate legal counsel and outside legal experts should be consulted at all phases of a sensitive investigation.

As a general rule, in the United States, a private company can monitor the electronic (and physical) actions of its employees. Consent is not always required (depending on the situation and the physical location of the employee), nor is prior notification. In any situation, however, legal advice should be obtained prior to monitoring employees, especially if that monitoring is initiated or increased in response to an incident. Prior notification of monitoring and informed consent by the employees will make the situation clearer and might also act as a deterrent.

Government agencies, including contractors employed by them in some situations, generally have much stricter rules as to the type of monitoring they can conduct. The law is not clear on this, and agencies often have differing interpretations and implementations of their right to monitor. Again, proper legal advice is critical.

Private companies outside the United States have different requirements. European Union privacy laws might make it difficult for the company to monitor email, for example. The situation is even less clear when the traffic or data crosses national boundaries.

Case Study

This particular case illustrates many of the points discussed in this chapter. It is not meant to be representative because insider attacks can vary widely, but it does demonstrate some of the pitfalls inherent to investigating an insider.

A firewall administrator was suspected of using an anonymous account to post harassing emails to a web bulletin board. The email account was a free web-based email service (such as Hotmail or Yahoo! Mail). The account in question had been used by the employee in the past to post to other boards (such as technical and computer-gaming discussions).

The message headers indicated that the source address of the postings corresponded to the corporate web proxy server, indicating that the messages had been sent from a company computer. The employee was interviewed and confronted. He refused to discuss the incident and was terminated. A team of consultants was hired to perform forensics examinations of the employee's computer and to audit the firewalls to ensure that no modifications had been made to them.

- The employee was interviewed by the head of physical security. This person had a background in law enforcement but was not technically skilled. Based on transcripts of the interview, the employee probably felt threatened by the interviewer. Some of the more technical questions asked during the interview might have been misunderstood by one or both persons. For example, the employee was asked whether he had any kind of remote access to the firewalls, and he stated that he had none. In fact, he did have dial-in access. However, based on the specific way the question was stated, it was possible that the employee interpreted it as asking if he had any *unauthorized* remote access. As the investigation progressed, it became clear that almost nothing obtained as a result of this interview was usable. The key point is that interviewing a potential suspect requires qualified and skilled personnel and should not be attempted randomly.

- The employee was terminated following the interview. By terminating him immediately, however, the company lost any leverage it might have had to gain his cooperation. When further examination revealed no conclusive evidence that the employee was the source of the postings, the company could have become liable in a wrongful-termination lawsuit. The decision to terminate the employee was made as a direct result of the interview and was made without input from the corporate legal or incident response teams. As a general rule, suspected employees should not be terminated unless there is overwhelming evidence. It is usually better to place them on administrative leave pending the results of the investigation. This both avoids potential lawsuits over wrongful termination and can be used to persuade the employee to cooperate with the investigation.

- The consulting team was not requested until two weeks after the final posting. Forensics examinations were unable to produce conclusive evidence that the employee had made the postings. All members of the employee's team had their computers examined as well. Because other people had knowledge of the incident, their computers demonstrated that they had visited the bulletin board. However, no forensics evidence existed that any employee had posted. Forensics, to be successful, requires that the computer be seized and examined as soon as possible following the incident. Logs, temporary files, cache, and history files are quickly overwritten during normal use.

continues

continued

- Although the postings resolved the source address back to the corporate proxy server, the firewalls were not logging all outbound HTTP traffic. In addition, logs were only maintained for one month and then were deleted. By the time the investigation took place, no logs were available to further resolve the source of the posting back to a specific computer. In addition, even if the firewall logs had been available, the company did not maintain DHCP logs. It would have been virtually impossible to tie an IP address in the firewall log to a specific workstation. Logs are one of the key sources of evidence. They must be backed up and archived offline. Again, the delay in initiating the investigation resulted in a lack of evidence.

- One of the postings was made during a weekend. The company had no records, however, that could track which employees had been present in the building during that period. Although the company had electronic badge access to the offices, it was common practice, especially on weekends when the air conditioning was turned off, for the first employee in to block the doors open with a fire extinguisher. It was therefore impossible to demonstrate whether the suspect employee (or any other employees) were physically able to make this particular posting. Physical security logs are often the only way to put a person at a computer.

- The decision to call in outside consultants to do the investigation was extremely useful. Regardless of the technical skills of the consultants or the internal incident response personnel, the fact that the suspect was a firewall administrator (and an ad-hoc member of the incident response team) created the potential for a conflict of interest (or at least the perception of one). By bringing in outside consultants to audit the affected systems, the company was able to demonstrate that it was willing to do an independent audit of the incident and that no one, not even members of the incident response team, was above suspicion. The use of external auditors, who might report to persons outside the normal incident response team, can be valuable in demonstrating a degree of due care and diligence in the investigation.

The company responded to the bulletin board by stating that it had investigated the incident and terminated the employee responsible. The bulletin board then deleted the email account. No further harassing emails were received from the company. However, because all members of the team were aware of the scope of the investigation, this might simply be a case in which the person responsible simply stopped his actions because he knew he was being monitored.

Conclusion

Insider attacks, like any computer incident, have the potential to be business crippling. Senior management must be involved with the investigation and needs to make those business decisions (such as whether to terminate or prosecute) that will guide the investigation process while preserving the end goal of helping the *business* respond to the attack.

As previously discussed, insider attacks are especially challenging for an incident response team. The attackers might know of the investigation (and, even worse, might actually be part of the team). They have access to the most sensitive systems and data in the company, and they are in a position to exploit that data. The incident response process should contain procedures for detecting and investigating insider attacks, including, when appropriate, the specific criteria for requesting external assistance.

11

The Human Side
of Incident Response

by Terry Gudaitis, Ph.D.

THE CONCERN FOR INFORMATION SECURITY IS GROWING nationwide and worldwide as more companies, financial institutions, organizations, governments, and individuals rely on computers to maintain, increase, and advance their businesses. The problems of computer misuse, computer sabotage, and hacking are issues for everyone, professionally or personally, who uses the Internet or is attached to a company network. Individuals, small companies, and organizations not affiliated with technology sometimes assume that they cannot be harmed or targeted by computer criminals. Of course, everyone can be a target for hackers, even the little guy. Although the attacks are technical, people are being hurt, people are being affected, and more importantly, people are still the perpetrators. The weapons of choice might be technical, but the fingers on the keyboards are still human.

The primary response services in the information security industry include technical solutions (such as PKI and VPN), technical preventions (such as firewalls and IDSs), and incident response programs. Although the current services offer a wide array of technical solutions to prevent damaging incidents, these incidents are still committed by human beings. Ironically, although the damage is being done by humans, all of the typical solutions for mitigating information security incidents are technical based. The addition of behavioral science–based investigative techniques must be integrated into an effective incident response program to develop a more complete and successful solution to information security issues.

To comprehensively protect sensitive information from modification, destruction, and disclosure, the science of studying human beings, the organizations for which they work, and the society in which they live must be assessed. Even the companies that purchase a great deal of technology-based protection for their systems will continue to have the problems based on human behavior and human beings. The best firewall built cannot prevent the person with legitimate access from causing harm. Human-based protection must be incorporated into an overall security package because more than 60% of attacks are coming from the inside. Human-based incident response techniques must be incorporated into an overall incident response program.

Although there are numerous established technical means to assist a company in protecting sensitive information and data, the same level of behavior-based techniques is not being utilized. The techniques from the fields of criminology, sociology, behavioral science, and human communication should play a complimentary role with computer science and information technology to more successfully secure the integrity of data and information. Behavioral science and profiling tools focus on the assessment, investigation, education, and development of human beings, the companies for which they work, and the society in which they live. The purpose of this chapter is to demonstrate how behavioral science methodologies can be combined with existing technical investigative techniques to combat cybercrime and fit within an incident response team. The behavioral assessment methods used in incident response closely parallel the six-stage incident response methodology outlined in Chapter 3, "A Methodology for Incident Response."

Integration of the Social Sciences into Incident Response

Almost every day a TV news report, newspaper, or Internet news story will report an incident of hacking, computer abuse, or cybercrime. Everyone is getting hit, and it is not just web site defacement of government sites or other "nuisance" attacks. The recent onslaught of distributed denial-of-service attacks, identity thefts, virus releases, and online credit card thefts has demonstrated an increase in the sophistication of attacks and the capability to attack large, successful American and European companies—as well as individuals. To combat these types of incidents, most corporations and government organizations have formed or contracted incident response teams.

In most cases, the incident response teams are sufficiently staffed with technically skilled individuals. Incident response teams follow established polices and procedures for incident handling, and they attempt to limit the scope and magnitude of the incident, prevent the incident from escalating, restore necessary systems, and conduct investigations. The primary tools in the incident response team box are technical. However, to restore the business to normal operations, to identify the attacker(s), or to capture the attacker(s), the capabilities of an incident response team need to expand far beyond the technical expertise of the team members. The successful conclusion (or prevention) of an attack sometimes has more to do with having the capability to handle the human aspects of incident response than the technical aspects.

Understanding the human aspects of incident response is critical to forming, training, and applying the talents of an incident response team to an incident. These human-based issues can be described as those aspects of incident response that fall outside the scope of technical experience and skill. The human aspects of incident response revolve around people: the victims, the employees, the stockholders, the executives, and of course, the perpetrators. If an incident response team does not understand the human or people perspectives when commencing the investigation of an incident, the incident response team is already behind the curve. This lesson has been learned from years of conventional criminal investigation.

A good homicide investigation does not rely on the results of lab tests; the investigation includes eyewitness interviews, the use of informants, victim statements, sketch artists, interrogation of suspects, and criminal or psychological profiling of the perpetrator. The investigator must also consider peripheral aspects of the case, as follows:

1. Possible media exposure
2. Visibility of the case within the police department
3. Interaction with the district attorney's office
4. The political aspects of a high-visibility case
5. Public reaction and safety
6. Behaviors and the emotional state of the survivors' or victims' families
7. Interaction with the suspects' attorneys
8. The proper collection of evidence and maintaining a chain of custody
9. Possible multiple jurisdictions involved in the investigation (which could include local, state, county, and/or federal investigators)
10. The vigilant collection of circumstantial evidence to be used in a grand jury hearing or trial

It is not unusual for homicide detectives, at some point in their careers, to become overwhelmed with a case. Extremely long work hours, time away from their own families, emotional involvement with a case, and obsessive thought about a case can lead investigators down a path of personal issues (such as fatigue, health issues, divorce, depression). These are the human- or people-based issues of investigating conventional crimes. A parallel set of issues exists for incident response teams and the experts who make up incident response teams.

The human aspects of incident response can make or break a case . . . and perhaps make or break a company. Just as the experienced homicide detective uses every tool available, whether it is the forensics lab or the street informant, the incident response team of today must use every tool available. A state-of-the-art incident response team must also realize the peripheral issues surrounding an incident and be equally experienced in anticipating and dealing with them. Most of these peripheral issues are human based and do require an additional or different set of investigation and response skills.

This chapter is divided into four sections and delves into four human aspects of incident response. The four sections are cybercrime profiling (the psychological profiling of attackers), insiders (attackers who are inside your organization), dealing with incident victims, incident response team fatigue and stress.

Part I: Cybercrime Profiling

Most everyone has seen the movie *The Silence of the Lambs* or the more recently released *Hannibal*. Each of these popular movies familiarized the public with the established discipline of criminal profiling. The methodology of psychological or criminal profiling has been used for more than two decades to assist investigators and forensic analysts in incident investigation. In the early 1970s, several now well-known FBI special agents (for example, John Douglas, Leo Hazelwood, and Robert Ressler) created and developed conventional crime-profiling techniques. They focused on the psychological profiling of serial killers, serial rapists, and serial arsonists. Their techniques have been validated and expanded over the years to include the profiling of kidnapping cases, single or unrelated homicides, and other conventional (or nontechnical crimes).

The various social scientific and profiling techniques used to assess people have been widely accepted in the conventional investigative world. Psychological profiling has been utilized in law enforcement and in the intelligence community for assessing individuals, groups, and cultures and for solving crimes. The behavioral information and profiles provided to investigators have supplemented forensic data, hard scientific data, and otherwise technically gathered data. Hard scientific information gathered by medical examiners, ballistics experts, demolitions specialists, DNA experts, and other laboratory analysts is both used by and supplemented by profilers. The profilers provide that extra tool in the box that looks at the crime, the crime scene, the victim, and the perpetrator from a behavioral or psychological perspective. This profiling tool can be utilized during all six stages of incident response, depending on who or what is being assessed.

The very basic concept behind profiling is that people are creatures of habit and form behavioral patterns. Individuals might not even be aware of some of their own patterns. Behind each pattern is also a motive, a reason why, or a catalyst that spurs on the behavior. Uncovering and understanding these patterns is critical to forming a useful criminal profile.

There are two simple ways to define profiling:

Definition #1:
Profiling is the process by which an incident is evaluated and assessed from a behavioral perspective to provide social scientific insight into the individual or individuals who might have committed the specific act(s) or offense(s).

Definition #2:
Profiling is the process by which a crime scene is observed, evaluated, and assessed from behavioral, criminological, anthropological, victimological, and psychological perspectives to provide social scientific insight into the individual or individuals who might have committed the specific offense or offenses.

The concept behind profiling is that weapons do not commit crimes, people do. Thus, those individuals who commit cybercrimes are the roots of the problem, not the advancing technologies. If the problem is primarily human driven, the solution must include, in part, a human solution. As criminal profiling increases the size of the conventional investigative toolbox, similar behavior-based methodologies can be used to enhance the number of tools used to combat breaches of information security. Human-based data gathering, assessment, and cybercrime profiling need to be synthesized and incorporated in conjunction with the information security techniques applied by incident response teams.

What is Cybercrime Profiling (CCP)?

CCP, in its purest form, is simply an extension or adaptation of conventional criminal profiling applied to the cybercrime scene. CCP uses all the same data-gathering techniques as conventional criminal profiling, but it has applied the methodology to the technical incident. In conventional crime profiling, the profiler would look to the forensics experts, the medical examiner, the detectives, and the crime victim to collect information about a case. The strategy of the cybercrime profiler is much the same. The cybercrime profiler turns to the system administrator, the incident response team members, the firewall expert, and perhaps the virus expert for the same type of input and information. The cybercrime profiler is searching for those same patterns that the perpetrator left behind that could assist the technical incident responders in mitigating the incident, predicting the attacker's next move, or even identifying the attacker. In these examples, cybercrime profiling would be an integral part of Stage 2, detection. CCP can be broadly defined as follows:

> The investigation, analysis, assessment, and reconstruction of data (from behavioral, psychological, criminological, anthropological, and victimological perspectives) that has been extracted from computer systems, networks, media (such as tape, discs, digital, and audio), and physical security logs (such as badge readers, cameras, and biometric devices) as well as from human-based systems (such as corporate policies, organizational procedures, and organizational culture/climate).

Why Is CCP Used as Part of Incident Response?

As previously stated, CCP works in conjunction with and supplements incident response and technical cyberforensics. CCP is recommended as an added aspect of the incident response team for the following reasons:

1. The combination of technical science and social science is a powerful one.
2. The problems associated with information security and incident response are based in human behavior. The integration of technical and behavioral science is necessary; you cannot forget about half of the problem.

3. Profiling provides a distinct investigative perspective.

4. CCP creates an effective multilayered approach to cybercrime investigation and mitigation.

There are many times when an incident, surprisingly enough, will not have a great deal of technical data on which to base an investigation. When email threats are sent or postings are made to message boards, anonymizers and other techniques are typically used to cloak the identity and the technical trail of an attacker. These are the types of cases in which it is certainly appropriate for a profiler to be engaged.

Cybercrime profilers might also look for data in places where the technical team typically does not, or they might provide information to the victim of the incident that the technical team frequently overlooks. Important data might be available through a human resources department of an organization. For example, most HR departments house all employee and former employee records, including complaints, disciplinary actions, and resumes. HR departments are also typically well versed in the corporate culture and climate. They know when layoffs have taken place, when management changes have occurred, and when other things relating to employees have taken place within the organization. Understanding and having access to this type of information about a company might provide leads or clues as to why an incident occurred and who might be responsible. Public relations departments, physical security departments, and finance departments also might be relevant and hold critical information pertinent to the case.

When Is CCP Used?

Although CCP is mostly seen as an aspect of incident response to profile "who done it," there are a few other applications. Overall in the scheme of information security, CCP is used in three basic ways, fitting into all six stages of incident response as described in Chapter 3:

1. As a cybercrime prevention tool (Stage 1)

2. As a postincident or postmortem assessment tool (Stage 6)

3. As an Incident Response tool (Stages 2–5)

Preparation and Prevention

As a cybercrime preparation or prevention tool, CCP is used to identify vulnerabilities within an organization and hopefully to prevent an incident from happening. CCP can be used in various ways to add to the existing technical methods used to prevent attacks. The focus of profiling, preattack, is to basically think like or assess the motivations of a would-be attacker. White hat hackers or ethical hackers do this from a technical perspective. Profiling can be used as a precursor to or as preparation for conducting ethical social engineering tests. Constructing scenarios to run against call centers, organizations, and other critical parts of a company using emotional or psychological strategies is effective in uncovering potential human-based vulnerabilities. Of course, the information gained from an effective psychologically based social engineering task (for example, account data, passwords, user IDs) can be passed to the ethical hacking team for further exploitation.

CCP can also be used to construct an organizational profile of a company, corporation, or agency. To conduct "preventative profiling," information about an organization and its employees, policies, structure, size, departments, industry, and internal workings needs to be assessed. Due to the interdependence of individuals, organizations, departments within organizations, and the trends that occur in society, the relationships and connections between those elements must be analyzed because they are all synthesized and linked via computers, networks, the Internet, and intranets.

Every organization goes through difficult times, and every organization has a distinct culture. Understanding and profiling the corporate culture and climate can provide the organization with an understanding of when the probability of attack might be higher or lower. One method of identifying the more probable times of attack is to identify the *hot spots* within the organization. The hot spots are those times during the year when the organization experiences the most stress, anxiety, or change, the times of the year when the employees, the stockholders, the investors, or the customers might become uneasy, disgruntled, tense, or on the flipside, more successful or more public. For example, in some organizations, the hot spots might include the timeframe when performance evaluations and bonuses are conducted; in other organizations, it might be during the annual or quarterly reports. Some organizations report the most unrest during times of downsizing or critical management change; other organizations experience stress during acquisitions, mergers, or physical location changes. These times of stress typically correspond to increased incidents; about three to four months after a hot spot occurs, an organization is more likely to experience an attack, most likely from an insider.

Another hot spot catalyst is when the organization attains publicity or becomes prominent in the news. Organizations that have become household names or are otherwise well known are frequent targets for attack. When an organization's public relations department or marketing department prepares a big media spread or when a company is doing so well financially that it gets a lot of attention from Wall Street and is reported in the news, this publicity (positive or negative) heightens the probability of attack. If these hot spots are understood, they are predictable. Thus, enhanced security measures can be put in place during these times of higher incident probability.

CCP can likewise be applied to the preparation for and prevention of incidents by assisting in the candidate screening or hiring process. No organization wants to hire people who will steal, cheat, conduct industrial espionage, or otherwise sabotage the company. Specifically, companies are very aware of the damage that highly technical people can do to their organization with skill, access, and in some cases, even authorization. There are many theories and many approaches to employee screening, including background investigations, polygraph tests, and interviews that seem like interrogations. Some organizations have no hiring process and seem to hire anyone who appears to be breathing and have a pulse. Most companies do not want to hire hackers or crackers; however, they are not sure how to weed out people who are capable of doing damage but won't from those who are capable of doing damage and would—either for money, kicks, or revenge. Just as CCP can assist a company in profiling an organization for vulnerabilities, the methodologies of profiling can be used to assist organizations in developing interview strategies and techniques to weed out those who might do an organization damage.

Postmortem or Follow-Up

Just as CCP can be applied to incident preparation and prevention, profiling or assessing an incident from a human perspective can provide both the incident response team and the client with useful postincident recommendations. This postmortem assessment is part of Stage 6, follow-up. The three applications of human-based assessment techniques for postmortem assessment are as follows:

1. Continuing the process and flow of the incident response capability

2. Evaluating the communication and behavior of the incident response team members as well as the communication with the client

3. Contributing human-based recommendations to prevent the incident from reoccurring

Although the incident response team leader or manager is frequently responsible for maintaining the skill sets of the response team and managing the successful conclusion of an incident, this team leader is typically focusing on the successful technical solution of the incident. In some cases, even though the technical issues are resolved, human beings might have been adversely affected and might still feel victimized by the incident. Specifically in cyberstalking cases and cyberthreat cases, victims of these types of crimes don't usually go back to business as usual just because their stalker was identified and caught or because their system was restored. The victims have emotional and psychological issues that need postincident attention and perhaps counseling. This particular subject will be discussed in more detail in Part III of this chapter.

It is always recommended, but infrequent, that incident response teams sit down after an incident is closed to discuss what went well and what did not go so well. When teams walk through this process, again, the focus is primarily targeted to how well the team members used their technical prowess to go after the attacker, patch the holes, and locate other vulnerabilities, or how fast they were able to restore the system to functionality. One aspect that the human side of incident response can bring to the table is an assessment of the communication between team members as well as an assessment of how well team members communicated with the client or victim. Developing trusting and open interpersonal relationships with clients is an important, if not critical, part of incident response. During the course of an incident, it is highly likely that someone will be briefing a manager or someone within the attacked organization who is not highly technical but who needs to understand the incident and its implications. It is imperative that an incident response team be able to discuss the incident in highly technical terms as well as break down it in plain language so that a public relations specialist can prepare to answer questions from the media if needed.

Working an incident from the human perspective also provides an added dimension to the list of recommendations and suggestions provided to the client postincident. Human-based recommendations might include recommendations regarding employee policy changes, physical security observations, and social engineering prevention strategies. For example, if an insider committed an incident, there might be relevant suggestions to make regarding the organization's hiring procedures or termination processes.

Incident Response—Detection, Containment, Eradication, and Recovery

The most recognized time when CCP is used is during the heat of an ongoing incident. At this stage, profiling can assist in the identification, investigation, interrogation, and prosecution of the perpetrator. Cybercrime profiling can supplement Stage 2, detection, by trying to ascertain what is going on and who the perpetrator might be. Profiling can supplement Stage 3, containment, by helping to limit the extent of the attack damage or compromise committed by the perpetrator. Profiling and behavioral assessment might be able to assist in the isolation or eradication of the cause of the attack, assisting the technical team during Stage 4, eradication. Finally, by understanding the attack or incident from a psychological or behavioral perspective, profiling techniques might be able to supplement the recovery process, as described in Stage 5. The goals of the profiler during an incident, however, are driven by the needs of the client. Each client has distinct needs that could vary widely. The goals of CCP include the following:

- Narrowing the suspect pool (insider or outsider)
- Identifying the actual perpetrator
- Identifying whether the incident was caused by a single attacker or multiple perpetrators
- Assessing the organization and determining the attacker's motivation and additional vulnerabilities or attack targets
- Assessing the scope of the incident and the impact on employees, customers, stockholders, managers, and public perception
- Predicting the perpetrator's behavior or next move
- Providing consultation to the victim(s)
- Assisting in the sharing of information between organizational departments
- Using the profile to generate more questions or answers about the incident and who might be involved
- Supplementing the interview or interrogation process if suspects are revealed
- Assisting in the evidence collection and prosecution process
- Providing suggestions and follow-up advice postincident

The sooner CCP can be brought into an investigation the better. Again, just as in conventional crime cases, it is more difficult to assess a case when it's cold or when it has been ongoing for some time.

The Methodology of CCP

The assessment methodologies used in cyberprofiling are very similar to those used in conventional criminal profiling. The actual methodology of CCP, as in conventional criminal profiling, is a mix of science and art. CCP is grounded in behavioral science but utilizes the subjective experience of the profiler in addition to the art of interpretation. In general, there are four foundational steps or processes to work through when profiling a cybercrime case. The four foundational steps are as follows:

1. Conducting a case overview
2. Performing triage
3. Analysis and profiling
4. Conducting the technical interview

Case Overview

The basics of a CPP case overview include the following:

1. The identification of modus operandi (MO).
2. The determination and identification of a signature.
3. A content analysis.
4. Pattern recognition of the attack.
5. An assessment of the technical aspects of the attack.
6. Extension of research and search for related information.
7. A victimological assessment.
8. The determination of linkage. Each data set within a case and related to a case is independent until multiple cases can be linked together.

The goal of this first step, which is part of the detection stage, is to get a handle on what is going on, what has the attacker done, how has the attacker committed the offense, and what some of the patterns and details are that jump out at the beginning.

Modus Operandi

Modus operandi (MO) is a mechanism by which the perpetrator commits his or her crime. It is a learned behavior, and it can change over time as the individual changes, grows, and develops. The MO can be considered a pattern, allowing for some variance. It is important, however, to understand the basic behavioral pattern of the perpetrator. An example of an MO in conventional crime can be found in the case of the Boston Strangler. In that case, the strangler not only strangled all his victims but also included the process of selecting females living alone in apartment buildings as victims and the mode and ruse of entry to his victims' apartments as "maintenance." An MO in cybercrime might include the use of email to launch extortion demands after which the attacker consistently compromises systems by using known vulnerabilities in networks and assuming that most companies are not current on their patches. The attacker's MO also might include the use of root kit.

Assessing and constructing the MO of a computer attack is useful in determining not only who might have conducted the attack but also what the person's skill sets are, his or her attack preferences, and what some of the attacker's vulnerabilities might be. In the case of the extortion attempts, the MO indicates that the attacker's most likely vulnerability might be his next step, which is the voice or face-to-face communication with the company to collect the demanded payment. The MO in that case highlights the attacker's technical skills and abilities; the entire attack is extremely technical and, according to the technical members of the incident response team, very well executed. There is no indication of comfort or evidence of confidence in interpersonal communication.

Signature

Signature is what the perpetrator has to do to fulfill self-needs. It is an unnecessary addition to the completion of the actual crime. The signature of a crime or of the criminal typically does not change from one crime to the next. For example, in the case of the Boston Strangler, his signature was tying bows around the bodies made from the victims' clothing items (such as stockings or scarves) found in their apartments. The big, sometimes elaborate bows made by the Boston Strangler were not necessary to the actual completion of his crime. He could have strangled his victims without conducting this last behavior, but it was his signature. It was something he had to do for emotional or psychological reasons.

The signature is distinctive, and in most cases, there is some form of a signature. It might be difficult to detect or a bit obtuse, but there is some distinguishing factor in most behaviors—including the behavior of hackers! Various signatures found in cybercrimes include comment lines in virus code, email address names/aliases, screen names, stylistic components of emails and message board postings, and graphic characteristics in web defacements. The establishment and identification of a signature is one of the best ways to tie cases together or to establish linkage.

The Style of the Technical Attack

The style of the technical attack includes components that might relate directly to the MO and the signature. These stylistic components include the manner in which the perpetrator used the attack tools. In conventional crime, stylistic components of a crime might include things like what type of binding materials were used during an abduction (rope, duct tape, handcuffs) or in what style the ransom note was written (pen and ink, script versus printing, paragraph divisions, margins, typed, and so on) In cybercrime investigation and incident response, the stylistic components might be contained in captured virus code. Part of the style of a virus attack might include what the actual code looks like, how spaces are used in the program, how the logic of the code flows, and how elegant the code is. Understanding the style of the code might provide insight regarding who authored the code. In one case, virus code was captured, and the style of the programming was that all the lines of code were jammed together with no spaces and no indentation between lines. This style of programming was characteristic in the mid-to-late 1970s and early 1980s. Space was at a premium, and every available space was valuable. Thus, programmers who learned to program during this timeframe valued space, and many continued to program using this indicative style. Estimating the educational timeframe of the virus writer can provide an educated prediction of the virus writer's age. Assessing age on only the evidence of space is not recommended, but this is useful data and is a worthwhile observation to note.

Victimology

Victimology is the study of the victim or the target. It is necessary and important when investigating an incident to understand why a particular victim was targeted. Studying the victim might provide clues as to who the attacker is by virtue of who was intended to receive harm. In cybercrime investigation, ascertaining who the victim is might include both human and inanimate objects (such as the systems, networks, web servers, laptops). It is possible that an incident might include the compromise of a system or an email account to send harassing or threatening messages to a human victim. In that case, there are two victims: the compromised system and account and the person receiving the threats. Understanding who the person is and why someone might have wanted to inflict fear or harm on him or her might become a very personal and disclosive process. Interviewing the victim must be conducted with the utmost confidentiality and respect. It is also recommended that the victim be interviewed more than once and with a variety of interviewing strategies.

Content Analysis

Content analysis as a social scientific tool has been around since the early 1900s. This interpretation and assessment technique primarily was used by anthropologists, rhetoricians, and literary scholars. Varied and early types of content analysis have been used in academic settings since Socrates and Aristotle. Used in profiling, content analysis is the assessment of the actual contents or matter of the evidence available in a crime scene. By conducting a cursory content analysis of a crime scene, the profiler begins to get a more robust picture of what actually took place. In conventional profiling, a content analysis would certainly be conducted on a ransom note, an extortion letter, or a bank robbery note. At this stage, the literal interpretation is important to understand. What does the note or letter actually say? What do the kidnappers want? How much money are the extortionists asking for? How does the bank robber want the money, in 20s, in 100s? In the case of cybercrime profiling, the same goal applies.

In cases of computer crime, a content analysis would be conducted on virus code, cyberstalking emails, threatening message board postings, files of compromised systems, and particularly in forensics cases in which entire drives are imaged. The same types of questions apply to computer crime as to conventional crime. What is the virus attempting to do to the OS? What does the cyberstalker want? Who specifically is the message board poster threatening, an individual or an organization? What are the names of the files that were compromised? What are the contents or categories of data on the imaged system?

Content analysis will be revisited later in the profiling process. At this stage, it is imperative to understand the plain presentation of the facts. At a later stage, more facets of content analysis will emerge that will include subjective interpretation.

Pattern Recognition

Pattern recognition is the search for and recognition of any repeating components of a crime that have occurred within the same crime or case. Identifying patterns within the same case could provide insight regarding the identity of the attacker, the motivation of the attacker, or when the attacker might strike next. When it becomes very apparent in the course of an investigation that the same attacker is responsible for the crime, looking for patterns within the individual's attack can assist investigators and incident responders. Pattern recognition is a useful tool to use in cases of stalking, both conventional stalking and cyberstalking. In most cases of stalking, it is apparent that there is one perpetrator and typically one victim. The stalker might behave in ways that reveal a pattern to his or her actions. A cyberstalker's pattern might be the time of day emails are sent to the victim, or a pattern might reveal that the stalker is more active on Wednesdays than on any other day of the week. In conventional cases, this type of information might be very important in the maintenance of victim safety. In cyberstalking cases, this information is likewise central to maintaining the safety and well being of the victim, but this information might provide timeframes to set up sniffers, trace-backs, and other technical trap and trace methods.

Linkage

Linkage is the natural extension of pattern recognition. Linkage is the search for and recognition of any repeating components of a crime that might also have occurred in other crimes. Identifying links between different cases is historically a foundational part of linking and identifying serial crime cases. Similarities in MO, signature, stylistic components, victims, or the contents of attacks might indicate the presence of a recidivist criminal. On the other hand, extreme dissimilarities in attack patterns might indicate that there are multiple attackers or a group. Patterns can be found in any aspect of the incident. Patterns could include the time of day the compromises were conducted as well as whom was targeted. In serial crime cases, the study of the victims as well as pattern recognition can uncover the victim MO of the killer. In the example of the infamous serial killer Ted Bundy, his pattern or preference was to target young, brunette, college women.

Using linkage as a profiling tool in incident response is only slightly different from its use in conventional crime investigation. Firewall logs, email headers, server logs, timestamps, and Internet histories are only a few places where patterns can be uncovered.

Sometimes the link is discovered by looking outside of the obvious or outside the technical data and logs. For example, in one serial denial-of-service attack case, the victim company was being attacked multiple times over the course of six months. The company did not know whether the attacks were related. However, linkage identified that the company was being attacked only after the company received positive attention in the media. The company's public relations department provided the information for identifying the pattern. Specifically, the company was attacked every time its PR department issued a press release. The positive attention appeared to be the catalyst for the attacks. The next question, of course, was who would attack a company after good press? A disgruntled employee? An activist group? A competitor? In this case, it turned out to be a competitor.

Research

After completing the seven foundational information-gathering stages presented in the preceding sections (MO, signature, the style of the technical attack, victimological assessment, content analysis, pattern recognition, and linkage), the last step in this first phase of profiling is to take all the data and information collected from this cursory review and search for more data. Search for related information that might be relevant to the case. Related case research is most easily first conducted on the Internet. Using any pertinent information, an open-source collection on the Internet and World Wide Web can be conducted. Incident response case data might provide screen names, email addresses, IP addresses, names, places, and other pointers. It is surprising how many people (including perpetrators) use and reuse favorite addresses and names. People are known to choose one screen name and use the same name on several message boards. People use the same initials or a variation of their email address in other correspondence identifiers. An enormous amount of information is available online, and it is worthwhile to play sleuth and surf for additional information that might be very germane to a case.

Performing Triage

The next step in the profiling process is to conduct a full-scale triage on the case. After the case overview is completed, the incident response team and cybercrime profiler should have a good feel for the case. It is possible, however, that at this stage, the incident responders might have to clarify some findings and points to the client or the victim. Triage in the incident response arena can best be defined as the sorting and defining of critical incident components, and it is part of detection, containment, and eradication. Completing the triage process usually assists the cybercrime profiler and incident responder in accurately answering questions posed by the client or victim. There are six steps in the triage process:

1. Validation of the incident category (threat, stalking, harassment, denial of service, compromise)

2. Establishment of bonafides

3. Assessment of the threat level

4. Assessment of the level of potential violence

5. Communication and establishment of goals with the victim

6. Communication strategy with the attacker

Validation of the Incident Category

The first component of triage is to validate the type or category of incident. It is not infrequent or unusual for a client or victim to call an incident response team for assistance and start the conversation by saying, "I am being cyberstalked and I need help," or "I think a disgruntled employee has just launched an attack on us by taking down our firewalls." After conducting the case overview, the incident type should be fairly clear, and sometimes it does not match the original description provided by the client or victim. It is not remarkable for someone to call with the belief that he or she is being cyberstalked when the actual incident category is cyberharassment or even spam. Accurately labeling the incident at this point will assist the profiler and the incident responders in shaping the expectations of the client as well as educating the client or victim to the actual circumstances. One of the unfortunate situations is when a victim or a client misreads the incident. Inappropriate actions can be taken (sometimes by the client) that might negatively affect the case.

Establishment of Bonafides

When everyone seems to agree with the incident category, one more variable must be validated. The establishment of bonafides means making sure that the information provided is accurate and that the information has come from accurate sources. This is a regrettable step to have to go through, but at this point, further responding to a bogus case would be a terrible waste of time, energy, and money. Just as people fabricate being the victim of all sorts of crimes—even sexual assault—some cybercrimes have likewise been fabricated by victims. Whether the motivation is to seek and attain attention or is a byproduct of severe manic depression, there are cases in which individuals have invented their own cyberharassers, cyberstalkers, and death threats. Validation of provided information is necessary. There have also been cases in which the perpetrator has actually been one of the information technology experts providing logs and incident data to the incident response team. Of course, not all the relevant data made it to the hands of the incident response team. Check, recheck, and question any anomalies in data acquisition.

Level of Threat

When the bonafides of an incident and a victim have been validated, the next most critical assessment to conduct is the level of threat. The victim must be given an indication of how threatening the attacker is and what can be done to minimize the threat. Again, in cases of incident response, the victim can be human (an individual or an organization) or inanimate. When the CCP is dealing with a human victim— whether that victim is an individual, a group of individuals, or all employees within an organization—the following might be some of the elements of threat:

1. What is the geographic proximity of the attacker to the victim?
2. Are the words or actions of the attacker becoming more aggressive?
3. Is there any evidence that the attacker has committed this type of crime in the past?
4. How many attackers do there appear to be?
5. Are the attacks organized or disorganized?
6. Are the attacks or actions of the attacker happening more frequently?

Depending on the level of threat assessed, the victims might need special assistance. For example, if an individual has received multiple threats that are increasing in veracity, enhanced physical security might be recommended. If an organization or its employees are threatened, the appropriate follow-up might be to involve local law enforcement, and likewise, an increase in physical security precautions might be recommended. On the technical side, the incident response team members might be simultaneously providing various methods of increasing information security.

Level of Violence

If the threat level is assessed as being high, there is potential for violence. The assessment of the type of violence likely and the level of violence probable should be reported and responded to as quickly as possible. Physical security departments should be contacted immediately, and private security and law enforcement might also be brought in at this juncture. Regardless of the system restoration process or any network damage related to the incident, the safety and well being of employees should be the top priority of all organizations.

Communication and Establishment of Goals with the Victim

When both the threat and violence preventative measures have been implemented, ongoing communication with the victim is essential. The incident response team must understand the goals of the investigation. It is possible that the client will simply want the systems restored and the victims protected, with little to no actual investigation. The client might also choose to have the incident investigated to a level that determines whether the attack originated from the inside or the outside. It is also possible that the client will want a full investigation, including identifying the perpetrator. Regardless of what goal the client has, all aspects of the investigation must be conducted as if the case were going to court. Collection of evidence, documentation of records, and due diligence on the technical side as well as the human side must be conducted. It is always possible that the client will change his or her mind and later decide to prosecute or investigate to a fuller extent.

The client or the victim must also realize the potential consequences of the investigation. What happens if the incident response team actually identifies the perpetrator and the person is revealed to be a vice president in the company? How does the client want to deal with human resources issues such as termination or disciplinary action? How does the client want to deal with possible media attention? How does the client want to deal with the affect that the incident and the revelation of the perpetrator are going to have on employees and morale? Answers to these questions and a host of others must be answered before actions are taken.

Communication Strategy with the Attacker

One possibility is that the client will want the attacker to be identified. There are many ways to go about conducting the "who done it" part of the investigation. One potential suggestion is to commence communication with the attacker. Whether the attacker is attempting to extort money, harass an employee, or post intellectual property information on the Internet, it is possible to learn more about the perpetrator by actually attempting contact. Computer crimes units in law enforcement must be very careful when using this technique because it might be illegal and considered entrapment. Commercial incident response teams do have more legal room to maneuver in this manner, but the client must provide explicit permission. The following are some of the issues that must be discussed and decided before any incident responder attempts to communicate with a potential attacker:

1. How is initial contact with the potential attacker going to be made?
2. For what purpose is the attacker going to be contacted?
3. Where is the attacker going to be contacted? On a message board? An IM session? Via email?
4. When should the attacker be contacted?
5. What is going to be communicated to the attacker?
6. What is the overall goal of the communication?

This last question might be the most important. Is the purpose of contacting the attacker to attain additional information? Is it to attain a certain piece of information? Or is it to establish an electronic form of communication that can be traced?

In one case, contact with the attacker served several purposes. The case was originally called in as a cyberstalking case. However, after performing triage, it was assessed as a multiple harassment case. The victim was receiving repeated and numerous emails every day that were threatening and harassing. At first glance, the victim assumed one person was stalking her, but after completing the first few steps of the case overview process, it became apparent that the emails were originating from multiple people. Someone had posted the victim's email address on the web and encouraged others to harass her. The victim was barraged with emails. The contents of one repeat harasser were particularly disturbing. The client wanted to know where (geographically) this specific harasser was located. It was assessed that if this harasser was local to the victim, she would be in more imminent danger than if the harasser was geographically in another state. Caution had to be exercised; people are mobile. Thus, the level of threat would not decrease to zero just because the harasser is found to live hundreds of miles away. The threat probability would just decrease as compared to the level of threat if the harasser were local. At any rate, the goal was to find the location of the one harasser.

The victim provided permission to use all means possible to find this harasser's location. After conducting some research using the harasser's email address, contact was made via a message board with only one strategy in mind: to get him to discuss something local to his current geographic location. The secondary goal was to get him to disclose where his home was located. The entire communication process took three days. The harasser did end up being almost 800 miles away from the victim, but his actual identity was not ascertained. After this combination of technical incident response techniques and profiling techniques, the victim's online identity was altered, extra security measures were put in place, and the case was closed.

Profiling and Analysis

Although the processes of case overview and triage are important building blocks in establishing a profile, the real nuts and bolts of the CCP methodology are steeped in this next section. There is some overlap or expansion of ideas and components presented within the case overview and triage sections. However, the establishment of a good (and accurate) profile must incorporate much more than a surface level assessment of a case. Profiling is a process that is context driven and is perhaps more ethnographic in nature than statistical. A profile that is accurate—and thus useful—is created from the specific crime scene and incorporates elements from the immediate surrounding context. Profiling is done on a case-by-case basis to deductively draw conclusions from the data as opposed to inductively force fitting a new situation into a template created by prior cases.

To build, expand, and increase the accuracy of a profile, four cybercrime elements must be layered onto the data and information already compiled: the physical MO, the psychological MO, the addition of technical data assessment, and the actual profile.

The Physical MO

The physical MO characterizes tangible items that the attacker displays or reveals while committing the offense. These items are sensory apparent when assessing an incident (that is, they are heard, seen, spoken, felt). The code and comment lines in virus code can be seen; the words, grammar, and syntax of email text can be seen; the names of the compromised files also can be viewed, as can the contents of any logs. The language used in emails, postings, and files also can be interpreted as heard or spoken. Although in these examples the attacker chooses to verbalize in writing, the words can still be read out loud. When read aloud, the tempo, inflection, and emotive value of the written language can sometimes expose added meaning. The physical MO contains three major categories: frequency or time pattern analysis, in-depth content analysis, and linguistic analysis.

Frequency or Time Pattern Analysis   The physical MO includes an aspect of frequency or time pattern analysis. Earlier in the profiling process, components such as pattern recognition and linkage might have already started the foundation for the complete time pattern analysis. Time pattern analysis begins by cataloging or databasing time-relevant data. Logs, email headers, message board dates, forensics reports, and other timestamp records all provide the data to compile information for a time pattern analysis. All available time-related data should be recorded, such as month, year, date, day of the week, and time. When recording time, remember to record it consistently; some timestamps might use Eastern Standard Time, some Pacific Time, and some Greenwich Time. Other time- or frequency-related data found, for example, in the Internet cache might include the actual number of web sites visited, how many times they were visited, and over what time period. Collecting and analyzing this data can provide insight as to the behavioral habits and activity level of the attacker or the suspect.

In-Depth Content Analysis   The physical MO also includes a more in-depth aspect of content analysis. Although a cursory content analysis was conducted during the case overview (which focused on the literal and factual aspects of evidence), this more in-depth content analysis takes a closer look at those literal words. This content analysis is conducted, among many reasons, to establish a behavioral baseline of the attacker. This content analysis begins by taking the evidence apart word by word, phrase by phrase, and assessing the content for subjects, topics, names, categories, themes, or issues. The breadth and depth of topic or subject matter knowledge might be assessed as well. Although the obvious place to use this type of analysis is on written text (such as emails or postings), this technique can also be used to assess the content of imaged drives in a forensics case; the content of copied, stolen, or damaged files; the filenames of damaged sites; and any residual the attacker might leave behind such as the graffiti on a defaced web site. The content analysis should also include an assessment of the attacker's technical expertise or demonstrated expertise in any other field.

Linguistic Analysis   The final part of completing the physical MO is to conduct a linguistic analysis of the evidence. Once again, each word and each phrase must be picked apart and analyzed for any meaning. A linguistic assessment of the evidence would include the language used (such as English, Spanish, or Russian), the writing style, word choice, grammar, syntax, and punctuation. The emotive value of the words must be assessed as well as the emotive impact of phrases or sentences. For example, although the word "kill" might appear in an email, without context, the word might or might not have emotive power. Other linguistic elements might surface during this assessment such as the use of colloquialisms, shorthand, acronyms, regionalisms, and typos.

An enormous amount of information is contained in language, which reveals information about the author. One way to look at both content analysis and linguistic analysis is to ask, "Out of all the words in all the languages, why did this attacker choose these? And why are they combined in this fashion?" People also tend to be creatures of habit, and certain stylistic elements are invisible or unimportant to most people. Luckily, this includes the crackers, cyberstalkers, harassers, and other cyberdeviants.

Psychological MO

The psychological MO might be the most difficult piece to assess and put together. The psychological MO focuses on the behavioral and psychological factors of the attacker. This piece of the profiling process is sometimes conducted last, after all data is collected and all other analyses have been conducted. The purpose of this part is to gain enough insight into the psychological or characterological structure of the attacker that predicting attacker behavior might be possible. The psychological MO is also an important addition to the threat level and violence level probabilities. This is also the time when the profiler gets the closest to climbing inside the head of the criminal. The assessments and conclusions drawn from this section must be done conservatively and carefully. In most cases, this psychological assessment is being conducted without any direct interaction with the attacker (unless communication was established with the attacker). Thus, the assessment is called a "remote" assessment and should be conducted with assiduousness.

The psychological MO has 12 variables; they are the attacker's predatory needs, target/victim MO, need to control, acceleration, escalation, level of success, self-needs fulfilled, level of premeditation, level of self-control, ability to relate to others, sociocultural issues, and environmental needs. Each variable is described in the following sections. To some extent, although these variables are defined and listed individually, there is a great deal of overlap and synthesis between the concepts. When dealing with human behavior and psychology, it is sometimes difficult to split out variables that are mutually exclusive or exhaustive.

Predatory Needs   The attacker's predatory needs include the level to which the person has to prey on someone or something to achieve the desired satisfaction. Predatory needs might include the desire to instill fear, incite rage, achieve emotional control over someone, or achieve technical control over something.

Target/Victim MO   The attacker's target victim MO is a more in-depth assessment of the victimology of the targets. The attacker's choice of targets might also include both human and technical targets.

Need to Control   The attacker's need to control is analyzed. Assessment of the data might reveal insight into the attacker's psychological need to control the actual attack, the victim(s), and the consequences of the attack. The factor of control provides psychological insight regarding the stability of the attacker. A lack of control could indicate attacker vulnerability and perhaps even the potential to make mistakes in subsequent incidents.

Acceleration The attacker's acceleration relates to the rate at or frequency with which he or she conducts the attacks. Time pattern analysis can provide the basic information to address this variable. Stalkers who increase the number of emails or communications to their victims over time would demonstrate an increase in acceleration.

Escalation The attacker's escalation relates to the potency, power, or vigor with which the attacks are progressing. An example of escalation would be an attacker who starts out by simply posting complaints about a company on a message board and then over time escalates to posting threats to company officers. Typically, if the attacker is escalating, the probable threat and/or violence levels might increase.

Level of Success The attacker's level of success is just that—how successful the attacker is. If the assessed goal of the attacker was to compromise a particular system and that goal was achieved, the attacker can be deemed to have a high level of success. There are many instances in which the attacker might not know his or her actual level of success. For example, if the goal is to frighten or scare an individual via death threats, unless the attacker actually sees the reaction of the victim, the attacker might not have an accurate grasp on the level of success. It may be possible, however, to assess what the attacker might believe.

Self-Needs Fulfilled It might not be possible to assess the attacker's self-needs might in every case. It is difficult to analyze what exactly anyone's needs are at any given time. However, if it can be ascertained that the attacker needs to feel important or feel power through committing criminal acts, the success level of the attack might be able to contribute to the assessment of this variable. If an attacker's self-needs are not met, more activity might be predicted for the attacker to achieve his or her needs.

Level of Premeditation The attacker's level of premeditation reveals how organized and thoughtful the attacker was prior to the actual incident. A high level of premediation might indicate a more controlled and sophisticated attacker. It might also indicate a certain experience level.

Level of Self-Control The attacker's level of self-control reflects the attacker's ability to control his or her behaviors before, during, and after an incident. The level of self-control might also include the ability of the attacker to control his or her emotions and risk-taking ability. If an attacker gets to the point where he or she cannot exercise self-control, the ability to predict the attacker's behavior is diminished.

Ability to Relate to Others   The attacker's ability to relate to others indicates his or her level of social skills, social or interpersonal appropriateness, and ability to form "normal" relationships with others. Even though the attacker might be conducting a purely technical attack, there may be technical "fingerprints" left at the crime scene that would provide insight to the attacker's interactive capabilities.

Sociocultural Issues   The attacker's sociocultural issues correspond to how the attacker relates to society and to certain cultures. Depending on the data, language cues and linguistic elements might reveal from where geographically or culturally the attacker originates.

Environmental Needs   The attacker's environmental needs indicate the environment in which the attacker is comfortable and desires to operate. In some cases, the attacker is environmentally comfortable launching attacks from public places such as cybercafes; other attackers must be in the comfort of their own homes or spaces.

Adding the Technical Piece

In addition to synthesizing the profile data emerging from the physical MO and the psychological MO, CCP must include the technical assessment of the incident. The technical experts on the incident response team should be questioned throughout the profiling process. Information about the technical parts of the attack that contribute to the construction of a profile might include the following: How technically skilled is the attacker? How long did this attack take to complete from beginning to end? What security measures did the attacker have to circumvent? Are there more sophisticated ways to conduct the same type of attack? What are the unusual parts of the attack? Could the attack have been prevented? Did the attack take any inside knowledge? Does it appear that one person could have launched this attack alone? Literally, there are probably hundreds of questions to ask the technical experts; the specific case will drive the types of questions that are appropriate.

The Final Profile

Constructing the final profile of the attacker or attackers is done by synthesizing all the data and information collected through the stages of the profiling process. From this data, a profile of the attacker will emerge. The final profile contains as much demographic and psychological information as possible. There is no template, and the depth of each profile as well as the type of information contained therein will differ from case to case. See Figure 11.1 for a chart with the types of information that make up the profile.

Establishing the Profile(s)

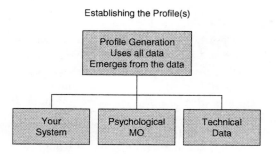

Figure 11.1   Final profile information.

As part of the incident response report, the profile should be presented as additional investigative information and should not be considered fact. The final profile, although generated using both qualitative and quantitative methods, is subjective in nature, and if the behavioral profiler is provided additional information or different information, it is possible that the final profile could change. Additional information collected via profiling might also enhance the methods chosen to question individuals, search for suspects, predict possible future behavior of the attacker(s), and question and assess the perpetrators when identified.

Profile Validation   When possible, it is important to validate the accuracy of the profiles. In instances in which the perpetrator is identified, a postincident assessment should take place to evaluate the validity of the profile provided before the final identification of the perpetrator. A great deal can be learned and gained from reviewing why a profile matched the actual attacker or why a profile did not match. Although the science of psychological profiling has been around for decades and has been validated over the years, cybercrime profiling is still in its infancy. The heuristic value gained from a postincident analysis of profiling accuracy is crucial to the development and advancement of the discipline of cybercrime profiling.

Psychological Profiling: Myths and Legends

For the discipline of cybercrime profiling to gain momentum and credibility, some common myths and legends must be dismissed. As demonstrated in the previous pages, profiling is not done through some type of psychic ability nor are tarot cards or crystal balls used. Developing a profile is not conducted as depicted in the movie *The Silence of the Lambs* or on the TV show *Profiler*.

Another popular myth is that psychological profiling or criminal profiling is conducted by giving subjects psychological tests. The art and science of profiling does not include the clinical aspects of diagnosis. Quite honestly, a cybercrime profiler should not focus on nor care whether the attacker is clinically depressed, is bipolar, or has any other psychological disorders. The cybercrime profiler must concentrate on the behavior of the attacker, regardless what or how the attacker might be feeling. The attacker him- or herself might not even know how he or she is feeling.

The most popular myth is that there is some type of hacker or attacker profile that describes what attackers look like and who they are. It would be extremely beneficial for companies and organizations to have a quick answer to their problems with threats and hackers. The development of a criminal profile of a hacker using psychological assessment tools and demographics (that is, he's a white male, 25 to 42 years old, middle management level, divorced, egocentric, and wears green tennis shoes) could be that quick fix. However, there is no profile of a hacker, there is no profile of an insider who intrudes or damages a company's system, there is no profile to help establish preventative measures against cybercrimes, and there never will be a single "silver bullet" profile or simple answer to the question, "What type of person commits computer crime?" Nor is a profile derived by collecting data from prior cases, as in a compilation of psychological testing data and demographic data.

Profiles are created on an individual, case-by-case basis. Thus, there are many reasons why a single profile cannot and should not be developed from psychological testing data or prior case data. First and foremost, human beings are far too complex. If a profile template is generated from prior data (such as jailhouse interviews, psychological testing data, demographics of convicted criminals), the conclusion is not a true profile but a review of characteristics from a subset of individuals (those who were there and those who agreed to participate in interviews and tests). As an aside, the reliability of self-reports also needs to be questioned.

Finally, "profiling is not studying data and taking a generalization and applying it to a specific offense" (Turvey, 1997, p. 3). Using generalizations is dangerous. For example, a researcher might interview and test disgruntled employees and discover that a statistical majority were divorced and/or clinically depressed at the time of the offense. To then generalize and draw the conclusion that divorced, depressed people are more likely to be disgruntled and do damage is not valid. The lack of face validity, criterion validity, predictive validity, and common sense will indicate that many, many people in this country are divorced and are probably depressed over the divorce, but these variables do not make them disgruntled employees who might constitute an insider threat. People are dynamic and life is dynamic, thus incentives, motivations, beliefs, methods of attack, and circumstances change over time as well. Each incident is a case to be worked in context.

Understanding the Attackers

So, what does an attacker look like? Popular media and culture want us to believe that hackers are all under 20 years old with blue hair, too many earrings, and droopy pants. Psychiatrists want us to believe that hackers are disgruntled, depressed, disloyal employees. Other scientists want us to believe that hackers have a disorder called Aspberger's Syndrome, a light form of autism. That's just not the case. Perpetrators of computer crime come in all shapes and sizes and with all disorders or no disorders. As previously discussed, there are no demographics that provide a "profile" of a hacker. Don't buy into the stereotype of what a hacker looks like and who it must be. It is crucial for the incident response team not to have any preconceived notions or to cave into management's belief that the "weird sys admin guy" is probably the insider who hacked the system. There are three major reasons why a single hacker or attacker profile will not be generated: incident variance, motivational variance, and perpetrator variance.

Incident Variance

There are many different types of cybercrimes. Even within the categories of cybercrime, there is no evidence to support the theory that all cyberstalkers fit a certain demographic or psychological profile, nor do all data sabotagers look, act, or think a certain way. The following is an abbreviated list of distinct types of cybercrime:

- Incident variance
- Cyberstalking
- Child pornography
- Industrial espionage
- Extortion
- Illegal gambling
- Theft of proprietary information
- Insider trading
- Cyberthreats
- Malicious code/virus
- Discrimination and harassment
- Sabotage of data and/or networks
- Copyright violations
- Financial fraud
- Denial of service
- Pirating software
- System penetration
- Insider attacks

Motivational Variance

Differing motivations is the second reason why a single profile cannot be developed by psychological testing or by creating a profiling template. The motivations to commit these offenses are broad in scope and different for each individual. Motivating factors might include revenge, financial instability, thrill seeking, fun, intellectual challenge, goal fulfillment, greed, fear, stress, rebellion, protest, believed justification, extortion, blackmail, and the list goes on. Those who commit computer crimes are hackers, crackers, individuals, groups, terrorists, disgruntled employees, former employees, terminated employees, industrial spies, government spies, contractors, competitor informants, members of organized crime, and those who have a cause or reason to protest.

Perpetrator Variance

The third reason why a single hacker profile cannot be generated is due to the variance of individuals: emotionally, intellectually, psychologically, and culturally. People are dynamic and life is dynamic, thus incentives, motivations, beliefs, methods of attack, and circumstances change over time as well. Cybercrimes have been committed by all types of people from all around the world. The only general statement that can be made accurately at this juncture is that the majority of cybercrimes are committed by males. Types of perpetrator variance include gender, ethnicity, race, level of technical ability, level of social skill, and cross-cultural variance. Perpetrators might be working alone or with others, they could be insiders or outsiders, and their ages have also varied.

Part II: Insider Attacks

Many current surveys and research studies indicate that human beings—and primarily "insiders"—are the cause of most computer attacks. In addition to the issue of an "inside job" is the fact that an insider could help an outsider gain access. Outside hackers with inside knowledge can likewise cause a great deal of expensive damage to the network, can cause time and cost damage for those who have to spend their time assessing and rebuilding the destroyed parts, and can damage the reputation of a company. All security breaches cost an employer, even the ones not defined as being "data destructive."

Although attacks conducted purely by outsiders can certainly wreak havoc, the inside job is perceived to be destructive to the organization. This is probably a psychological factor—no one wants to believe that "one of our own" could do such a terrible thing. An insider-gone-bad shatters the perception (however false it might be) that when employees join the ranks of an organization, they are a loyal part of the family. The public has witnessed this type of reaction every time a new spy is uncovered in the CIA or at the FBI. The truth of the matter is that no matter what organization people work for, they are still just people. Perhaps they are mostly good people, but some will become a risk and a threat to the organization by conducting insider attacks.

Most agencies, corporations, and organizations prepare for and try to prevent insider attacks. Corporations have attorneys and technical experts who advise and implement deterrents. The most popular deterrents include the signing of nondisclo-sure agreements, noncompete agreement, and nonsolicitation agreements; participation in ongoing ethics training; and participation in training programs that focus on corpo-rate policies and rules, including computer use policies. The preceding answers and ideas to prevent insider incidents are mostly ineffective and antiquated; some are even humorous. Lawyers can't stop insider incidents with wordy agreements, new policies, and more documents for employees to sign.

Technical and physical security policies, as developed in Stage 1 (preparation), try to prevent the loss of sensitive data by monitoring employees online and by implementing security badges, cameras, biometric devices, and locked or secured areas. Technology can't stop insiders with legitimate access. All the monitoring in the world cannot pre-vent the best and the brightest from accessing data or sabotaging an internal system. Some of these insiders are the ones with legitimate, authorized access to sensitive pro-jects anyway. The truly deviant do not care that they have signed documents. They feel entitled to the data. Other clever thieves and criminals will go about taking insider advantage without technically doing anything to violate the signed agreements. The obvious and the inept will be detected, and some of the less sophisticated attempts to use proprietary data or to violate a patent will be found out. Agreements and nondis-closures will only reinforce to those who are already honest and noncriminal to remain honest. The clever, the slick, and the sophisticated are getting away with murder—well, maybe theft—and will continue to behave in criminal and destructive ways.

Some of the government agencies and defense contractors implement polygraph tests, rigorous background investigations, and psychological screening tests before hir-ing. Some of these same agencies continually require an update to all these vetting strategies throughout an individual's employment. Once again, however, the news has indicated that even in the most rigid screening environments, such as the CIA and the FBI, spies are still hired, and insiders have turned spy and not been detected for years even with their follow-up security checks. Although background investigations can discover the obvious problems upfront (those with prior criminal histories and arrest records), generally speaking, the majority of people in the world who are active hack-ers, attackers, and crackers have not been arrested for a computer crime—or any crime. Therefore, a background investigation for the purposes of uncovering a would-be hacker before hiring the individual is almost a moot point.

The polygraph test is yet another misplaced idea for vetting hacker insiders. Although in many instances the polygraph is a useful tool, it usually works best for those who don't know how to beat it by doing breathing and heart-rate control exer-cises, those who don't feel guilty or inherently wrong about something they might have done, those who don't have respect for or fear of the polygraph process itself, or those who don't register conclusive results because their physiological responses were inconsistent across the exam. The point is that many hackers do not believe what they are doing is wrong, and thus they will not feel guilt or register a change on the poly-graph. Insiders who are there to conduct industrial espionage might be trained in how to beat a polygraph. If there is any doubt as to the capability of people to beat the polygraph, remember that there were East Germans, Cubans, and Soviets who all passed polygraphs during the Cold War and were still spies for their host countries, even though they were screened by our law enforcement and intelligence agencies.

On a business level, the polygraph can be an expensive and time-consuming tool that has very low probability of generating useful results for finding bad insiders. Even if inside attackers could be screened out during the hiring process, many insiders turn bad after they have been with the organization for a period of time. Career changes, job changes, management changes, position and responsibility changes, as well as other personal, nonrelated work pressures appear and can provide the catalysts for people to change. People might become disgruntled or greedy, have a need for revenge, feel entitlement, or experience many other things that would provide the motivation to launch an insider attack.

One method used to screen employees, contractors, new hires, potential hires, and temporary workers is the use psychological instruments and batteries. Some of the more popular instruments include the Minnesota Multiphasic Personality Inventory (MMPI), the California Personality Inventory (CPI), the Adjective Checklist (ACL), and even the Myers–Briggs Type Indicator, which is actually not a clinical assessment tool. Clinically assessing and then "profiling" an individual as he or she is prescreened for hire into a company can provide the employer with some personality traits and characteristics. However, it is not legal to administer clinical testing that would indicate a mental disability, according to the guidelines established by the Americans with Disabilities Act of 1992 and the Rehabilitation Act of 1973 (sections 503 and 504). Clinical assessments that lead to identifying a mental disorder or impairment (which are listed in the Diagnostic and Statistical Manual of Mental Disorders, currently the DSM5) are defined as medical examinations, and under the law, employers cannot require medical exams until after an applicant has been given a conditional job offer (section 501, Rehabilitation Act of 1973; 29 U.S.C.A. section 791 [g], 1994; section 504, 29 U.S.C.A. sections 793 [d], 794 [d], 1994). Clinical assessments are not legally permissible during a prehiring phase when these types of tools would be the most useful.

The other problem with using psychological instruments is that the profile of a "good employee" must be derived by testing a sample of good employees and then screening the potential ones against the desired scores of the established ones. Clinical data identifying the characteristics of a good employee might be available, depending on the test, but many employees test well and start out as good employees. These good employees can, over time and because of certain life circumstances, turn into disgruntled employees, as stated earlier. The other issue is that many of the variables that determine a good employee are the same variables that have been used by those who conduct psychological tests to describe a good hacker (such as excellent technical skills, introverted, unsophisticated interpersonal skills, compulsive Internet users).

Another issue regarding clinical instruments is the ability of the test taker to falsify answers. Faking responses based uon the obviousness of the questions—and the fact that many of these assessments have been in use for decades—might enable the test taker to choose the response that is "appropriate." It is not difficult to select the proper

Likert scale answers to questions such as, "I have disturbing thoughts," "The world is confusing," "I feel rage easily," and "I have violent urges." These tests are so transparent and have been around for so long that even the layperson who has never had a course in psychology can easily figure out what the question is asking.

Specifically, the problem of criminal attacks on computers is extremely complicated due to the perpetrators coming from both the inside and outside of a particular company. In addition, the motivations, rationales, and methods of attack differ not only between insiders and outsiders but on an individual basis. Even though hackers have been stereotyped as introverts and socially inept, many use the MO of social engineering to obtain the information needed to break and enter. An additional complication, specifically with labeling hackers as introverts, involves the definition of introversion itself and the testing tools used to categorize introverts versus extraverts. In everyday use, and in line with the nonclinical Myers-Briggs Type Indicator, extraversion and introversion have been linked to a person's interpersonal sociability. Extraverts are social, outgoing, friendly, and open. Introverts are interpersonally shy, withdrawn, reserved, and reticent. When assessing or profiling hackers and potential disgruntled employees, it might be easy to socially categorize them as introverts due to their lack of desire for interpersonal communication with others face to face. However, communication modes in our society have changed. There is a shift in social behavior from communication face to face to social interaction over the Internet. These hackers are very social, using chat rooms, bulletin boards, and other online communications networks. Thus, these computer communicators are both directing their energies toward others as well as generating a high degree of focus toward an object outside themselves—the computer itself. The vehicle and means of communication have been socially altered, but the clinical tests have not been likewise altered to reflect the cultural and societal shift.

Some insider attacks also occur after an employee has been terminated, so no amount of vetting, screening, assessing, or testing upfront during the hiring process could predict or prevent a former employee from launching an attack with his or her still fully intact insider knowledge. This concept of a former employee with insider knowledge is also tangentially related to the inside-out attack. The *inside-out attack* is when an individual on the inside is either knowingly or unknowingly providing someone on the outside with inside information. This particular type of incident is difficult to investigate because on the onset it appears that the attack has been launched from an external source. However, as the investigation progresses, it becomes apparent that the attacker could have only compromised those systems or servers with some inside help or knowledge. After the inside link is detected, the incident becomes far more complicated to investigate. The person on the inside "assisting" the incident response team could end up to be the wayward insider.

The last issue related to insider problems concerns the insider who is really hired by, paid by, and trained by organized crime, foreign intelligence agencies, or other groups for the sole purpose of infiltrating an organization. Don't forget that an insider can technically also include business partners, teaming partners, joint ventures, subcontractors, and other partnerships. A review of recent organized crime cases, for example, Operation Uptick, revealed a vast and complex organized crime scheme in the stock brokerage and investment industry in New York City. Any legitimate companies affiliated with the front companies were duped into believing in their validity; all of their sensitive and proprietary information was being used for insider-trading purposes and stock trade "pump and dump" schemes. So there are instances in which companies acquire insiders or others who get inside information by virtue of business partnerships and affiliations. Certainly, due diligence can be conducted on any company to validate its legitimacy, and this should be done. There are people and entities out there, however, who are extremely experienced and good at creating facades and conning even the most discriminating people.

Why Insiders Attack

So, what can organizations do? The first thing every corporation, agency, or business needs to understand is the "why." Why do insiders attack? There are too many possible motives to cover every case of why an insider attacks. In general, however, there are eight motivational categories: greed, no perceived choice, revenge or retribution, entitlement, curiosity, challenge or ego, serious business, and accident.

Greed

Some insiders just want to make money. The lure of selling data or stealing property fulfills their need to make more money than their salary allows. Insider trading and other financial or stock manipulation schemes (using insider information) are a common byproduct of greed.

No Perceived Choice—Had to Do It

Due to personal circumstances, perhaps totally unrelated to the job or the employer, some insiders find themselves in unrecoverable financial situations. The only perceived way out of ruin is to take what the company has to offer and sell it, exploit it, or use it to turn a profit. Those who find themselves believing that they "had to do it" are sometimes in debt and cannot afford their basic living expenses—even though those expenses might not be in any way extravagant. Divorce, gambling, poor investments, extreme medical bills, or other life changes are only some of the reasons why people find themselves in what they perceive to be dire straits. In some cases, the insiders might want to believe that they are only "borrowing" from their employer. In other cases, the insiders feel so positively about the employer they were compromising and stealing from that they felt they were treating their employer as they would their family—leaning on the resources that are available.

Revenge or Retribution

Other insiders conduct attacks against their employers for pure revenge or retribution. At some point, the employee feels that he or she has not been treated fairly by a specific manager or even by the company as a whole. Anger, frustration, rage, and anxieties build, finally exploding into an attack. In some cases, these insiders target the person(s) that they have perceived treated them unfairly or badly, and in some cases, the incident is targeted toward the entire company. The choice of whether to make the attack personal against someone or more generally against the reputation or name of the organization depends on who the attacker believes should experience the consequences.

Entitlement

Similar to the motive of revenge is the motive of entitlement. Insiders who attack because of entitlement might believe they were unfairly overlooked for that raise, that promotion, or that bonus. This insider might feel that the employer is just too incompetent to recognize true hard work and brilliance; thus the insider feels entitled to give him- or herself a bonus.

Curiosity

Many inside incidents, particularly those defined as "unauthorized use of systems," are a result of a Curious George–type just poking around to see what he or she can get into. Although this type of behavior violates most computer-use policies and may even be illegal, many of these insiders really do not believe they are doing anything wrong. These curious intruders might not damage anything, copy anything, delete anything, or take anything.

Challenge or Ego

An extension of the curious are those who crack into systems for the challenge, the fun, and to enhance their egos. These insiders are driven by their technical prowess and the desire to demonstrate it, if only to themselves. Again, this type of behavior violates computer-use policies and likewise might be considered illegal.

Serious Business

Insiders who are there for the sole purpose of exploiting the organization are engaged in serious business. Employees who are linked to organized crime or who are part of industrial espionage are there to do serious harm and damage. Corporate sabotage, intelligence gathering, and theft are only a few of the reasons these employees are walking the halls. They have been employed by their "true employer" for the single reason of gathering, stealing, or planting information within your organization. These insiders are extremely difficult to spot, are near impossible to account for, and are very well versed and professional concerning their business of sabotage.

Accident

Some insiders create incidents but do so purely by accident or because of naivety. Many honest people who have no intent to do harm to themselves, others, or their employer inadvertently end up being the perpetrator of an incident. These insiders are perhaps not aware of the corporate policies and rules or maybe acted in a way that is not covered in the policy. People post things to the Internet that they should not, sometimes with the best of intentions. People talk to other people, not realizing that they are disclosing proprietary information. Accidents also happen to firewalls and servers. An incorrectly written protocol or a PERL or JAVA program with errors can create problems that might, in fact, look as if someone was attempting to do malicious damage to the organization.

Possible Solutions

So what can companies and organizations do to lessen the chance of an insider attack? There are certain things that an organization can do on the human level to reduce vulnerability, increase security awareness, and perhaps prevent an incident from occurring. One recommendation is to train and educate all employees regarding organizational policies for acceptable computer use. Training does help, and it also ensures that the organization is doing its best to educate the employees regarding security. Training courses will not cure the problem, but it is one piece of a multilayered security approach.

Another recommendation is to maintain the mound of legal paperwork that most new employees sign at the commencement of their employment. Although these legal documents and nondisclosure agreements don't necessarily act as a deterrent, the maintenance of these documents is important for the company.

Do not overreact or overprotect when it comes to online access or network access. Some companies deny Internet access and external email privileges to their employees. This is not the answer. Restricting or prohibiting Internet or email access with the outer world is at best antiquated and will eventually take a toll on business.

Conduct an overall organizational assessment to ascertain where your company's hot spots are and when you are most at risk for attack. Some of the most common warning signs of insider attacks waiting to happen include times of mergers, acquisitions, or downsizing; management changes (though sometimes this can be good); post performance evaluation time; bonus, promotion, or raise time; and geographic relocation of physical office space—particularly if people are being relocated into cubicles from offices or are being moved from a single office to a shared office. Any change that alters the reality or the environment or forces employees into a different thought process is cause for pause. People do react to stress; unfortunately, it's not always in a constructive way.

Extend an organizational assessment to include an Internet and web search of your company's name and other critical aspects of your business. Understanding how easy it is to obtain information on an individual or an organization is the first step toward better protection. Conducting an open-source collection on your company or assessing its message boards is a good way to take the temperature of the corporate culture in a very public and noninvasive way. The information on the public Internet is just that—public. No one should have the assumption that posting something is private.

Conduct a physical assessment of your facilities and work environments. Many environmental factors might actually promote or encourage online misbehavior. Again, changes in environment can affect employees. Other considerations for a physical security review include things like clean air circulation, appropriate ventilation, and heating and cooling systems. All these precautions promote the well-being of an employee and decrease stress.

In light of all the stumbling blocks concerning the use of psychological assessments as a prescreening tool to identify potential cybercriminals, the concept of a prehiring evaluation is sound. There are other types of behavioral assessment instruments, defined as nonclinical tests, that could be used to determine job suitability based on skills, education, and occupational experience. There are also nonclinical instruments that measure personality and behavioral characteristics. Although not as powerful as a clinical instrument from a pure psychological perspective, these tools, for not only legal reasons, are better suited for employee selection. These nonclinical assessments not only focus on job suitability and skills, they do not contain the obvious psychiatry-laden questions that are easily picked out and answered "appropriately."

The real answer to preventing insider attacks is the ability to understand your corporate culture. An in-depth understanding of an organization can be obtained and should be conducted as part of Stage 1, preparation.

Investigating Insiders

One of the more difficult investigations to conduct is the incident that involves an insider or group of insiders. Incident response teams should be very well trained and educated as to the company's corporate policies regarding the treatment of insiders and should consult with an attorney regarding the legal rights of an insider. There are three considerations to always keep in mind when conducting an internal investigation:

1. Everyone might be a suspect because the perpetrator is on the inside.

2. The revelation that an incident was perpetrated by an insider might cause extra stress and worry for other employees and management. (People might become anxious or paranoid and might view the investigation as a witch hunt.)

3. The manner in which the investigation is handled is a reflection on both the incident response team and the company.

In most cases, if an insider is suspected, two other departments must be brought into to investigation: human resources and physical security. Both of these departments have access to information that might assist the incident response team in the investigation. These departments might also play active roles in supporting the ongoing components or results of the investigation (such as interviewing suspects, issuing disciplinary notices, or conducting terminations). The legal counsel should also be present and consulted during the phases of an insider investigation.

If insiders need to be questioned or interviewed as part of the investigation, this process should be well planned, well executed, and well documented. The incident response team members need to have a well-rounded skill set in addition to having computer skills, firewall knowledge, various OS backgrounds, and virus knowledge. The IT incident response team members should be well versed in interview techniques and should have excellent interpersonal skills.

Employees who are suspects and others who have incident-related information might need to be interviewed. As the investigator, you should be able to structure the entire interviewing process. Incident responders should have the following information before any interviewing takes place:

1. The names of those employees who need to be interviewed.

2. The people who will be conducting the interviews: Are they from the company's physical security or HR department or from the incident response team?

3. A consistent and nonthreatening approach to all interviewees. Figure out exactly what is going to be said, what the purpose of the interview is, and what will be told to the interviewees.

4. An appropriate place to conduct the interviews without interruptions.

5. Times and dates of the interviews and approximately how long each one will initially last. Follow-up interviews can be conducted a later time.

6. The order of the interviewees: Who should be interviewed before whom?

7. The selection and presence of a third party as a witness during all interviews.

The questions asked during the interviews should be a mix of technical- and behavioral-based questions—again, prepared well in advance of the interviews. Preparation and planning do not mean you should exclude open discussion or taking a different tactic during an interview session. Good investigators will conduct each interview slightly differently because the interviewees are all individuals and are different. Flexibility and thinking on your feet are also essential.

All interviews, even those conducted over the phone, should be documented. Records of these interviews might end up as evidence; therefore, the discussions must be documented as accurately as possible. The following are some of the things that should be recorded as part of the documentation process:

1. The interview data, time, and place

2. The arrival time of the interviewee

3. The names of the interviewee, the interviewer, and the witness

4. The questions asked and the answers provided

5. Any observations that might be considered nonverbal

6. The time at which the interview ended

7. Whether the interviewee is a candidate for a follow-up interview

During this interview process, the reputation of the interviewees must be maintained. Some interviewees will feel as though they are being singled out or picked on, or they might believe that because they are being questioned in relation to an incident, their career and job will be negatively affected. Management needs to participate in this process to alleviate any fears. All interviews and treatment of employees must be done with utmost respect and decorum—even the interviews with the prime suspects.

The seasoned incident response team not only knows how to communicate well across departments, it knows when and with whom to communicate. The incident response team should have a "need to know" policy. Many mistakes are made by inexperienced incident response teams when they announce the problem to everyone with a technical background who will listen. Unfortunately, one of the technical experts being so helpful might be the attacker. Tipping the perpetrator off to the investigation is sure to ruin the chances of a successful outcome. A clear chain of communication is a requirement. Human nature sometimes indicates that we trust those around us and those with whom we work. There have been too many documented incidents of insiders who have been the perpetrators of cyberincidents.

Part III: Incident Victims

The victim of the attack is not just the system or individual being stalked; there are some additional or peripheral victims who also are affected by incidents of cybercrime. In incident response, it is important not only to discover the threat and the technical means of penetration, but to understand what the reactions will be to this incident—from other employees, the executives, the stockholders, the competitors, the public, advertisers, new recruits, current clients, and potential customers. Like the fallout of a conventional crime that affects more than just the victim, an information security breach does not end when all the systems are rebooted, scanned, fixed, and secured. Understanding and assessing all of the victims of an attack is critical to all stages of the investigation and incident response process (see Chapter 3 for details regarding the six-stage methodology).

Anyone who has ever been a victim of a violent crime knows that the victim who was attacked or assaulted is not the only victim. A woman who is raped in her neighborhood while jogging is clearly the victim. However, others are also affected by this horrendous crime, including the victim's family, her friends, and her neighbors who always thought the neighborhood was safe. As this case breaks on the news, more people will be affected: the community and perhaps even her colleagues at work. This incident might even impact sex-crime investigators, sexual assault laws, and women's rights groups. The impact of a cybercrime incident could have the same domino effect.

Typically, when an incident occurs, the fundamental and sometimes only focus is on the box, system, network, or server compromised. There are far more issues and implications, however, than the damaged or compromised system. Putting the technical issues aside, here is a list of potential human victims:

1. The individual(s) targeted or the actual victim(s)
2. The family, friends, and guardians of the target
3. Members of the organization
4. The "C-levels" (that is, the CEO, CIO, CFO)
5. The corporate board
6. The stockholders
7. The employees
8. The customers
9. The public
10. Members of the industry as a whole

Take, for example, any of the publicized distributed denial-of-service attacks in the news lately. The flood of packets that took down the servers did not make the servers themselves the only victims. The organizations had to deal with the media and the public nature of the attacks; the C-levels had to adjust their schedules, business plans, and goals to focus on recovery; the stocks were affected; the customers were affected; and ultimately the public's perception of online business was affected. The success or failure to bring the perpetrators to justice will likewise have an impact on the victims. Questions and concerns will arise: What if the perpetrators did more damage than we thought? What if the attackers disclose information to the public that we do not want out there? The ability of an incident response team to understand the big picture—including the political, public, financial, business, and future ramifications of an incident—distinguishes the inexperienced incident response team from the premiere incident response team.

In addition to DDOS attacks, viruses, and server compromises, many cases of cybercrime target an individual or a group of people within an organization. Even though the weapon is technical, the real affect of the crime resembles a conventional crime. Whether the technical attack is classified as cyberstalking, cyberharassment, or a threat, the victim is clearly a human being. Incident response teams must have a qualified individual as part of the team to understand the variables that enter the picture when a person is the target of computer crime. Having an incident response team member who is just good with people is not enough. Cases of cyberstalking do go to court. The team member who deals with the human side of incident response should have the credentials to stand up in court as an expert witness, have the capability to provide depositions, and be well versed in victim counseling. In some instances, an incident response team might have to deal with the manager, spouse, family, or parents of a victim and interview and counsel them, too. The one thing an incident response team cannot do is make victims feel worse or neglected or fail to provide them with the best possible consultation, particularly when it would affect their psychological and mental well-being or their physical safety. In the cases in which children have been the victims of terrible cyberharassment cases or cyberpornography cases, law enforcement should be called in immediately.

Here are some of the decisions or options for a victim of cybercrime:

1. Contracting or enlisting the assistance of a physical security detail.

2. Asking for additional police checks on residences and places of employment. Usually, local law enforcement is able to work in some extra security checks during regular neighborhood patrols.

3. Attaining the services of an employee-assistance program, which typically has counselors on staff for both psychological counseling and financial counseling.

4. Seeking therapy or psychiatric counseling in a private setting.

These options can be implemented on a short-term or long-term basis, as dictated by both the victim and the progression of the case. The following paragraphs discuss an example of how a victim was mishandled in a cyberstalking case.

An incident response team was called in to investigate a case of cyberstalking. A female employee had been receiving increasingly frightening emails for almost three months. She finally told her boss, and the incident response team was called into investigate. The inexperienced incident response team went to work contacting the sender's ISP, tracking the email account, looking at firewall logs, and employing all the other appropriate technical investigation tactics. The team scoured the Internet, looking for other places this stalker might have used his address or a similar name in a screen name. The team was bound and determined to identify her stalker. However, no one ever made appropriate contact with the human resources department, no one made appropriate contact with the legal department (remember, stalking is a crime), no one asked whether the victim felt threatened, and no one was able to make that assessment because all the focus was on the technical trail. As a result, no one called the physical security department or employee assistance to help the victim.

The incident response team was eventually able to identify the cyberstalker, and it was another employee of the company. The investigation took almost three weeks, and in the meantime, she was left to her own devices. She had trouble sleeping, trouble concentrating, could barely do her work, and did not feel safe anywhere. The company and the incident response team failed to provide her with appropriate support during this incident. Even after the cyberstalker was identified and terminated, the victim's fears and stress continued. The incident response team was long gone by this point and did not even realize that just because the perpetrator was caught, it did not mean the entirety of the case was over. This unfortunate result could have been avoided.

It is important to understand the dynamics of what a victim might experience in order to provide better assistance and consultation during all stages of incident response. Most people can probably imagine what it must be like to be stalked in the conventional sense, an individual physically being stalked by another individual. Imagine the stalker lurking outside your home or your office, following you to the store, and perhaps leaving notes on your car and letters in your mailbox. The dynamics of the cyberstalker are similar but in many ways are also very different. The victim's emotional and psychological reaction to cyberstalking differs, generally speaking, from a victim's reaction to conventional stalking. Victims of cyberstalking tend to experience higher levels of paranoia, the perception that there is no safe haven, a higher level of suspicion (the perpetrator is perceived to be anywhere, everywhere, anyone, and everyone), and a fear of other intrusions.

All of these victim reactions make sense. Most of the time, in a conventional stalking case, the victim knows who his or her stalker is or at least knows what the stalker looks like because stalkers typically show themselves or are seen lurking around. The victim of cyberstalking typically does not know who the stalker is or what he or she looks like. The cyberstalker is cloaked behind the anonymity of the Internet and might only stalk or communicate via email. Thus, the reactions of paranoia and seeing everyone as a suspect make sense. If the victim cannot see the stalker, everyone is suspect.

Because the threats are coming in via email, sometimes the victims perceive that they have no safe haven. Victims of conventional stalking, although in a state of constant fear, do report that they have places where they feel safer. These safe havens might be a friend's home, the office, or traveling on business or for pleasure—somewhere where the stalker does not surface or does not appear to surface. The cyberstalking victim feels that, because the Internet is everywhere and you can carry a laptop home, on business trips, to the office, and really wherever you go, there is no real safe place away. If the victim is to continue to function in an electronic world, conduct business, and communicate with friends and family, most believe they cannot sacrifice or give up email. Even victims who have changed addresses are still found by their stalkers.

Due to the perception of no safe haven, many victims of cyberstalking experience increased anxiety and a type of depression. They have reported sleep problems, eating difficulties, and other physical manifestations of stress. The victims of conventional stalking are fearful of being physically harmed or killed by their stalker, and this, of course, is enormously straining. The victims of cyberstalking likewise fear physical harm, but they also assume that their cybersavvy stalker will also infiltrate other areas of their life, like cracking into their bank accounts or somehow cracking into their computers and having access to all their emails and personal documents.

Victims of cyberstalking tend to report the cases later than victims of conventional stalking. This lapse in time is understandable but also can present problems for an incident response team. People are consistently more likely to report a strange person skulking around and looking out of place than to report the receipt of one odd email. People get strange and odd email all the time; between advertisements, solicitations, and just plain nuisance mail, a lot of junk gets delivered. Sometimes an email arrives that is clearly not intended for the recipient. No big deal. However, after a few more seemingly wrong emails arrive, the victims still do not typically report the harassment. Not until the stalker either accelerates or escalates to a level that would make the hair on anyone's neck stand up do the cyber victims generally report this type of crime. In many cases, the victim has actually corresponded with the stalker, not realizing what would eventually come to be.

Part IV: Human Side of Incident Response

So far, the point of this chapter is how and why to add the human side to incident response investigation techniques. This section is going to shift gears slightly and focus on the incident responders themselves. First, what is an incident responder? Who might likely end up in this type of job? What kind of hours do these responders keep? Understanding the personalities and the dynamics of an incident response team is also critical to its success. Incident response teams are similar in dynamics to firefighters and SWAT teams. They consist of bright, highly energized people who like to think, solve problems, be challenged, and respond in a time of crisis. Incident responders themselves live for the incident and the uncertainty. Every incident is different, exciting, and new. The one thing that incident responders do not realize or ever focus on is the physiological and psychological strain being placed on them and the people around them. Fatigue, stress, dehydration, sleep depravation, and lack of food are common byproducts of responders working a long, involved incident.

When the incident response hotline rings, the responders kick into motion. This is the fun part of the job—incident investigation. People become incident responders because they respond well to pressurized situations and like the adrenaline boost that surges during times of crisis. Not only do responders like the initial excitement of a case, they hang on much longer than they should without appropriate rest, food, and water. When an incident carries on for more than 48 hours, incident responders start to suffer from sleep deprivation. During the course of that first 48 hours, these team members are not likely to stop for a healthy meal or a drink near enough to water to maintain proper hydration. The stresses and challenges of the case are probably catching up with everyone. Between fatigue and a lack of food, sleep, and water, combined with the normal frustrations of the investigation itself, the incident response team is wiped out by now. Well before getting to this stage at 48 hours, the team was possibly starting to operate slower, starting to think less clearly and slower, and perhaps even starting to make a few minor mistakes. Decision-making skills and the ability to make good judgments are adversely related to lack of sleep, food, and water. It is sometimes difficult for the team members to realize they are experiencing symptoms of exhaustion. Communication begins to break down between the team when everyone is tired, hungry, and probably a bit cranky.

In addition to the responder's issues of fatigue, it is a good idea to recognize that although 48 hours might go by in a flash for the responder, his or her friends, family members, and other colleagues might need to be in touch. During long-standing incidents, incident responders have been known to remain at the office for hours and hours or even days at a stretch. Firefighters and police officers know that their family lives and personal lives can suffer dramatically due to their intense work schedule.

To prevent some of these problems from occurring, incident response teams should do the following:

1. Create policies that encourage shift work during long hours.

2. Have on site provisions for a few days (juices, bottled water, food).

3. Have fly-away kits prepared with a mini version of certain provisions so that when the team is on the road, the bag already contains sustenance.

4. Have a quiet room somewhere or maybe part of the lab to have cot, couch, or resting place for the team.

5. Make sure there is scheduled time for all the responders to call home or friends to maintain contact.

The maintenance of a physically and mentally healthy incident response team is too important not to consider. The successful closure of a case might depend on it.

Summary

The overall cost and concern for information security is immense. Incident response teams are sprouting up in greater number within organizations and as specialty service divisions of information security companies. So far, the tools of incident response have been technical. Human- and behavior-based solutions and tools must be integrated into the technical models to combat the spectrum of threats facing individuals and organizations today.

Cybercrime profiling and other behavioral assessment techniques can be used in conjunction with technical tools to prevent, predict, and mitigate incidents. Profiling can be utilized throughout the incident response process and can supplement each of the six stages of response: preparation, detection, containment, eradication, recovery, and follow-up. Although the methodologies of cybercrime profiling have been integrated with incident response, social scientific tools applied to the issues of computer crime have not been fully tapped. Within the disciplines of criminology, behavioral science, psychology, and anthropology, more research needs to be conducted to enhance our knowledge about changing world cultures and communication, changes in technology and how that changes human behavior, how technology effects society, and how organizations are impacted by the transformations stemming from a rapidly changing and advancing technological world.

The combination of technical science and social science is a powerful one, and it can be applied and utilized within the field of incident response. Over the years, the synthesis of technical science and social science has provided a significant boost to conventional criminal investigation, interview and interrogation techniques, and even crime prevention. The same fusion can provide technical specialists and incident response teams with an added perspective and thus perhaps an additional solution. The fields of information technology and behavioral science rarely meet, and when they do, their perspectives, methodologies, and paradigms are very different. However, it is when these differences blend and begin to complement one another that more comprehensive solutions and advancements are made.

12

Traps and Deceptive Measures

FOR YEARS, INFORMATION SECURITY PROFESSIONALS AND OTHERS have been attempting to fight computer crime and misuse. Few would disagree that despite the emergence of new standards and technology (including better intrusion detection technology, sophisticated third-party authentication methods, advanced encryption algorithms, improved procedures, more types of professional certification, and other new approaches and developments), computer crime and misuse are actually becoming worse. Why?

Many potential explanations exist; one particularly plausible one is that security professionals' approaches almost invariably lag behind the approaches used by those who attack systems and networks. Attackers constantly develop new methods and tools. Security professionals keep using what they consider to be "tried and true" countermeasures—countermeasures that might or might not counter the most recent types of threats. Worse yet, security professionals often do not understand who is attacking them as well as how and why. Fortunately, methods designed to identify attackers and how they do what they do are available. Among the most interesting and potentially useful of these methods are traps and deception. In this chapter, we'll look into types of deceptive measures and traps that can be used, consider the advantages and disadvantages of using deceptive measures and traps, delve into a few specific types, and finally explore how each can be used during the process of responding to incidents. First, let's consider some basic definitions.

About Traps and Deceptive Measures

Traps and deceptive measures are measures that appear to be real systems, services, environments, and so forth, but they're not. Deceptive measures are designed to cause people who attack and misuse systems and networks to obtain false information or to interact with virtual or other nonreal environments in which they can do little, if any, harm. A "trap" is designed to keep an attacker in one place (that is, one system or one application and so forth) so that the behavior and actions of the attacker can be recorded and analyzed, possibly (but not necessarily) for the purpose of use as evidence in a court of law. *Deceptive measures* are thus broader in scope; *traps* are one of several types of deceptive measures. Traps and deceptive measures encompass a wide range of methods and tools, of which honeypots, automated messages, Trojaned commands, and virtual environments are some of the best known.

Honeypots

We will first consider what honeypots are and why they are used.

What Are Honeypots?

In the most fundamental sense, a *honeypot* is a computer designed to attract attackers. The computer is not a real server; it is not intended for legitimate users. It appears, however, to be a real server or service by blending in with the normal environment. It performs and responds as users expect; if properly designed and implemented, it should not disrupt the computing environment. If the honeypot incorporates a trap element, this element is not obvious. At the same time, a honeypot logs everything that an attacker or potential attacker does.

Goal

The major goal of honeypots is rather simple—to have an adversary find and use a tempting environment that is so credible that the adversary devotes considerable attention to it. All the while, "white hat" personnel are monitoring and recording what the adversary does, but the adversary does not notice the monitoring and recording activity (provided, of course, that the honeypot is designed and implemented correctly). Another possible goal is to gather evidence (possibly legal evidence), as discussed in a later part of this chapter.

Automated Messages

Automated messages are messages[1] sent to a user when usage of a system or application is suspicious. As mentioned in Chapter 3, "A Methodology for Incident Response," many attacks occur during nonworking hours. An ingenious system administrator or someone else could configure a system to display an intimidating login message (for example, whenever someone tries to login between midnight and 5 a.m. and possibly also on weekends). Alternatively, a message might appear minutes or hours after a user has logged in. A user might, for instance, attempt to do something suspicious, such as enter the `rpcinfo` and `showmount` commands. This might trigger the display of an automated message on the user's screen.

The intimidating message might, at a minimum, warn against unauthorized usage. In a more extreme case, this message might ask the person who is attempting to log in to call a certain phone number to provide positive identification. Consider the following possible messages:

"Do not continue to attempt to log in to this system unless you are a legitimate user. Our policy is to prosecute all unauthorized access to this and other systems. Everything you are doing on this system is being monitored."

"We have traced the origin of your connection and are verifying whether the connection is legitimate."

"You are using an account that has not been used in so long that we consider your access pattern suspicious—please call 415-445-4545 to verify your identity immediately."

Goal

The rationale of automated messages is to capitalize on the desire of most attackers to remain anonymous. Many times, the first thing an attacker who breaks into a UNIX or Linux system will do is enter the `who` command to determine who is on the compromised system at that time. If it appears that the system administrator is logged in, many attackers will log out immediately. When a message such as one of the preceding is displayed, attackers are likely to think they have been discovered, prompting them to move on to other systems.

---

1. Chapter 7, "Legal Issues," discusses the importance of having system warning banners, banners that are displayed during logins. Automated messages go beyond logon banners in that they are context dependent and are displayed any time after the login banner appears to the time the user logs out.

Implementing Automated Messages

Implementing automated messages usually is not difficult. The easiest implementation methods include integrating messages into login script execution or the `lastlogin` message in UNIX and Linux. Scheduling one or more message displays via a cron job in UNIX and Linux or an at/Task Scheduler job in Windows NT or Windows 2000 is another alternative. Some significant hurdles exist, however, the most notable of which is a lack of existing tools that provide suitable automated message-generation support capability. Another is the difficulty of making messages look contextually plausible. An attacker who repeatedly receives the identical message will quickly learn that the message is bogus. It is important, therefore, to ensure that a variety of contextually plausible messages will be displayed.

Trojaned Commands

Still another approach is using Trojaned commands. This section discusses what Trojaned commands are and how they can be used.

What Are Trojaned Commands?

Certain commands are used disproportionately by attackers who are "door knob rattling" (that is, using methods that provide information about potential victim systems). The following are some possible target commands:

- `finger`
- `rwho`
- `rpcinfo`
- `showmount`
- `nslookup`

The "white hat" community often counters the threat that such commands pose by disabling these commands altogether. Instead of disabling dangerous commands, however, it might in some circumstances be prudent to modify them to provide misinformation. For example, someone who uses `finger` on a potential victim machine might obtain output that shows that root is using the system, something that normally intimidates potential attackers. Similarly, the output might show a list of users on the system, all of which represent bogus accounts set up to provide an alarm if an attacker logs in to any of them. Most importantly, however, all command usage (including the time of command entry, the source address, and so forth) can be logged.

Goal

The major goal of using Trojaned commands is making systems and networks harder to attack by deceiving actual and potential attackers. By providing attackers with bogus user names, bogus IP addresses, and so forth, use of this deception method can considerably elevate the work factor necessary to successfully attack systems.

Evaluation

One of the major advantages of using Trojaned commands is the simplicity of this approach. All a person has to do is modify existing commands. (This, of course, depends on the availability of source code.) Furthermore, no special machines are necessary; Trojaned commands can be used on any non-honeypot server!

One of the major disadvantages, however, is that only a limited subset of commands is suitable. It makes sense to use the Trojan commands approach with commands such as `finger` and `rpcinfo`, but most commands that a normal user would use are not suitable. Consider, for example, what would have to be done to cause bogus output to be displayed when the `mount` or `net use` commands are entered. Additionally, there is a real risk of disruption when legitimate users enter one or more trojaned commands. Legitimate users can enter any of the commands that are more suitable for use with this approach; the output they receive is likely to cause a flood of help desk calls and waste the users' time (causing frustration and possibly hostility). Finally, it takes considerable time and ingenuity to set up Trojaned commands that are credible to attackers. If a potential attacker uses `finger` on a system once and then again two hours later, finding exactly the same list of users and session characteristics, the attacker will quickly realize that something is wrong. The attacker then might post a message warning other would-be attackers, thus rendering the use of Trojaned commands useless.

Virtual Environments

The next alternative we will consider is the use of virtual environments.

What Are Virtual Environments?

Virtual environments are special, safe environments (usually in the form of special shell environments) that are set up after users log in. These environments are normally created by execution of shell scripts for a special account, often one that has already been compromised and to which an attacker is likely to return. The normal authentication program is used when anyone tries to gain access to a system, but to create a virtual environment, one replaces the normal login shell with a special one.

One of the most fascinating tales in the entire computer and information security arena is the story of "Berferd[2]," a Dutch attacker who regularly broke into a system at AT&T Bell Laboratories several years ago. Bill Cheswick, then a researcher at AT&T Bell Laboratories, noticed these attacks and set up a "jail (virtual) environment" for him. Thinking that he had gained a root shell, Berferd logged in to the victim system time after time. In reality, however, he was in a virtual environment in which his access was severely limited. All the while, Berferd's actions were being recorded; Cheswick traced the source of the attacks to the Netherlands.

---

2. Cheswick, William, and Steven Bellovin. *Firewalls and Internet Security: Repelling the Wily Hacker.* Addison Wesley, 1994.

Goal

The main goal of virtual environments is to create a safe environment for logins so that the actions of attackers can be recorded and analyzed. Receiving prompt notification that an attacker is once again active on a system is yet another possible goal.

How to Implement Virtual Environments

Implementing virtual environments does not need to be complicated. Cheswick originally used a small set of programs and alterations to the MIPS operating system. A normal UNIX or Linux system, however, is likely to be easier to use and certainly as functional in setting up a jail environment. You need to add at least one line such as the following to the /etc/passwd file, such as:

```
admin:*:111:111:ADMIN:/home/admin:/home/admin/root_sh
```

An unpassworded entry (or, in some cases, an easy-to-guess password) for each account must then be added to the shadow password file.

The key to successful jail environments is the shell environment created after a login. The root_sh shell must make the attackers believe they are in a real environment. Entering **cd ..**, for example, must ostensibly move the attackers to the parent directory of what appears to be the current working directory. The content of all files within directories such as /, /bin, /sbin, /dev/, /etc/, /usr, /var, /tmp, and others must be credible. All output from the user interaction in the jail environment can be sent to /var/log/hacker.log or another path, depending on the particular version of UNIX or Linux used.

Evaluation

Jail environments are particularly useful when attackers have been repeatedly breaking into systems but the decision to keep the systems running and connected to the network has been made. Jail environments can allow people dealing with the break-ins to record the actions of the perpetrators without additional appreciable risk to systems and networks. One of the downsides is that building credible jail environments can be difficult. With two major exceptions—both of which are commercial firewalls that place apparent attackers in a special, artificial environment rather than simply dropping packets—jail environment shells are not available in the public domain. Creating a custom shell for this purpose that will fool most attackers generally requires a great amount of effort and expertise. Additionally, whoever creates a jail environment shell must be careful to avoid security flaws that could allow attackers to break out of this shell, escalate privileges, initiate a core dump, and other undesirable outcomes.

Advantages and Limitations of Traps and Deceptive Measures

Regardless of the particular instantiation, traps and deceptive measures offer both advantages and disadvantages. This section of the chapter considers both.

Advantages

In the broadest sense, traps and deceptive measures deserve consideration because they represent a departure from traditional information and computer/information security countermeasures. Many security professionals are convinced that these traditional measures, such as password policies, password filters, system auditing, and so on, have lost much of their luster and effectiveness over time. Too often, attackers' strategies for attacking systems and networks are successful on the first try. If we could understand the behavior of perpetrators as they engage in unauthorized activity, however, we might be able to provide appropriate countermeasures. Traps and deceptive measures are particularly promising in this regard. Consider the potential benefits discussed in the following sections.

Providing a Moving Target

Traps and deceptive measures, in effect, can provide a moving target for attackers. A victim host on one day might be a bogus host the next day. A legitimate service, environment, or command can be changed. Attackers must now modify their goals and targets if they are to be successful in their efforts.

Increasing the Time and Work Factor Associated with Attacking Systems

In what is already widely regarded as the definitive paper on honeypots, Douglas Moran points out that attackers often allocate a certain amount of time to each target in an attempt to lower the probability of being detected.[3] If attackers spend their time in confusion or misdirection by reaching a bogus server, service, application, directory, and so on, time is more likely to run out. Additionally, if attackers have to discriminate between what is real and what is bogus as they engage in their efforts, the work factor is likely to increase. The likely result is fewer systems attacked and quite possibly fewer successful attacks.

Reducing the Potential for Damage

In World War II, fighting forces launched *drones*, decoy aircraft designed to draw fire away from normal aircraft. Various forms of deceptive measures can serve as *virtual drones* that help keep attackers away from valuable systems, services, and resources. Similarly, deploying decoy servers, services, and resources can also provide an early glimpse into attacker activities and types of tools (including any new tools) used. The result is a better ability to protect systems and networks by being able to deploy additional evasive measures before attacks actually reach the intended victim systems.

---

3. Moran, Douglas. "Effective deployment of honeypots against internal and external threats." *Information Security Bulletin*, 2000, Vol. 5, Issue 8, pp. 27–34.

Providing More Time for a Well-Planned, Efficient Response

The likelihood that attackers' efforts might be derailed or slowed is an advantage for security professionals. Instead of having to make instant decisions, they might now have the luxury of more time to plan a proper course of action, which in turn can lead to a more efficient and satisfactory incident response effort.

Providing Information that Traditional Tools Miss

Traps and deceptive measures also can record information that traditional tools such as intrusion detection systems (IDSs) and firewalls miss. Despite the fact that many IDSs seem to be improving in their detection capabilities, they nevertheless invariably miss a sizeable portion of attacks. Someone who has bypassed firewall defenses and then evaded intrusion-detection measures might next connect to a server or service that looks interesting. If the server or service is bogus, however, security staff and others will immediately learn of the presence of an attacker. Traps and deceptive measures are particularly valuable in discovering insider attacks, incidents that current IDSs are particularly poor in recognizing. Bogus servers (honeypots) are also valuable in helping determine when an attacker is performing network scans. Attackers typically deploy a variety of scanning methods—but in particular slow scanning—to avoid detection. Placing several bogus servers that yield data concerning scans can lead to the capability to correlate data across these servers. The benefit is the capability to conclusively identify that a scan has been launched within one's network. A honeypot sometimes is the only way to identify internal attacks.

Decreasing Attackers' Confidence

Another potential benefit of traps and deceptive measures is that, if deployed properly, they can lower the confidence of attackers. Attackers might not only wonder why they are not experiencing as much success as usual, they might also lose face if others learn that they have spent time attacking decoy systems, services, and resources. Loss of confidence can result in a reduction or cessation of attacks.

Yielding Intelligence Data

In a series of "Know your Enemy" papers, Lance Spitzner[4] argues that to truly secure systems, you must know who your enemy is and what the enemy can and is likely to do. Spitzner argues that honeypots provide an excellent way to "know your enemy."

Providing a Wake-Up Call to Management

The last advantage discussed here relates to educating and motivating management concerning security-related threats and their consequences. Security professionals can talk eloquently with management about the many security-related threats that are present as well as the ways these threats can be countered, but management's reaction typically is

---

4. Spitzner, Lance. www.enteract.com/~lspitz/honeypot.html, 2000.

disappointing. Data and observations from use of traps and deceptive measures often provide a wake-up call to management that something is wrong and danger is imminent. Traps and deceptive measures provide data that management generally finds more real and believable in contrast to something more obtuse such as the results of a risk analysis.

Limitations

Most traps and deceptive measures also have several inherent limitations, which are presented in the following sections.

Effort and Resources Required

Only the very naïve believe that you can set up a trap or other deceptive measure and then leave it alone until you are ready to harvest the results. These measures almost invariably necessitate closer monitoring—and greater attention to aspects such as where within a network they are placed—than normal systems. At the very minimum, the value of the information that these measures provide is generally very fleeting. Failing to promptly harvest this information is likely to render the information of little value. As will be discussed shortly, traps and deceptive measures need to be dynamic in nature to be credible, which generally requires a greater level of effort to implement. Additionally, any host on which traps or other deceptive measures are placed is a potential target of attack.

Difficulty of Creating Traps and Deceptive Measures with Sufficient Credibility

The problem of creating traps and deceptive measures that will genuinely fool attackers is one of the greatest obstacles to their deployment. Many attackers have years of experience and can see right through poorly designed or poorly implemented traps and deceptive measures. The sophistication of these implementations is extremely variable. More sophisticated implementations are more complete in every detail, have better logging, are fundamentally more secure[5] against attacks (and subversion attempts), and so forth. Less sophisticated implementations are laughable even to novice attackers. One of the potential advantages of buying commercial software to trap and deceive attackers is that such software is usually considerably higher in credibility.

The "Boomerang Factor"

Any computing platform on which some kind of trap or deceptive measure is implemented is a potential target of attack. An attacker does not need to be able to determine whether or not a particular system runs deceptive services to be able to compromise that system's security and then launch attacks on other systems. For example, an attacker might want to use a host that runs deception services to initiate

---

5. In fact, one of the chief characteristics of a good trap/deceptive measure is greater ability to resist attempts to attack and/or subvert the measure.

vulnerability scans, to be a Warez server, or to launch attacks on other systems. If the host that runs deception services is within an organization's internal network and if an attacker compromises that host's security, the attacker is now in a prime position to compromise other hosts within that network.

Case Study: A Honeypot Backfires on a Security Firm

According to www.theregister.co.uk, a New Zealand security company's use of a honeypot backfired on it. The company deployed a honeypot to monitor attacker activity but did little more than set up a poorly protected web server with no real data among its other web servers. A well-known cracker discovered that FrontPage had not been completely deinstalled from the honeypot web server and then exploited a vulnerability in a FrontPage extension to deface the web server. He then used access to the honeypot to gain access to critical systems deployed by the company. To add insult to injury, another attacker accessed and defaced the honeypot web server sometime afterward.

Someone from the company later admitted that the honeypot should have been connected to a separate network segment from which access to other systems should not have been possible. He also prescribed better monitoring efforts as well as suitable policies and procedures concerning the use of honeypots.

Difficulty in Integrating into the Overall Computing and Networking Environment

Integrating traps and deceptive measures into mainstream computing and networking environments is still another potentially significant challenge. In most organizations, achieving operational continuity is one of the highest goals. Bogus services and servers can be disruptive, however. A bogus server designed to "draw fire," for example, can be the target of many simultaneous DoS attacks, which can overload the network. Bogus servers that send logs and other data to other hosts can potentially flood the other hosts with data during times of intense activity. Furthermore, IP addresses must be allocated to bogus servers, but IP address space within an organization's network(s) might be scarce. Finally, users who stumble onto traps and deceptive measures and attempt to access or use them might not only experience work disruptions, they might also overwhelm help desk personnel with questions or requests for assistance. They might even also become suspects of an investigation—a potential witch hunt with many negative consequences!

Focus: Honeypots

Honeypots are currently the most popular of all traps and deceptive measures. Accordingly, we'll take a detailed look at some of the main issues related to honeypots and their use. The meaning of "honeypot," however, is not universally agreed upon, so we'll start by exploring what kinds of implementations might be called honeypots.

Deception Servers Versus Deception Hosts

Earlier in this chapter, we proposed a definition of a honeypot. In his previously cited paper on honeypots, however, Douglas Moran propounds that the term "honeypot" is ill-advised. First, according to Moran, "honeypot" is an inadequately defined term in that it can mean almost anything. Additionally, in many people's minds, the term "honeypot" conjures the impression of entrapment, something that is highly undesirable. He instead prefers to use the terms "deception server" and "deception host."

According to Moran, a *deception server* emulates one or more network services, delivering protocol-level interactions without the actual content normally provided during such interactions. Different platforms, such as UNIX, Linux, NetWare, and Windows NT/2000, can be emulated. It is also possible to use scripting to provide realistic responses when attackers connect to deception servers. Trojaned commands, according to Moran's definition, are one type of deception server.

In contrast, Moran defines a *deception host* as a normal host that has bogus content (for example, files with interesting names and content such as bogus personnel files) as well as monitoring capabilities. A deception host, for example, can store *treasures*, data or applications that motivate attackers into staying connected to that host. A virtual jail environment, according to Moran, would thus really be something that is within or part of a deception host.

Despite the eloquence of Moran's definitions, we will continue to use the term "honeypot" in a broader sense than Moran does. We will use "honeypot" to refer to decoy systems designed to attract attackers instead of distinguishing between deception servers and deception hosts.

How Legal and Ethical are Honeypots?

How legal are honeypots? This question has, to the best of our knowledge, never been tested in a court of law. If set up properly (as explained shortly), honeypots do not appear to violate any law in any country. The best thing to do, however, is to consult with your organization's legal department.

What about ethics and privacy issues? Critics of honeypots are often quick to point out that these measures potentially invade people's privacy—they capture every keystroke of people who essentially have been tricked. Worrying about ethics is admirable, but these critics too often forget that law enforcement often uses sting operations to solve difficult cases. Little protest occurs except on behalf of criminals who have been caught red-handed.

Much of the answer to this ethical dilemma actually depends on how the honeypot is set up and run. Honeypots can and should, for example, display the same warning banner as other systems—a warning banner that cautions would-be users that everything they do will be monitored. Goading or inviting would-be attackers to connect to honeypots, on the other hand, not only is likely to be viewed negatively in a court of law, it also presents serious ethical problems.

continues

continued

Examples of honeypot deployments that are ethically controversial include recording chat sessions on a bogus chat server that anyone might in good faith visit, setting up bogus financial transactions in which credit card numbers can be entered (because people expect privacy and safety in the use of credit card numbers), and running programs that create reverse connections to read files on the perpetrator's computer(s). Remember from Chapter 3 that being attacked does not justify subsequent counterattacks on your part. No matter what you do, unfortunately, invasion of privacy is always a potential risk, but this risk is by no means limited to the use of honeypots.

Initial Considerations

As you can see by now, successfully deploying traps and deceptive measures requires anticipating and resolving many issues long before these measures are deployed. Setting up honeypots, in particular, requires a considerable amount of planning. Let's now turn our attention to the many initial considerations with which you will have to deal if you want to successfully deploy honeypots.

Policy

Throughout this book, we have emphasized the importance of policy in incident response. The relationship of policy to deploying honeypots is particularly important. Policy considerations potentially apply not only to computer and information security policy but also potentially to human relations and legal policy provisions. In the case of computer and information security policy, it is particularly important for any provisions to be understood and followed. For example, an organization's computer and information security policy is likely to require that all systems owned by the organization display a warning banner for each login. Any host used for traps and deceptive measures must therefore display such a warning banner. Additionally, a computer and information security policy might prescribe certain safeguards and archiving requirements for log data. If so, these safeguards and archiving procedures must be put in place for all data harvested from traps and deceptive measures.

Dealing with human relations and legal policies is likely to prove even more complex. An employee-oriented company, for example, might expressly forbid the use of deception in dealing with employees. Could something like a honeypot nevertheless be used? The answer depends on the judgment of managers, most likely managers from the human relations and legal department. Again, just as in the case of almost every other matter related to incident response, obtaining the input, buy-in, and (often) permission of the human relations and legal departments is necessary.

Purpose

It is also important to clearly define the purpose and objectives of deploying honeypots long before any honeypot is ever deployed. The case study presented earlier in this chapter concerning the compromise of a honeypot shows what happens when objectives are not clearly defined. Behind every honeypot should be a written, clearly described statement of mission. One possible mission might be to discover new attacks before they become widespread. Another might be to obtain information about suspected insider attacks that have been occurring recently. The statement of mission should also include an estimate of how long the honeypot will be deployed as well as where it will be deployed, issues that we will consider in more detail shortly.

Approvals

After a statement of mission for each honeypot is in place, each honeypot should be approved by the management of any department or function (for example, legal) that has partial or full jurisdiction over activities involving honeypot deployment. Be careful—an unauthorized honeypot deployment can be extremely career limiting! Approval should be written, as should be any restrictions imposed on the use of honeypots.

Procedures

As in the case of other facets of incident response, having written procedures to govern activities related to honeypot deployment is essential to the success of any honeypot effort. The following are some areas that procedures should address:

- Data access and reporting—who gets access to honeypot data and what level of reporting to management is required.
- Monitoring—how often honeypot data must be inspected.
- Data archiving—any data archiving procedures.
- Inspection and maintenance—checking the security condition of each honeypot.
- Longevity—the maximum life of the honeypot and what must be done to clean up the honeypot when its life cycle is complete.
- Security administration—how administrators will gain secure remote access.
- Testing—what kinds of tests need to be conducted and how often.
- Incident response—what to do if the honeypot itself is compromised. Before running a honeypot, you should define a process for determining when to terminate an attacker's access as well as who must be notified and under what conditions.

Deployment Considerations

After initial issues have been resolved, you need to consider where and how honeypots need to be deployed. The following sections deal with these critical issues.

What Type(s)?

One of the more difficult decisions is what type of honeypot (if any) to deploy. In other words, what kinds of services, data, and features will each honeypot fake? One of the easiest courses of action is to simply fake one or more of the following widely attacked services[6]:

- `systat`
- `ftp`
- `telnet`
- `dns`
- `gopher`
- `http`
- `sunrpc`
- `nntp`
- `locator` (in Windows 9X, Windows NT, and Windows 2000)
- `nbsession` (in Windows 9X, Windows NT, and Windows 2000)
- `imap`

Alternatively, you might leave a host's configuration and services alone for the most part (after, of course, you have made it sufficiently secure) and instead assign that host an attractive name. The particular name assigned to the host will depend on numerous factors. Keeping the name contextually plausible is particularly important. If the names of other servers within a subnet are corp001, corp002, corp003, and so on, assigning a name of "sneezy" to a honeypot within the same subnet is probably not too smart. If, on the other hand, an insider has apparently been looking for potential targets of embezzlement, a name such as "financeserve" might be appropriate. The choice of a name is thus a matter of judgment (although "PeopleSoft" somehow always seems to work!). One nice thing about naming honeypots is that if one name does not work (that is, fails to attract sufficient attention) changing the name is generally trivial.

---

6. It is essential, of course, that all systems house honeypots that run only the bare minimum of services needed. Any service running on any system can potentially be exploited to allow unauthorized access to the system, escalation of privileges, and so forth. This principle does not apply to "faked" services, however. A honeypot should run as many faked services as needed.

What Kind of Appearance?

What kind of appearance should a honeypot have? How should it look and feel to an attacker? The best answer is that the look and feel of a honeypot should be in accordance with the purpose of the honeypot. Some honeypots need to look very polished to avoid standing out among other systems with elaborate user interfaces, sophisticated graphics design, and so on. Others (for example, within a research and development organization) might need to look more roughshod to be credible. Note that if you implement a honeypot using commercial honeypot software or a honeypot toolkit, much of the look and feel of the honeypot is likely to be predetermined by the software or tool used.

Should all honeypots that an organization deploys have the same look and feel? The answer once again is that it depends. Some organizations roll out complete honeypot farms (honeypots that have distributed functionality) using honeypots that all have the same look and feel. The rationale is that an organization's servers often have a similar look and feel, so attackers who reach honeypots that are similar in this manner are more likely to be deceived. Others feel that having the same look and feel can help tip off attackers that they have reached bogus machines and/or services, and thus you should deploy honeypots with a range of different appearances and behaviors.

Quality of Deception

In his classic paper on honeypots, Douglas Moran proposes ways of measuring the quality of honeypot deception. For a given deception host, he says that the quality of deception depends on "convincing content, variable content, and faithful representation of the platform." "Convincing content" is a function of how hard or how long the attacker will search for information that interests him. Attackers are likely to use grep and other commands to locate files of potential interest, but they are not likely to devote much time to most files that simply contain a single word of interest but no other interesting content. Better deception translates in part to the fact that attackers take the time to read files or execute applications on a honeypot because they appear to be what the attackers are looking for. "Variable content" is similar, except that the variety in content from file to file on a honeypot is instead what keeps attackers on the honeypot. "Faithful representation of the platform" means that a honeypot system and its services work in the same way that the faked system/service/application typically works, even though the environment is a fake one.

What Platform(s)?

Another important deployment issue is deciding what particular platform (UNIX, Linux, Windows NT, Windows 2000, Novell, or whatever) to use. Unfortunately, any issue that concerns the choice of an operating system usually quickly deteriorates into a "religious war"—one in which facts are ignored and emotions run rampant.

All things considered, we believe that UNIX is generally most suitable for honeypot deployment due to its combination of security, performance, and modifiability. Major flavors of UNIX such as Solaris and HP-UX have become markedly better in their security capabilities over the years. The vendors, too, have become more responsive in developing security solutions (including patches). In contrast, many other operating systems (such as Windows NT and the various flavors of Linux) are not as mature; security vulnerabilities have historically been more numerous (even though patches usually become available not too long after these vulnerabilities are discovered). Additionally, UNIX (and to some degree Linux) offers performance advantages if implemented on a suitable hardware platform. Finally, UNIX (and also Linux) offers a high degree of modifiability. Not only it is possible to obtain the source code for many tools and routines that can be useful for traps and deceptive measures, Unix also offers a rich set of functions and system calls that programmers can use during development. These things said, it is also important to understand that if a honeypot is supposed to look and act like a Windows 2000 server, there really is no other practical way[7] to achieve the desired look and feel than to deploy a Windows 2000 platform. Additionally, certain honeypot tools run only on certain platforms (for example, Solaris).

You need to harden the operating system you use as much as possible.[8] Although a discussion about hardening UNIX (or any other operating system) is outside the scope of this book, at a minimum, you will need to delete unnecessary services (in /etc/services in some flavors of UNIX, /etc/inetd.conf in others), modify the /etc/inittab file to run your host no higher than runlevel 2 (in most UNIX systems), and delete all passwords except for the root password and the unprivileged account(s) to which root users must first log in before using su to obtain a root shell. You can then install the tools or routines needed to implement the honeypot.

How Many?

In principle, security needs should be the main driver of the number of honeypots to be deployed. Suppose, for example, that a business has been losing a considerable amount of money due to multiple attacks and that the "crown jewel" servers are highly at risk. The most logical first step, of course, is to tighten the security of these servers (for example, through carefully configured packet filters). In this example, however, it might be wise to deploy many dozens of honeypots throughout the company's network to provide reconnaissance concerning the nature of possible malicious activity and the degree to which it might be occurring. In another case, a company might want to place only one honeypot in a demilitarized zone (DMZ) to determine the kinds of externally initiated attacks that are likely to occur.

---

7. Some might disagree with this statement; it is possible to use a tool such as VMWare to run Windows NT on a Linux platform.

8. The same principle applies to any other operating system you might use. SANS (www.sans.org) publishes step-by-step guidelines for hardening Solaris, Linux, Windows NT and Windows 2000.

The quantity of honeypots needed also depends on many other variables, one of the biggest of which is the cost of the platforms that house the honeypots. Sometimes you can get by with older hardware platforms that nobody wants (and that are thus cheap or possibly even free), but sometimes you can't. Certain commercial honeypot implementations require higher ended (and thus more expensive) hardware, for example. Additionally, relevant variables that affect the number of honeypots deployed include the cost of any commercial software needed; the personnel costs associated with creating, installing, maintaining, and monitoring each honeypot; the availability of IP addresses; and possibly others.

Where Should You Place Each Honeypot?

The best answer (not intended to be frivolous) to this question is that honeypots should be placed where they are needed. In general, if externally initiated attacks are currently the major impetus for honeypot deployment, you should place the honeypot(s) on a DMZ—preferably an external DMZ (in front of the firewall), as shown in Figure 12.1. If the major interest concerns activity within an internal network, honeypots can be dispersed throughout this network, perhaps one in every subnet (if subnets are used). In general, we have found that dispersing honeypots works better (in terms of the number of hits that each honeypot receives), but like everything else, this is not always true.

Additionally, it is important to ensure that any honeypot . . .

- Is router-addressable. (Otherwise, it will be reachable only by hosts within the same local network.)
- Has a static address. (Otherwise, it will be difficult for attackers to stumble onto the honeypot and return to it afterward.)
- Does not remain in any single location too long, unless being in that location results in a satisfactory number of hits. "If at first you don't succeed, try, try again."

Security of the Honeypot Itself

As mentioned earlier in this chapter, any honeypot is also a potential victim. It thus must be sufficiently secure in all ways except in the functions that must be open to attackers. These functions must be self-contained so that attackers cannot break out of them and gain access to a system and its resources. Security, of course, can never be absolute. You must therefore assume that, sooner or later, a dedicated attacker can and will break any honeypot's defenses. Accordingly, it is important to avoid placing critical or sensitive services, applications, and data on the same physical platform as a honeypot. It is best to devote each physical platform on which a honeypot resides to honeypot functionality. In other words, secure the honeypot as well as you can but avoid taking unnecessary chances with the things that are most valuable.

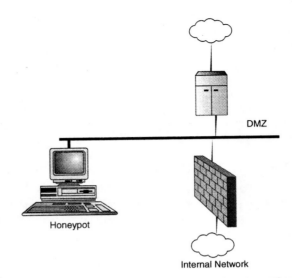

Figure 12.1 Possible placement of a honeypot to trap external attackers.

Finally, ensure that any log data that honeypots produce is well protected. Giving log files obscure names and making them into hidden files might help a little, but both of these measures are little more than examples of efforts designed to achieve "security by obscurity." Assigning strong permissions (for example, so that they are not accessible in any way, especially via read and/or write permissions, only by the superuser) is a better measure. Frequently harvesting the data is probably the most effective measure (so that if anyone alters or deletes log data, you already have him or her), but make sure any remote connections to honeypots for the purpose of data transfer are via an encrypted channel (for example, a virtual private network or secure shell). An organization might want to place IDS engines around a honeypot to assess its security, as one would place these engines around a firewall.

Getting Honeypots Noticed

You might or might not want to get a particular honeypot widely noticed. A reason for *not* wanting a honeypot to be widely noticed is to obtain some realistic data concerning the severity of the threat to hosts within your network. If you refrain from giving any special clues to potential attackers, any attacks that occur are likely to represent a realistic level of attack activity rather than one that results from drawing attention to systems within your network. Another reason is that a very deceptive honeypot might generate entirely too much activity. The result might be a massive network clog. Additionally, it is probably not even necessary to advertise the presence of a honeypot to get it attacked. Josephine Schwabel, Nick Rohring, Mike Hall, and Eugene Schultz[9] placed a Linux-based honeypot in a university network without doing any advertising of the presence of the honeypot whatsoever. The honeypot soon started receiving scores of attacks anyway. Remember, there are individuals who are desperately in need of a life! They appear to do little more each day than to scan and then attack systems indiscriminately.

Plan B is to deliberately draw others' attention to the honeypot(s). The motive, in this case, often varies from attracting a number of attackers for the purpose of conducting a network trace on each connection, to identifying a range of attack signatures or tools, to identifying the presence or attack signature of one particular person. One way to ethically draw attention to honeypots is to briefly install a web browser in the honeypot and then visit a variety of web sites. With all the sniffers over the Internet, you'd be surprised to learn how many attackers will pick up the honeypot's IP address. Another way is to post to newsgroups with content such as "I don't understand very much about security, but I need to secure my server—can you give me some advice?" Still another way is to do a cleartext remote login into a bogus account on the honeypot from several locations. It is important, however, to refrain from inviting, challenging, or taunting anyone into attacking the honeypot—to do so is not only ethically questionable but also possibly against the law.

Evaluation

When each honeypot implementation is finished, take the time to evaluate the honeypot to ensure that it meets requirements before actually deploying it. Does it do what it is supposed to do? Does the implemented honeypot conform to your organization's computer and information security policy? Has the honeypot been implemented with adequate consideration for security? Is the honeypot credible? What are the current security-related weaknesses, and what (if anything) can be done to counter them? One of the main reasons many honeypots are less successful than anticipated is failure to perform an evaluation of this nature.

Testing

A final deployment consideration is testing. It is not a good idea to deploy any honeypot without testing it first. After all, the honeypot might have security-related vulnerabilities of which you are not aware. An attacker might be able to exploit these vulnerabilities to subvert your honeypot (and perhaps also your network and everything within it!). Running a vulnerability scanner such as Nessus or nMap is a good first step. If the honeypot passes a vulnerability scan, it is a good idea to next conduct

9. Schwabel, Josephine, et. al. "Lessons learned from deploying a honey pot." *Information Security Bulletin,* 2000, Vol. 5, Issue 10, pp. 23–36.

some penetration tests against the honeypot. (We assume, of course, that anyone who conducts a vulnerability scan or penetration test will be wise enough to first obtain written permission from management.) It is important to view testing as part of the honeypot life cycle; hacking tools and attack techniques are constantly becoming more sophisticated. A honeypot that passes a vulnerability scan or penetration test today might not be able to pass in a few months. Additionally, new vulnerabilities, some of which could be exploited in honeypots, are constantly being identified.

Now that we have covered initial considerations and deployment issues, let's turn our attention on how honeypots are implemented. The next section addresses this issue.

Honeypots as Legal Evidence?

One of the most interesting controversies concerning honeypots is whether they can be used as evidence in legal proceedings. Considerable folklore but little fact surrounds this issue. To the best of our knowledge, there is no legal precedent concerning whether or not evidence gleaned from honeypots is admissible.

Suppose that no laws are broken in setting up and running one or more honeypot(s) and that the evidence from honeypots is gathered and handled properly. In theory, the evidence should be legally admissible. This speculation might be moot, however. Lance Spitzner, someone to whom we referred earlier in this chapter, believes that any discussion of issues concerning legal evidence from honeypots is irrelevant. He says that honeypots should *not* be used to *apprehend* attackers; rather, they should be deployed to discover what attackers are doing without them recognizing that they are being observed and studied. Others disagree, saying that the magnitude of the cybercrime problem is so great that any legal means to identify and convict computer criminals should be used.

Case Study: The Deception Tool Kit (DTK)

DTK[10] is one of the most widely known and used honeypot toolkits. The following section looks at DTK as an example of how to implement a honeypot.

About DTK

With DTK, you can build your own custom honeypot implementation. DTK runs "state machine" scripts—that is, scripts that fake the various states involved in connecting to services—on ports of your choice. Consider, for example, the nature of a Simple Mail Transfer Protocol (SMTP) connection on TCP port 25:

1. The sender sends 'HELO <server name>' as an introduction; the <server name> is a string identifying the name of the sender.

---

10. This tool is available from a number of web sites, including www.all.net and www.packetstormsecurity.org.

2. A 'MAIL FROM: <e-mail address>' that specifies the email address of the original sender of the message is then sent.

3. The sender sends 'RCPT TO: <e-mail address>', where <e-mail address> is the address of the email recipient.

4. The 'DATA' command followed by all the data in the email message, including headers appended to the message by intermediate servers as well as the text, is sent.

5. A 'QUIT' command is sent.

RFC-compliant SMTP implementations include these five states in the order shown here. DTK allows someone to create a fake mail service by implementing state files that emulate all of these states. Mail is not the only service that DTK can fake, however. DTK can also fake systat, chargen, ftp, telnet, time, domain, tftp, finger, http, pop-3, exec, rlogin, rshell, nfs, and others.

Functionality

In addition to being able to fake services, DTK logs a considerable amount of data. It not only timestamps and records each connection attempt (whether or not it is successful), it also records every keystroke entered. Log data are sent by default to /dtk/log. Sample output appears in Figure 12.2.

Additionally, DTK can provide an alert in the form of an email message, a pager signal, or a message written to a console, if an attack occurs.

How DTK Works

DTK is a Perl script implementation that runs on UNIX hosts (although it can be ported to other operating systems). It can run as a standalone background process (based on inetd, the inet daemon), or it can replace inetd with a special Perl script, listen.pl. It has at least one state-machine script for each to-be-faked port, but it can easily be modified to include more detailed emulation of services.

```
72.14.4.222 13067 110 2000/07/12 10:41:03 27017 176:1 listen.pl S0 Init
72.14.4.222 13067 110 2000/0712 10:41:03 27017 176:1 listen.pl S0 NoInput
128.8.30.5 1063 110 2000/08/13 11:58:36 31394 176:2 listen.pl S0 Init
128.8.30.5 1063 110 2000/08/13 11:58:40 31394 176:2 listen.pl S0 PASS^M
128.8.30.5 1063 110 2000/08/13 11:58:46 31394 176:2 listen.pl S0 USER smith^M
128.8.30.5 1063 110 2000/08/13 11:58:53 31394 176:2 listen.pl S0 PASS smith^M
128.8.30.5 1063 110 2000/08/13 11:58:02 31394 176:2 listen.pl S0 USER smith^M
128.8.30.5 1063 110 2000/08/13 11:58:09 31394 176:2 listen.pl S0 PASS password^M
128.8.30.5 1063 110 2000/08/13 11:58:11 31394 176:2 listen.pl S0 ^M
128.8.30.5 1063 110 2000/08/13 11:58:13 31394 176:2 listen.pl S0 ^M
128.8.30.5 1063 110 2000/08/13 11:58:15 31394 176:2 listen.pl S0 QUIT^M
128.8.30.5 1063 110 2000/08/13 11:58:15 31394 176:2 listen.pl S0 WeClose
```

Figure 12.2 Sample DTK log data.

An Evaluation of DTK

The fact that we have discussed DTK in this chapter should not be construed as an endorsement of this tool, that we think it is *the* honeypot tool you should use. In the long run, it is generally best to buy a tried and proven commercial honeypot, one that not only offers high quality deception but that also is very difficult to compromise. DTK, however, is an excellent tool for getting started with honeypots—to learn how to set one up, deploy it, and monitor the activity that occurs. Some of the positives of DTK include easy installation, the fact that it delivers only bogus services, its modifiability and extensibility (see the following sidebar), its low CPU consumption, its capability to log a considerable amount of information (including timestamped keystrokes), and the fact that Fred Cohen, the author/developer of this tool, has imposed very reasonable terms and conditions of usage.

DTK is not perfect. Disadvantages include portability problems (it is not as easy to port DTK as might be expected), the fact that creating warning banners is difficult, the fact that the log file (/dtk/log) format is difficult to read, and the limited degree of realism that can be achieved with DTK. The last point is particularly important. When you set up a DTK server, it looks and feels like a DTK server. DTK is very simple and straightforward; experienced attackers are almost certain to detect that they are connected to a DTK server and thus make their exit quickly. DTK proponents respond, however, that by making other (non-honeypot) systems look and feel more like DTK, this problem can at least be solved to some degree.

An Example of DTK's Modifiability

DTK's modifiability is one of the best things about it. Suppose, for example, you want to expand deception capabilities to 100 hosts. The following script will cause DTK to monitor the first 100 addresses within a certain class C subnet. This script creates 100 new entries in the /etc/sysconfig/network-scripts directory.

```
RANGE="128.0.0"
for I in 1 2 3 4 5 6 7 8 9 10 … 96 97 98 99 100
do
echo "DEVICE=eth0:$(i)
IPADDR=$(RANGE).$(i)
NETMASK=255.255.255.100
NETWORK=$(RANGE).100
BROADCAST=$(RANGE).100
ONBOOT="yes" > /etc/sysconfig/network-scripts/ifcfg-eth0:$(i)
echo -n "$(i) "
```

Putting Honeypots into Perspective

Are honeypots a valuable tool in the war against cybercrime and computer misuse? Some say no. Critics often say that it is better to simply shut down services than to run on dangerous ports. Others say that honeypots are a form of "poor man's security," that they provide a way for an organization with few security controls to achieve at least some degree of security. Others view honeypots as a type of intrusion detection measure. Remember that most IDSs are not very proficient in detecting certain kinds of attacks, especially insider attacks. Honeypots, on the other hand, are well suited to detecting insider attacks. Still others view honeypots as measures that serve a security control function; they protect against undesired access to systems and networks or at least slow this kind of access down.

We are confident that honeypots are capable of meeting a wide range of needs. They can, for example, serve as both an intrusion detection measure and a kind of deterrent to attackers by slowing attackers' efforts. They might also be useful in reconnaissance efforts: learning what attackers are doing, what they are trying to attack, and how often and how hard they are doing it. We do not view honeypots as mainstream security-control measures, however, but rather as *adjuncts* to these measures. They do not really stop attacks, although they can deter and deflect attackers' efforts. They can also provide an early indication that attacks against systems and networks are occurring as well as information about the patterns of the attacks.

We would also like to once again emphasize that it is unwise to deploy honeypots without considerable planning. Setting up suitable precautions in the event that Murphy's Law prevails is imperative. What if attackers compromise the honeypot? What if bona fide users connect to the honeypot and become confused? Consider also that a honeypot might provide conclusive evidence that someone in your organization, possibly even a senior manager, is involved in malicious or downright illegal activity. What should your next step be? It is critical to carefully analyze and solve these and other similar issues well in advance of any honeypot deployment.

Integrating Traps and Deceptive Measures into Incident Response

What relationship do traps and deceptive measures have to incident response? We've already provided a few answers to this question (for example, that traps and deceptive measures provide more time to develop an optimal incident response strategy after an incident has been detected). This final section of the chapter addresses this question in terms of stages of the PDCERF incident response methodology.

Detection

By now, the value of traps and deceptive measures as detection measures should be obvious. The actions of attackers who stumble onto honeypots can provide a valuable indication that an attack on one or more networks (and the systems therein) is underway. Although they do not directly indicate attacks on bona fide systems, deceptive measures can prompt security and other professionals to look more closely at what is occurring within systems and networks.

Preparation

Preparation involves getting ready for incident response efforts. Traps and deceptive measures can greatly help in this stage because well-designed measures of this nature can provide early indications of new attacks and threats. Incident response staff can brace for such new attacks and threats by obtaining appropriate tools, ensuring that incident response procedures are updated, and so on.

Containment

As we said in Chapter 3, deciding what to do after detecting a security-related incident is critical. One option is to allow the attack on victim hosts to continue; another option is to shut the attack off by shutting down the victim system(s) or disconnecting from the network. Traps and deceptive measures fit nicely with the first option.

Traps and deceptive measures have often been deployed as part of a delaying strategy during an ongoing attack. Their function is to distract the attackers to allow for more time to trace their connections and to close the vulnerabilities that have been exploited on other potential victim systems. If an attack occurs, for example, a honeypot with elaborate monitoring capabilities can be implemented to record all of the attacker's keystrokes and perhaps even to gather any attack tools while the attacker engages in all kinds of futile actions.

Another potentially valuable role of traps and deceptive measures during incident response is the capability to better protect one or more critical servers during an attack. If attackers have targeted a critical server such as finance.corp.com, you can take this host offline or rename it and move it to another part of your network. Next you can bring up a honeypot named finance.corp.com in the victim host's place. Any attacks on finance.corp.com will now be directed at the honeypot, not the critical system. This swap-out strategy can help minimize loss and disruption (and worry) when security-related incidents occur. Similarly, if someone is trying to break into a UNIX system that has no valuable resources or services, it might be prudent to create a jail environment on that system for the attacker to log in to.

Follow-Up

Traps and deceptive measures are also potentially useful in the follow-up stage of incident response. Suppose, for example, that an internal honeypot attracts a huge number of connections from your organization's employees. Furthermore, suppose you discover that the employees' activity is not unauthorized; rather, they are scanning the network looking for underutilized hosts so they can run resource-intensive programs on these hosts. Perhaps your organization's computer-usage policy should be changed as a result of the usage patterns that the honeypot has detected. Similarly, suppose a host that supports a jail environment is repeatedly attacked by someone who, by all appearances, is an expert attacker. If the attacker breaks the host's defenses and then launches attacks against other systems from the compromised host, it would be wise to revise the procedures for jail environment operations afterward. It might be better to shut down a host that supports a jail environment earlier, as soon as indications that the host is the target of a sophisticated attack surface.

Summary

Traps and deceptive measures are measures that seem to be real systems, services, applications, environments, and so on, but they're not. Deceptive measures are intended to provide false information to attackers and mislead them so that they do not focus their attacks on real systems and the network.

A trap is supposed to make an attacker stay in one place so that data concerning the attacker's actions can be gathered. Major types of traps and deceptive measures include honeypots, computers designed to lure attackers, automated messages, messages sent to a user when usage of a system or application appears to be unauthorized or anomalous, trojaned commands, commands that provide misinformation, jail environments, and special shell environments that appear to be bona fide environments.

Some of the advantages of traps and deception include providing a moving target, increasing the time and work factor involved in attacking systems, reducing the likelihood of damage to systems and networks, allowing more time to plan a suitable course of action, providing data that traditional tools generally miss, diminishing attackers' confidence, yielding intelligence data, and helping to educate and motivate management concerning security problems and solutions. Some disadvantages include the amount of work and resources required in a successful deception effort, the challenge of setting up credible deception measures, the possibility that these measures could backfire, and the challenge of integrating traps and deception measures into the IT mainstream.

This chapter focused more on honeypots than on any other type of traps and deceptive measures because of their growing popularity. We emphasized that careful planning in terms of conforming each honeypot deployment to an organization's policy, defining the purpose of each honeypot, obtaining necessary approvals, and developing appropriate procedures for operation of honeypots is critical. Resolving deployment issues—the type and quantity of honeypots used, the look and feel of each honeypot, the platform that houses each honeypot, where the honeypot(s) will be placed within the network, and how each honeypot will be secured—is also essential.

You will also have to decide whether or not to advertise each honeypot. Performing a security evaluation and testing each honeypot to help ensure that it will be able to withstand attacks are both necessary in a successful honeypot deployment. We took a brief look at the Deception Tool Kit (DTK), which provides fake services using state-machine scripts written in Perl. DTK logs timestamped keystrokes and can even provide real-time alerts that attacker activity is occurring. Honeypots cannot be considered mainstream security measures, but they supplement these measures well by deterring and deflecting attacks as well as by providing data that often cannot be obtained elsewhere.

Traps and deceptive measures are useful in four of the six stages of incident response, namely the preparation, detection, containment, and follow-up stages. Being able to swap out a victim machine or account with a bogus one is particularly valuable in containing attacks. Traps and deceptive measures can also provide valuable "lessons learned" for incident response efforts by providing data that can be used in modifying policies and procedures as well as in other ways.

13

Future Directions in Incident Response

PREDICTING THE FUTURE IS FRAUGHT WITH PERIL, but some advances in the field of incident response appear to be logical and predictable. Human nature being what it is, some of the most desperately needed improvements are years away at best, but the field is maturing, and many of the worst problems, such as legal and technical issues, have been addressed.

Although many of the details of incident response are likely to change (some dramatically), the overall focus of the discipline remains the same—providing organizations with an appropriate response to a security incident that addresses human, technical, and business factors. Although automated tools and improved laws might assist in this goal, the final responsibility lies with management's capability to view incident response as a problem for the organization, related to its goals, and not simply a computer problem.

Technical Advances

As technology changes, the field of incident response will change accordingly. Some of the changes will ease the response team's job by automating or simplifying tasks; others will make it more difficult by placing more sophisticated tools and techniques in the hands of offenders. Automated hacking tools, trojans, and worms are now readily available to attackers. Although most of these are easily detectable and relatively unsophisticated, they are far more widespread than in the past. Programming tools are also available to customize them to escape detection or to provide, for example, encrypted control traffic.

Intrusion Detection

The field of intrusion detection has changed dramatically. Although raw packet logging tools are still available, the sheer volume of traffic makes them difficult to use in most environments. Increasingly, companies are turning to specialized tools that can detect common attacks, log the traffic, and alert the administrator.

Most IDSs currently are signature based. Like antivirus tools, the IDS has a database of common attack patterns. When the software detects a similar pattern, it issues an alert. The disadvantages of this are obvious. First, like antivirus software, it can only detect attacks that are already known. The system must be constantly updated to keep the signature database current. Second, some attacks are indistinguishable from normal traffic. Port scans, for example, can be set up to scan a range of ports randomly and at a very slow rate. If the scan comes below a certain rate, the IDS might not recognize it as a scan.

There is significant research on new methods of intrusion detection based not on signature but on anomalies. These tools detect network traffic that is different from normal patterns. The difficulty with this is defining normal and abnormal traffic. Although this research is promising, anomaly-detection software still is subject to the major disadvantages of signature tools. Both are difficult to configure to avoid either missing attacks or flooding the administrator with false alarms. IDSs, however, are valuable to detect simple attacks by the so-called "script kiddies." As such, they can free up the security staff to concentrate on more significant attacks.

Intrusion detection either can be based on the network, where it listens to network traffic and attempts to detect an attack, or can be installed directly on a critical host. On the host server, it looks for changes to critical files. Arguably, antivirus software is a form of host-based intrusion detection. Microsoft is also now including a feature that tracks changes to library files (dynamic linked libraries, or DLLs) and that can allow the user to revert to a previous version of the file if an application (or attacker) modifies a file. No security is built into this feature; it is primarily to allow users to recover from changes made by installing new applications. A similar feature with appropriate access controls could be the basis for an improved host-based intrusion-detection system.

There are a number of significant limitations to IDS, including both false positives and negatives. A signature-based system can be set to detect certain forms of attack. However, it might not be able to distinguish between a password-guessing attack on a server and a user who has simply forgotten his or her password. Similarly, some denial-of-service attacks can consist of legitimate requests for service but in such large numbers that the server cannot process the requests. The IDS should be able to distinguish between large traffic and actual attacks. One actual example of false alarms is provided in the following sidebar.

False Alarms from Intrusion Detection

A client contacted us about an attempted intrusion. The client had installed IDS software among its critical servers and was detecting what appeared to be attempts to log on to a Windows NT domain. The logon attempts appeared to be coming from within the network but from a remote (international) site. No one from that site had permission to access the domain.

A review of the logs revealed that the logon attempts were actually an attempt to access network resources within the domain. However, the resources did not appear to be available (and, according to the client, did not exist). Further investigation tracked the logon attempts back to a number of workstations. The attempts, however, were occurring at a time when no one was physically at the workstation.

Further analysis revealed that the workstations were attempting to access an antivirus software update server. The client then stated that the same contractor had configured all the workstations. Contact with the contractor confirmed that it had installed antivirus software and automatically updated it prior to shipping the computers. By coincidence, the antivirus server had the same Windows domain name as a critical server at the client site. The contractor had failed to disable automatic updates, so the workstations were periodically polling the client network and attempting to access the antivirus update on this critical server.

There is a specific class of attacks known as *stealth scans*. In these attacks, the traffic is specifically designed to come at an extremely slow rate. The IDS will not be able to differentiate between the scan traffic and other legitimate traffic occurring simultaneously.

There also might be problems with IDS on switched networks. On standard Ethernet networks, all nodes can monitor all traffic. Deploying an IDS is simply a matter of placing a monitoring station on an unused node. In switched networks, however, traffic might be passed directly from one node, through the switch, to the destination. The IDS station would not be able to monitor the traffic. Most switches have provisions for a port on the switch to monitor traffic, but this might impact the performance of the switch or the IDS engine.

There might also be problems monitoring traffic that is encrypted. Although at some point, the packet headers must be in plain text, this will only serve to catch some attacks. For example, an attack against a web server application might consist of a series of commands for the web server to execute. The commands will be contained in the data section of the packet. If the packets are encrypted when they pass by the IDS monitor, it will be unable to detect the attack.

Finally, capturing traffic is a relatively straightforward practice. Deploying the IDS engine can be fairly simple, and even applying the rule sets might not be especially difficult. However, if the volume of traffic is large, analyzing the output and actually understanding what is occurring on the network is far from a simple task. The specifics of traffic analysis are clearly outside the scope of this book, but interested readers should consult other texts such as those by Marcus Ranum (for example, *Web Security Sourcebook,* John Wiley & Sons) or Stephen Northcutt (*Network Intrusion Detection*).

Automated Response

There is considerable interest in automating some portion of the response process. For example, the IDS system can isolate attackers into a controlled environment where they can do no harm and can be observed. The attacks can be automatically blocked. However, there is a desire in the discipline to make the process even more automatic.

An automated system can choose from many possible responses:

- It can shut down the system under attack.
- It can place the attacker into a "virtual jail" where additional information can be gathered.
- It can send a message back to the attacker or to his or her ISP.
- It can shut down the connection and block all further connections from that address for a period of time.
- It can require additional authentication to allow the session to continue.
- It can attempt some sort of traceback.
- It can attempt some sort of counterattack.

Periodically, stories appear in the popular press alleging that corporations are using automated tools to counterattack intruders. For example, one such story read, "In the U.S., firms are increasingly using hacking tools to attack the systems of hackers. Thirty-two percent of Fortune 500 companies have installed counteroffensive software, according to a survey by security consultancy WarRoom Research. Tactics include launching trojan horse attacks to damage and disable a hacker's computer, and automated scripts that can erase an attacker's hard drive or hijack email."[1]

It is unlikely, however, that this is actually occurring. Although there have been such reports, none of them have been substantiated. The authors also have no knowledge of any such systems in use by any private corporation, government, or military organization. WarRoom Research stated that this report had its roots in testimony to the U.S. Congress several years ago and is frequently taken out of context.

This is not to say, however, that there is no place for automated tools. Some intrusion-detection software, for example, will automatically block any traffic from an IP address if it detects an attack. Personal IDS is becoming more common as home users are increasingly using high-speed, always-on connections. One example is Black Ice Defender. This tool can be configured to automatically do a DNS lookup on incoming packets. It supports logging of attacks and can automatically block suspicious addresses for 24 hours. The user can then choose to manually block an address indefinitely. Some corporations have developed tools that will extract the data from IDS logs and automatically produce a letter or email to the ISP.

An organization must be extremely careful, however, when deploying any kind of automated system. An increased reliance on automation can lead to increased predictability. This, in turn, might allow the system to be defeated or bypassed more easily. The system itself might be subject to attack, or an attacker could actually use the automated response to create problems for a third party by simulating attacks from that party's network.

---

1. Madeline Bennett, *High-Tech Vigilantes Face Legal Threat*, www.zdnet.com/zdnn/
stories/news/0,4586,2716730,00.html.

That being said, some form of automated response, despite its inherent limitations, is one of the few long-term approaches to incident response that truly offers a unique solution to the problem of managing large numbers of attacks.

Experimental Tracing Methods

Chapter 6, "Tracing Network Attacks," discussed methods of tracing network attacks. Any number of problems and challenges can make this a difficult problem. The intruder can "leapfrog" through multiple hosts in multiple jurisdictions. Tracing such an attack requires cooperation from each organization along the way. Some attacks (including most denial-of-service attacks) support "spoofed" addresses, so the investigator must track a packet from hop-to-hop. To counter some of these issues, there is ongoing research regarding new methods of tracing attacks. None of these is near deployment, and some might require changes in the TCP/IP protocol, so a solution to this problem will not be immediately available. A complete discussion of this research is outside the scope of this book (and would probably be obsolete almost immediately), but some of these methods are described in the following sections.

DOS Tracker

Internet MCI developed this tool. It runs on the routers within a company and automatically traces packets back to their original source (ignoring spoofed addresses). The tool is primarily designed for ISPs because it must be installed on each router.

An early version of this tool was used in 1996 to trace a SYN flood attack against a California company back through a Canadian educational institution and finally to a California university. Although the specific attacker was not found, discovery of the route allowed ISPs to block the flood. The program is available for free download at `ftp.mci.net/outgoing/dostrack742812.tar`.

Intrusion Detection and Isolation Protocol (IDIP)

The Defense Advanced Research Projects Agency (DARPA) is funding research to combine IDSs with firewalls and routers to develop an automated defense system that can be deployed on an intranet. The components will communicate in real time to detect and respond to attacks. The current project is a cooperative effort between Trusted Information Systems, Boeing, and UC Davis.

IDIP is the common protocol used within this network to communicate between components. This protocol keeps track of packets at each router interface and can track a stream of traffic back to the source. Once more, the limitation is obvious; the protocol only is useful if it is deployed on the router.

Forensics Tools

The field of computer forensics has changed dramatically from its first roots. Investigators are using automated tools to capture and analyze the data. Because mass storage has become extremely cheap, it is no longer feasible to conduct a complete sector-by-sector examination of very large mass-storage devices. It is not unusual for investigations to involve media of over a terabyte. Only automation can reduce this to workable proportions.

It is likely that these tools will continue to evolve. Only time will tell whether a fully automated tool will produce acceptable evidence, but the tools are sure to be challenged in future cases. The probable outcome is that a standard set of tools will emerge, and forensics recovery using these tools will become as acceptable as fingerprinting.

Law enforcement agencies have begun the development of tools to detect pornographic images on large media. These tools are limited in that, at the present time, they can only search for known images. However, promising technologies involving image recognition could make it possible to, for example, identify all images on a drive that have certain characteristics or that contain a given person's face. These tools can also search images or streaming media for corporate logos or proprietary trademarks.

Encryption

In recent years, the U.S. government has moderated its views on the export of strong encryption. At the same time, however, other agencies have warned that the spread of strong encryption technologies could make it more difficult to investigate and prosecute crime. Other governments regulate the use of cryptography, limiting it to certain industries, insisting on a key escrow scheme, or even prohibiting its use entirely. It is unlikely, however, that such regulations will keep strong encryption out of the hands of determined criminals.

As encryption becomes more available, it will be used more often by people involved in computer security incidents. One example of this is the use of encrypted control traffic in denial-of-service attacks. These attacks are covered in more detail later in this chapter. Some of the distributed denial-of-service (DDOS) tools available allow the controller to use encryption to control "zombie" computers. Back Orifice 2000 also uses encrypted control traffic in an effort to evade intrusion-detection software.

Although much has been made recently of advances in breaking encryption algorithms, there is no sign that encryption is becoming more vulnerable. 56-bit DES can be brute-forced using dedicated processors in a reasonable amount of time (depending on the processor, a matter of days or less), but stronger algorithms are readily available. Even using Triple-DES changes the key length from 56 to 112 bits, dramatically increasing the effort required to brute force. At the present time, it is not feasible to brute force attack Triple-DES, and other algorithms are even more robust.

It is likely that encryption will be more widely used in the future. It is equally unlikely that advances in cryptographic techniques will make it easier to break strong encryption. Investigators, therefore, will have to contend with this issue. As discussed in previous chapters, one extremely effective way to deal with this problem is to utilize well-written policies that address the use of both authorized and unauthorized encryption on company computers. Even if the contents of the file cannot be read, the simple fact that encryption was used might be sufficient for the purposes of the investigation.

Social Advances

Although advances in technology might assist the incident response team, this is often a two-edged sword. The rapid pace of technology and the increase in networking also make the attacker's job easier. The same is true of changes in nontechnical areas. Changes in legal statutes and precedents might make it easier to prosecute or to improve international or interjurisdictional cooperation. Changes might also introduce new risks (as in the case of some of the privacy regulations).

Legal Issues

One of the major challenges in incident response has been the coordination of legal efforts across jurisdictions. Major steps have been taken to alleviate this, but the problems remain. The Council on Europe treaty discussed in Chapter 7, "Legal Issues," is a good example of this.

There are still major jurisdictions in the world, however, where laws against hacking are either nonexistent or poorly enforced. Agencies might not have the technical skills or the infrastructure to investigate these crimes. Cliff Stoll, in his classic book *The Cuckoo's Egg*, gives excellent examples of the difficulties in coordinating an investigation across international borders. He also illustrates the problems in doing a phone trace in a country where the switches are still manual.

It would be nice to state that the situation has improved, and it has in many locations. However, there are still other areas where the state of affairs is much the same. For example, following the outbreak of the Love Bug worm in early 2000, investigators detained people in the Philippines. At the time, there was no law on the books that prohibited the writing or release of a computer virus in that country.

Consumer protection and privacy laws will also continue to impact incident response. Financial and healthcare organizations are now required to protect personal information. The European Union has extensive privacy regulations that, among other things, prohibit the transfer of personal data to any country that does not explicitly comply with the EU regulation.

Cooperative Response

One of the major problems with large-scale incident response is securing the cooperation of all the parties involved, especially where multiple legal and political jurisdictions are concerned. Incident response tends to be insular, limited to the specific organization involved (and perhaps local law enforcement agencies).

Large-scale, cooperative efforts could be the single most effective step in improving incident response. Unfortunately, these do not appear likely in the short term. Politics—at all levels, including corporate, national, international, and within organizations—makes it difficult to formalize a cooperative process. Lack of resources (both in terms of money and trained personnel) might impede these efforts as well, and it is likely that attackers will continue to choose venues that cannot or will not cooperate as the source of their attacks.

There might also be issues with the disposition, ownership, and release of information gathered during incidents. Technical information about the networks or the attack could be dangerous if released. Private information about individuals or organizational proprietary data might be protected in some jurisdictions and not in others.

Education

In recent years, the growth of the computer security field has prompted a similar growth in formal education programs. It is now possible to study information security as a discipline at the graduate level. James Madison University in Virginia offers a program that leads to a Master of Science in Computer Science (MSCS) with a concentration computer security.[2] The program consists of a number of seven-week Internet-based classes. Students have up to six years to complete the program. Other educational institutions appear to be following suit.

JMU also sponsors the Center for Research in Information Systems Security Education (CRISSE, www.crisse.org), which facilitates information security education through all levels of education including K–12, undergraduate, graduate, and doctoral. Part of the activities of the center includes the sponsorship of an annual conference called the National Colloquium for Information Systems Security Education in conjunction with other educational institutions and government agencies. The 2001 colloquium was held at George Mason University and counted the Critical Information Assurance Office, Ernst & Young, George Mason University, Idaho State University, ISC2, James Madison University, Microsoft Corporation, the National Security Agency, and Virginia Center for Innovative Technology among its sponsors.

Conferences are also presenting courses in incident response. Systems Administration, Networking, and Security (SANS, www.sans.org), for example, now offers specific tracks in incident response at most of its conferences. The MIS Training Institute (MISTI, www.misti.com) covers incident response in both its conferences and its executive symposiums.

---

2. More information is available on the JMU web site at www.infosec.jmu.edu/program/html/program.htm.

The Progress of the Profession

One major advance in the field of incident response is the rise of incident response as a professional discipline. Incidents are increasingly handled by dedicated teams, either part of the company or external consultants. This trend really began as a response to the Morris Internet worm and has continued as organizations recognize that security-related incidents are here to stay and can cripple an organization. Law enforcement agencies have established specific teams to deal with security incidents, including forensics specialists and legal experts versed in the intricacies of computer crime and international law. The press has discovered that security incidents make good news, so companies and agencies have been forced to deal publicly with issues that, until recently, might have been brushed under the rug.

There is an international organization of incident response teams, the Forum of Security and Incident Response Teams (FIRST). Established in 1990, FIRST now has more than 90 members. These members include corporate teams (representing internal incident response teams), government agencies (representing either an entire national government, such as Australia, or an agency, such as NASA), consulting companies (that provide external incident response support), and nonprofit teams (such as the Computer Emergency Response Coordination Center [CERT/CC] discussed in Chapter 1, "An Introduction to Incident Response"). More details about FIRST are available at www.first.org.

Whereas early incidents were primarily handled by a combination of general law enforcement agents and systems administrators, major incidents today might involve a multiagency task force teamed with incident response teams from national agencies, Internet service providers, and major corporations. The FBI, U.S. Secret Service, New Scotland Yard, and many state and local law enforcement agencies now have dedicated computer incident investigators. Unfortunately, getting these agencies involved requires that the incident violate a certain statute and that, quite frankly, a law enforcement representative (such as a U.S. attorney) deem the incident worthy of investigation and prosecution.

Certification

A number of professional certifications are available in the field of computer security. Although most of these do not directly equate to incident response, they are applicable to it in many ways and illustrate the continuing trend toward specialization in the field. It is likely that certifications will become more important as the field of incident response (and computer security in general) matures.

CISSP

The Certified Information Systems Security Professional, or CISSP, is the oldest certification program in the field of computer security. The program is offered by the Information Systems Security Consortium (ISC2, www.isc2.org). The certification is modeled after the certified public accountant program and consists of a requirement of three years of experience, a test covering 10 subject areas, and a requirement for continuing education. The 10 subject areas, called the Common Body of Knowledge (CBK) are covered in the following sidebar. CISSPs must also agree to abide by a code of ethics.

ISC2 Code of Ethics

ISC2 requires that candidates for the CISSP and SSCP examinations agree to a code of ethics. This code is arguably the de facto standard code of ethics for information security professionals. The code is reproduced in its entirety here:

> "All information systems security professionals who are certified by (ISC)[2] recognize that such certification is a privilege that must be both earned and maintained. In support of this principle, all Certified Information Systems Security Professionals (CISSPs) commit to fully support this Code of Ethics. CISSPs who intentionally or knowingly violate any provision of the Code will be subject to action by a peer review panel, which may result in the revocation of certification.

> "There are only four mandatory canons in the code. By necessity, such high-level guidance is not intended to substitute for the ethical judgement of the professional.

> "Additional guidance is provided for each of the canons. While this guidance may be considered by the Board in judging behavior, it is advisory rather than mandatory. It is intended to help the professional in identifying and resolving the inevitable ethical dilemmas that will confront him/her."

Code of Ethics Preamble:

- Safety of the commonwealth, duty to our principals, and to each other requires that we adhere, and be seen to adhere, to the highest ethical standards of behavior.

- Therefore, strict adherence to this code is a condition of certification.

Code of Ethics Canons:

- Protect society, the commonwealth, and the infrastructure.

- Act honorably, honestly, justly, responsibly, and legally.

- Provide diligent and competent service to principals.

- Advance and protect the profession.

Objectives for Guidance:

- Give guidance for resolving good versus good and bad versus bad dilemmas.

- Encourage right behavior.

  For example, teaching, valuing the certificate, and "Walking"

- Discourage certain common but egregious behavior.

Protect Society, the Commonwealth, and the Infrastructure:

- Promote and preserve public trust and confidence in information and systems.

- Promote the understanding and acceptance of prudent information security measures.

- Preserve and strengthen the integrity of the public infrastructure.

- Discourage unsafe practice.

Act Honorably, Honestly, Justly, Responsibly, and Legally:

- Tell the truth; make all stakeholders aware of your actions on a timely basis.

- Observe all contracts and agreements, expressed or implied.

- Treat all constituents fairly. In resolving conflicts, consider public safety and duties to principals, individuals, and the profession in that order.

- Give prudent advice; avoid raising unnecessary alarm or giving unwarranted comfort. Take care to be truthful, objective, cautious, and within your competence.

- When resolving differing laws in different jurisdictions, give preference to the laws of the jurisdiction in which you render your service.

Provide Diligent and Competent Service to Principals:

- Preserve the value of their systems, applications, and information.

- Respect their trust and the privileges that they grant you.

- Avoid conflicts of interest or the appearance thereof.

- Render only those services for which you are fully competent and qualified.

Advance and Protect the Profession:

- Sponsor for professional advancement those best qualified. All other things equal, prefer those who are certified and who adhere to these canons. Avoid professional association with those whose practices or reputation might diminish the profession.

- Take care not to injure the reputation of other professionals through malice or indifference.

- Maintain your competence; keep your skills and knowledge current. Give generously of your time and knowledge in training others.[3]

---

3. Information Systems Security Consortium Code of Ethics, www.isc2.org.

The certification has been criticized as not technical enough, but the CISSP is targeted specifically at managers. Hands-on administrators can earn the Systems Security Certified Practitioner certification. This exam is directed at network and security administrators. ISC2 differentiates the two as follows:

"The CISSP certification identifies you as a security professional who has met a certain standard of knowledge and experience and who continues to keep his/her knowledge current and relevant to what is happening the field of Information Security. CISSPs must have a minimum of three years experience in one or more of the 10 CBK domains. The CISSP program certifies IT professionals who are responsible for developing the information security policies, standards, and procedures and managing their implementation across an organization.

"The SSCP certification identifies you as a security practitioner who has met a certain standard of knowledge and experience and who continues to keep his/her knowledge current and relevant to what is happening in the practice of Information Security. SSCPs must have a minimum of one year of experience on one or more of the seven CBK domains. The certification is targeted at network and systems security administrators. Network and systems security administrators provide day-to-day support of the security infrastructure."[4]

ISC2 Common Body of Knowledge

ISC2 has recognized 10 major areas in the field of information security. Although none of them equates directly to incident response, all have some applicability. The 10 areas are as follows:

- Access control

- Computer operations security

- Cryptography

- Application program security

- Risk management and business continuity planning

- Communications security

- Computer architecture and systems security

- Physical security

- Policy, standards, and organization

- Law, investigation, and ethics

4. Information Systems Security Consortium, *SSCP White Paper,* www.isc2.org/sscp/index.html.

The SSCP certification program recognizes a slightly different version of the Common Body of Knowledge because it is oriented more toward administrators than managers. The seven areas covered by the SSCP exam are as follows:

- Access controls

- Administration

- Auditing and monitoring

- Risk, response, and recovery

- Cryptography

- Data communications

- Malicious code[5]

Although certification is not currently a requirement by any organization for employment, it is increasingly becoming a discriminator, and many employment advertisements state that certification is an asset. Some consulting organizations are now advertising the number of CISSPs on staff.

SANS

The SANS Institute has recently begun a certification program. In 1999, SANS formed the Global Incident and Analysis Center (GIAC) to gather and analyze Y2K incident data. In late 2000, SANS announced a certification program as part of this center. GIAC certification begins with a course called "SANS Security Essentials," designed to prepare professionals for the subject area modules. The GIAC Security Essentials Certification (GSEC) covers security basics but assumes that students have some familiarity with computers and networking concepts.

Six subject area modules provide in-depth training in specialized subjects. These courses assume the student has a basic working knowledge of each area:

- Firewalls, Perimeter Protection, and VPNs: GIAC Certified Firewall Analyst (GCFW)

- Intrusion Detection in Depth: GIAC Certified Intrusion Analyst (GCIA)

- Advanced Incident Handling and Hacker Exploits: GIAC Certified Incident Handler (GCIH)

- Securing Windows: GIAC Certified Windows Security Administrator (GCNT)

- Securing UNIX: GIAC Certified UNIX Security Administrator (GCUX)

5. Information Systems Security Consortium, www.isc2.org.

Following the successful completion of the GSEC and at least one subject area module, students are eligible to sit for the GIAC Security Engineer (GSE) certification. Training consists of a combination of coursework offered at the conferences, practical exercises, and an examination. Recertification is required periodically, depending on the subject area. The recertification period ranges from one to four years; professionals must retake the certification examination.

Forensics

The major certifying body in the field of computer forensics is the International Association for Computer Investigative Specialists (IACIS, www.cops.org). Membership in IACIS is limited to law enforcement personnel. The organization offers a two-year certification program for investigators called the Certified Forensics Computer Examiner (CFCE). The major advantage to CFCE certification is that it has been recognized by legal precedent as specifying a certain level of expertise. This makes it much simpler to introduce a CFCE as an expert witness in litigation.

Until recently, CFCE certification has been limited to IACIS members (and by extension, to law enforcement only). In March of 2001, however, IACIS announced an external certification program in which the CFCE program will be offered to nonmembers.

This certification program consists of a series of hands-on tests in which the applicant must recover data from floppy and hard disks, followed by an examination on forensics techniques and procedures. The disks must be examined and reports prepared that indicate that the applicant used proper forensics and investigative measures. The entire process (six floppy disks, one hard disk, and the examination) must be completed within five months. IACIS offers a training program for its members, but no instruction is available for nonmembers.

Other Certifications

Other certification programs are available that do not directly relate to the field of information security. For example, a person can become a Certified Fraud Examiner (CFE) or a Certified Information Systems Auditor (CISA). Most of these programs have their roots in financial audit and were originally designed to support an audit program.

The Nature of Incidents

It is extremely difficult to predict how future incidents will differ from current trends because the data on current trends is so incomplete. Although some evidence might suggest that external attacks are becoming more common (as discussed in Chapter 10, "Responding to Insider Attacks"), personal experience tends to imply that insiders continue to dominate (at least the most serious). Recent years have seen a rise in virus and worm incidents and new motivations for attacks (such as "hacktivism").

Viruses and Worms

Viruses and worms are nothing new. In 1988, the Morris worm brought virtually the entire Internet to a halt. At that time, however, the Internet was restricted to a few government agencies and academic institutions. The effect on the average person or business was nonexistent. This is no longer possible.

Ten years after the Morris worm, the Melissa worm hit. Melissa was the first worm with the capability to spread itself over a network. Since then, variants and copies of this worm have emerged. All tend to infect the host computer and then spread by mailing infected emails to other computers. Most are programmed in Visual Basic. Although they are not technically viruses in that they do not infect a specific file or program, many do require that certain programs be installed in order to run. For example, both Melissa and the I Love You worm required Microsoft Outlook to propagate.

Although the antivirus community has been quick, in all of these cases, to develop tools to detect, quarantine, and clean these viruses, the rate at which they can spread is phenomenal. Company email servers have been crippled by the shear volume of the attacks. Some companies have even disconnected their mail servers in an attempt to prevent the spread of the virus. This, however, both prevents users from getting antiviral updates and also accomplishes a complete denial-of-service attack against the corporate network. Even if the virus does not gain hold, the company is completely shut down for the period.

Virus writers (with the exception of Robert T. Morris) have traditionally been viewed by law enforcement as nuisances not worthy of prosecution. This has changed. The FBI launched massive investigations following the outbreaks of both Melissa and the Love Bug. This will almost certainly continue as new viruses emerge.

Insider Attacks

Chapter 10 discussed some recent statistics that tend to indicate that external attacks are becoming more prevalent. This might, in fact, be a function of better detection or the widespread virus/worm outbreaks in the last few years. Insider attacks are still recognized as the most potentially damaging for all the reasons previously given.

Because most office workers now have personal computers on their desktops—and most of these have connections both to the company network and the Internet—the potential for abuse is extraordinary. A malicious employee can use "tunneling" technology to send and receive encrypted data over open ports, regardless of the firewall configuration. These attacks are covered in more detail in Chapter 11, "The Human Side of Incident Response." They are almost impossible to detect and even more difficult to block.

Some corporations have expressed concern over the use of a secure sockets layer (SSL) in web sites because they cannot monitor the traffic. However, blocking SSL will raise concerns with employees because then they cannot access e-commerce sites or do online banking from their corporate computers. Even some news and informational sites require SSL. If a company chooses to do this, it must first establish a policy that states that the company computers and network connections are for business use only and that *no* personal use is allowed.

The trend, however, is in the other direction. Most companies accept some level of personal use, provided it does not impact business. Accepting this, however, does introduce some additional risk, and businesses must be prepared to address this.

New Internet services can also introduce risk. Yahoo! now offers a service called the Yahoo! Briefcase (`http://briefcase.yahoo.com`). This service allows users to store up to 30MB of files on Yahoo! servers, accessible anywhere from a web browser. If an employee wants to steal data from the organization, he or she can now do it through the web browser and download it later from outside the organization. It will be almost impossible to detect unless the organization is specifically looking for (or blocking) connections to these sites.

Another dangerous trend is the widespread use of personal systems (such as personal data assistants). Malicious users can download large amounts of data to these devices, which can be easily concealed and removed from the site. Some of these devices support wireless communication, either by wireless radio frequency modems or by infrared technology.

Also newly available are removable storage devices. For example, there are now devices that plug into the universal serial bus (USB) port on a computer. Agate Technologies (`www.agatetech.com`) makes a USB hard drive about the size of a key fob. When plugged into the USB port, it appears to the computer as an additional hard drive. These drives can hold up to 64MB of data.

External Attacks

The most recent trend in external attacks has been in denial of service. Security expert Bill Cheswick describes this as "the last computer security problem."[6] When all the patches are applied, when all the firewalls are in place, when all the software is completely secure, denial-of-service attacks are still possible.

The CIA model discussed in the Chapter 1 recognizes that information must be available to be useful. It is more than that, however. There are now businesses that have no physical presence to their customers outside of the Internet. The financial loss to an online merchant when customers cannot access the site is staggering. Individuals are now buying and selling stock over the Internet. Although it might be frustrating to one person not to be able to buy or sell, it could mean major losses for the brokerage houses. One can even postulate an incident in which a person can artificially manipulate a stock price simply by denying others the opportunity to trade.

6. From a talk given by Bill Cheswick at the Cannes security conference. Copies of the slides were available on his web page at `http://cm.bell-labs.com/who/ches/talks/index.html`.

The costs in lost revenue are difficult to measure when customers cannot get into the site to buy. The intangible losses, in which new customers simply decide to go somewhere else, cannot be quantified. Even organizations that do not directly do business over the Internet can be affected. Their employees cannot exchange email with clients or suppliers. They can't access patches or updated software. It is even possible that the loss of network connectivity might overload or slow other communications networks, and the phone service into a company might be affected.

Distributed denial-of-service attacks were discussed in earlier chapters. Until recently, a company under attack could simply add more capacity. It was likely that a corporation could quickly have more capacity than the attacker could overwhelm. With distributed attacks, however, an attacker can easily have more available bandwidth than the victim. As personal broadband systems become more widespread, the number of available agent computers increases dramatically. It will be easy for an attacker to compromise a few dozen home machines with DSL service and quickly overwhelm a T-1 connection. The suggestions in the following sidebar might help prevent these attacks, but they require that Internet service providers implement certain controls.

DDOS

Distributed denial-of-service attacks were described in earlier chapters. Here are a few steps that users, companies, and Internet service providers can take to help prevent their severity:

1. **Patch vulnerable systems and maintain the patch level.** To exploit a system as a zombie, the system must first be compromised.

2. **Use antivirus software on personal computers.** Although the attacks are not technically viruses, the attack techniques are often detected and blocked by AV software.

3. **Use a personal firewall on home-use systems.** Do this especially if a personal system is always connected to the Internet through a cable modem or DSL. This software will also assist in blocking zombie attacks.

4. **Use ingress filtering on firewalls.** A firewall should never accept packets that appear to come from either an internal address or a nonroutable address. This will block many of the spoofed packets.

5. **Use egress filtering on border routers.** A border router should never allow outbound packets that do not appear to come from the internal network. This will help prevent internal computers from being used to launch attacks on other networks.

6. **Maintain a good relationship with service providers.** If an attack is occurring, the ISP can block the traffic upstream or can divert traffic. An alternate ISP can also keep connectivity alive even during an attack.

Another recent trend in external attacks has been to attack the corporation by compromising internal (or virtually internal) clients. For example, Microsoft had an incident in late 2000 in which a personal computer owned by a Microsoft employee and used to access the internal network was compromised by a trojan horse program. The attacker potentially had access to the entire internal Microsoft network through the company's own virtual private network.

Firewalls and external controls have become very robust and, provided that they are maintained and patched, all but impossible to breach. However, more companies are allowing employees to telecommute or are providing access to workers who travel. These computers are much more difficult to secure because the company does not have day-to-day control, and the computers might be exposed to any number of attacks, unprotected by any kind of firewall (or even an antivirus program). A trojan program can initiate connections or can wait for the VPN client to establish a tunnel and then gather information about the internal network or even spread itself to other computers. When the attacker has access to an internal computer, he or she can tunnel traffic in both directions over a permitted port such as HTTP.

Two Major Internet Incidents

In November of 1988, an Internet worm began spreading across what was then the ARPAnet. The worm used a bug in the UNIX *sendmail* program to gain root access to computers. If the program had been patched, it used a buffer overflow in the *finger* daemon. The program contained some rudimentary encryption in the source code to hide its commands and make reverse engineering more difficult. Over a period of about a week, the program spread to more than 2,000 computers, estimated to be approximately 10% of the ARPAnet at the time.

The program manifested itself by creating multiple connections to other networked computers. In doing so, it produced a large number of system processes, slowing the infected machines to a near halt. Investigators from the military community (the owner of ARPAnet), educational institutions, and law enforcement agencies worked to develop a countermeasure and to discover the identity of the author. The investigation was unprecedented and worked primarily through personal contacts. At the time of the incident, computer security was still an extremely small field, and specialists in it were rare. Almost everyone knew everyone else.

In early 1990, a jury in Syracuse, New York, found Robert T. Morris guilty of creating and spreading the worm. He was sentenced to probation, community service, and a fine.

The first week of May 2000, a computer virus called the Love Bug began spreading across personal computers. The program was technically a worm, not a virus, because it did not actually infect another program. The worm spread by sending infected emails of itself—with the subject line "I Love You"—to all members of a computer's address book. It also changed the user's Internet home page and downloaded and installed an executable program.

Reaction to this worm was swift. The major antivirus vendors issued updates to their products within hours of its release. Corporations instituted quarantine programs to isolate infected computers and to filter out suspected emails. Although the worm still spread quickly, infection rates varied widely. Personal users were hit heavily, as were some companies and government organizations; others were virtually unaffected.

The U.S. Federal Bureau of Investigation immediately began an investigation of the incident. Working with Interpol, it traced the probable source of the program to the Philippines. It then coordinated with the Philippines National Bureau of Investigation to arrest a suspect within a week. That suspect was charged in the incident, although the charges were eventually dropped based on the lack of applicable laws in the Philippines.

The contrast between these two incidents is striking. Although both were massive denial-of-service attacks against the Internet, the Morris worm was investigated primarily by amateurs. There was no dedicated computer crime section in the FBI, and few organizations had incident response teams. The Love Bug, however, had immediate attention by dedicated computer crime investigators worldwide. International cooperation was significant, whereas it was not a major factor in the Morris incident. Finally, although the Morris worm infected a larger percentage of the Internet, the all-pervasive nature of the network in the year 2000 ensured that a much greater number of users were affected, even if it was only by a network slowdown trying to get email or access virus update files.

Conclusion

The rise of computing and networking power has dramatically impacted nearly everyone. Even if its effects are not direct, the changes in business practices and the growth of new businesses have reshaped the economies of industrialized nations. The Internet boom, for better or worse, created massive wealth all over the world.

We have also seen the democratization of computing power. At the time of this writing, an average person can purchase a computer with a processor speed of 1.5GHz. This provides that person with computing power previously only available to major corporations and, before that, to large government agencies. This spread of power benefits the user, of course, but it also has potential to make the attackers' jobs easier. For example, passwords are rapidly approaching the point at which they are trivial to guess. With this kind of raw processing speed, a computer can guess all variations on an eight-character password in a matter of days if not hours.

The origins of computer incident response can be traced to the Hanover Hackers case described by Cliff Stoll. That incident was a case of espionage by foreigners (if not a foreign government) against U.S. agencies and corporations. Corporate espionage via the Internet now occurs daily. Theft of data and computing resources is commonplace. Identity theft has become much easier now that so much information and commerce is available on the Internet. The past two years have seen massive worm attacks across the Internet, affecting thousands (some authorities say millions) of users.

It is not hard to postulate new, nontraditional attacks. Distributed denial of service is an excellent example. The actual attack is a classic DoS attack, using old tools. Attacking someone using other computers is also not new. But combining these techniques is a major advance and represents a fundamental shift in the nature of the attack, not just the magnitude.

Similarly, one could envision, for example, antiglobalization protestors placing child pornography on corporate web sites in an attempt to embarrass or discredit large corporations. A person could short sell a large amount of stock and then place illegal materials on corporate computers and call the FBI.

Financial institutions have been urged (if not regulated) to form incident response teams. A letter from the Federal Deposit Insurance Corporation in 2000 stated, "Management should prepare a formal, written recovery plan and form an incident response team. If there is an attack on a computer system, the incident response team should be prepared to take appropriate action."[7]

An organization must be prepared to respond to a computer incident, just as it must be prepared to react to a natural disaster. Companies have always had plans for how to react when a robber shows up at the door with a gun. They should be equally prepared to respond when the robber shows up at the web server with a computer.

---

7. FDIC letter to all financial institutions, October 3, 2000, www.fdic.gov/news/news/financial/2000/fil0067.html.

RFC-2196

Site Security Handbook

Status of this Memo

This memo provides information for the Internet community. It does not specify an Internet standard of any kind. Distribution of this memo is unlimited.

Abstract

This handbook is a guide to developing computer security policies and procedures for sites that have systems on the Internet. The purpose of this handbook is to provide practical guidance to administrators trying to secure their information and services. The subjects covered include policy content and formation, a broad range of technical system and network security topics, and security incident response.

Table of Contents

1. Introduction

This document provides guidance to system and network administrators on how to address security issues within the Internet community. It builds on the foundation provided in RFC 1244 and is the collective work of a number of contributing authors. Those authors include Jules P. Aronson (aronson@nlm.nih.gov), Nevil Brownlee (n.brownlee@auckland.ac.nz), Frank Byrum (byrum@norfolk.infi.net), Joao Nuno Ferreira (ferreira@rccn.net), Barbara Fraser (byf@cert.org), Steve Glass (glass@ftp.com), Erik Guttman (erik.guttman@eng.sun.com), Tom Killalea (tomk@nwnet.net), Klaus-Peter Kossakowski (kossakowski@cert.dfn.de), Lorna Leone (lorna@staff.singnet.com.sg), Edward P. Lewis (Edward.P.Lewis.1@gsfc.nasa.gov), Gary Malkin (gmalkin@xylogics.com), Russ Mundy (mundy@tis.com), Philip J. Nesser (pjnesser@martigny.ai.mit.edu), and Michael S. Ramsey (msr@interpath.net).

In addition to the principle writers, a number of reviewers provided valuable comments. Those reviewers include: Eric Luiijf (`luiijf@fel.tno.nl`), Marijke Kaat (`marijke.kaat@sec.nl`), Ray Plzak (`plzak@nic.mil`) and Han Pronk (`h.m.pronk@vka.nl`).

A special thank you goes to Joyce Reynolds, ISI, and Paul Holbrook, CICnet, for their vision, leadership, and effort in the creation of the first version of this handbook. It is the working group's sincere hope that this version will be as helpful to the community as the earlier one was.

1.1 Purpose of This Work

This handbook is a guide to setting computer security policies and procedures for sites that have systems on the Internet (however, the information provided should also be useful to sites not yet connected to the Internet). This guide lists issues and factors that a site must consider when setting their own policies. It makes a number of recommendations and provides discussions of relevant areas.

This guide is only a framework for setting security policies and procedures. In order to have an effective set of policies and procedures, a site will have to make many decisions, gain agreement, and then communicate and implement these policies.

1.2 Audience

The audience for this document includes system and network administrators, and decision makers (typically "middle management") at sites. For brevity, we will use the term "administrator" throughout this document to refer to system and network administrators.

This document is not directed at programmers or those trying to create secure programs or systems. The focus of this document is on the policies and procedures that need to be in place to support the technical security features that a site may be implementing.

The primary audience for this work are sites that are members of the Internet community. However, this document should be useful to any site that allows communication with other sites. As a general guide to security policies, this document may also be useful to sites with isolated systems.

1.3 Definitions

For the purposes of this guide, a "site" is any organization that owns computers or network-related resources. These resources may include host computers that users use, routers, terminal servers, PCs or other devices that have access to the Internet. A site may be an end user of Internet services or a service provider such as a mid-level network. However, most of the focus of this guide is on those end users of Internet services. We assume that the site has the ability to set policies and procedures for itself with the concurrence and support from those who actually own the resources. It will be assumed that sites that are parts of larger organizations will know when they need to consult, collaborate, or take recommendations from, the larger entity.

The "Internet" is a collection of thousands of networks linked by a common set of technical protocols which make it possible for users of any one of the networks to communicate with, or use the services located on, any of the other networks (FYI4, RFC 1594).

The term "administrator" is used to cover all those people who are responsible for the day-to-day operation of system and network resources. This may be a number of individuals or an organization.

The term "security administrator" is used to cover all those people who are responsible for the security of information and information technology. At some sites this function may be combined with administrator (above); at others, this will be a separate position.

The term "decision maker" refers to those people at a site who set or approve policy. These are often (but not always) the people who own the resources.

1.4 Related Work

The Site Security Handbook Working Group is working on a User's Guide to Internet Security. It will provide practical guidance to end users to help them protect their information and the resources they use.

1.5 Basic Approach

This guide is written to provide basic guidance in developing a security plan for your site. One generally accepted approach to follow is suggested by Fites, et. al. [Fites 1989] and includes the following steps:

1. Identify what you are trying to protect.
2. Determine what you are trying to protect it from.
3. Determine how likely the threats are.
4. Implement measures which will protect your assets in a cost-effective manner.
5. Review the process continuously and make improvements each time a weakness is found.

Most of this document is focused on item 4 above, but the other steps cannot be avoided if an effective plan is to be established at your site. One old truism in security is that the cost of protecting yourself against a threat should be less than the cost of recovering if the threat were to strike you. Cost in this context should be remembered to include losses expressed in real currency, reputation, trustworthiness, and other less obvious measures. Without reasonable knowledge of what you are protecting and what the likely threats are, following this rule could be difficult.

1.6   Risk Assessment

1.6.1   General Discussion

One of the most important reasons for creating a computer security policy is to ensure that efforts spent on security yield cost-effective benefits. Although this may seem obvious, it is possible to be mislead about where the effort is needed. As an example, there is a great deal of publicity about intruders on computers systems; yet most surveys of computer security show that, for most organizations, the actual loss from "insiders" is much greater.

Risk analysis involves determining what you need to protect, what you need to protect it from, and how to protect it. It is the process of examining all of your risks, then ranking those risks by level of severity. This process involves making cost-effective decisions on what you want to protect. As mentioned above, you should probably not spend more to protect something than it is actually worth.

A full treatment of risk analysis is outside the scope of this document. [Fites 1989] and [Pfleeger 1989] provide introductions to this topic. However, there are two elements of a risk analysis that will be briefly covered in the next two sections:

1. Identifying the assets
2. Identifying the threats

For each asset, the basic goals of security are availability, confidentiality, and integrity. Each threat should be examined with an eye to how the threat could affect these areas.

1.6.2   Identifying the Assets

One step in a risk analysis is to identify all the things that need to be protected. Some things are obvious, like valuable proprietary information, intellectual property, and all the various pieces of hardware; but, some are overlooked, such as the people who actually use the systems. The essential point is to list all things that could be affected by a security problem.

One list of categories is suggested by Pfleeger [Pfleeger 1989]; this list is adapted from that source:

1. Hardware: CPUs, boards, keyboards, terminals, workstations, personal computers, printers, disk drives, communication lines, terminal servers, routers.
2. Software: source programs, object programs, utilities, diagnostic programs, operating systems, communication programs.
3. Data: during execution, stored on-line, archived off-line, backups, audit logs, databases, in transit over communication media.
4. People: users, administrators, hardware maintainers.
5. Documentation: on programs, hardware, systems, local administrative procedures.
6. Supplies: paper, forms, ribbons, magnetic media.

1.6.3 Identifying the Threats

Once the assets requiring protection are identified, it is necessary to identify threats to those assets. The threats can then be examined to determine what potential for loss exists. It helps to consider from what threats you are trying to protect your assets.

The following are classic threats that should be considered. Depending on your site, there will be more specific threats that should be identified and addressed.

1. Unauthorized access to resources and/or information

2. Unintended and/or unauthorized Disclosure of information

3. Denial of service

2. Security Policies

Throughout this document there will be many references to policies. Often these references will include recommendations for specific policies. Rather than repeat guidance in how to create and communicate such a policy, the reader should apply the advice presented in this chapter when developing any policy recommended later in this book.

2.1 What Is a Security Policy and Why Have One?

The security-related decisions you make, or fail to make, as administrator largely determines how secure or insecure your network is, how much functionality your network offers, and how easy your network is to use. However, you cannot make good decisions about security without first determining what your security goals are.

Until you determine what your security goals are, you cannot make effective use of any collection of security tools because you simply will not know what to check for and what restrictions to impose.

For example, your goals will probably be very different from the goals of a product vendor. Vendors are trying to make configuration and operation of their products as simple as possible, which implies that the default configurations will often be as open (i.e., insecure) as possible. While this does make it easier to install new products, it also leaves access to those systems, and other systems through them, open to any user who wanders by.

Your goals will be largely determined by the following key tradeoffs:

1. Services offered versus security provided—Each service offered to users carries its own security risks. For some services the risk outweighs the benefit of the service and the administrator may choose to eliminate the service rather than try to secure it.

2. Ease of use versus security—The easiest system to use would allow access to any user and require no passwords; that is, there would be no security. Requiring passwords makes the system a little less convenient, but more secure. Requiring device-generated one-time passwords makes the system even more difficult to use, but much more secure.

3. Cost of security versus risk of loss—There are many different costs to security: monetary (i.e., the cost of purchasing security hardware and software like firewalls and one-time password generators), performance (i.e., encryption and decryption take time), and ease of use (as mentioned above). There are also many levels of risk: loss of privacy (i.e., the reading of information by unauthorized individuals), loss of data (i.e., the corruption or erasure of information), and the loss of service (e.g., the filling of data storage space, usage of computational resources, and denial of network access). Each type of cost must be weighed against each type of loss.

Your goals should be communicated to all users, operations staff, and managers through a set of security rules, called a "security policy." We are using this term, rather than the narrower "computer security policy" since the scope includes all types of information technology and the information stored and manipulated by the technology.

2.1.1 Definition of a Security Policy

A security policy is a formal statement of the rules by which people who are given access to an organization's technology and information assets must abide.

2.1.2 Purposes of a Security Policy

The main purpose of a security policy is to inform users, staff and managers of their obligatory requirements for protecting technology and information assets. The policy should specify the mechanisms through which these requirements can be met. Another purpose is to provide a baseline from which to acquire, configure and audit computer systems and networks for compliance with the policy. Therefore an attempt to use a set of security tools in the absence of at least an implied security policy is meaningless.

An Appropriate Use Policy (AUP) may also be part of a security policy. It should spell out what users shall and shall not do on the various components of the system, including the type of traffic allowed on the networks. The AUP should be as explicit as possible to avoid ambiguity or misunderstanding. For example, an AUP might list any prohibited USENET newsgroups. (Note: Appropriate Use Policy is referred to as Acceptable Use Policy by some sites.)

2.1.3 Who Should be Involved When Forming Policy?

In order for a security policy to be appropriate and effective, it needs to have the acceptance and support of all levels of employees within the organization. It is especially important that corporate management fully support the security policy process otherwise there is little chance that they will have the intended impact. The following is a list of individuals who should be involved in the creation and review of security policy documents:

1. Site security administrator
2. Information technology technical staff (e.g., staff from computing center)
3. Administrators of large user groups within the organization (e.g., business divisions, computer science department within a university, etc.)

4. Security incident response team

5. Representatives of the user groups affected by the security policy

6. Responsible management

7. Legal counsel (if appropriate)

The list above is representative of many organizations, but is not necessarily comprehensive. The idea is to bring in representation from key stakeholders, management who have budget and policy authority, technical staff who know what can and cannot be supported, and legal counsel who know the legal ramifications of various policy choices. In some organizations, it may be appropriate to include EDP audit personnel. Involving this group is important if resulting policy statements are to reach the broadest possible acceptance. It is also relevant to mention that the role of legal counsel will also vary from country to country.

2.2 What Makes a Good Security Policy?

The characteristics of a good security policy are:

1. It must be implementable through system administration procedures, publishing of acceptable use guidelines, or other appropriate methods.

2. It must be enforceable with security tools, where appropriate, and with sanctions, where actual prevention is not technically feasible.

3. It must clearly define the areas of responsibility for the users, administrators, and management.

The components of a good security policy include:

1. Computer Technology Purchasing Guidelines which specify required, or preferred, security features. These should supplement existing purchasing policies and guidelines.

2. A Privacy Policy which defines reasonable expectations of privacy regarding such issues as monitoring of electronic mail, logging of keystrokes, and access to users' files.

3. An Access Policy which defines access rights and privileges to protect assets from loss or disclosure by specifying acceptable use guidelines for users, operations staff, and management. It should provide guidelines for external connections, data communications, connecting devices to a network, and adding new software to systems. It should also specify any required notification messages (e.g., connect messages should provide warnings about authorized usage and line monitoring, and not simply say "Welcome").

4. An Accountability Policy which defines the responsibilities of users, operations staff, and management. It should specify an audit capability, and provide incident handling guidelines (i.e., what to do and who to contact if a possible intrusion is detected).

5. An Authentication Policy which establishes trust through an effective password policy, and by setting guidelines for remote location authentication and the use of authentication devices (e.g., one-time passwords and the devices that generate them).

6. An Availability statement which sets users' expectations for the availability of resources. It should address redundancy and recovery issues, as well as specify operating hours and maintenance down-time periods. It should also include contact information for reporting system and network failures.

7. An Information Technology System & Network Maintenance Policy which describes how both internal and external maintenance people are allowed to handle and access technology. One important topic to be addressed here is whether remote maintenance is allowed and how such access is controlled. Another area for consideration here is outsourcing and how it is managed.

8. A Violations Reporting Policy that indicates which types of violations (e.g., privacy and security, internal and external) must be reported and to whom the reports are made. A non-threatening atmosphere and the possibility of anonymous reporting will result in a greater probability that a violation will be reported if it is detected.

9. Supporting Information which provides users, staff, and management with contact information for each type of policy violation; guidelines on how to handle outside queries about a security incident, or information which may be considered confidential or proprietary; and cross-references to security procedures and related information, such as company policies and governmental laws and regulations.

There may be regulatory requirements that affect some aspects of your security policy (e.g., line monitoring). The creators of the security policy should consider seeking legal assistance in the creation of the policy. At a minimum, the policy should be reviewed by legal counsel.

Once your security policy has been established it should be clearly communicated to users, staff, and management. Having all personnel sign a statement indicating that they have read, understood, and agreed to abide by the policy is an important part of the process. Finally, your policy should be reviewed on a regular basis to see if it is successfully supporting your security needs.

2.3 Keeping the Policy Flexible

In order for a security policy to be viable for the long term, it requires a lot of flexibility based upon an architectural security concept. A security policy should be (largely) independent from specific hardware and software situations (as specific systems tend to be replaced or moved overnight). The mechanisms for updating the policy should be clearly spelled out. This includes the process, the people involved, and the people who must sign-off on the changes.

It is also important to recognize that there are exceptions to every rule. Whenever possible, the policy should spell out what exceptions to the general policy exist. For example, under what conditions is a system administrator allowed to go through a user's files. Also, there may be some cases when multiple users will have access to the same userid. For example, on systems with a "root" user, multiple system administrators may know the password and use the root account.

Another consideration is called the "Garbage Truck Syndrome." This refers to what would happen to a site if a key person was suddenly unavailable for his/her job function (e.g., was suddenly ill or left the company unexpectedly). While the greatest security resides in the minimum dissemination of information, the risk of losing critical information increases when that information is not shared. It is important to determine what the proper balance is for your site.

3. Architecture

3.1 Objectives

3.1.1 Completely Defined Security Plans

All sites should define a comprehensive security plan. This plan should be at a higher level than the specific policies discussed in chapter 2, and it should be crafted as a framework of broad guidelines into which specific policies will fit.

It is important to have this framework in place so that individual policies can be consistent with the overall site security architecture. For example, having a strong policy with regard to Internet access and having weak restrictions on modem usage is inconsistent with an overall philosophy of strong security restrictions on external access.

A security plan should define: the list of network services that will be provided; which areas of the organization will provide the services; who will have access to those services; how access will be provided; who will administer those services; etc.

The plan should also address how an incident will be handled. Chapter 5 provides an in-depth discussion of this topic, but it is important for each site to define classes of incidents and corresponding responses. For example, sites with firewalls should set a threshold on the number of attempts made to foil the firewall before triggering a response. Escalation levels should be defined for both attacks and responses. Sites without firewalls will have to determine if a single attempt to connect to a host constitutes an incident. What about a systematic scan of systems?

For sites connected to the Internet, the rampant media magnification of Internet related security incidents can overshadow a (potentially) more serious internal security problem. Likewise, companies who have never been connected to the Internet may have strong, well defined, internal policies but fail to adequately address an external connection policy.

3.1.2 *Separation of Services*

There are many services which a site may wish to provide for its users, some of which may be external. There are a variety of security reasons to attempt to isolate services onto dedicated host computers. There are also performance reasons in most cases, but a detailed discussion is beyond the scope of this document.

The services which a site may provide will, in most cases, have different levels of access needs and models of trust. Services which are essential to the security or smooth operation of a site would be better off being placed on a dedicated machine with very limited access (see Section 3.1.3 "deny all" model), rather than on a machine that provides a service (or services) which has traditionally been less secure, or requires greater accessibility by users who may accidentally suborn security.

It is also important to distinguish between hosts which operate within different models of trust (e.g., all the hosts inside of a firewall and any host on an exposed network).

Some of the services which should be examined for potential separation are outlined in section 3.2.3. It is important to remember that security is only as strong as the weakest link in the chain. Several of the most publicized penetrations in recent years have been through the exploitation of vulnerabilities in electronic mail systems. The intruders were not trying to steal electronic mail, but they used the vulnerability in that service to gain access to other systems.

If possible, each service should be running on a different machine whose only duty is to provide a specific service. This helps to isolate intruders and limit potential harm.

3.1.3 *Deny All / Allow All*

There are two diametrically opposed underlying philosophies which can be adopted when defining a security plan. Both alternatives are legitimate models to adopt, and the choice between them will depend on the site and its needs for security.

The first option is to turn off all services and then selectively enable services on a case by case basis as they are needed. This can be done at the host or network level as appropriate. This model, which will hereafter be referred to as the "deny all" model, is generally more secure than the other model described in the next paragraph. More work is required to successfully implement a "deny all" configuration as well as a better understanding of services. Allowing only known services provides for a better analysis of a particular service/protocol and the design of a security mechanism suited to the security level of the site.

The other model, which will hereafter be referred to as the "allow all" model, is much easier to implement, but is generally less secure than the "deny all" model. Simply turn on all services, usually the default at the host level, and allow all protocols to travel across network boundaries, usually the default at the router level. As security holes become apparent, they are restricted or patched at either the host or network level.

Each of these models can be applied to different portions of the site, depending on functionality requirements, administrative control, site policy, etc. For example, the policy may be to use the "allow all" model when setting up workstations for general use, but adopt a "deny all" model when setting up information servers, like an email hub. Likewise, an "allow all" policy may be adopted for traffic between LAN's internal to the site, but a "deny all" policy can be adopted between the site and the Internet.

Be careful when mixing philosophies as in the examples above. Many sites adopt the theory of a hard "crunchy" shell and a soft "squishy" middle. They are willing to pay the cost of security for their external traffic and require strong security measures, but are unwilling or unable to provide similar protections internally. This works fine as long as the outer defenses are never breached and the internal users can be trusted. Once the outer shell (firewall) is breached, subverting the internal network is trivial.

3.1.4   Identify Real Needs for Services

There is a large variety of services which may be provided, both internally and on the Internet at large. Managing security is, in many ways, managing access to services internal to the site and managing how internal users access information at remote sites.

Services tend to rush like waves over the Internet. Over the years many sites have established anonymous FTP servers, gopher servers, wais servers, WWW servers, etc. as they became popular, but not particularly needed, at all sites. Evaluate all new services that are established with a skeptical attitude to determine if they are actually needed or just the current fad sweeping the Internet.

Bear in mind that security complexity can grow exponentially with the number of services provided. Filtering routers need to be modified to support the new protocols. Some protocols are inherently difficult to filter safely (e.g., RPC and UDP services), thus providing more openings to the internal network. Services provided on the same machine can interact in catastrophic ways. For example, allowing anonymous FTP on the same machine as the WWW server may allow an intruder to place a file in the anonymous FTP area and cause the HTTP server to execute it.

3.2   Network and Service Configuration

3.2.1   Protecting the Infrastructure

Many network administrators go to great lengths to protect the hosts on their networks. Few administrators make any effort to protect the networks themselves. There is some rationale to this. For example, it is far easier to protect a host than a network. Also, intruders are likely to be after data on the hosts; damaging the network would not serve their purposes. That said, there are still reasons to protect the networks. For example, an intruder might divert network traffic through an outside host in order to examine the data (i.e., to search for passwords). Also, infrastructure includes more than the networks and the routers which interconnect them. Infrastructure also includes network management (e.g., SNMP), services (e.g., DNS, NFS, NTP, WWW), and security (i.e., user authentication and access restrictions).

The infrastructure also needs protection against human error. When an administrator misconfigures a host, that host may offer degraded service. This only affects users who require that host and, unless that host is a primary server, the number of affected users will therefore be limited. However, if a router is misconfigured, all users who require the network will be affected. Obviously, this is a far larger number of users than those depending on any one host.

3.2.2 Protecting the Network

There are several problems to which networks are vulnerable. The classic problem is a "denial of service" attack. In this case, the network is brought to a state in which it can no longer carry legitimate users' data. There are two common ways this can be done: by attacking the routers and by flooding the network with extraneous traffic. Please note that the term "router" in this section is used as an example of a larger class of active network interconnection components that also includes components like firewalls, proxy-servers, etc.

An attack on the router is designed to cause it to stop forwarding packets, or to forward them improperly. The former case may be due to a misconfiguration, the injection of a spurious routing update, or a "flood attack" (i.e., the router is bombarded with unroutable packets, causing its performance to degrade). A flood attack on a network is similar to a flood attack on a router, except that the flood packets are usually broadcast. An ideal flood attack would be the injection of a single packet which exploits some known flaw in the network nodes and causes them to retransmit the packet, or generate error packets, each of which is picked up and repeated by another host. A well chosen attack packet can even generate an exponential explosion of transmissions.

Another classic problem is "spoofing." In this case, spurious routing updates are sent to one or more routers causing them to misroute packets. This differs from a denial of service attack only in the purpose behind the spurious route. In denial of service, the object is to make the router unusable; a state which will be quickly detected by network users. In spoofing, the spurious route will cause packets to be routed to a host from which an intruder may monitor the data in the packets. These packets are then re-routed to their correct destinations. However, the intruder may or may not have altered the contents of the packets.

The solution to most of these problems is to protect the routing update packets sent by the routing protocols in use (e.g., RIP-2, OSPF). There are three levels of protection: clear-text password, cryptographic checksum, and encryption. Passwords offer only minimal protection against intruders who do not have direct access to the physical networks. Passwords also offer some protection against misconfigured routers (i.e, routers which, out of the box, attempt to route packets). The advantage of passwords is that they have a very low overhead, in both bandwidth and CPU consumption. Checksums protect against the injection of spurious packets, even if the intruder has direct access to the physical network. Combined with a sequence number, or other unique identifier, a checksum can also protect again "replay" attacks, wherein an old (but valid at the time) routing update is retransmitted by either an intruder or a misbehaving router. The most security is provided by complete encryption of sequenced, or uniquely identified, routing updates. This prevents an intruder from determining the topology of the network. The disadvantage to encryption is the overhead involved in processing the updates.

RIP-2 (RFC 1723) and OSPF (RFC 1583) both support clear-text passwords in their base design specifications. In addition, there are extensions to each base protocol to support MD5 encryption.

Unfortunately, there is no adequate protection against a flooding attack, or a misbehaving host or router which is flooding the network. Fortunately, this type of attack is obvious when it occurs and can usually be terminated relatively simply.

3.2.3 *Protecting the Services*

There are many types of services and each has its own security requirements. These requirements will vary based on the intended use of the service. For example, a service which should only be usable within a site (e.g., NFS) may require different protection mechanisms than a service provided for external use. It may be sufficient to protect the internal server from external access. However, a WWW server, which provides a home page intended for viewing by users anywhere on the Internet, requires built-in protection. That is, the service/protocol/server must provide whatever security may be required to prevent unauthorized access and modification of the Web database.

Internal services (i.e., services meant to be used only by users within a site) and external services (i.e., services deliberately made available to users outside a site) will, in general, have protection requirements which differ as previously described. It is therefore wise to isolate the internal services to one set of server host computers and the external services to another set of server host computers. That is, internal and external servers should not be co-located on the same host computer. In fact, many sites go so far as to have one set of subnets (or even different networks) which are accessible from the outside and another set which may be accessed only within the site. Of course, there is usually a firewall which connects these partitions. Great care must be taken to ensure that such a firewall is operating properly.

There is increasing interest in using intranets to connect different parts of a organization (e.g., divisions of a company). While this document generally differentiates between external and internal (public and private), sites using intranets should be aware that they will need to consider three separations and take appropriate actions when designing and offering services. A service offered to an intranet would be neither public, nor as completely private as a service to a single organizational subunit. Therefore, the service would need its own supporting system, separated from both external and internal services and networks.

One form of external service deserves some special consideration, and that is anonymous, or guest, access. This may be either anonymous FTP or guest (unauthenticated) login. It is extremely important to ensure that anonymous FTP servers and guest login userids are carefully isolated from any hosts and file systems from which outside users should be kept. Another area to which special attention must be paid concerns anonymous, writable access. A site may be legally responsible for the content of publicly available information, so careful monitoring of the information deposited by anonymous users is advised.

Now we shall consider some of the most popular services: name service, password/key service, authentication/proxy service, electronic mail, WWW, file transfer, and NFS. Since these are the most frequently used services, they are the most obvious points of attack. Also, a successful attack on one of these services can produce disaster all out of proportion to the innocence of the basic service.

3.2.3.1 *Name Servers (DNS and NIS(+))*

The Internet uses the Domain Name System (DNS) to perform address resolution for host and network names. The Network Information Service (NIS) and NIS+ are not used on the global Internet, but are subject to the same risks as a DNS server. Name-to-address resolution is critical to the secure operation of any network. An attacker who can successfully control or impersonate a DNS server can re-route traffic to subvert security protections. For example, routine traffic can be diverted to a compromised system to be monitored; or, users can be tricked into providing authentication secrets. An organization should create well known, protected sites to act as secondary name servers and protect their DNS masters from denial of service attacks using filtering routers.

Traditionally, DNS has had no security capabilities. In particular, the information returned from a query could not be checked for modification or verified that it had come from the name server in question. Work has been done to incorporate digital signatures into the protocol which, when deployed, will allow the integrity of the information to be cryptographically verified (see RFC 2065).

3.2.3.2 *Password/Key Servers (NIS(+) and KDC)*

Password and key servers generally protect their vital information (i.e., the passwords and keys) with encryption algorithms. However, even a one-way encrypted password can be determined by a dictionary attack (wherein common words are encrypted to see if they match the stored encryption). It is therefore necessary to ensure that these servers are not accessible by hosts which do not plan to use them for the service, and even those hosts should only be able to access the service (i.e., general services, such as Telnet and FTP, should not be allowed by anyone other than administrators).

3.2.3.3 *Authentication/Proxy Servers (SOCKS, FWTK)*

A proxy server provides a number of security enhancements. It allows sites to concentrate services through a specific host to allow monitoring, hiding of internal structure, etc. This funneling of services creates an attractive target for a potential intruder. The type of protection required for a proxy server depends greatly on the proxy protocol in use and the services being proxied. The general rule of limiting access only to those hosts which need the services, and limiting access by those hosts to only those services, is a good starting point.

3.2.3.4 Electronic Mail Electronic mail (email) systems have long been a source for intruder break-ins because email protocols are among the oldest and most widely deployed services. Also, by its very nature, an email server requires access to the outside world; most email servers accept input from any source. An email server generally consists of two parts: a receiving/sending agent and a processing agent. Since email is delivered to all users, and is usually private, the processing agent typically requires system (root) privileges to deliver the mail. Most email implementations perform both portions of the service, which means the receiving agent also has system privileges. This opens several security holes which this document will not describe. There are some implementations available which allow a separation of the two agents. Such implementations are generally considered more secure, but still require careful installation to avoid creating a security problem.

3.2.3.5 World Wide Web (WWW) The Web is growing in popularity exponentially because of its ease of use and the powerful ability to concentrate information services. Most WWW servers accept some type of direction and action from the persons accessing their services. The most common example is taking a request from a remote user and passing the provided information to a program running on the server to process the request. Some of these programs are not written with security in mind and can create security holes. If a Web server is available to the Internet community, it is especially important that confidential information not be co-located on the same host as that server. In fact, it is recommended that the server have a dedicated host which is not "trusted" by other internal hosts.

Many sites may want to co-locate FTP service with their WWW service. But this should only occur for anon-ftp servers that only provide information (ftp-get). Anon-ftp puts, in combination with WWW, might be dangerous (e.g., they could result in modifications to the information your site is publishing to the web) and in themselves make the security considerations for each service different.

3.2.3.6 File Transfer (FTP, TFTP) FTP and TFTP both allow users to receive and send electronic files in a point-to-point manner. However, FTP requires authentication while TFTP requires none. For this reason, TFTP should be avoided as much as possible.

Improperly configured FTP servers can allow intruders to copy, replace and delete files at will, anywhere on a host, so it is very important to configure this service correctly. Access to encrypted passwords and proprietary data, and the introduction of Trojan horses are just a few of the potential security holes that can occur when the service is configured incorrectly. FTP servers should reside on their own host. Some sites choose to co-locate FTP with a Web server, since the two protocols share common security considerations. However, the practice isn't recommended, especially when the FTP service allows the deposit of files (see section on WWW above). As mentioned in the opening paragraphs of section 3.2.3, services offered internally to your site should not be co-located with services offered externally. Each should have its own host.

TFTP does not support the same range of functions as FTP, and has no security whatsoever. This service should only be considered for internal use, and then it should be configured in a restricted way so that the server only has access to a set of predetermined files (instead of every world-readable file on the system). Probably the most common usage of TFTP is for downloading router configuration files to a router. TFTP should reside on its own host, and should not be installed on hosts supporting external FTP or Web access.

*3.2.3.7 **NFS*** The Network File Service allows hosts to share common disks. NFS is frequently used by diskless hosts who depend on a disk server for all of their storage needs. Unfortunately, NFS has no built-in security. It is therefore necessary that the NFS server be accessible only by those hosts which are using it for service. This is achieved by specifying which hosts the file system is being exported to and in what manner (e.g., read-only, read-write, etc.). File systems should not be exported to any hosts outside the local network since this will require that the NFS service be accessible externally. Ideally, external access to NFS service should be stopped by a firewall.

3.2.4 Protecting the Protection

It is amazing how often a site will overlook the most obvious weakness in its security by leaving the security server itself open to attack. Based on considerations previously discussed, it should be clear that: the security server should not be accessible from off-site; should offer minimum access, except for the authentication function, to users on-site; and should not be co-located with any other servers. Further, all access to the node, including access to the service itself, should be logged to provide a "paper trail" in the event of a security breach.

3.3 Firewalls

One of the most widely deployed and publicized security measures in use on the Internet is a "firewall." Firewalls have been given the reputation of a general panacea for many, if not all, of the Internet security issues. They are not. Firewalls are just another tool in the quest for system security. They provide a certain level of protection and are, in general, a way of implementing security policy at the network level. The level of security that a firewall provides can vary as much as the level of security on a particular machine. There are the traditional trade-offs between security, ease of use, cost, complexity, etc.

A firewall is any one of several mechanisms used to control and watch access to and from a network for the purpose of protecting it. A firewall acts as a gateway through which all traffic to and from the protected network and/or systems passes. Firewalls help to place limitations on the amount and type of communication that takes place between the protected network and the other network (e.g., the Internet, or another piece of the site's network).

A firewall is generally a way to build a wall between one part of a network, a company's internal network, for example, and another part, the global Internet, for example. The unique feature about this wall is that there needs to be ways for some traffic with particular characteristics to pass through carefully monitored doors ("gateways"). The difficult part is establishing the criteria by which the packets are allowed or denied access through the doors. Books written on firewalls use different terminology to describe the various forms of firewalls. This can be confusing to system administrators who are not familiar with firewalls. The thing to note here is that there is no fixed terminology for the description of firewalls.

Firewalls are not always, or even typically, a single machine. Rather, firewalls are often a combination of routers, network segments, and host computers. Therefore, for the purposes of this discussion, the term "firewall" can consist of more than one physical device. Firewalls are typically built using two different components, filtering routers and proxy servers.

Filtering routers are the easiest component to conceptualize in a firewall. A router moves data back and forth between two (or more) different networks. A "normal" router takes a packet from network A and "routes" it to its destination on network B. A filtering router does the same thing but decides not only how to route the packet, but whether it should route the packet. This is done by installing a series of filters by which the router decides what to do with any given packet of data.

A discussion concerning capabilities of a particular brand of router, running a particular software version is outside the scope of this document. However, when evaluating a router to be used for filtering packets, the following criteria can be important when implementing a filtering policy: source and destination IP address, source and destination TCP port numbers, state of the TCP "ack" bit, UDP source and destination port numbers, and direction of packet flow (i.e.. A->B or B->A). Other information necessary to construct a secure filtering scheme are whether the router reorders filter instructions (designed to optimize filters, this can sometimes change the meaning and cause unintended access), and whether it is possible to apply filters for inbound and outbound packets on each interface (if the router filters only outbound packets then the router is "outside" of its filters and may be more vulnerable to attack). In addition to the router being vulnerable, this distinction between applying filters on inbound or outbound packets is especially relevant for routers with more than 2 interfaces. Other important issues are the ability to create filters based on IP header options and the fragment state of a packet. Building a good filter can be very difficult and requires a good understanding of the type of services (protocols) that will be filtered.

For better security, the filters usually restrict access between the two connected nets to just one host, the bastion host. It is only possible to access the other network via this bastion host. As only this host, rather than a few hundred hosts, can get attacked, it is easier to maintain a certain level of security because only this host has to be protected very carefully. To make resources available to legitimate users across this firewall, services have to be forwarded by the bastion host. Some servers have forwarding built in (like DNS-servers or SMTP-servers), for other services (e.g., Telnet, FTP, etc.), proxy servers can be used to allow access to the resources across the firewall in a secure way.

A proxy server is way to concentrate application services through a single machine. There is typically a single machine (the bastion host) that acts as a proxy server for a variety of protocols (Telnet, SMTP, FTP, HTTP, etc.) but there can be individual host computers for each service. Instead of connecting directly to an external server, the client connects to the proxy server which in turn initiates a connection to the requested external server. Depending on the type of proxy server used, it is possible to configure internal clients to perform this redirection automatically, without knowledge to the user, others might require that the user connect directly to the proxy server and then initiate the connection through a specified format.

There are significant security benefits which can be derived from using proxy servers. It is possible to add access control lists to protocols, requiring users or systems to provide some level of authentication before access is granted. Smarter proxy servers, sometimes called Application Layer Gateways (ALGs), can be written which understand specific protocols and can be configured to block only subsections of the protocol. For example, an ALG for FTP can tell the difference between the "put" command and the "get" command; an organization may wish to allow users to "get" files from the Internet, but not be able to "put" internal files on a remote server. By contrast, a filtering router could either block all FTP access, or none, but not a subset.

Proxy servers can also be configured to encrypt data streams based on a variety of parameters. An organization might use this feature to allow encrypted connections between two locations whose sole access points are on the Internet.

Firewalls are typically thought of as a way to keep intruders out, but they are also often used as a way to let legitimate users into a site. There are many examples where a valid user might need to regularly access the "home" site while on travel to trade shows and conferences, etc. Access to the Internet is often available but may be through an untrusted machine or network. A correctly configured proxy server can allow the correct users into the site while still denying access to other users.

The current best effort in firewall techniques is found using a combination of a pair of screening routers with one or more proxy servers on a network between the two routers. This setup allows the external router to block off any attempts to use the underlying IP layer to break security (IP spoofing, source routing, packet fragments), while allowing the proxy server to handle potential security holes in the higher layer protocols. The internal router's purpose is to block all traffic except to the proxy server. If this setup is rigidly implemented, a high level of security can be achieved.

Most firewalls provide logging which can be tuned to make security administration of the network more convenient. Logging may be centralized and the system may be configured to send out alerts for abnormal conditions. It is important to regularly monitor these logs for any signs of intrusions or break-in attempts. Since some intruders will attempt to cover their tracks by editing logs, it is desirable to protect these logs. A variety of methods is available, including: write once, read many (WORM) drives; papers logs; and centralized logging via the "syslog" utility. Another technique is to use a "fake" serial printer, but have the serial port connected to an isolated machine or PC which keeps the logs.

Firewalls are available in a wide range of quality and strengths. Commercial packages start at approximately $10,000US and go up to over $250,000US. "Home grown" firewalls can be built for smaller amounts of capital. It should be remembered that the correct setup of a firewall (commercial or homegrown) requires a significant amount of skill and knowledge of TCP/IP. Both types require regular maintenance, installation of software patches and updates, and regular monitoring. When budgeting for a firewall, these additional costs should be considered in addition to the cost of the physical elements of the firewall.

As an aside, building a "home grown" firewall requires a significant amount of skill and knowledge of TCP/IP. It should not be trivially attempted because a perceived sense of security is worse in the long run than knowing that there is no security. As with all security measures, it is important to decide on the threat, the value of the assets to be protected, and the costs to implement security.

A final note about firewalls. They can be a great aid when implementing security for a site and they protect against a large variety of attacks. But it is important to keep in mind that they are only one part of the solution. They cannot protect your site against all types of attack.

4.   Security Services and Procedures

This chapter guides the reader through a number of topics that should be addressed when securing a site. Each section touches on a security service or capability that may be required to protect the information and systems at a site. The topics are presented at a fairly high level to introduce the reader to the concepts.

Throughout the chapter, you will find significant mention of cryptography. It is outside the scope of this document to delve into details concerning cryptography, but the interested reader can obtain more information from books and articles listed in the reference section of this document.

4.1   Authentication

For many years, the prescribed method for authenticating users has been through the use of standard, reusable passwords. Originally, these passwords were used by users at terminals to authenticate themselves to a central computer. At the time, there were no networks (internally or externally), so the risk of disclosure of the clear text password was minimal. Today, systems are connected together through local networks, and these local networks are further connected together and to the Internet. Users are logging in from all over the globe; their reusable passwords are often transmitted across those same networks in clear text, ripe for anyone in-between to capture. And indeed, the CERT★ Coordination Center and other response teams are seeing a tremendous number of incidents involving packet sniffers which are capturing the clear text passwords.

With the advent of newer technologies like one-time passwords (e.g., S/Key), PGP, and token-based authentication devices, people are using password-like strings as secret tokens and pins. If these secret tokens and pins are not properly selected and protected, the authentication will be easily subverted.

4.1.1 One-Time passwords

As mentioned above, given today's networked environments, it is recommended that sites concerned about the security and integrity of their systems and networks consider moving away from standard, reusable passwords. There have been many incidents involving Trojan network programs (e.g., telnet and rlogin) and network packet sniffing programs. These programs capture clear text hostname/account name/password triplets. Intruders can use the captured information for subsequent access to those hosts and accounts. This is possible because 1) the password is used over and over (hence the term "reusable"), and 2) the password passes across the network in clear text.

Several authentication techniques have been developed that address this problem. Among these techniques are challenge-response technologies that provide passwords that are only used once (commonly called one-time passwords). There are a number of products available that sites should consider using. The decision to use a product is the responsibility of each organization, and each organization should perform its own evaluation and selection.

4.1.2 Kerberos

Kerberos is a distributed network security system which provides for authentication across unsecured networks. If requested by the application, integrity and encryption can also be provided. Kerberos was originally developed at the Massachusetts Institute of Technology (MIT) in the mid 1980s. There are two major releases of Kerberos, version 4 and 5, which are for practical purposes, incompatible.

Kerberos relies on a symmetric key database using a key distribution center (KDC) which is known as the Kerberos server. A user or service (known as "principals") are granted electronic "tickets" after properly communicating with the KDC. These tickets are used for authentication between principals. All tickets include a time stamp which limits the time period for which the ticket is valid. Therefore, Kerberos clients and server must have a secure time source, and be able to keep time accurately.

The practical side of Kerberos is its integration with the application level. Typical applications like FTP, telnet, POP, and NFS have been integrated with the Kerberos system. There are a variety of implementations which have varying levels of integration. Please see the Kerberos FAQ available at `http://www.ov.com/misc/krb-faq.html` for the latest information.

4.1.3 Choosing and Protecting Secret Tokens and PINs

When selecting secret tokens, take care to choose them carefully. Like the selection of passwords, they should be robust against brute force efforts to guess them. That is, they should not be single words in any language, any common, industry, or cultural acronyms, etc. Ideally, they will be longer rather than shorter and consist of pass phrases that combine upper and lower case character, digits, and other characters.

Once chosen, the protection of these secret tokens is very important. Some are used as pins to hardware devices (like token cards) and these should not be written down or placed in the same location as the device with which they are associated. Others, such as a secret Pretty Good Privacy (PGP) key, should be protected from unauthorized access.

One final word on this subject. When using cryptography products, like PGP, take care to determine the proper key length and ensure that your users are trained to do likewise. As technology advances, the minimum safe key length continues to grow. Make sure your site keeps up with the latest knowledge on the technology so that you can ensure that any cryptography in use is providing the protection you believe it is.

4.1.4 *Password Assurance*

While the need to eliminate the use of standard, reusable passwords cannot be over-stated, it is recognized that some organizations may still be using them. While it's rec-ommended that these organizations transition to the use of better technology, in the mean time, we have the following advice to help with the selection and maintenance of traditional passwords. But remember, none of these measures provides protection against disclosure due to sniffer programs.

1. The importance of robust passwords—In many (if not most) cases of system penetration, the intruder needs to gain access to an account on the system. One way that goal is typically accomplished is through guessing the password of a legitimate user. This is often accomplished by running an automated password cracking program, which utilizes a very large dictionary, against the system's password file. The only way to guard against passwords being disclosed in this manner is through the careful selection of passwords which cannot be easily guessed (i.e., combinations of numbers, letters, and punctuation characters). Passwords should also be as long as the system supports and users can tolerate.

2. Changing default passwords—Many operating systems and application programs are installed with default accounts and passwords. These must be changed imme-diately to something that cannot be guessed or cracked.

3. Restricting access to the password file—In particular, a site wants to protect the encrypted password portion of the file so that would-be intruders don't have them available for cracking. One effective technique is to use shadow passwords where the password field of the standard file contains a dummy or false pass-word. The files containing the legitimate passwords are protected elsewhere on the system.

4. Password aging—When and how to expire passwords is still a subject of contro-versy among the security community. It is generally accepted that a password should not be maintained once an account is no longer in use, but it is hotly debated whether a user should be forced to change a good password that's in active use. The arguments for changing passwords relate to the prevention of the continued use of penetrated accounts. However, the opposition claims that fre-quent password changes lead to users writing down their passwords in visible areas (such as pasting them to a terminal), or to users selecting very simple pass-words that are easy to guess. It should also be stated that an intruder will proba-bly use a captured or guessed password sooner rather than later, in which case password aging provides little if any protection. While there is no definitive

answer to this dilemma, a password policy should directly address the issue and provide guidelines for how often a user should change the password. Certainly, an annual change in their password is usually not difficult for most users, and you should consider requiring it. It is recommended that passwords be changed at least whenever a privileged account is compromised, there is a critical change in personnel (especially if it is an administrator!), or when an account has been compromised. In addition, if a privileged account password is compromised, all passwords on the system should be changed.

5. Password/account blocking—Some sites find it useful to disable accounts after a predefined number of failed attempts to authenticate. If your site decides to employ this mechanism, it is recommended that the mechanism not "advertise" itself. After disabling, even if the correct password is presented, the message displayed should remain that of a failed login attempt. Implementing this mechanism will require that legitimate users contact their system administrator to request that their account be reactivated.

6. A word about the finger daemon—By default, the finger daemon displays considerable system and user information. For example, it can display a list of all users currently using a system, or all the contents of a specific user's .plan file. This information can be used by would-be intruders to identify usernames and guess their passwords. It is recommended that sites consider modifying finger to restrict the information displayed.

4.2 Confidentiality

There will be information assets that your site will want to protect from disclosure to unauthorized entities. Operating systems often have built-in file protection mechanisms that allow an administrator to control who on the system can access, or "see," the contents of a given file. A stronger way to provide confidentiality is through encryption. Encryption is accomplished by scrambling data so that it is very difficult and time consuming for anyone other than the authorized recipients or owners to obtain the plain text. Authorized recipients and the owner of the information will possess the corresponding decryption keys that allow them to easily unscramble the text to a readable (clear text) form. We recommend that sites use encryption to provide confidentiality and protect valuable information.

The use of encryption is sometimes controlled by governmental and site regulations, so we encourage administrators to become informed of laws or policies that regulate its use before employing it. It is outside the scope of this document to discuss the various algorithms and programs available for this purpose, but we do caution against the casual use of the UNIX crypt program as it has been found to be easily broken. We also encourage everyone to take time to understand the strength of the encryption in any given algorithm/product before using it. Most well-known products are well-documented in the literature, so this should be a fairly easy task.

4.3   Integrity

As an administrator, you will want to make sure that information (e.g., operating system files, company data, etc.) has not been altered in an unauthorized fashion. This means you will want to provide some assurance as to the integrity of the information on your systems. One way to provide this is to produce a checksum of the unaltered file, store that checksum offline, and periodically (or when desired) check to make sure the checksum of the online file hasn't changed (which would indicate the data has been modified).

Some operating systems come with checksumming programs, such as the UNIX sum program. However, these may not provide the protection you actually need. Files can be modified in such a way as to preserve the result of the UNIX sum program! Therefore, we suggest that you use a cryptographically strong program, such as the message digesting program MD5 [ref], to produce the checksums you will be using to assure integrity.

There are other applications where integrity will need to be assured, such as when transmitting an email message between two parties. There are products available that can provide this capability. Once you identify that this is a capability you need, you can go about identifying technologies that will provide it.

4.4   Authorization

Authorization refers to the process of granting privileges to processes and, ultimately, users. This differs from authentication in that authentication is the process used to identify a user. Once identified (reliably), the privileges, rights, property, and permissible actions of the user are determined by authorization.

Explicitly listing the authorized activities of each user (and user process) with respect to all resources (objects) is impossible in a reasonable system. In a real system certain techniques are used to simplify the process of granting and checking authorization(s).

One approach, popularized in UNIX systems, is to assign to each object three classes of user: owner, group and world. The owner is either the creator of the object or the user assigned as owner by the super-user. The owner permissions (read, write and execute) apply only to the owner. A group is a collection of users which share access rights to an object. The group permissions (read, write and execute) apply to all users in the group (except the owner). The world refers to everybody else with access to the system. The world permissions (read, write and execute) apply to all users (except the owner and members of the group).

Another approach is to attach to an object a list which explicitly contains the identity of all permitted users (or groups). This is an Access Control List (ACL). The advantage of ACLs are that they are easily maintained (one central list per object) and it's very easy to visually check who has access to what. The disadvantages are the extra resources required to store such lists, as well as the vast number of such lists required for large systems.

4.5 Access

4.5.1 *Physical Access*

Restrict physical access to hosts, allowing access only to those people who are supposed to use the hosts. Hosts include "trusted" terminals (i.e., terminals which allow unauthenticated use such as system consoles, operator terminals and terminals dedicated to special tasks), and individual microcomputers and workstations, especially those connected to your network. Make sure people's work areas mesh well with access restrictions; otherwise they will find ways to circumvent your physical security (e.g., jamming doors open).

Keep original and backup copies of data and programs safe. Apart from keeping them in good condition for backup purposes, they must be protected from theft. It is important to keep backups in a separate location from the originals, not only for damage considerations, but also to guard against thefts.

Portable hosts are a particular risk. Make sure it won't cause problems if one of your staff's portable computer is stolen. Consider developing guidelines for the kinds of data that should be allowed to reside on the disks of portable computers as well as how the data should be protected (e.g., encryption) when it is on a portable computer.

Other areas where physical access should be restricted is the wiring closets and important network elements like file servers, name server hosts, and routers.

4.5.2 *Walk-up Network Connections*

By "walk-up" connections, we mean network connection points located to provide a convenient way for users to connect a portable host to your network.

Consider whether you need to provide this service, bearing in mind that it allows any user to attach an unauthorized host to your network. This increases the risk of attacks via techniques such as IP address spoofing, packet sniffing, etc. Users and site management must appreciate the risks involved. If you decide to provide walk-up connections, plan the service carefully and define precisely where you will provide it so that you can ensure the necessary physical access security.

A walk-up host should be authenticated before its user is permitted to access resources on your network. As an alternative, it may be possible to control physical access. For example, if the service is to be used by students, you might only provide walk-up connection sockets in student laboratories.

If you are providing walk-up access for visitors to connect back to their home networks (e.g., to read e-mail, etc.) in your facility, consider using a separate subnet that has no connectivity to the internal network.

Keep an eye on any area that contains unmonitored access to the network, such as vacant offices. It may be sensible to disconnect such areas at the wiring closet, and consider using secure hubs and monitoring attempts to connect unauthorized hosts.

4.5.3 Other Network Technologies

Technologies considered here include X.25, ISDN, SMDS, DDS and Frame Relay. All are provided via physical links which go through telephone exchanges, providing the potential for them to be diverted. Crackers are certainly interested in telephone switches as well as in data networks!

With switched technologies, use Permanent Virtual Circuits or Closed User Groups whenever this is possible. Technologies which provide authentication and/or encryption (such as IPv6) are evolving rapidly; consider using them on links where security is important.

4.5.4 Modems

4.5.4.1 Modem Lines Must Be Managed
Although they provide convenient access to a site for its users, they can also provide an effective detour around the site's firewalls. For this reason it is essential to maintain proper control of modems.

Don't allow users to install a modem line without proper authorization. This includes temporary installations (e.g., plugging a modem into a facsimile or telephone line overnight).

Maintain a register of all your modem lines and keep your register up to date. Conduct regular (ideally automated) site checks for unauthorized modems.

4.5.4.2 Dial-in Users Must Be Authenticated
A username and password check should be completed before a user can access anything on your network. Normal password security considerations are particularly important (see section 4.1.1).

Remember that telephone lines can be tapped, and that it is quite easy to intercept messages to cellular phones. Modern high-speed modems use more sophisticated modulation techniques, which makes them somewhat more difficult to monitor, but it is prudent to assume that hackers know how to eavesdrop on your lines. For this reason, you should use one-time passwords if at all possible.

It is helpful to have a single dial-in point (e.g., a single large modem pool) so that all users are authenticated in the same way.

Users will occasionally mis-type a password. Set a short delay—say two seconds—after the first and second failed logins, and force a disconnect after the third. This will slow down automated password attacks. Don't tell the user whether the username, the password, or both, were incorrect.

4.5.4.3 Call-back Capability
Some dial-in servers offer call-back facilities (i.e., the user dials in and is authenticated, then the system disconnects the call and calls back on a specified number). Call-back is useful since if someone were to guess a username and password, they are disconnected, and the system then calls back the actual user whose password was cracked; random calls from a server are suspicious, at best. This

does mean users may only log in from one location (where the server is configured to dial them back), and of course there may be phone charges associated with their call-back location.

This feature should be used with caution; it can easily be bypassed. At a minimum, make sure that the return call is never made from the same modem as the incoming one. Overall, although call-back can improve modem security, you should not depend on it alone.

4.5.4.4 *All Logins Should Be Logged*

All logins, whether successful or unsuccessful should be logged. However, do not keep correct passwords in the log. Rather, log them simply as a successful login attempt. Since most bad passwords are mistyped by authorized users, they only vary by a single character from the actual password. Therefore if you can't keep such a log secure, don't log it at all.

If Calling Line Identification is available, take advantage of it by recording the calling number for each login attempt. Be sensitive to the privacy issues raised by Calling Line Identification. Also be aware that Calling Line Identification is not to be trusted (since intruders have been known to break into phone switches and forward phone numbers or make other changes); use the data for informational purposes only, not for authentication.

4.5.4.5 *Choose Your Opening Banner Carefully*

Many sites use a system default contained in a message of the day file for their opening banner. Unfortunately, this often includes the type of host hardware or operating system present on the host. This can provide valuable information to a would-be intruder. Instead, each site should create its own specific login banner, taking care to only include necessary information.

Display a short banner, but don't offer an "inviting" name (e.g., University of XYZ, Student Records System). Instead, give your site name, a short warning that sessions may be monitored, and a username/password prompt. Verify possible legal issues related to the text you put into the banner.

For high-security applications, consider using a "blind" password (i.e., give no response to an incoming call until the user has typed in a password). This effectively simulates a dead modem.

4.5.4.6 *Dial-out Authentication*

Dial-out users should also be authenticated, particularly since your site will have to pay their telephone charges.

Never allow dial-out from an unauthenticated dial-in call, and consider whether you will allow it from an authenticated one. The goal here is to prevent callers using your modem pool as part of a chain of logins. This can be hard to detect, particularly if a hacker sets up a path through several hosts on your site.

At a minimum, don't allow the same modems and phone lines to be used for both dial-in and dial-out. This can be implemented easily if you run separate dial-in and dial-out modem pools.

4.5.4.7 Make Your Modem Programming as "Bullet-proof" as Possible

Be sure modems can't be reprogrammed while they're in service. At a minimum, make sure that three plus signs won't put your dial-in modems into command mode!

Program your modems to reset to your standard configuration at the start of each new call. Failing this, make them reset at the end of each call. This precaution will protect you against accidental reprogramming of your modems. Resetting at both the end and the beginning of each call will assure an even higher level of confidence that a new caller will not inherit a previous caller's session.

Check that your modems terminate calls cleanly. When a user logs out from an access server, verify that the server hangs up the phone line properly. It is equally important that the server forces logouts from whatever sessions were active if the user hangs up unexpectedly.

4.6 Auditing

This section covers the procedures for collecting data generated by network activity, which may be useful in analyzing the security of a network and responding to security incidents.

4.6.1 What to Collect

Audit data should include any attempt to achieve a different security level by any person, process, or other entity in the network. This includes login and logout, super user access (or the non-UNIX equivalent), ticket generation (for Kerberos, for example), and any other change of access or status. It is especially important to note "anonymous" or "guest" access to public servers.

The actual data to collect will differ for different sites and for different types of access changes within a site. In general, the information you want to collect includes: username and hostname, for login and logout; previous and new access rights, for a change of access rights; and a timestamp. Of course, there is much more information which might be gathered, depending on what the system makes available and how much space is available to store that information.

One very important note: do not gather passwords. This creates an enormous potential security breach if the audit records should be improperly accessed. Do not gather incorrect passwords either, as they often differ from valid passwords by only a single character or transposition.

4.6.2 Collection Process

The collection process should be enacted by the host or resource being accessed. Depending on the importance of the data and the need to have it local in instances in which services are being denied, data could be kept local to the resource until needed or be transmitted to storage after each event.

There are basically three ways to store audit records: in a read/write file on a host, on a write-once/read-many device (e.g., a CD-ROM or a specially configured tape drive), or on a write-only device (e.g., a line printer). Each method has advantages and disadvantages.

File system logging is the least resource intensive of the three methods and the easiest to configure. It allows instant access to the records for analysis, which may be important if an attack is in progress. File system logging is also the least reliable method. If the logging host has been compromised, the file system is usually the first thing to go; an intruder could easily cover up traces of the intrusion.

Collecting audit data on a write-once device is slightly more effort to configure than a simple file, but it has the significant advantage of greatly increased security because an intruder could not alter the data showing that an intrusion has occurred. The disadvantage of this method is the need to maintain a supply of storage media and the cost of that media. Also, the data may not be instantly available.

Line printer logging is useful in system where permanent and immediate logs are required. A real time system is an example of this, where the exact point of a failure or attack must be recorded. A laser printer, or other device which buffers data (e.g., a print server), may suffer from lost data if buffers contain the needed data at a critical instant. The disadvantage of, literally, "paper trails" is the need to keep the printer fed and the need to scan records by hand. There is also the issue of where to store the, potentially, enormous volume of paper which may be generated.

For each of the logging methods described, there is also the issue of securing the path between the device generating the log and actual logging device (i.e., the file server, tape/CD-ROM drive, printer). If that path is compromised, logging can be stopped or spoofed or both. In an ideal world, the logging device would be directly attached by a single, simple, point-to-point cable. Since that is usually impractical, the path should pass through the minimum number of networks and routers. Even if logs can be blocked, spoofing can be prevented with cryptographic checksums (it probably isn't necessary to encrypt the logs because they should not contain sensitive information in the first place).

4.6.3 Collection Load

Collecting audit data may result in a rapid accumulation of bytes so storage availability for this information must be considered in advance. There are a few ways to reduce the required storage space. First, data can be compressed, using one of many methods. Or, the required space can be minimized by keeping data for a shorter period of time with only summaries of that data kept in long-term archives.

One major drawback to the latter method involves incident response. Often, an incident has been ongoing for some period of time when a site notices it and begins to investigate. At that point in time, it's very helpful to have detailed audit logs available. If these are just summaries, there may not be sufficient detail to fully handle the incident.

4.6.4 Handling and Preserving Audit Data

Audit data should be some of the most carefully secured data at the site and in the backups. If an intruder were to gain access to audit logs, the systems themselves, in addition to the data, would be at risk.

Audit data may also become key to the investigation, apprehension, and prosecution of the perpetrator of an incident. For this reason, it is advisable to seek the advice of legal council when deciding how audit data should be treated. This should happen before an incident occurs.

If a data handling plan is not adequately defined prior to an incident, it may mean that there is no recourse in the aftermath of an event, and it may create liability resulting from improper treatment of the data.

4.6.5 Legal Considerations

Due to the content of audit data, there are a number of legal questions that arise which might need to be addressed by your legal counsel. If you collect and save audit data, you need to be prepared for consequences resulting both from its existence and its content.

One area concerns the privacy of individuals. In certain instances, audit data may contain personal information. Searching through the data, even for a routine check of the system's security, could represent an invasion of privacy.

A second area of concern involves knowledge of intrusive behavior originating from your site. If an organization keeps audit data, is it responsible for examining it to search for incidents? If a host in one organization is used as a launching point for an attack against another organization, can the second organization use the audit data of the first organization to prove negligence on the part of that organization?

The above examples are meant to be comprehensive, but should motivate your organization to consider the legal issues involved with audit data.

4.7 Securing Backups

The procedure of creating backups is a classic part of operating a computer system. Within the context of this document, backups are addressed as part of the overall security plan of a site. There are several aspects to backups that are important within this context:

1. Make sure your site is creating backups.

2. Make sure your site is using offsite storage for backups. The storage site should be carefully selected for both its security and its availability.

3. Consider encrypting your backups to provide additional protection of the information once it is off-site. However, be aware that you will need a good key management scheme so that you'll be able to recover data at any point in the future. Also, make sure you will have access to the necessary decryption programs at such time in the future as you need to perform the decryption.

4. Don't always assume that your backups are good. There have been many instances of computer security incidents that have gone on for long periods of time before a site has noticed the incident. In such cases, backups of the affected systems are also tainted.

5. Periodically verify the correctness and completeness of your backups.

5. Security Incident Handling

This chapter of the document will supply guidance to be used before, during, and after a computer security incident occurs on a host, network, site, or multi-site environment. The operative philosophy in the event of a breach of computer security is to react according to a plan. This is true whether the breach is the result of an external intruder attack, unintentional damage, a student testing some new program to exploit a software vulnerability, or a disgruntled employee. Each of the possible types of events, such as those just listed, should be addressed in advance by adequate contingency plans.

Traditional computer security, while quite important in the overall site security plan, usually pays little attention to how to actually handle an attack once one occurs. The result is that when an attack is in progress, many decisions are made in haste and can be damaging to tracking down the source of the incident, collecting evidence to be used in prosecution efforts, preparing for the recovery of the system, and protecting the valuable data contained on the system.

One of the most important, but often overlooked, benefits for efficient incident handling is an economic one. Having both technical and managerial personnel respond to an incident requires considerable resources. If trained to handle incidents efficiently, less staff time is required when one occurs.

Due to the world-wide network most incidents are not restricted to a single site. Operating systems vulnerabilities apply (in some cases) to several millions of systems, and many vulnerabilities are exploited within the network itself. Therefore, it is vital that all sites with involved parties be informed as soon as possible.

Another benefit is related to public relations. News about computer security incidents tends to be damaging to an organization's stature among current or potential clients. Efficient incident handling minimizes the potential for negative exposure.

A final benefit of efficient incident handling is related to legal issues. It is possible that in the near future organizations may be held responsible because one of their nodes was used to launch a network attack. In a similar vein, people who develop patches or workarounds may be sued if the patches or workarounds are ineffective, resulting in compromise of the systems, or, if the patches or workarounds themselves damage systems. Knowing about operating system vulnerabilities and patterns of attacks, and then taking appropriate measures to counter these potential threats, is critical to circumventing possible legal problems.

The sections in this chapter provide an outline and starting point for creating your site's policy for handling security incidents. The sections are:

1. Preparing and planning (what are the goals and objectives in handling an incident).

2. Notification (who should be contacted in the case of an incident).

   Local managers and personnel

   Law enforcement and investigative agencies

   Computer security incidents handling teams

Affected and involved sites

Internal communications

Public relations and press releases

3. Identifying an incident (is it an incident and how serious is it).
4. Handling (what should be done when an incident occurs).

Notification (who should be notified about the incident)

Protecting evidence and activity logs (what records should be kept from before, during, and after the incident)

Containment (how can the damage be limited)

Eradication (how to eliminate the reasons for the incident)

Recovery (how to reestablish service and systems)

Follow Up (what actions should be taken after the incident)

5. Aftermath (what are the implications of past incidents).
6. Administrative response to incidents.

The remainder of this chapter will detail the issues involved in each of the important topics listed above, and provide some guidance as to what should be included in a site policy for handling incidents.

5.1 Preparing and Planning for Incident Handling

Part of handling an incident is being prepared to respond to an incident before the incident occurs in the first place. This includes establishing a suitable level of protections as explained in the preceding chapters. Doing this should help your site prevent incidents as well as limit potential damage resulting from them when they do occur. Protection also includes preparing incident handling guidelines as part of a contingency plan for your organization or site. Having written plans eliminates much of the ambiguity which occurs during an incident, and will lead to a more appropriate and thorough set of responses. It is vitally important to test the proposed plan before an incident occurs through "dry runs." A team might even consider hiring a tiger team to act in parallel with the dry run. (Note: a tiger team is a team of specialists that try to penetrate the security of a system.)

Learning to respond efficiently to an incident is important for a number of reasons:

1. Protecting the assets which could be compromised
2. Protecting resources which could be utilized more profitably if an incident did not require their services
3. Complying with (government or other) regulations
4. Preventing the use of your systems in attacks against other systems (which could cause you to incur legal liability)
5. Minimizing the potential for negative exposure

As in any set of pre-planned procedures, attention must be paid to a set of goals for handling an incident. These goals will be prioritized differently depending on the site. A specific set of objectives can be identified for dealing with incidents:

1. Figure out how it happened.
2. Find out how to avoid further exploitation of the same vulnerability.
3. Avoid escalation and further incidents.
4. Assess the impact and damage of the incident.
5. Recover from the incident.
6. Update policies and procedures as needed.
7. Find out who did it (if appropriate and possible).

Due to the nature of the incident, there might be a conflict between analyzing the original source of a problem and restoring systems and services. Overall goals (like assuring the integrity of critical systems) might be the reason for not analyzing an incident. Of course, this is an important management decision; but all involved parties must be aware that without analysis the same incident may happen again.

It is also important to prioritize the actions to be taken during an incident well in advance of the time an incident occurs. Sometimes an incident may be so complex that it is impossible to do everything at once to respond to it; priorities are essential. Although priorities will vary from institution to institution, the following suggested priorities may serve as a starting point for defining your organization's response:

1. Priority one—protect human life and people's safety; human life always has precedence over all other considerations.
2. Priority two—protect classified and/or sensitive data. Prevent exploitation of classified and/or sensitive systems, networks or sites. Inform affected classified and/or sensitive systems, networks or sites about already occurred penetrations. (Be aware of regulations by your site or by government.)
3. Priority three—protect other data, including proprietary, scientific, managerial and other data, because loss of data is costly in terms of resources. Prevent exploitations of other systems, networks or sites and inform already affected systems, networks or sites about successful penetrations.
4. Priority four—prevent damage to systems (e.g., loss or alteration of system files, damage to disk drives, etc.). Damage to systems can result in costly down time and recovery.
5. Priority five—minimize disruption of computing resources (including processes). It is better in many cases to shut a system down or disconnect from a network than to risk damage to data or systems. Sites will have to evaluate the trade-offs between shutting down and disconnecting, and staying up. There may be service agreements in place that may require keeping systems up even in light of further damage occurring. However, the damage and scope of an incident may be so extensive that service agreements may have to be over-ridden.

An important implication for defining priorities is that once human life and national security considerations have been addressed, it is generally more important to save data than system software and hardware. Although it is undesirable to have any damage or loss during an incident, systems can be replaced. However, the loss or compromise of data (especially classified or proprietary data) is usually not an acceptable outcome under any circumstances.

Another important concern is the effect on others, beyond the systems and networks where the incident occurs. Within the limits imposed by government regulations it is always important to inform affected parties as soon as possible. Due to the legal implications of this topic, it should be included in the planned procedures to avoid further delays and uncertainties for the administrators.

Any plan for responding to security incidents should be guided by local policies and regulations. Government and private sites that deal with classified material have specific rules that they must follow.

The policies chosen by your site on how it reacts to incidents will shape your response. For example, it may make little sense to create mechanisms to monitor and trace intruders if your site does not plan to take action against the intruders if they are caught. Other organizations may have policies that affect your plans. Telephone companies often release information about telephone traces only to law enforcement agencies.

Handling incidents can be tedious and require any number of routine tasks that could be handled by support personnel. To free the technical staff it may be helpful to identify support staff who will help with tasks like: photocopying, faxing, etc.

5.2 Notification and Points of Contact

It is important to establish contacts with various personnel before a real incident occurs. Many times, incidents are not real emergencies. Indeed, often you will be able to handle the activities internally. However, there will also be many times when others outside your immediate department will need to be included in the incident handling. These additional contacts include local managers and system administrators, administrative contacts for other sites on the Internet, and various investigative organizations. Getting to know these contacts before incidents occur will help to make your incident handling process more efficient.

For each type of communication contact, specific "Points of Contact" (POC) should be defined. These may be technical or administrative in nature and may include legal or investigative agencies as well as service providers and vendors. When establishing these contacts, it is important to decide how much information will be shared with each class of contact. It is especially important to define, ahead of time, what information will be shared with the users at a site, with the public (including the press), and with other sites.

Settling these issues are especially important for the local person responsible for handling the incident, since that is the person responsible for the actual notification of others. A list of contacts in each of these categories is an important time saver for this person during an incident. It can be quite difficult to find an appropriate person during an incident when many urgent events are ongoing. It is strongly recommended that all relevant telephone numbers (also electronic mail addresses and fax numbers) be included in the site security policy. The names and contact information of all individuals who will be directly involved in the handling of an incident should be placed at the top of this list.

5.2.1 Local Managers and Personnel

When an incident is under way, a major issue is deciding who is in charge of coordinating the activity of the multitude of players. A major mistake that can be made is to have a number of people who are each working independently, but are not working together. This will only add to the confusion of the event and will probably lead to wasted or ineffective effort.

The single POC may or may not be the person responsible for handling the incident. There are two distinct roles to fill when deciding who shall be the POC and who will be the person in charge of the incident. The person in charge of the incident will make decisions as to the interpretation of policy applied to the event. In contrast, the POC must coordinate the effort of all the parties involved with handling the event.

The POC must be a person with the technical expertise to successfully coordinate the efforts of the system managers and users involved in monitoring and reacting to the attack. Care should be taken when identifying who this person will be. It should not necessarily be the same person who has administrative responsibility for the compromised systems since often such administrators have knowledge only sufficient for the day to day use of the computers, and lack in-depth technical expertise. Another important function of the POC is to maintain contact with law enforcement and other external agencies to assure that multi-agency involvement occurs. The level of involvement will be determined by management decisions as well as legal constraints.

A single POC should also be the single person in charge of collecting evidence, since as a rule of thumb, the more people that touch a potential piece of evidence, the greater the possibility that it will be inadmissible in court. To ensure that evidence will be acceptable to the legal community, collecting evidence should be done following predefined procedures in accordance with local laws and legal regulations.

One of the most critical tasks for the POC is the coordination of all relevant processes. Responsibilities may be distributed over the whole site, involving multiple independent departments or groups. This will require a well coordinated effort in order to achieve overall success. The situation becomes even more complex if multiple sites are involved. When this happens, rarely will a single POC at one site be able to adequately coordinate the handling of the entire incident. Instead, appropriate incident response teams should be involved.

The incident handling process should provide some escalation mechanisms. In order to define such a mechanism, sites will need to create an internal classification scheme for incidents. Associated with each level of incident will be the appropriate POC and procedures. As an incident is escalated, there may be a change in the POC which will need to be communicated to all others involved in handling the incident. When a change in the POC occurs, the old POC should brief the new POC in all background information.

Lastly, users must know how to report suspected incidents. Sites should establish reporting procedures that will work both during and outside normal working hours. Help desks are often used to receive these reports during normal working hours, while beepers and telephones can be used for out of hours reporting.

5.2.2 Law Enforcement and Investigative Agencies

In the event of an incident that has legal consequences, it is important to establish contact with investigative agencies (e.g, the FBI and Secret Service in the U.S.) as soon as possible. Local law enforcement, local security offices, and campus police departments should also be informed as appropriate. This section describes many of the issues that will be confronted, but it is acknowledged that each organization will have its own local and governmental laws and regulations that will impact how they interact with law enforcement and investigative agencies. The most important point to make is that each site needs to work through these issues.

A primary reason for determining these points of contact well in advance of an incident is that once a major attack is in progress, there is little time to call these agencies to determine exactly who the correct point of contact is. Another reason is that it is important to cooperate with these agencies in a manner that will foster a good working relationship, and that will be in accordance with the working procedures of these agencies. Knowing the working procedures in advance, and the expectations of your point of contact is a big step in this direction. For example, it is important to gather evidence that will be admissible in any subsequent legal proceedings, and this will require prior knowledge of how to gather such evidence. A final reason for establishing contacts as soon as possible is that it is impossible to know the particular agency that will assume jurisdiction in any given incident. Making contacts and finding the proper channels early on will make responding to an incident go considerably more smoothly.

If your organization or site has a legal counsel, you need to notify this office soon after you learn that an incident is in progress. At a minimum, your legal counsel needs to be involved to protect the legal and financial interests of your site or organization. There are many legal and practical issues, a few of which are:

1. Whether your site or organization is willing to risk negative publicity or exposure to cooperate with legal prosecution efforts.

2. Downstream liability—if you leave a compromised system as is so it can be monitored and another computer is damaged because the attack originated from your system, your site or organization may be liable for damages incurred.

3. Distribution of information—if your site or organization distributes information about an attack in which another site or organization may be involved or the vulnerability in a product that may affect ability to market that product, your site or organization may again be liable for any damages (including damage of reputation).

4. Liabilities due to monitoring—your site or organization may be sued if users at your site or elsewhere discover that your site is monitoring account activity without informing users.

Unfortunately, there are no clear precedents yet on the liabilities or responsibilities of organizations involved in a security incident or who might be involved in supporting an investigative effort. Investigators will often encourage organizations to help trace and monitor intruders. Indeed, most investigators cannot pursue computer intrusions without extensive support from the organizations involved. However, investigators cannot provide protection from liability claims, and these kinds of efforts may drag out for months and may take a lot of effort.

On the other hand, an organization's legal council may advise extreme caution and suggest that tracing activities be halted and an intruder shut out of the system. This, in itself, may not provide protection from liability, and may prevent investigators from identifying the perpetrator.

The balance between supporting investigative activity and limiting liability is tricky. You'll need to consider the advice of your legal counsel and the damage the intruder is causing (if any) when making your decision about what to do during any particular incident.

Your legal counsel should also be involved in any decision to contact investigative agencies when an incident occurs at your site. The decision to coordinate efforts with investigative agencies is most properly that of your site or organization. Involving your legal counsel will also foster the multi-level coordination between your site and the particular investigative agency involved, which in turn results in an efficient division of labor. Another result is that you are likely to obtain guidance that will help you avoid future legal mistakes.

Finally, your legal counsel should evaluate your site's written procedures for responding to incidents. It is essential to obtain a "clean bill of health" from a legal perspective before you actually carry out these procedures.

It is vital, when dealing with investigative agencies, to verify that the person who calls asking for information is a legitimate representative from the agency in question. Unfortunately, many well intentioned people have unknowingly leaked sensitive details about incidents, allowed unauthorized people into their systems, etc., because a caller has masqueraded as a representative of a government agency. (Note: this word of caution actually applies to all external contacts.)

A similar consideration is using a secure means of communication. Because many network attackers can easily re-route electronic mail, avoid using electronic mail to communicate with other agencies (as well as others dealing with the incident at hand). Non-secured phone lines (the phones normally used in the business world) are also frequent targets for tapping by network intruders, so be careful!

There is no one established set of rules for responding to an incident when the local government becomes involved. Normally (in the U.S.), except by legal order, no agency can force you to monitor, to disconnect from the network, to avoid telephone contact with the suspected attackers, etc. Each organization will have a set of local and national laws and regulations that must be adhered to when handling incidents. It is recommended that each site be familiar with those laws and regulations, and identify and get to know the contacts for agencies with jurisdiction well in advance of handling an incident.

5.2.3   Computer Security Incident Handling Teams

There are currently a number of Computer Security Incident Response teams (CSIRTs) such as the CERT Coordination Center, the German DFN-CERT, and other teams around the globe. Teams exist for many major government agencies and large corporations. If such a team is available, notifying it should be of primary consideration during the early stages of an incident. These teams are responsible for coordinating computer security incidents over a range of sites and larger entities. Even if the incident is believed to be contained within a single site, it is possible that the information available through a response team could help in fully resolving the incident.

If it is determined that the breach occurred due to a flaw in the system's hardware or software, the vendor (or supplier) and a Computer Security Incident Handling team should be notified as soon as possible. This is especially important because many other systems are vulnerable, and these vendor and response team organizations can help disseminate help to other affected sites.

In setting up a site policy for incident handling, it may be desirable to create a subgroup, much like those teams that already exist, that will be responsible for handling computer security incidents for the site (or organization). If such a team is created, it is essential that communication lines be opened between this team and other teams. Once an incident is under way, it is difficult to open a trusted dialogue between other teams if none has existed before.

5.2.4   Affected and Involved Sites

If an incident has an impact on other sites, it is good practice to inform them. It may be obvious from the beginning that the incident is not limited to the local site, or it may emerge only after further analysis.

Each site may choose to contact other sites directly or they can pass the information to an appropriate incident response team. It is often very difficult to find the responsible POC at remote sites and the incident response team will be able to facilitate contact by making use of already established channels.

The legal and liability issues arising from a security incident will differ from site to site. It is important to define a policy for the sharing and logging of information about other sites before an incident occurs.

Information about specific people is especially sensitive, and may be subject to privacy laws. To avoid problems in this area, irrelevant information should be deleted and a statement of how to handle the remaining information should be included. A clear statement of how this information is to be used is essential. No one who informs a site of a security incident wants to read about it in the public press. Incident response teams are valuable in this respect. When they pass information to responsible POCs, they are able to protect the anonymity of the original source. But, be aware that, in many cases, the analysis of logs and information at other sites will reveal addresses of your site.

All the problems discussed above should be not taken as reasons not to involve other sites. In fact, the experiences of existing teams reveal that most sites informed about security problems are not even aware that their site had been compromised. Without timely information, other sites are often unable to take action against intruders.

5.2.5 Internal Communications

It is crucial during a major incident to communicate why certain actions are being taken, and how the users (or departments) are expected to behave. In particular, it should be made very clear to users what they are allowed to say (and not say) to the outside world (including other departments). For example, it wouldn't be good for an organization if users replied to customers with something like, "I'm sorry the systems are down, we've had an intruder and we are trying to clean things up." It would be much better if they were instructed to respond with a prepared statement like, "I'm sorry our systems are unavailable, they are being maintained for better service in the future."

Communications with customers and contract partners should be handled in a sensible, but sensitive way. One can prepare for the main issues by preparing a checklist. When an incident occurs, the checklist can be used with the addition of a sentence or two for the specific circumstances of the incident.

Public relations departments can be very helpful during incidents. They should be involved in all planning and can provide well constructed responses for use when contact with outside departments and organizations is necessary.

5.2.6 Public Relations—Press Releases

There has been a tremendous growth in the amount of media coverage dedicated to computer security incidents in the United States. Such press coverage is bound to extend to other countries as the Internet continues to grow and expand internationally. Readers from countries where such media attention has not yet occurred, can learn from the experiences in the U.S. and should be forewarned and prepared.

One of the most important issues to consider is when, who, and how much to release to the general public through the press. There are many issues to consider when deciding this particular issue. First and foremost, if a public relations office exists for the site, it is important to use this office as liaison to the press. The public relations office is trained in the type and wording of information released, and will help to assure that the image of the site is protected during and after the incident (if possible). A public relations office has the advantage that you can communicate candidly with them, and provide a buffer between the constant press attention and the need of the POC to maintain control over the incident.

If a public relations office is not available, the information released to the press must be carefully considered. If the information is sensitive, it may be advantageous to provide only minimal or overview information to the press. It is quite possible that any information provided to the press will be quickly reviewed by the perpetrator of the incident. Also note that misleading the press can often backfire and cause more damage than releasing sensitive information.

While it is difficult to determine in advance what level of detail to provide to the press, some guidelines to keep in mind are:

1. Keep the technical level of detail low. Detailed information about the incident may provide enough information for others to launch similar attacks on other sites, or even damage the site's ability to prosecute the guilty party once the event is over.

2. Keep the speculation out of press statements. Speculation of who is causing the incident or the motives are very likely to be in error and may cause an inflamed view of the incident.

3. Work with law enforcement professionals to assure that evidence is protected. If prosecution is involved, assure that the evidence collected is not divulged to the press.

4. Try not to be forced into a press interview before you are prepared. The popular press is famous for the "2 am" interview, where the hope is to catch the interviewee off guard and obtain information otherwise not available.

5. Do not allow the press attention to detract from the handling of the event. Always remember that the successful closure of an incident is of primary importance.

5.3   Identifying an Incident

5.3.1   Is It Real?

This stage involves determining if a problem really exists. Of course many if not most signs often associated with virus infection, system intrusions, malicious users, etc., are simply anomalies such as hardware failures or suspicious system/user behavior. To assist in identifying whether there really is an incident, it is usually helpful to obtain and use any detection software which may be available. Audit information is also extremely useful, especially in determining whether there is a network attack. It is extremely important to obtain a system snapshot as soon as one suspects that something is wrong. Many incidents cause a dynamic chain of events to occur, and an initial system snapshot may be the most valuable tool for identifying the problem and any source of attack. Finally, it is important to start a log book. Recording system events, telephone conversations, time stamps, etc., can lead to a more rapid and systematic identification of the problem, and is the basis for subsequent stages of incident handling.

There are certain indications or "symptoms" of an incident that deserve special attention:

1. System crashes.

2. New user accounts (the account RUMPLESTILTSKIN has been unexpectedly created), or high activity on a previously low usage account.

3. New files (usually with novel or strange file names, such as data.xx or k or .xx).

4. Accounting discrepancies (in a UNIX system you might notice the shrinking of an accounting file called /usr/admin/lastlog, something that should make you very suspicious that there may be an intruder).

5. Changes in file lengths or dates (a user should be suspicious if .EXE files in an MS DOS computer have unexplainably grown by over 1800 bytes).

6. Attempts to write to system (a system manager notices that a privileged user in a VMS system is attempting to alter RIGHTSLIST.DAT).

7. Data modification or deletion (files start to disappear).

8. Denial of service (a system manager and all other users become locked out of a UNIX system, now in single user mode).

9. Unexplained, poor system performance.

10. Anomalies ("GOTCHA" is displayed on the console or there are frequent unexplained "beeps").

11. Suspicious probes (there are numerous unsuccessful login attempts from another node).

12. Suspicious browsing (someone becomes a root user on a UNIX system and accesses file after file on many user accounts).

13. Inability of a user to log in due to modifications of his/her account.

By no means is this list comprehensive; we have just listed a number of common indicators. It is best to collaborate with other technical and computer security personnel to make a decision as a group about whether an incident is occurring.

5.3.2 Types and Scope of Incidents

Along with the identification of the incident is the evaluation of the scope and impact of the problem. It is important to correctly identify the boundaries of the incident in order to effectively deal with it and prioritize responses.

In order to identify the scope and impact a set of criteria should be defined which is appropriate to the site and to the type of connections available. Some of the issues include:

1. Is this a multi-site incident?

2. Are many computers at your site affected by this incident?

3. Is sensitive information involved?

4. What is the entry point of the incident (network, phone line, local terminal, etc.)?

5. Is the press involved?

6. What is the potential damage of the incident?

7. What is the estimated time to close out the incident?

8. What resources could be required to handle the incident?

9. Is law enforcement involved?

5.3.3 Assessing the Damage and Extent

The analysis of the damage and extent of the incident can be quite time consuming, but should lead to some insight into the nature of the incident, and aid investigation and prosecution. As soon as the breach has occurred, the entire system and all of its components should be considered suspect. System software is the most probable target. Preparation is key to be able to detect all changes for a possibly tainted system. This includes checksumming all media from the vendor using a algorithm which is resistant to tampering. (See section 4.3.)

Assuming original vendor distribution media are available, an analysis of all system files should commence, and any irregularities should be noted and referred to all parties involved in handling the incident. It can be very difficult, in some cases, to decide which backup media are showing a correct system status. Consider, for example, that the incident may have continued for months or years before discovery, and the suspect may be an employee of the site, or otherwise have intimate knowledge or access to the systems. In all cases, the pre-incident preparation will determine what recovery is possible.

If the system supports centralized logging (most do), go back over the logs and look for abnormalities. If process accounting and connect time accounting is enabled, look for patterns of system usage. To a lesser extent, disk usage may shed light on the incident. Accounting can provide much helpful information in an analysis of an incident and subsequent prosecution. Your ability to address all aspects of a specific incident strongly depends on the success of this analysis.

5.4 Handling an Incident

Certain steps are necessary to take during the handling of an incident. In all security-related activities, the most important point to be made is that all sites should have policies in place. Without defined policies and goals, activities undertaken will remain without focus. The goals should be defined by management and legal counsel in advance.

One of the most fundamental objectives is to restore control of the affected systems and to limit the impact and damage. In the worst case scenario, shutting down the system, or disconnecting the system from the network, maybe the only practical solution.

As the activities involved are complex, try to get as much help as necessary. While trying to solve the problem alone, real damage might occur due to delays or missing information. Most administrators take the discovery of an intruder as a personal challenge. By proceeding this way, other objectives as outlined in the local policies may not always be considered. Trying to catch intruders may be a very low priority, compared to system integrity, for example. Monitoring a hacker's activity is useful, but it might not be considered worth the risk to allow the continued access.

5.4.1 Types of Notification and Exchange of Information

When you have confirmed that an incident is occurring, the appropriate personnel must be notified. How this notification is achieved is very important to keeping the event under control both from a technical and emotional standpoint. The circumstances should be described in as much detail as possible, in order to aid prompt acknowledgment and understanding of the problem. Great care should be taken when determining to which groups detailed technical information is given during the notification. For example, it is helpful to pass this kind of information to an incident handling team as they can assist you by providing helpful hints for eradicating the vulnerabilities involved in an incident. On the other hand, putting the critical knowledge into the public domain (e.g., via USENET newsgroups or mailing lists) may potentially put a large number of systems at risk of intrusion. It is invalid to assume that all administrators reading a particular newsgroup have access to operating system source code, or can even understand an advisory well enough to take adequate steps.

First of all, any notification to either local or off-site personnel must be explicit. This requires that any statement (be it an electronic mail message, phone call, fax, beeper, or semaphone) providing information about the incident be clear, concise, and fully qualified. When you are notifying others that will help you handle an event, a "smoke screen" will only divide the effort and create confusion. If a division of labor is suggested, it is helpful to provide information to each participant about what is being accomplished in other efforts. This will not only reduce duplication of effort, but allow people working on parts of the problem to know where to obtain information relevant to their part of the incident.

Another important consideration when communicating about the incident is to be factual. Attempting to hide aspects of the incident by providing false or incomplete information may not only prevent a successful resolution to the incident, but may even worsen the situation.

The choice of language used when notifying people about the incident can have a profound effect on the way that information is received. When you use emotional or inflammatory terms, you raise the potential for damage and negative outcomes of the incident. It is important to remain calm both in written and spoken communications.

Another consideration is that not all people speak the same language. Due to this fact, misunderstandings and delay may arise, especially if it is a multi-national incident. Other international concerns include differing legal implications of a security incident and cultural differences. However, cultural differences do not only exist between countries. They even exist within countries, between different social or user groups. For example, an administrator of a university system might be very relaxed about attempts to connect to the system via telnet, but the administrator of a military system is likely to consider the same action as a possible attack.

Another issue associated with the choice of language is the notification of non-technical or off-site personnel. It is important to accurately describe the incident without generating undue alarm or confusion. While it is more difficult to describe the incident to a non-technical audience, it is often more important. A non-technical description may be required for upper-level management, the press, or law enforcement liaisons. The importance of these communications cannot be underestimated and may make the difference between resolving the incident properly and escalating to some higher level of damage.

If an incident response team becomes involved, it might be necessary to fill out a template for the information exchange. Although this may seem to be an additional burden and adds a certain delay, it helps the team to act on this minimum set of information. The response team may be able to respond to aspects of the incident of which the local administrator is unaware. If information is given out to someone else, the following minimum information should be provided:

1. Time zone of logs, . . . in GMT or local time
2. Information about the remote system, including host names, IP addresses and (perhaps) user IDs
3. All log entries relevant for the remote site
4. Type of incident (what happened, why should you care)

If local information (i.e., local user IDs) is included in the log entries, it will be necessary to sanitize the entries beforehand to avoid privacy issues. In general, all information which might assist a remote site in resolving an incident should be given out, unless local policies prohibit this.

5.4.2 *Protecting Evidence and Activity Logs*

When you respond to an incident, document all details related to the incident. This will provide valuable information to yourself and others as you try to unravel the course of events. Documenting all details will ultimately save you time. If you don't document every relevant phone call, for example, you are likely to forget a significant portion of information you obtain, requiring you to contact the source of information again. At the same time, recording details will provide evidence for prosecution efforts, providing the case moves in that direction. Documenting an incident will also help you perform a final assessment of damage (something your management, as well as law enforcement officers, will want to know), and will provide the basis for later phases of the handling process: eradication, recovery, and follow-up "lessons learned."

During the initial stages of an incident, it is often infeasible to determine whether prosecution is viable, so you should document as if you are gathering evidence for a court case. At a minimum, you should record:

1. All system events (audit records)
2. All actions you take (time tagged)
3. All external conversations (including the person with whom you talked, the date and time, and the content of the conversation)

The most straightforward way to maintain documentation is keeping a log book. This allows you to go to a centralized, chronological source of information when you need it, instead of requiring you to page through individual sheets of paper. Much of this information is potential evidence in a court of law. Thus, when a legal follow-up is a possibility, one should follow the prepared procedures and avoid jeopardizing the legal follow-up by improper handling of possible evidence. If appropriate, the following steps may be taken:

1. Regularly (e.g., every day) turn in photocopied, signed copies of your logbook (as well as media you use to record system events) to a document custodian.

2. The custodian should store these copied pages in a secure place (e.g., a safe).

3. When you submit information for storage, you should receive a signed, dated receipt from the document custodian.

Failure to observe these procedures can result in invalidation of any evidence you obtain in a court of law.

5.4.3 Containment

The purpose of containment is to limit the extent of an attack. An essential part of containment is decision making (e.g., determining whether to shut a system down, disconnect from a network, monitor system or network activity, set traps, disable functions such as remote file transfer, etc.).

Sometimes this decision is trivial; shut the system down if the information is classified, sensitive, or proprietary. Bear in mind that removing all access while an incident is in progress obviously notifies all users, including the alleged problem users, that the administrators are aware of a problem; this may have a deleterious effect on an investigation. In some cases, it is prudent to remove all access or functionality as soon as possible, then restore normal operation in limited stages. In other cases, it is worthwhile to risk some damage to the system if keeping the system up might enable you to identify an intruder.

This stage should involve carrying out predetermined procedures. Your organization or site should, for example, define acceptable risks in dealing with an incident, and should prescribe specific actions and strategies accordingly. This is especially important when a quick decision is necessary and it is not possible to first contact all involved parties to discuss the decision. In the absence of predefined procedures, the person in charge of the incident will often not have the power to make difficult management decisions (like to lose the results of a costly experiment by shutting down a system). A final activity that should occur during this stage of incident handling is the notification of appropriate authorities.

5.4.4 Eradication

Once the incident has been contained, it is time to eradicate the cause. But before eradicating the cause, great care should be taken to collect all necessary information about the compromised system(s) and the cause of the incident as they will likely be lost when cleaning up the system.

Software may be available to help you in the eradication process, such as anti-virus software. If any bogus files have been created, archive them before deleting them. In the case of virus infections, it is important to clean and reformat any media containing infected files. Finally, ensure that all backups are clean. Many systems infected with viruses become periodically re-infected simply because people do not systematically eradicate the virus from backups. After eradication, a new backup should be taken.

Removing all vulnerabilities once an incident has occurred is difficult. The key to removing vulnerabilities is knowledge and understanding of the breach.

It may be necessary to go back to the original distribution media and re-customize the system. To facilitate this worst case scenario, a record of the original system setup and each customization change should be maintained. In the case of a network-based attack, it is important to install patches for each operating system vulnerability which was exploited.

As discussed in section 5.4.2, a security log can be most valuable during this phase of removing vulnerabilities. The logs showing how the incident was discovered and contained can be used later to help determine how extensive the damage was from a given incident. The steps taken can be used in the future to make sure the problem does not resurface. Ideally, one should automate and regularly apply the same test as was used to detect the security incident.

If a particular vulnerability is isolated as having been exploited, the next step is to find a mechanism to protect your system. The security mailing lists and bulletins would be a good place to search for this information, and you can get advice from incident response teams.

5.4.5 Recovery

After the cause of an incident has been eradicated, the recovery phase defines the next stage of action. The goal of recovery is to return the system to normal. In general, bringing up services in the order of demand to allow a minimum of user inconvenience is the best practice. Understand that the proper recovery procedures for the system are extremely important and should be specific to the site.

5.4.6 Follow-Up

When you believe that a system has been restored to a "safe" state, it is still possible that holes, and even traps, could be lurking in the system. One of the most important stages of responding to incidents is also the most often omitted, the follow-up stage. In the follow-up stage, the system should be monitored for items that may have been missed during the cleanup stage. It would be prudent to utilize some of the tools mentioned in Chapter 7 as a start. Remember, these tools don't replace continual system monitoring and good systems administration practices.

The most important element of the follow-up stage is performing a postmortem analysis. Exactly what happened, and at what times? How well did the staff involved with the incident perform? What kind of information did the staff need quickly, and how could they have gotten that information as soon as possible? What would the staff do differently next time?

After an incident, it is prudent to write a report describing the exact sequence of events: the method of discovery, correction procedure, monitoring procedure, and a summary of lesson learned. This will aid in the clear understanding of the problem. Creating a formal chronology of events (including time stamps) is also important for legal reasons.

A follow-up report is valuable for many reasons. It provides a reference to be used in case of other similar incidents. It is also important to, as quickly as possible, obtain a monetary estimate of the amount of damage the incident caused. This estimate should include costs associated with any loss of software and files (especially the value of proprietary data that may have been disclosed), hardware damage, and manpower costs to restore altered files, reconfigure affected systems, and so forth. This estimate may become the basis for subsequent prosecution activity. The report can also help justify an organization's computer security effort to management.

5.5   Aftermath of an Incident

In the wake of an incident, several actions should take place. These actions can be summarized as follows:

1. An inventory should be taken of the systems' assets, (i.e., a careful examination should determine how the system was affected by the incident).

2. The lessons learned as a result of the incident should be included in revised security plan to prevent the incident from re-occurring.

3. A new risk analysis should be developed in light of the incident.

4. An investigation and prosecution of the individuals who caused the incident should commence, if it is deemed desirable.

If an incident is based on poor policy, and unless the policy is changed, then one is doomed to repeat the past. Once a site has recovered from and incident, site policy and procedures should be reviewed to encompass changes to prevent similar incidents. Even without an incident, it would be prudent to review policies and procedures on a regular basis. Reviews are imperative due to today's changing computing environments.

The whole purpose of this post mortem process is to improve all security measures to protect the site against future attacks. As a result of an incident, a site or organization should gain practical knowledge from the experience. A concrete goal of the post mortem is to develop new proactive methods. Another important facet of the aftermath may be end user and administrator education to prevent a reoccurrence of the security problem.

5.6   Responsibilities

5.6.1   Not Crossing the Line

It is one thing to protect one's own network, but quite another to assume that one should protect other networks. During the handling of an incident, certain system vulnerabilities of one's own systems and the systems of others become apparent. It is quite easy and may even be tempting to pursue the intruders in order to track them. Keep in mind that at a certain point it is possible to "cross the line," and, with the best of intentions, become no better than the intruder.

The best rule when it comes to propriety is to not use any facility of remote sites which is not public. This clearly excludes any entry onto a system (such as a remote shell or login session) which is not expressly permitted. This may be very tempting; after a breach of security is detected, a system administrator may have the means to "follow it up," to ascertain what damage is being done to the remote site. Don't do it! Instead, attempt to reach the appropriate point of contact for the affected site.

5.6.2 Good Internet Citizenship

During a security incident there are two choices one can make. First, a site can choose to watch the intruder in the hopes of catching him; or, the site can go about cleaning up after the incident and shut the intruder out of the systems. This is a decision that must be made very thoughtfully, as there may be legal liabilities if you choose to leave your site open, knowing that an intruder is using your site as a launching pad to reach out to other sites. Being a good Internet citizen means that you should try to alert other sites that may have been impacted by the intruder. These affected sites may be readily apparent after a thorough review of your log files.

5.6.3 Administrative Response to Incidents

When a security incident involves a user, the site's security policy should describe what action is to be taken. The transgression should be taken seriously, but it is very important to be sure of the role the user played. Was the user naive? Could there be a mistake in attributing the security breach to the user? Applying administrative action that assumes the user intentionally caused the incident may not be appropriate for a user who simply made a mistake. It may be appropriate to include sanctions more suitable for such a situation in your policies (e.g., education or reprimand of a user) in addition to more stern measures for intentional acts of intrusion and system misuse.

6. Ongoing Activities

At this point in time, your site has hopefully developed a complete security policy and has developed procedures to assist in the configuration and management of your technology in support of those policies. How nice it would be if you could sit back and relax at this point and know that you were finished with the job of security. Unfortunately, that isn't possible. Your systems and networks are not a static environment, so you will need to review policies and procedures on a regular basis. There are a number of steps you can take to help you keep up with the changes around you so that you can initiate corresponding actions to address those changes. The following is a starter set and you may add others as appropriate for your site.

1. Subscribe to advisories that are issued by various security incident response teams, like those of the CERT Coordination Center, and update your systems against those threats that apply to your site's technology.

2. Monitor security patches that are produced by the vendors of your equipment, and obtain and install all that apply.

3. Actively watch the configurations of your systems to identify any changes that may have occurred, and investigate all anomalies.

4. Review all security policies and procedures annually (at a minimum).

5. Read relevant mailing lists and USENET newsgroups to keep up to date with the latest information being shared by fellow administrators.

6. Regularly check for compliance with policies and procedures. This audit should be performed by someone other than the people who define or implement the policies and procedures.

7. Tools and Locations

This chapter provides a brief list of publicly available security technology which can be downloaded from the Internet. Many of the items described below will undoubtedly be surpassed or made obsolete before this document is published.

Some of the tools listed are applications such as end user programs (clients) and their supporting system infrastructure (servers). Others are tools that a general user will never see or need to use, but may be used by applications, or by administrators to troubleshoot security problems or to guard against intruders.

A sad fact is that there are very few security conscious applications currently available. Primarily, this is caused by the need for a security infrastructure which must first be put into place for most applications to operate securely. There is considerable effort currently taking place to build this infrastructure so that applications can take advantage of secure communications. Most of the tools and applications described below can be found in one of the following archive sites:

1. CERT Coordination Center `ftp://info.cert.org:/pub/tools`

2. DFN-CERT `ftp://ftp.cert.dfn.de/pub/tools/`

3. Computer Operations, Audit, and Security Tools (COAST)
   `coast.cs.purdue.edu:/pub/tools`

It is important to note that many sites, including CERT and COAST are mirrored throughout the Internet. Be careful to use a "well known" mirror site to retrieve software, and to use verification tools (md5 checksums, etc.) to validate that software. A clever cracker might advertise security software that has intentionally been designed to provide access to data or systems.

Tools

COPS

DES

Drawbridge

identd (not really a security tool)

ISS

Kerberos

logdaemon

lsof

MD5

PEM

PGP

rpcbind/portmapper replacement

SATAN

sfingerd

S/KEY

smrsh

ssh

swatch

TCP-Wrapper

tiger

Tripwire★

TROJAN.PL

8. Mailing Lists and Other Resources

It would be impossible to list all of the mail-lists and other resources dealing with site security. However, these are some "jump-points" from which the reader can begin. All of these references are for the "INTERNET" constituency. More specific (vendor and geographical) resources can be found through these references.

Mailing Lists

1. CERT(TM) Advisory

   Send mail to: `cert-advisory-request@cert.org`

   Message Body: subscribe cert <FIRST NAME> <LAST NAME>

   A CERT advisory provides information on how to obtain a patch or details of a workaround for a known computer security problem. The CERT Coordination Center works with vendors to produce a workaround or a patch for a problem, and does not publish vulnerability information until a workaround or a patch is available. A CERT advisory may also be a warning to our constituency about ongoing attacks (e.g., "CA-91:18.Active.Internet.tftp.Attacks").

CERT advisories are also published on the USENET newsgroup: comp.security.announce

CERT advisory archives are available via anonymous FTP from info.cert.org in the /pub/cert_advisories directory.

2. VIRUS-L List

   Send mail to: `listserv%lehiibm1.bitnet@mitvma.mit.edu`

   Message Body: subscribe virus-L FIRSTNAME LASTNAME

   VIRUS-L is a moderated mailing list with a focus on computer virus issues. For more information, including a copy of the posting guidelines, see the file "virus-l.README," available by anonymous FTP from cs.ucr.edu.

3. Internet Firewalls

   Send mail to: `majordomo@greatcircle.com`

   Message Body: subscribe firewalls user@host

   The Firewalls mailing list is a discussion forum for firewall administrators and implementors.

USENET newsgroups

1. comp.security.announce

   The comp.security.announce newsgroup is moderated and is used solely for the distribution of CERT advisories.

2. comp.security.misc

   The comp.security.misc is a forum for the discussion of computer security, especially as it relates to the UNIX(r) Operating System.

3. alt.security

   The alt.security newsgroup is also a forum for the discussion of computer security, as well as other issues such as car locks and alarm systems.

4. comp.virus

   The comp.virus newsgroup is a moderated newsgroup with a focus on computer virus issues. For more information, including a copy of the posting guidelines, see the file "virus-l.README," available via anonymous FTP on info.cert.org in the /pub/virus-l directory.

5. comp.risks

   The comp.risks newsgroup is a moderated forum on the risks to the public in computers and related systems.

World-Wide Web Pages

1. `http://www.first.org/`

   Computer Security Resource Clearinghouse. The main focus is on crisis response information; information on computer security-related threats, vulnerabilities, and solutions. At the same time, the Clearinghouse strives to be a general index to computer security information on a broad variety of subjects, including general risks, privacy, legal issues, viruses, assurance, policy, and training.

2. `http://www.telstra.com.au/info/security.html`

   This Reference Index contains a list of links to information sources on Network and Computer Security. There is no implied fitness to the Tools, Techniques and Documents contained within this archive. Many if not all of these items work well, but we do not guarantee that this will be so. This information is for the education and legitimate use of computer security techniques only.

3. `http://www.alw.nih.gov/Security/security.html`

   This page features general information about computer security. Information is organized by source and each section is organized by topic. Recent modifications are noted in What's New page.

4. `http://csrc.ncsl.nist.gov`

   This archive at the National Institute of Standards and Technology's Computer Security Resource Clearinghouse page contains a number of announcements, programs, and documents related to computer security.

★ CERT and Tripwire are registered in the U.S. Patent and Trademark Office

9. References

The following references may not be available in all countries.

[Appelman, et. al., 1995] Appelman, Heller, Ehrman, White, and McAuliffe, "The Law and The Internet," USENIX 1995 Technical Conference on UNIX and Advanced Computing, New Orleans, LA, January 16-20, 1995.

[ABA, 1989] American Bar Association, Section of Science and Technology, "Guide to the Prosecution of Telecommunication Fraud by the Use of Computer Crime Statutes," American Bar Association, 1989.

[Aucoin, 1989] R. Aucoin, "Computer Viruses: Checklist for Recovery," Computers in Libraries, Vol. 9, No. 2, Pg. 4, February 1989.

[Barrett, 1996] D. Barrett, "Bandits on the Information Superhighway," O'Reilly & Associates, Sebastopol, CA, 1996.

[Bates, 1992] R. Bates, "Disaster Recovery Planning: Networks, Telecommunications and Data Communications," McGraw-Hill, 1992.

[Bellovin, 1989] S. Bellovin, "Security Problems in the TCP/IP Protocol Suite," Computer Communication Review, Vol 19, 2, pp. 32-48, April 1989.

[Bellovin, 1990] S. Bellovin, and M. Merritt, "Limitations of the Kerberos Authentication System," Computer Communications Review, October 1990.

[Bellovin, 1992] S. Bellovin, "There Be Dragon," USENIX: Proceedings of the Third Usenix Security Symposium, Baltimore, MD. September, 1992.

[Bender, 1894] D. Bender, "Computer Law: Evidence and Procedure," M. Bender, New York, NY, 1978-present.

[Bloombecker, 1990] B. Bloombecker, "Spectacular Computer Crimes," Dow Jones- Irwin, Homewood, IL. 1990.

[Brand, 1990] R. Brand, "Coping with the Threat of Computer Security Incidents: A Primer from Prevention through Recovery," R. Brand, 8 June 1990.

[Brock, 1989] J. Brock, "November 1988 Internet Computer Virus and the Vulnerability of National Telecommunications Networks to Computer Viruses," GAO/T-IMTEC-89-10, Washington, DC, 20 July 1989.

[BS 7799] British Standard, BS Tech Cttee BSFD/12, Info. Sec. Mgmt, "BS 7799 : 1995 Code of Practice for Information Security Management," British Standards Institution, London, 54, Effective 15 February 1995.

[Caelli, 1988] W. Caelli, Editor, "Computer Security in the Age of Information," Proceedings of the Fifth IFIP International Conference on Computer Security, IFIP/Sec '88.

[Carroll, 1987] J. Carroll, "Computer Security," 2nd Edition, Butterworth Publishers, Stoneham, MA, 1987.

[Cavazos and Morin, 1995] E. Cavazos and G. Morin, "Cyber-Space and The Law," MIT Press, Cambridge, MA, 1995.

[CCH, 1989] Commerce Clearing House, "Guide to Computer Law," (Topical Law Reports), Chicago, IL., 1989.

[Chapman, 1992] B. Chapman, "Network(In) Security Through IP Packet Filtering," USENIX: Proceedings of the Third UNIX Security Symposium, Baltimore, MD, September 1992.

[Chapman and Zwicky, 1995] B. Chapman and E. Zwicky, "Building Internet Firewalls," O'Reilly and Associates, Sebastopol, CA, 1995.

[Cheswick, 1990] B. Cheswick, "The Design of a Secure Internet Gateway," Proceedings of the Summer Usenix Conference, Anaheim, CA, June 1990.

[Cheswick1] W. Cheswick, "An Evening with Berferd In Which a Cracker is Lured, Endured, and Studied," AT&T Bell Laboratories.

[Cheswick and Bellovin, 1994] W. Cheswick and S. Bellovin, "Firewalls and Internet Security: Repelling the Wily Hacker," Addison-Wesley, Reading, MA, 1994.

[Conly, 1989] C. Conly, "Organizing for Computer Crime Investigation and Prosecution," U.S. Dept. of Justice, Office of Justice Programs, Under Contract Number OJP-86-C-002, National Institute of Justice, Washington, DC, July 1989.

[Cooper, 1989] J. Cooper, "Computer and Communications Security: Strategies for the 1990s," McGraw-Hill, 1989.

[CPSR, 1989] Computer Professionals for Social Responsibility, "CPSR Statement on the Computer Virus," CPSR, Communications of the ACM, Vol. 32, No. 6, Pg. 699, June 1989.

[CSC-STD-002-85, 1985] Department of Defense, "Password Management Guideline," CSC-STD-002-85, 12 April 1985, 31 pages.

[Curry, 1990] D. Curry, "Improving the Security of Your UNIX System," SRI International Report ITSTD-721-FR-90-21, April 1990.

[Curry, 1992] D. Curry, "UNIX System Security: A Guide for Users and Systems Administrators," Addison-Wesley, Reading, MA, 1992.

[DDN88] Defense Data Network, "BSD 4.2 and 4.3 Software Problem Resolution," DDN MGT Bulletin #43, DDN Network Information Center, 3 November 1988.

[DDN89] DCA DDN Defense Communications System, "DDN Security Bulletin 03," DDN Security Coordination Center, 17 October 1989.

[Denning, 1990] P. Denning, Editor, "Computers Under Attack: Intruders, Worms, and Viruses," ACM Press, 1990.

[Eichin and Rochlis, 1989] M. Eichin, and J. Rochlis, "With Microscope and Tweezers: An Analysis of the Internet Virus of November 1988," Massachusetts Institute of Technology, February 1989.

[Eisenberg, et. al., 89] T. Eisenberg, D. Gries, J. Hartmanis, D. Holcomb, M. Lynn, and T. Santoro, "The Computer Worm," Cornell University, 6 February 1989.

[Ermann, Williams, and Gutierrez, 1990] D. Ermann, M. Williams, and C. Gutierrez, Editors, "Computers, Ethics, and Society," Oxford University Press, NY, 1990. (376 pages, includes bibliographical references).

[Farmer and Spafford, 1990] D. Farmer and E. Spafford, "The COPS Security Checker System," Proceedings of the Summer 1990 USENIX Conference, Anaheim, CA, Pgs. 165-170, June 1990.

[Farrow, 1991] Rik Farrow, "UNIX Systems Security," Addison-Wesley, Reading, MA, 1991.

[Fenwick, 1985] W. Fenwick, Chair, "Computer Litigation, 1985: Trial Tactics and Techniques," Litigation Course Handbook Series No. 280, Prepared for distribution at the Computer Litigation, 1985: Trial Tactics and Techniques Program, February-March 1985.

[Fites 1989] M. Fites, P. Kratz, and A. Brebner, "Control and Security of Computer Information Systems," Computer Science Press, 1989.

[Fites, Johnson, and Kratz, 1992] Fites, Johnson, and Kratz, "The Computer Virus Crisis," Van Hostrand Reinhold, 2nd edition, 1992.

[Forester and Morrison, 1990] T. Forester, and P. Morrison, "Computer Ethics: Tales and Ethical Dilemmas in Computing," MIT Press, Cambridge, MA, 1990.

[Foster and Morrision, 1990] T. Forester, and P. Morrison, "Computer Ethics: Tales and Ethical Dilemmas in Computing," MIT Press, Cambridge, MA, 1990. (192 pages including index.)

[GAO/IMTEX-89-57, 1989] U.S. General Accounting Office, "Computer Security - Virus Highlights Need for Improved Internet Management," United States General Accounting Office, Washington, DC, 1989.

[Garfinkel and Spafford, 1991] S. Garfinkel, and E. Spafford, "Practical Unix Security," O'Reilly & Associates, ISBN 0-937175-72-2, May 1991.

[Garfinkel, 1995] S. Garfinkel, "PGP: Pretty Good Privacy," O'Reilly & Associates, Sebastopol, CA, 1996.

[Garfinkel and Spafford, 1996] S. Garfinkel and E. Spafford, "Practical UNIX and Internet Security," O'Reilly & Associates, Sebastopol, CA, 1996.

[Gemignani, 1989] M. Gemignani, "Viruses and Criminal Law," Communications of the ACM, Vol. 32, No. 6, Pgs. 669-671, June 1989.

[Goodell, 1996] J. Goodell, "The Cyberthief and the Samurai: The True Story of Kevin Mitnick-And The Man Who Hunted Him Down," Dell Publishing, 1996.

[Gould, 1989] C. Gould, Editor, "The Information Web: Ethical and Social Implications of Computer Networking," Westview Press, Boulder, CO, 1989.

[Greenia, 1989] M. Greenia, "Computer Security Information Sourcebook," Lexikon Services, Sacramento, CA, 1989.

[Hafner and Markoff, 1991] K. Hafner and J. Markoff, "Cyberpunk: Outlaws and Hackers on the Computer Frontier," Touchstone, Simon & Schuster, 1991.

[Hess, Safford, and Pooch] D. Hess, D. Safford, and U. Pooch, "A Unix Network Protocol Security Study: Network Information Service," Texas A&M University.

[Hoffman, 1990] L. Hoffman, "Rogue Programs: Viruses, Worms, and Trojan Horses," Van Nostrand Reinhold, NY, 1990. (384 pages, includes bibliographical references and index.)

[Howard, 1995] G. Howard, "Introduction to Internet Security: From Basics to Beyond," Prima Publishing, Rocklin, CA, 1995.

[Huband and Shelton, 1986] F. Huband, and R. Shelton, Editors, "Protection of Computer Systems and Software: New Approaches for Combating Theft of Software and Unauthorized Intrusion," Papers presented at a workshop sponsored by the National Science Foundation, 1986.

[Hughes, 1995] L. Hughes Jr., "Actually Useful Internet Security Techniques," New Riders Publishing, Indianapolis, IN, 1995.

[IAB-RFC1087, 1989] Internet Activities Board, "Ethics and the Internet," RFC 1087, IAB, January 1989. Also appears in the Communications of the ACM, Vol. 32, No. 6, Pg. 710, June 1989.

[Icove, Seger, and VonStorch, 1995] D. Icove, K. Seger, and W. VonStorch, "Computer Crime: A Crimefighter's Handbook," O'Reilly & Associates, Sebastopol, CA, 1995.

[IVPC, 1996] IVPC, "International Virus Prevention Conference '96 Proceedings," NCSA, 1996.

[Johnson and Podesta] D. Johnson, and J. Podesta, "Formulating A Company Policy on Access to and Use and Disclosure of Electronic Mail on Company Computer Systems."

[Kane, 1994] P. Kane, "PC Security and Virus Protection Handbook: The Ongoing War Against Information Sabotage," M&T Books, 1994.

[Kaufman, Perlman, and Speciner, 1995] C. Kaufman, R. Perlman, and M. Speciner, "Network Security: PRIVATE Communication in a PUBLIC World," Prentice Hall, Englewood Cliffs, NJ, 1995.

[Kent, 1990] S. Kent, "E-Mail Privacy for the Internet: New Software and Strict Registration Procedures will be Implemented this Year," Business Communications Review, Vol. 20, No. 1, Pg. 55, 1 January 1990.

[Levy, 1984] S. Levy, "Hacker: Heroes of the Computer Revolution," Delta, 1984.

[Lewis, 1996] S. Lewis, "Disaster Recovery Yellow Pages," The Systems Audit Group, 1996.

[Littleman, 1996] J. Littleman, "The Fugitive Game: Online with Kevin Mitnick," Little, Brown, Boston, MA., 1996.

[Lu and Sundareshan, 1989] W. Lu and M. Sundareshan, "Secure Communication in Internet Environments: A Hierarchical Key Management Scheme for End-to-End Encryption," IEEE Transactions on Communications, Vol. 37, No. 10, Pg. 1014, 1 October 1989.

[Lu and Sundareshan, 1990] W. Lu and M. Sundareshan, "A Model for Multilevel Security in Computer Networks," IEEE Transactions on Software Engineering, Vol. 16, No. 6, Page 647, 1 June 1990.

[Martin and Schinzinger, 1989] M. Martin, and R. Schinzinger, "Ethics in Engineering," McGraw Hill, 2nd Edition, 1989.

[Merkle] R. Merkle, "A Fast Software One Way Hash Function," Journal of Cryptology, Vol. 3, No. 1.

[McEwen, 1989] J. McEwen, "Dedicated Computer Crime Units," Report Contributors: D. Fester and H. Nugent, Prepared for the National Institute of Justice, U.S. Department of Justice, by Institute for Law and Justice, Inc., under contract number OJP-85-C-006, Washington, DC, 1989.

[MIT, 1989] Massachusetts Institute of Technology, "Teaching Students About Responsible Use of Computers," MIT, 1985-1986. Also reprinted in the Communications of the ACM, Vol. 32, No. 6, Pg. 704, Athena Project, MIT, June 1989.

[Mogel, 1989] Mogul, J., "Simple and Flexible Datagram Access Controls for UNIX-based Gateways," Digital Western Research Laboratory Research Report 89/4, March 1989.

[Muffett, 1992] A. Muffett, "Crack Version 4.1: A Sensible Password Checker for Unix."

[NCSA1, 1995] NCSA, "NCSA Firewall Policy Guide," 1995.

[NCSA2, 1995] NCSA, "NCSA's Corporate Computer Virus Prevention Policy Model," NCSA, 1995.

[NCSA, 1996] NCSA, "Firewalls & Internet Security Conference '96 Proceedings," 1996.

[NCSC-89-660-P, 1990] National Computer Security Center, "Guidelines for Formal Verification Systems," Shipping list no.: 89-660-P, The Center, Fort George G. Meade, MD, 1 April 1990.

[NCSC-89-254-P, 1988] National Computer Security Center, "Glossary of Computer Security Terms," Shipping list no.: 89-254-P, The Center, Fort George G. Meade, MD, 21 October 1988.

[NCSC-C1-001-89, 1989] Tinto, M., "Computer Viruses: Prevention, Detection, and Treatment," National Computer Security Center C1 Technical Report C1-001-89, June 1989.

[NCSC Conference, 1989] National Computer Security Conference, "12th National Computer Security Conference: Baltimore Convention Center, Baltimore, MD, 10-13 October, 1989: Information Systems Security, Solutions for Today—Concepts for Tomorrow," National Institute of Standards and National Computer Security Center, 1989.

[NCSC-CSC-STD-003-85, 1985] National Computer Security Center, "Guidance for Applying the Department of Defense Trusted Computer System Evaluation Criteria in Specific Environments," CSC-STD-003-85, NCSC, 25 June 1985.

[NCSC-STD-004-85, 1985] National Computer Security Center, "Technical Rationale Behind CSC-STD-003-85: Computer Security Requirements," CSC-STD-004-85, NCSC, 25 June 1985.

[NCSC-STD-005-85, 1985] National Computer Security Center, "Magnetic Remanence Security Guideline," CSC-STD-005-85, NCSC, 15 November 1985.

[NCSC-TCSEC, 1985] National Computer Security Center, "Trusted Computer System Evaluation Criteria," DoD 5200.28-STD, CSC-STD-001- 83, NCSC, December 1985.

[NCSC-TG-003, 1987] NCSC, "A Guide to Understanding DISCRETIONARY ACCESS CONTROL in Trusted Systems," NCSC-TG-003, Version-1, 30 September 1987, 29 pages.

[NCSC-TG-001, 1988] NCSC, "A Guide to Understanding AUDIT in Trusted Systems," NCSC-TG-001, Version-2, 1 June 1988, 25 pages.

[NCSC-TG-004, 1988] National Computer Security Center, "Glossary of Computer Security Terms," NCSC-TG-004, NCSC, 21 October 1988.

[NCSC-TG-005, 1987] National Computer Security Center, "Trusted Network Interpretation," NCSC-TG-005, NCSC, 31 July 1987.

[NCSC-TG-006, 1988] NCSC, "A Guide to Understanding CONFIGURATION MANAGEMENT in Trusted Systems," NCSC-TG-006, Version-1, 28 March 1988, 31 pages.

[NCSC-TRUSIX, 1990] National Computer Security Center, "Trusted UNIX Working Group (TRUSIX) rationale for selecting access control list features for the UNIX system," Shipping list no.: 90-076-P, The Center, Fort George G. Meade, MD, 1990.

[NRC, 1991] National Research Council, "Computers at Risk: Safe Computing in the Information Age," National Academy Press, 1991.

[Nemeth, et. al, 1995] E. Nemeth, G. Snyder, S. Seebass, and T. Hein, "UNIX Systems Administration Handbook," Prentice Hall PTR, Englewood Cliffs, NJ, 2nd ed. 1995.

[NIST, 1989] National Institute of Standards and Technology, "Computer Viruses and Related Threats: A Management Guide," NIST Special Publication 500-166, August 1989.

[NSA] National Security Agency, "Information Systems Security Products and Services Catalog," NSA, Quarterly Publication.

[NSF, 1988] National Science Foundation, "NSF Poses Code of Networking Ethics," Communications of the ACM, Vol. 32, No. 6, Pg. 688, June 1989. Also appears in the minutes of the regular meeting of the Division Advisory Panel for Networking and Communications Research and Infrastructure, Dave Farber, Chair, November 29-30, 1988.

[NTISSAM, 1987] NTISS, "Advisory Memorandum on Office Automation Security Guideline," NTISSAM COMPUSEC/1-87, 16 January 1987, 58 pages.

[OTA-CIT-310, 1987] United States Congress, Office of Technology Assessment, "Defending Secrets, Sharing Data: New Locks and Keys for Electronic Information," OTA-CIT-310, October 1987.

[OTA-TCT-606] Congress of the United States, Office of Technology Assessment, "Information Security and Privacy in Network Environments," OTA-TCT-606, September 1994.

[Palmer and Potter, 1989] I. Palmer, and G. Potter, "Computer Security Risk Management," Van Nostrand Reinhold, NY, 1989.

[Parker, 1989] D. Parker, "Computer Crime: Criminal Justice Resource Manual," U.S. Dept. of Justice, National Institute of Justice, Office of Justice Programs, Under Contract Number OJP-86-C-002, Washington, D.C., August 1989.

[Parker, Swope, and Baker, 1990] D. Parker, S. Swope, and B. Baker, "Ethical Conflicts: Information and Computer Science, Technology and Business," QED Information Sciences, Inc., Wellesley, MA. (245 pages).

[Pfleeger, 1989] C. Pfleeger, "Security in Computing," Prentice-Hall, Englewood Cliffs, NJ, 1989.

[Quarterman, 1990] J. Quarterman, "The Matrix: Computer Networks and Conferencing Systems Worldwide," Digital Press, Bedford, MA, 1990.

[Ranum1, 1992] M. Ranum, "An Internet Firewall," Proceedings of World Conference on Systems Management and Security, 1992.

[Ranum2, 1992] M. Ranum, "A Network Firewall," Digital Equipment Corporation Washington Open Systems Resource Center, June 12, 1992.

[Ranum, 1993] M. Ranum, "Thinking About Firewalls," 1993.

[Ranum and Avolio, 1994] M. Ranum and F. Avolio, "A Toolkit and Methods for Internet Firewalls," Trustest Information Systems, 1994.

[Reinhardt, 1992] R. Reinhardt, "An Architectural Overview of UNIX Network Security."

[Reinhardt, 1993] R. Reinhardt, "An Architectural Overview of UNIX Network Security," ARINC Research Corporation, February 18, 1993.

[Reynolds-RFC1135, 1989] The Helminthiasis of the Internet, RFC 1135, USC/Information Sciences Institute, Marina del Rey, CA, December 1989.

[Russell and Gangemi, 1991] D. Russell and G. Gangemi, "Computer Security Basics," O'Reilly & Associates, Sebastopol, CA, 1991.

[Schneier 1996] B. Schneier, "Applied Cryptography: Protocols, Algorithms, and Source Code in C," John Wiley & Sons, New York, second edition, 1996.

[Seeley, 1989] D. Seeley, "A Tour of the Worm," Proceedings of 1989 Winter USENIX Conference, Usenix Association, San Diego, CA, February 1989.

[Shaw, 1986] E. Shaw Jr., "Computer Fraud and Abuse Act of 1986," Congressional Record (3 June 1986), Washington, D.C., 3 June 1986.

[Shimomura, 1996] T. Shimomura with J. Markoff, "Takedown: The Pursuit and Capture of Kevin Mitnick, America's Most Wanted Computer Outlaw- by the Man Who Did It," Hyperion, 1996.

[Shirey, 1990] R. Shirey, "Defense Data Network Security Architecture," Computer Communication Review, Vol. 20, No. 2, Page 66, 1 April 1990.

[Slatalla and Quittner, 1995] M. Slatalla and J. Quittner, "Masters of Deception: The Gang that Ruled Cyberspace," Harper Collins Publishers, 1995.

[Smith, 1989] M. Smith, "Commonsense Computer Security: Your Practical Guide to Preventing Accidental and Deliberate Electronic Data Loss," McGraw-Hill, New York, NY, 1989.

[Smith, 1995] D. Smith, "Forming an Incident Response Team," Sixth Annual Computer Security Incident Handling Workshop, Boston, MA, July 25-29, 1995.

[Spafford, 1988] E. Spafford, "The Internet Worm Program: An Analysis," Computer Communication Review, Vol. 19, No. 1, ACM SIGCOM, January 1989. Also issued as Purdue CS Technical Report CSD-TR-823, 28 November 1988.

[Spafford, 1989] G. Spafford, "An Analysis of the Internet Worm," Proceedings of the European Software Engineering Conference 1989, Warwick England, September 1989. Proceedings published by Springer-Verlag as: Lecture Notes in Computer Science #387. Also issued as Purdue Technical Report #CSD-TR-933.

[Spafford, Keaphy, and Ferbrache, 1989] E. Spafford, K. Heaphy, and D. Ferbrache, "Computer Viruses: Dealing with Electronic Vandalism and Programmed Threats," ADAPSO, 1989. (109 pages.)

[Stallings1, 1995] W. Stallings, "Internet Security Handbook," IDG Books, Foster City CA, 1995.

[Stallings2, 1995] W. Stallings, "Network and InterNetwork Security," Prentice Hall, 1995.

[Stallings3, 1995] W. Stallings, "Protect Your Privacy: A Guide for PGP Users," PTR Prentice Hall, 1995.

[Stoll, 1988] C. Stoll, "Stalking the Wily Hacker," Communications of the ACM, Vol. 31, No. 5, Pgs. 484-497, ACM, New York, NY, May 1988.

[Stoll, 1989] C. Stoll, "The Cuckoo's Egg," ISBN 00385-24946-2, Doubleday, 1989.

[Treese and Wolman, 1993] G. Treese and A. Wolman, "X Through the Firewall, and Other Applications Relays," Digital Equipment Corporation, Cambridge Research Laboratory, CRL 93/10, May 3, 1993.

[Trible, 1986] P. Trible, "The Computer Fraud and Abuse Act of 1986," U.S. Senate Committee on the Judiciary, 1986.

[Venema] W. Venema, "TCP WRAPPER: Network monitoring, access control, and booby traps," Mathematics and Computing Science, Eindhoven University of Technology, The Netherlands.

[USENIX, 1988] USENIX, "USENIX Proceedings: UNIX Security Workshop," Portland, OR, August 29-30, 1988.

[USENIX, 1990] USENIX, "USENIX Proceedings: UNIX Security II Workshop," Portland, OR, August 27-28, 1990.

[USENIX, 1992] USENIX, "USENIX Symposium Proceedings: UNIX Security III," Baltimore, MD, September 14-16, 1992.

[USENIX, 1993] USENIX, "USENIX Symposium Proceedings: UNIX Security IV," Santa Clara, CA, October 4-6, 1993.

[USENIX, 1995] USENIX, "The Fifth USENIX UNIX Security Symposium," Salt Lake City, UT, June 5-7, 1995.

[Wood, et.al., 1987] C. Wood, W. Banks, S. Guarro, A. Garcia, V. Hampel, and H. Sartorio, "Computer Security: A Comprehensive Controls Checklist," John Wiley and Sons, Interscience Publication, 1987.

[Wrobel, 1993] L. Wrobel, "Writing Disaster Recovery Plans for Telecommunications Networks and LANS," Artech House, 1993.

[Vallabhaneni, 1989] S. Vallabhaneni, "Auditing Computer Security: A Manual with Case Studies," Wiley, New York, NY, 1989.

Security Considerations

This entire document discusses security issues.

Editor Information

Barbara Y. Fraser
Software Engineering Institute
Carnegie Mellon University
5000 Forbes Avenue
Pittsburgh, PA 15213
Phone: (412) 268-5010
Fax: (412) 268-6989
Email: byf@cert.org

B

Incident Response and Reporting Checklist

THIS CHECKLIST IS DESIGNED TO ENABLE INCIDENT response personnel to quickly assess and gather basic information about an incident. Although it does not contain specific instructions for how to respond to all incidents, it will assist the team in the detection and containment phases of the incident response process.

1. What is the nature of the emergency?
   a. Denial-of-service attack ☐
   b. Network intrusion ☐
   c. Insider attack ☐
   d. Virus, trojan horse, or worm ☐
   e. Other ☐
2. Did the attack result in a compromise of business data? ☐
3. Did the intruder gain root, administrator, or system access? ☐
4. When was the incident detected?
   Date:_____
   Time:_____

5. How was the incident detected?
    a. Intrusion detection system or audit logs ☐
    b. External complaint ☐
    c. User report ☐
    d. Antivirus software ☐
    e. Other ☐
6. When did the incident occur?

    Date:_____

    Time:_____
7. Is the incident ongoing? ☐
8. What are the current symptoms?
9. What business areas are affected?
10. What systems are affected?

    Gather as much data as possible about the systems, including the operating system, platform, applications, IP address, associated or suspected user IDs, most recent changes applied, and so on.
11. Are the affected systems still connected to the network? ☐

    Consider disconnecting the systems if possible.
12. Are backups of the affected systems available? ☐
13. Are the affected systems still at risk to attack? ☐

    Consider disconnecting the systems or securing the accounts if possible.
14. Will the systems potentially require forensics analysis? ☐

    Consider shutting down and securing the system for forensics imaging.

Index

Page numbers followed by *n* signify that the entry occurs in a footnote on that page.

Symbols

Page numbers followed by *n* signify that the entry occurs in a footnote on that page.

Page numbers followed by *n* signify that the entry occurs in a footnote on that page.

D

Page numbers followed by *n* signify that the entry occurs in a footnote on that page.

E

Page numbers followed by *n* signify that the entry occurs in a footnote on that page.

Page numbers followed by *n* signify that the entry occurs in a footnote on that page.

Page numbers followed by *n* signify that the entry occurs in a footnote on that page.

Page numbers followed by *n* signify that the entry occurs in a footnote on that page.

Page numbers followed by *n* signify that the entry occurs in a footnote on that page.

Page numbers followed by *n* signify that the entry occurs in a footnote on that page.

Page numbers followed by *n* signify that the entry occurs in a footnote on that page.

Page numbers followed by *n* signify that the entry occurs in a footnote on that page.

J-K

L

Page numbers followed by *n* signify that the entry occurs in a footnote on that page.

Page numbers followed by *n* signify that the entry occurs in a footnote on that page.

Page numbers followed by *n* signify that the entry occurs in a footnote on that page.

Page numbers followed by *n* signify that the entry occurs in a footnote on that page.

Page numbers followed by *n* signify that the entry occurs in a footnote on that page.

Q-R

Page numbers followed by *n* signify that the entry occurs in a footnote on that page.

S

Page numbers followed by *n* signify that the entry occurs in a footnote on that page.

Page numbers followed by n signify that the entry occurs in a footnote on that page.

Page numbers followed by *n* signify that the entry occurs in a footnote on that page.

Page numbers followed by *n* signify that the entry occurs in a footnote on that page.

Page numbers followed by *n* signify that the entry occurs in a footnote on that page.

Page numbers followed by n signify that the entry occurs in a footnote on that page.

Page numbers followed by *n* signify that the entry occurs in a footnote on that page.

VOICES THAT MATTER

HOW TO CONTACT US

VISIT OUR WEB SITE

WWW.NEWRIDERS.COM

On our web site, you'll find information about our other books, authors, tables of contents, and book errata. You will also find information about book registration and how to purchase our books, both domestically and internationally.

EMAIL US

Contact us at: **nrfeedback@newriders.com**

- If you have comments or questions about this book
- To report errors that you have found in this book
- If you have a book proposal to submit or are interested in writing for New Riders
- If you are an expert in a computer topic or technology and are interested in being a technical editor who reviews manuscripts for technical accuracy

Contact us at: **nreducation@newriders.com**

- If you are an instructor from an educational institution who wants to preview New Riders books for classroom use. Email should include your name, title, school, department, address, phone number, office days/hours, text in use, and enrollment, along with your request for desk/examination copies and/or additional information.

Contact us at: **nrmedia@newriders.com**

- If you are a member of the media who is interested in reviewing copies of New Riders books. Send your name, mailing address, and email address, along with the name of the publication or web site you work for.

BULK PURCHASES/CORPORATE SALES

If you are interested in buying 10 or more copies of a title or want to set up an account for your company to purchase directly from the publisher at a substantial discount, contact us at 800-382-3419 or email your contact information to corpsales@pearsontechgroup.com. A sales representative will contact you with more information.

WRITE TO US

New Riders Publishing
201 W. 103rd St.
Indianapolis, IN 46290-1097

CALL/FAX US

Toll-free (800) 571-5840
If outside U.S. (317) 581-3500
Ask for New Riders
FAX: (317) 581-4663

New
Riders

WWW.NEWRIDERS.COM

Solutions from experts you know and trust

www.informit.com

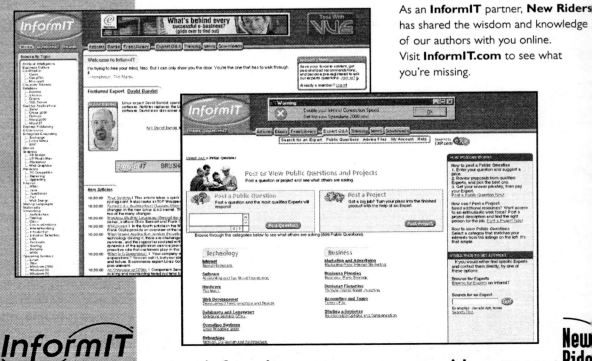

Colophon

The photograph on this cover was captured by PhotoLink and is an image of two bull elks fighting, entangling their antlers. During mating season, bull elk are prepared to use their antlers to fight other bulls to defend their harems of cows from rivals. In these fights, the weaker animal typically gives up, but occasionally one is injured. Bull elks are typically found in the Rocky Mountains of the United States. They often make a distinctive bugle sound, usually as a warning call targeted at other bulls that are getting too close to the harem. The bulls are protected from hunting in U.S. National Parks (such as Yellowstone and Rocky Mountain). The main beam of the elks' antlers can grow to as long as five feet.

This book was written and edited in Microsoft Word, and laid out in QuarkXPress. The fonts used for the body text are Bembo and MCPdigital. It was printed on 50# Husky Offset Smooth paper at VonHoffmann Graphics, Inc., in Owensville, MO. Prepress consisted of PostScript computer-to-plate technology (filmless process). The cover was printed at Moore Langen Printing in Terre Haute, Indiana, on Carolina, on 12pt, coated on one side.